THE REPUBLIC OF ARABIC LETTERS

THE REPUBLIC OF ARABIC LETTERS

Islam and the European Enlightenment

Alexander Bevilacqua

The Belknap Press of Harvard University Press

CAMBRIDGE, MASSACHUSETTS

LONDON, ENGLAND

2018

Interior design by Dean Bornstein

Library of Congress Cataloging-in-Publication Data
Names: Bevilacqua, Alexander, 1984– author.
Title: The republic of Arabic letters : Islam and the European enlightenment /
Alexander Bevilacqua.
Description: Cambridge, Massachusetts : The Belknap Press of
Harvard University Press, 2018. | Includes bibliographical references and index.
Identifiers: LCCN 2017031813 | ISBN 9780674975927 (alk. paper)
Subjects: LCSH: Islamic civilization—Study and teaching—Europe, Western. |
Enlightenment—Europe. | Europe—Civilization—Islamic influences. | Christian
scholars—Europe—History.
Classification: LCC CB251 .B426 2018 | DDC 909 / .09767—dc23
LC record available at https://lccn.loc.gov/2017031813

ما لا يُعلم كلّه لا يُترك كلّه فإنّ العلم بالبعض خير من الجهل بالكلّ

Abū'l-Fidā' (1321)

Quod totum sciri non potest, ne omittatur totum, siquidem Scientia partis melior est ignorantia totius.
Translation by Edward Pococke (1650)

What cannot totally be known, ought not to be totally neglected; for the Knowledge of a Part is better than the Ignorance of the Whole.
Translation by Simon Ockley (1718)

Semper praestat partem rei tenere, quam totam ignorare.
Translation by Johann Jacob Reiske (1770)

Contents

Illustrations follow page 126

Note on Terminology, Names, Transliteration, and Dates

In the era this book describes, Europeans lacked standardized terminology for identifying Muslims and their religious, cultural, and linguistic communities. The ancient but unspecific "Saracen," a name whose origin is as obscure as its use was widespread, was just one among many available designations. "Oriental" did not refer solely to Muslims: it could encompass all peoples of the Levant, including Jews and Christians, or even refer to all the peoples of Asia. Likewise, "Arab" could mean several things: sometimes it designated the nomadic desert Arabs, the Bedouin, sometimes the speakers of Arabic. (To call those who spoke or wrote in Arabic Arabs, as many Europeans did, was misleading, because Persians, Ottomans and many others used Arabic as well.) "Turks," too, could refer to Ottoman dynasts and subjects or else to speakers and writers of Turkish, or even, by synecdoche, to all Muslims (as in the expression, first attested in the sixteenth century, "to turn Turk"). This terminological complexity led, perhaps inevitably, to some ambiguity and overlap between terms. Thus, "the history of the Arabs" often meant the history of the Muslims—those medieval Muslims who had participated in Umayyad and Abbasid society. The non-Arab contribution was not properly acknowledged.

In this book I use "Islamic" rather than "Oriental," because the latter term, while probably the most frequently employed by its protagonists, seems far too imprecise to be useful. Nevertheless, the pages that follow look beyond the study of the religion of Islam. As a consequence, I use the term "Islamic" broadly, not just for religion but also to indicate Muslim cultural and intellectual production. Not all of this was religious in character; poetry, philosophy, and history all fall under the term. Marshall Hodgson coined the useful term "Islamicate" to refer to the cultural production of Muslim lands, including that of minorities, as opposed to the properly religious aspects of life, which he called "Islamic" (Marshall G. S. Hodgson, *The Venture of Islam: Conscience and History in a World Civilization* [Chicago, 1974], vol. 1). I have nonetheless avoided "Islamicate" because it has not taken hold outside the specialized circles of contemporary Islamic and Near Eastern studies (and perhaps not even there). As for the use of "Europe" and "European": the goal is to be as inclusive as possible, and to bring together Italian, German, Dutch, French, and English sources. My aim is not to dismiss national differences; the connections and parallels merely seemed more significant. "Western Christian" would have served as well.

The term "civilization" was first used only in the 1760s, but in this book I employ it to describe a notion that certainly emerged much earlier: the assumption that the sum total of a society's achievements in the arts and sciences could be described and evaluated. The thinkers profiled here were interested in assessing the relationship of Islam to what we might term cultural output, though their notion of it seems more accurately captured by the phrase "civilizational achievement." As for "culture": in my own usage, I have attempted, where possible, to qualify the slippery term with more specific attributes such as "intellectual" or "literary."

I use the vernacular names of humanist scholars (Reland, not Relandus), except when the Latin ones have gained currency in English (Golius, not van Gool). While Lodovico Marracci is mostly called Ludovico in the secondary literature, I have respected the way he spelled his name in autograph documents and vernacular publications. See, for instance, the letters at the Biblioteca Nazionale Centrale in Florence; and Lodovico Marracci, *L'ebreo preso per le buone* (Rome, 1701).

Transliteration of Arabic, Persian, and Turkish follows the simplified system of the *International Journal of Middle East Studies*. I have not included diacritics for words commonly used in English, such as "Muhammad." Likewise, I have used the English equivalents of Arabic names where they exist, rather than transliterations (Medina, not Madīna). The ʾ symbol stands for hamza, the glottal stop. The ʿ symbol stands for ayn, a throated consonant with no equivalent in English. In Arabic patronyms, "b." stands for "*ibn*" (son), so that the name ʿAlī b. Abī Ṭālib translates as ʿAlī, the son of Abū Ṭālib.

Calendar dates are Common Era unless otherwise indicated. The Islamic calendar is a lunar twelve-month calendar and begins in 622 CE, the year of Muhammad's flight to Medina, known as the hijra or hegira. Years in the Islamic calendar are referred to as AH for *Anno Hegirae*.

The Bible is quoted in the King James (Authorized) Version. Unless otherwise indicated, quotations from the Qur'an use the version of A. J. Arberry, *The Koran Interpreted* (London, 1955). All other translations are my own unless otherwise indicated, though I have consulted published translations where available.

List of Protagonists
(in chronological order by birth)

Edward Pococke (1604–1691). Chaplain to the English Levant Company at Aleppo and professor at Oxford. His *Specimen Historiæ Arabum* (1650) put European Arabic studies on a new footing. *(Chapters 3, 5)*

Lodovico Marracci (1612–1700). Member of the Order of the Mother of God and confessor to Pope Innocent XI (Odescalchi). He wrote a Latin translation of the Qur'an with critical notes drawn from five Arabic commentaries. *(Chapter 2)*

Barthélemy d'Herbelot (1625–1695). Supported by the Medici and King Louis XIV, this French scholar created the *Bibliothèque Orientale* (1697), a reference work about Islamic history and letters based on his reading in Arabic, Persian, and Turkish. *(Chapter 4)*

Richard Simon (1638–1712). French biblical scholar whose writings on Islam, which first appeared in the 1670s, drew analogies and connections with Christianity and emphasized that Muslim writers deserved to be studied like the good pagans of antiquity. *(Chapter 3)*

Antoine Galland (1646–1715). French interpreter, scholar, and translator. His posthumous fame derives from his translation of *The Thousand and One Nights,* the first into a Western language, but he was active in many areas, including manuscript collecting and numismatics. *(Chapters 1, 4)*

Eusèbe Renaudot (1646–1720). French scholar and diplomat who was especially interested in the history of the Eastern Churches and their liturgies. His work on Islamic history remained in manuscript. *(Chapter 5)*

Adriaan Reland (1676–1718). Dutch scholar of Oriental languages based in Utrecht. His short treatise *De Religione Mohammedica* (1705) advanced a fair-minded treatment of Islam and served as a manifesto of the new Arabic scholarship. *(Chapter 3)*

Simon Ockley (ca. 1679–1720). English scholar of Arabic who taught at Cambridge and wrote a two-volume *History of the Saracens* (1708 and 1718) that brought the early Arab conquests to the attention of English and European readers. *(Chapter 5)*

Charles-Louis de Secondat, Baron de La Brède et de Montesquieu (1689–1755). Political philosopher whose *Persian Letters* (1721) and *The Spirit of the Law* (1748) both touched on Islamic topics, renewing the concept of Oriental despotism. *(Chapter 6)*

François-Marie Arouet, known as Voltaire (1694–1778). Voltaire's treatment of Islam in his *Essai sur les mœurs* (1756) drew heavily on the writings of the European scholars of Arabic and turned their research into the knowledge of the French Enlightenment. *(Chapter 6)*

George Sale (ca. 1696–1736). The first translator of the Qur'an from Arabic into English. He lived in London and was not university educated. His *Koran* appeared in 1734 and became the standard English translation for both its scholarly and its literary accomplishment. *(Chapters 2, 3)*

Johann Jacob Reiske (1717–1774). German Arabist who attained an extraordinary mastery of Arabic sources, particularly historical ones. He failed to gain professional recognition, and much of his Arabic scholarship remained unpublished at his death. *(Chapter 5)*

Edward Gibbon (1737–1794). Gibbon treated the rise of Islam in volume 5 of *The History of the Decline and Fall of the Roman Empire,* which appeared in 1788. In many respects a student of the Republic of Arabic Letters, he nevertheless reproached Muslims for not having sufficiently absorbed the classical heritage. *(Chapter 6)*

List of Frequently Discussed
Arabic and Islamic Authors
(in chronological order)

Ibn Abī Zamanīn (936–1008). Andalusian jurist who produced a compendium (*mukhtaṣar*) of a Qur'an commentary by Yaḥyā b. Sallām. His work was especially popular in Iberia. (*Chapter 2*)

Gregorius Bar Hebraeus (1225 / 1226–1286). Christian scholar and saint of the Syriac Church. He wrote in Arabic and Syriac and was known in particular for his historical scholarship, of which he completed a summary in Arabic entitled *Mukhtaṣar ta'rīkh al-duwal* (Abridged history of dynasties). (*Chapters 3, 5*)

Pseudo-Wāqidī. The historian al-Wāqidī lived from about 747 / 748 to 823. Much later, a work entitled *Futūḥ al-Shām* (Conquests of Syria), compiled during the Crusades, was attributed to him. Its unidentified author is known as the pseudo-Wāqidī. (*Chapter 5*)

Abū'l-Fidā' (1273–1331). Ayyūbid prince of Ḥamā, in Syria, who wrote a universal history, *Mukhtaṣar fī akhbār al-bashar* (Concise history of mankind). (*Chapter 5*)

Al-Bayḍāwī (ca. second half of the thirteenth century to ca. early fourteenth century). Of Fars, in Persia, he compiled a one-volume abridgement of the Qur'an commentary by al-Zamakhsharī. It would become one of the most popular elucidations of the Qur'an in the Ottoman Empire. (*Chapter 2*)

Mīrkhwānd (1433 / 1434–1498). Scholar of Timurid Herat who wrote a seven-volume universal history in Persian, *Rawḍat al-ṣafā' fī sīrat al-anbiyā' wa'l-mulūk wa'l-khulafā'* (Garden of purity on the lives of prophets, kings, and caliphs), which was highly valued by later Persian and Ottoman readers. (*Chapters 1, 4*)

Kātib Çelebi (1609–1657). Ottoman scholar whose bibliography, *Kashf al-ẓunūn 'an asāmī al-kutub wa'l-funūn* (The clearing of doubts in the names of books and arts), offered the most comprehensive overview of Islamic books of his era. (*Chapter 2*)

THE REPUBLIC OF ARABIC LETTERS

INTRODUCTION

Around the time of his fifteenth birthday, in 1752, Edward Gibbon wanted to learn Arabic. The year before, he had discovered the Muslim conquests in English and French accounts. Yet his Oxford tutor "discouraged this childish fancy [and] neglected the fair occasion of directing the ardour of a curious mind," as Gibbon, who never took up the language, would recollect. The decision would haunt him in later years, when his great project of charting the decline of the Roman Empire led him beyond the confines of Western history and, via the entanglements of the Eastern Roman Empire, well into Asia and the histories of Muslim peoples. Though he could read sources in both Greek and Latin, Gibbon could not work autonomously on Islamic history. The ambition and scale of his historical vision outran his linguistic abilities, and he was well aware of the challenges he faced.[1]

The solution came from the European scholars of Arabic, writers whom Gibbon read and used in *The Decline and Fall of the Roman Empire:* George Sale, translator of the Qur'an; Simon Ockley, historian of the Arab conquests; Barthélemy d'Herbelot, creator of an encyclopedia of Islamic letters; and others. These authors, who people the footnotes of Gibbon's great work, provided him with the sources he was unable to read himself. They form an Enlightenment, now largely lost from view, in which Europeans learned Arabic and read Islamic manuscripts. This book offers a history of this Arabic-reading Enlightenment.

The seventeenth and eighteenth centuries saw a transformation in European knowledge of Islam and Islamic traditions. The imprecise and often incorrect body of notions available during the Middle Ages and the Renaissance gradually gave way to a vast and diverse set of translations, insights, and interpretations. At the same time, a new attitude developed toward the peoples and traditions of Islam. No longer seen as deeply alien, Muslims came to be appreciated, not just for their religious piety and military prowess, but also for their music and architecture, their social customs, the heroism of their histories, and even for their poetry and for the beauty of the Qur'an. At this time, Europeans first came to recognize the culture of Muslim lands as a holistic set of religious, intellectual, and literary traditions deserving respect and attention, and as an object of study that would yield intellectual, aesthetic, and even moral enrichment in a variety of fields.

European understandings of Islam changed, then, in two separate ways: on the one hand, Europeans studied a much wider range of sources of the Islamic intellectual tradition than ever before, and, on the other, they began to think and write about Islam with a fair-mindedness that had until then been at best the exception rather than the rule. The two developments, although related, were distinct. Some Europeans improved knowledge of Islam for polemical ends; they studied it in order to refute it more decisively. These were by no means the least influential writers. By contrast, sympathy did not always lead to deeper understanding, for others misrepresented Islam to make it seem more worthy of Christian esteem. Even so, the two processes—of study and of charitable reinterpretation—were linked. Generally speaking, those Europeans who learned Arabic and wrote about Islamic topics tended to hold a high opinion of Islamic letters, of their importance and originality; they even tended to overestimate the antiquity of Arabic, which increased its significance in their eyes. Together, the tradition of research and the effort at charitable reinterpretation laid the foundations of the modern Western understanding of Islam: many of the translations and interpretations first produced in this period persisted into the twentieth century.

This venture was undertaken only after global commerce brought Europeans into increased contact with the peoples, goods, languages, beliefs, and customs of Asia. This was the era of the chartered trading companies, and many European powers established a commercial presence abroad, not just in the Mediterranean but as far afield as the Coromandel Coast of India or Batavia, on the island of Java. European presence in the entrepôt cities of Istanbul, Izmir, and Aleppo, or in factories and settlements from North Africa to Southeast Asia, generated an increased awareness of the intellectual life of the Islamic city. If the merchants did not for the most part interest themselves in scholarly matters, they provided transportation and accommodation for those who traveled in pursuit of knowledge rather than profit. At the same time, Christian missionary efforts intensified European interactions with Muslim peoples.

The new knowledge of Islam was the product of studies undertaken by both Catholics and Protestants. Whether scholars, clergymen, or members of

religious orders, they all participated in a tradition of erudition that originated in the humanist movement of the Renaissance and extended across the
European continent and the British Isles (Map 1). These men competed
fiercely, and disagreed with vehemence, but they never duplicated one another's work, and they could agree across sectarian lines about what constituted
good research. They can be called a Republic of Arabic Letters: a working
community of scholars of different languages, political affiliations, and traditions of belief. Theirs was a province of the broader European Republic of
Letters (a period term), the continental scholarly community whose origins
dated to the time of Erasmus of Rotterdam, with shared rules of conduct and
goals.[2]

The translation movement described in this book was grounded in a perception of analogy between Western Christian and Islamic traditions. Analogy
was one of the chief intellectual tools that European scholars used to make
sense of Islamic history, religion, and letters and to make these intelligible to
their readers (Figure 1). In particular, one of their most powerful comparisons
was between Muslims and the "good pagans" of classical antiquity. The Christian tradition had, since the time of the Church Fathers, assimilated many
aspects of pre-Christian Greco-Roman literature and thought. In the seventeenth and eighteenth centuries, the presence of so much classical culture at
the heart of the Western tradition seemed to grant scholars permission to
study Islamic materials as well. Through an analogy with good paganism,
Europeans could validate their new interest in Islamic letters.[3]

European scholars also compared Islam to Christianity and to Judaism.
These comparisons were more ancient; they lay at the foundation of the polemical study of Islam in the Middle Ages. Christian writers then had aimed
to prove that Islam was not the product of a genuinely inspired revelation but
the forgery of an impostor who had confected it from bits and pieces of existing religions. This time around, however, the comparison served a different
function: to normalize Islam. Scholars argued that the God of the Qur'an was
the same God of the Christian Bible, and Islam came to seem to many a more
intellectually sound version of Christianity because it did not require belief in
the doctrine of the Trinity. The study of Islam became normatively decon-
taminated: Muhammad the impostor became Muhammad the legislator.

The scholars involved in the European study of African and Asian languages
thought they were expanding the approach of humanism—the scholarly

movement that had recovered the classics of Greece and Rome—to new literary traditions. For them, humanism was a universalist movement encompassing all the literary traditions of humankind. This sense of possibility and excitement is captured in some of their writings. In turn, they could and did use their knowledge of Islamic history and letters to reorient their understanding of their own place in world history, displacing themselves from its center.

One did not have to abandon one's own religious beliefs to take this intellectual step. Whether the European scholars of Arabic were clerics or laymen, they were not radical critics of their religion. They did not seek to overturn Christianity through their study of Islam. That antireligious readers ended up using the new knowledge of Islam to critique organized religion was an unintended consequence of their intellectual output; it had nothing to do with the original impetus for acquiring such knowledge. The Enlightenment understanding of Islam and Islamic culture was developed neither by the famous *philosophes* nor by the radical underground, but by a broader and less polemical group of researchers, who are the subject of this book: the thinkers who most intensively interacted with the written traditions of Islam.⁴

European scholars aiming to build a new understanding of Islam—for instance, to read the Qur'an as contemporary Muslims did—had to rely on the work of their Muslim counterparts in the areas of grammar, lexicography, commentary, compilation, abridgment, anthology, historiography (historical writing), biography, and more. Thus, many Islamic judgments about what mattered in the Islamic tradition were adopted by European scholars. With a remarkable naiveté, Europeans trusted information in Islamic sources, often taking their claims at face value. As a consequence, their new understanding was constructed with building blocks from the Islamic intellectual tradition.

The new knowledge allowed for an interpretation of Islamic letters as sophisticated as it was unprecedented in European history. This book is an account of this transformation, a new history of Islam and the European Enlightenment. It begins by relating how and why Islamic manuscripts were collected in great number all across Europe in the period beginning around 1600, then moves on to the process by which these manuscripts were spun into knowledge in learned and polite translations, editions, and histories. It considers the study of Islamic religion, first through the translation of the Qur'an published by the Italian Lodovico Marracci in 1698, and then through a broader look at how a new view of Islam emerged from the mid-seventeenth century to the early eighteenth. This new view was grounded both in a richer philological knowledge and in an effort to do justice to Islam—to extend intellectual charity to it. The investigation then moves to the study of Islamic history and letters broadly by examining the *Bibliothèque Orientale,* the masterpiece of the Frenchman Barthélemy d'Herbelot, published in Paris in 1697— the first true Western "encyclopedia" of Islamic culture—and then charting how the history of Islamic contributions to human civilization writ large was understood from mid-seventeenth to mid-eighteenth century. Chapter 6 investigates the impact of all of this research on the canonical, secular French and British Enlightenment of Montesquieu, Voltaire, and Gibbon. Readers like Voltaire and Gibbon adopted not just the raw materials but also the interpretations of the European scholars of Arabic, and wove them into the fabric of Enlightenment thought.[5]

The argument of this book relies on a combination of what were viewed until very recently as two distinct pursuits: intellectual history, on the one hand, and, on the other, the history of books and of reading. Only the use of this dual approach can reveal how new texts and new information transformed existing systems of knowledge. To the receptive reader, the impact of a new text could be as earth-shattering as that of a personal encounter with new places and peoples. In recent decades, cultural history has tended to consider the eyewitnessing of travelers to have been the most powerful disruption of inherited systems of thought. In contrast, this book reveals the immense transformative power of readerly experiences. The bookish encounters studied here reshaped long-standing Western intellectual traditions and biases.

The legacy of this new knowledge of Islamic history, religion, and letters was mixed. On the one hand, the achievements of European Islamic studies did not prevent the broader European turn to a patronizing view of Islam, as a religion and as a civilization, in the second half of the eighteenth century. On the other hand, these translations and interpretations lived on during the nineteenth-century age of empire. It has been insufficiently recognized that the foundations of the modern Western view of Islam were laid when a more equitable balance of power obtained between Western Christians and Muslims. Nineteenth-century European approaches to Islam had to contend with these earlier interpretations, for, through continual republication of certain works, such as Simon Ockley's history of the Arab conquests and George Sale's *Koran,* the Enlightenment understanding of Islam continued to reach new readers even in the nineteenth and twentieth centuries. These visions of Islam, born in a moment of intercultural possibility, continued to act in Western history even after that moment had passed.

Islam and the West from Muhammad to Mehmed the Conqueror

Intellectual relations between Christians and Muslims far predate the history recounted in these pages. Why did the translation movement described here not happen earlier? To understand how the intellectual projects of the seventeenth and eighteenth centuries diverged from what came before, it is necessary to cast a glance at the long history of Western Christian perceptions of Islam and of Muslims.

Islam was revealed—in the early seventh century CE—to a world already replete with religious beliefs and practices. Its first adherents were drawn from other religious communities: Zoroastrians, Jews, Christians, and polytheists. In the early years, this new belief system might have been of little concern to Christians living in Western Europe. Within a century of the revelation to Muhammad, however, Muslim armies had spread widely, and the political threat of Muslim invasion became real in such far-flung locations as Iberia, France, and Byzantium. As the Muslim empire expanded into territories that had long been Christian, and as Islam gained converts among Christians, the new religion began to impinge on the Western Christian worldview.[6]

Inevitably, Islam represented a theological problem as well as a political one. The first Christians to deal intellectually with Islam were not the members of Western Christendom but Christians of the Near East. Their writings on Islam—composed in Greek, Syriac, and Arabic—would influence later European interpreters. Medieval Christians categorized non-Christians as Jews, pagans, or heretics. The Jews, involved in the foundational events of Christianity, had a peculiar status of their own—associated in the Gospel of Matthew with the death of Jesus, they were viewed with suspicion and outright enmity, and resented for resisting conversion to Christianity. Pagans were defined as those who had not heard the Word of God; heretics had heard it yet persisted in not accepting it. Muslims did not fit neatly into any of these categories, but clearly they were not true believers. Yet their false creed enjoyed immense worldly success. Though the ways of divine Providence were often difficult to apprehend, Christian thinkers needed to grapple with the popularity of Islam. Was Islam a diabolical parody of Christianity, something the devil had concocted to mock true believers? Was the rise of Muslim empire a divine punishment, a scourge brought down on the Christian community of believers because they had sinned? Millenarian ideas about the coming of the end of the world also latched onto the rise of Islam. Was Muhammad the Antichrist? If so, the rise of Islam presaged the end of days.[7]

Medieval writers tried to fit Muslims into the history of the world, but the classical sources invested with most authority in the Western Christian tradition had little to say about the Arabs and nothing about Islam. Some creative scholars endowed Muslims with a genealogy going back to Abraham's son Ishmael, who was cast into the desert with his mother, the Egyptian slave girl Hagar. Because these writers considered Hagar and Ishmael to be the origin of the Arabs, they labeled Muslims "Hagarenes" or "Ishmaelites," that is, descendants of Hagar or of Ishmael. "Saracens," the most frequently used word for Muslims, was more an ethnic than a religious designation.[8]

Among the categories employed to understand Muhammad himself, the one that most influenced later tradition was that of false prophet, the figure against whom Jesus warns in the Sermon on the Mount, "Beware of false prophets, which come to you in sheep's clothing, but inwardly they are ravening wolves" (Matthew 7:15). The concept of false prophet was compatible with millenarianism: the New Testament foretold that false prophets would help bring about the Second Coming, the final era of history. Casting Muhammad as a false prophet who had cunningly misled his followers, Christian writers attempted to explain how this caravan trader had created such a successful religion.

Other attempts to discredit Muhammad included dismissing his moments of divine inspiration as nothing but epileptic fits or claiming that Islam achieved such widespread success because Muhammad had promised believers carnal delights in Heaven. As for the origins of the Qur'an, Muhammad was supposed to have been illiterate, but the Qur'an evinced detailed knowledge of both Judaism and Christianity. Muhammad claimed that the book was God's word as revealed to him by the angel Gabriel; Christian writers thought that he had forged it with the help of Jewish and Christian assistants.

Even the man who did most to advance the Christian study of Islam in the Middle Ages, Peter the Venerable, the abbot of Cluny, did not definitively state whether Muslims were pagans or heretics. He oversaw the translation of the Qur'an into Latin in twelfth-century Toledo; Iberia, a frontier between Muslim and Christian states, was especially well placed for such an effort. For Peter, who composed a number of writings against Islam, knowledge-making was not the ultimate goal; religious polemic and conversion were.[9]

Finally, Islam's central theological dogma, the unity of God, was a direct contradiction of the Trinitarian form of Christianity established at the Council of Nicaea in 325 CE. The Qur'an's statements about God's nature offered a direct rejoinder to the Christian concept. Sura 112 of the Qur'an, for instance, reads: "Say, 'He is God, One, God, the Everlasting Refuge, who has not begotten, and has not been begotten, and equal to Him is not any one.'" Although ancient unitarian heresies (such as Arianism) had been defeated, Islam represented the obdurate persistence of a belief that the Nicene Council had already sought to quash in the fourth century. In addition, the Muslim doctrine of the unity of God did not seem beyond the powers of human reason to apprehend, unlike the doctrine of the Trinity. This feature of Islam—its greater appeal to human reason in comparison to Trinitarian Christianity—would become salient once more in the seventeenth and eighteenth centuries.

The Renaissance and After

A European looking at a world map in the middle of the seventeenth century would have been struck by the transcontinental extent of lands governed or inhabited by Muslims. In that era, those domains stretched from Morocco to Malacca and from Timbuktu to Tashkent (Map 2). Three great Islamic dynasties flourished between the sixteenth and the eighteenth centuries: from east to west they were the Ottomans in the Balkans, Anatolia, the Levant, and North Africa; the Safavids in Persia; and the Mughals in northern India. Yet these empires were distinct, and they were not allied. The Ottomans and Mughals adhered to the Hanafi branch of Sunni Islam, whereas the Persians professed Twelver Shiism, a branch of Islam that the Ottomans condemned as heretical. Political enmity compounded this sectarian disagreement.[10]

The elegant craftsmanship of Muslim artisans had been known to Europeans for centuries. Textiles, carpets, jewelry, metalwork, ceramics, glassware, and illuminated books bespoke the cultural refinement of the peoples of this wide swath of the world.[11] Muslims had long been part of European history, from the medieval battles on European soil, such as Tours (also known as Poitiers, 732 CE), to the Crusades in the Holy Land and the Iberian wars that ended with the fall of Granada in 1492. In short, they were familiar foreigners.

At the level of thought and belief, moreover, most educated Europeans knew that Islam professed to be a replacement for Christianity, the final revelation of the Abrahamic God. The relative proximity of Muslims, their political, religious, and cultural achievements, and the geographical sweep of their states all impressed themselves on the European consciousness. At a time when Europeans were not yet the masters of the universe, there were good reasons to be interested in Muslims and their traditions.

The Ottoman Empire, geographically the closest to Europe of the three Muslim empires, was the one that most heavily influenced European understandings of Islam. In May 1453 the Ottomans, led by Mehmed II, conquered Constantinople and what remained of the Byzantine Empire, an event that put the study of Islam on the agenda for many European thinkers. The capture of the city founded by Constantine, the first Christian emperor, was widely perceived as a second fall of Rome. The destruction wrought by the Ottomans associated them in European minds with hostility to learning and culture. These parvenu conquerors appeared to many Europeans to be the enemy of the learned traditions of Christendom. In addition, the anti-Muslim rhetoric that had fueled the Crusades remained a powerful cultural force well into the Renaissance.[12]

The theological debates of the Protestant Reformation made European Christians more aware that their theology disagreed fundamentally with Islam's central creed—the unity of God.[13] In the sixteenth century, Muslims, who had often been described in broad ethnic terms, such as "Saracens," gained new religious identifiers, like "Mahometists." "Mahometist" had a precise meaning—a follower of Muhammad. Like the terms for Christian heresies (for instance, Arianism, Nestorianism, and Pelagianism, after Arius, Nestorius, and Pelagius), it bore the name of its founder. (In the sixteenth and seventeenth centuries, new theological movements were also named after founders: for example, Arminianism, Jansenism, and Socinianism after Jacobus Arminius, Cornelius Jansenius, and Faustus Socinus.) In other words, to European Christians the term "Mahometist" did not imply that Muslims adored Muhammad himself. The term "Muslims"—based on what believers are called in the Qur'an (*muslim,* pl. *muslimūn,* a noun with the same root as the word "Islam")—first came to be used in this period as well; it was introduced by European scholars of Arabic, though it was not widely adopted. This new salience of religion can be tracked in the imaginative literature of the period. For example, in the fifteenth- and early sixteenth-century romances of Matteo Maria Boiardo and Ludovico Ariosto, Christian and Saracen knights are hard to distinguish and follow the same code of honor. By contrast, the epic poems of Torquato Tasso and Edmund Spenser, both published in the late sixteenth century, are characterized by religious and ideological polarization.[14]

As a result of Islam's association with unitarianism, by the sixteenth century, if not earlier, the religion became a resource for those who questioned orthodox Western Christianity, whether Catholic or Protestant. Islam was so deeply associated with unitarianism in the minds of some Protestant Reformers that Adam Neuser, a German anti-Trinitarian, finally departed from his homeland for Istanbul, where he converted to Islam. The religion likewise held interest for such diverse readers as the Friulian miller Domenico Scandella, known as Menocchio, who was executed for heresy in 1600, and the early eighteenth-century English unitarian thinker John Toland, on whom more in Chapter 3. This renewed salience of Islam is also indicated by the Catholic Indices of Prohibited Books, which began as a Counter-Reformation measure: they banned both printed and manuscript versions of the Qur'an.[15]

The problem of how to classify Islam—as heresy, paganism, or alien religion—would continue into the Renaissance and after. This ambiguity, however, made the religion an interesting intellectual resource for thinking about foreign faiths and their relationship to Christianity. Its ambiguous categorization allowed the freedom to suggest new points of view, and, in particular, to argue that considering Islam alongside the classical cultures of antiquity was more relevant than contrasting it with Judaism or with Christian heresies.

A desire among some observers to understand Islam as a living religion predated the serious study of its written traditions. To some degree European travel writing even inspired later scholarly work in this area.[16] Since the late Middle Ages, Europeans had produced accounts of pilgrimages to the Holy Land and secular travels to Constantinople and beyond. In the late Renaissance, theorists of travel codified a veritable "art of travel" (*ars apodemica*) prescribing how learned travelers might gather knowledge on their journeys.[17] In the age of print, travel accounts spread knowledge of Muslim societies, peoples, and traditions to readers far and wide. These works dedicated much space to descriptions of manners and customs, and several important ones contained pictures of Muslim men and women, including clerics and mystics. These lively depictions testify not just to the intense European interest in Islam but also to the European capacity to consider it as a living and breathing phenomenon. The images illustrating books by Melchior Lorichs, Nicolas de Nicolay, and others were attempts to depict the tangible practices of Muslim believers (Figure 1). More than simply conveying information, travel narratives employed their descriptions of Muslim piety to moralize about the shortcomings of Christians: If heretics could be so pious, the argument ran, how could Christians not be inspired to outdo them?[18]

European travel writers praised other aspects of Muslim societies, such as their magnificence, charity, tolerance, and meritocracy. Muslim social institutions—charitable endowments of hospitals, for example—also impressed European visitors. The coexistence of different faiths within the Ottoman Empire seemed remarkable at a time when European states were much less religiously diverse and the continent was riven by sectarian violence and warfare, which lasted from about 1524 to 1648. From 1500 to 1700, dozens of published travel accounts of the Ottoman Empire, Safavid Persia, and Mughal India amounted to a large body of literature; during this same period, writings by Jesuit missionaries brought new knowledge of China to Europe.[19] But it was especially the lands of Islam that captured the European literary imagination, as demonstrated by the fact that plays set in the Ottoman Empire were by far more common than those on Indian or Chinese subjects.[20] Hindus, with their variety of deities, and their phallic lingam as an object of worship, seemed vastly more unfamiliar to Europeans than did Muslims, who recognized Jesus even if they denied that he was the incarnation of God.[21]

Arabic scholarship produced in Europe—the subject of this book—had a vexed relationship with European travel writing. As forms of expertise about Asia, the two were in direct competition. Moreover, they had different epistemological bases. If the scholars valued linguistic and philological knowledge above all, eyewitnessing was the supreme form of authority for travel writers. As a result, some scholars of Arabic, like d'Herbelot and Johann Jacob Reiske, excluded travel writing from their sources.[22] Others, like Richard Simon, Adriaan Reland, and Johann David Michaelis, employed travel writers whom they considered sufficiently learned and methodical and therefore trustworthy. Even so, to the end of the period Arabic scholarship and travel writing remained distinct undertakings, to the extent that some authors of the secular Enlightenment, such as Montesquieu, would rely on travel writing at the expense of the new Arabic scholarship altogether (see Chapter 6).

European Traditions of Knowledge

Beginning in the late sixteenth century, a number of European scholars set out to acquire Arabic and Islamic learning. The model for their activity was scholarly humanism, a movement that had begun in the fourteenth century with the recovery of Latin manuscripts, medieval copies of classical works that lay neglected or forgotten in monastic libraries across Europe. Soon enough, the humanist scholars sought Greek manuscripts as well, not restricting their searches to Italy or northern Europe, but pursuing them as far afield as monasteries in the Eastern Mediterranean. The end of the Byzantine Empire with the fall of Constantinople in 1453 brought emigrant Greek scholars and their manuscripts to Western Europe, enhancing the range of available sources. The humanist revival of Latin letters defined elite education in Europe for centuries, providing the curriculum for both a moral and a literary education from the fifteenth century through the eighteenth and beyond.[23]

In the Renaissance, humanist scholars broadened their studies beyond Greek and Latin to include Hebrew, not only because the Bible was written in it but also because it was widely considered the original language of humankind. What started as the recovery of Latin letters grew into an increasingly polyglot affair; trilingual colleges were founded in Louvain (1517) and Paris (1530). Hebrew made European men of learning familiar with a Levantine, Semitic language. It also put the Christian scholars of the Renaissance into a

complicated relationship with their Jewish contemporaries: they at once relied on them for their expertise and yet condescended to them on account of
their religious difference.

The European study of Hebrew led to the study of Arabic, as well as of
other Semitic languages, such as Aramaic (known as Chaldean); Syriac,
the language especially of Near Eastern Christians in late antiquity; Ge'ez
(known as Aethiopic); and Coptic. Knowledge of these languages was believed to enhance the understanding of Hebrew. Attention to Arabic could,
therefore, be justified not merely on polemical or missionary grounds but also
as a tool for understanding Christian Scripture itself.[24] In significant ways,
the study of Arabic followed the same path that the study of Hebrew had:
first the creation of grammars and dictionaries, then the gradual translation of
classical texts (the Hebrew Bible), on to the study of the Talmud and the
main rabbinical commentators on Scripture, and eventually to the study of
these writings as an end in itself. There were significant differences: the Jews
held a unique (and unenviable) place in Christian theology, and they had
lived on European soil in recent memory, or—in Italy, the Netherlands, the
Holy Roman Empire, and Poland-Lithuania—did so in the present. Their
lack of political clout, moreover, made them easier to dismiss than the
powerful and more distant Muslims.[25]

European scholars recognized (and, indeed, overestimated) the family relationship of Arabic to Hebrew, and many thought that Arabic could clarify
obscure Hebrew words. In addition, Arabic translations of the Bible existed
in the Levant, and Europeans hoped that gathering them might illuminate
obscure passages in the Hebrew Bible. The Complutensian Polyglot Bible,
completed in Alcalà de Henares, near Madrid, in 1517, and the three Polyglot
Bibles that followed were all the result of massive efforts of erudition and
typography, as well as piety; they were the scholarly equivalent of Gothic ca-
thedrals. Their goal was to bring together the biblical text in as many languages
as possible. The Paris and the London Polyglots both contained Arabic versions of the Bible.[26] Even if some scholars studied Arabic for its own sake, into
the nineteenth century others continued to consider Arabic together with
other Semitic languages, and especially as a resource for understanding biblical
Hebrew.

Arabic was also the tongue of several communities of Eastern Christians
and their liturgies and Bibles. Both Catholics and Protestants hoped to find

in the Eastern churches evidence of the antiquity of their own beliefs and tra-
ditions. The Catholic Church, in particular, whose missions to the Holy Land
had begun in the medieval period, sought to cultivate a special bond with the
Christian communities of the Eastern Mediterranean, even compelling the
Maronite Church of Mount Lebanon to join the Catholic Church in 1584.
The Maronite College in Rome would form a link between Europe and the
Christian Levant throughout the seventeenth and eighteenth centuries.[27]

Above all, both Catholic and Protestant Europeans studied Arabic
because they considered the language useful for shoring up their religious traditions. In an age of confessional states (states with an official religion), a
ruler's legitimacy was based on religious and political theology. Even so, the
interests that early modern scholars exhibited in practice were much broader
than the mandates they used to justify their scholarship. Alongside official
motivations, equally important ones were not articulated but can be recon-
structed by observing the scholars at work.[28] Attaining an objective view of
Islamic culture was not an explicit goal, but in their explorations, scholars
roamed well beyond the dictates of "utility," narrowly construed.

From the late sixteenth century to the late seventeenth, Europeans created
their own tools for the study of Arabic. The history of the early European
Arabists is one of penury and struggle with such basic problems as obtaining
manuscripts to study, mastering the lexical wealth of Arabic, and grasping the
complex rules of its grammar. Over time, collective sweat and toil made these
challenges less forbidding. The Dutch, especially, led the way. The great
Leiden scholar Joseph Scaliger left a small but significant donation of Arabic
books to the Leiden University Library, later enriched by a gift from his student Jacobus Golius. Scaliger, a man of many interests, had studied Arabic
and had even lived with his onetime Arabic teacher, Guillaume Postel.[29] The
Arabic grammar of the Dutch prodigy Thomas Erpenius, published in 1613,
was the standard reference into the early nineteenth century. For lexicography, Golius's *Lexicon Arabico-Latinum* (1653), a collation of several Arabic
dictionaries, including that of al-Jawharī, replaced such earlier efforts as the *Lexicon* of Franciscus Raphelengius. Scholars elsewhere worked toward the
same ends: the early English Arabist William Bedwell spent much of his life
working on a dictionary that was never published, and, in Milan, Antonio
Giggi translated al-Fīrūzābādī's dictionary, in 1632. Thanks especially to the
contributions of Erpenius and Golius, the problem of teaching correct Arabic

was in large measure solved by the middle of the seventeenth century. For the next two centuries, the instruments that they created would serve as vital references, and many of the protagonists of this book taught themselves Arabic from those pages.[30]

Traditionally, Oriental studies in the sixteenth and seventeenth centuries have been seen as a Protestant achievement, though more recent scholarship has recovered Catholic contributions. Catholic scholars of the seventeenth century produced one of the first Arabic dictionaries, a new translation of the Vulgate into Arabic, and, most importantly, the first accurate translation of the Qur'an into a European language, the history of which is recounted in Chapter 2. A Catholic scholar created a first Western encyclopedia of Islamic history and letters, the *Bibliothèque Orientale,* which is investigated in Chapter 4. This book integrates both Catholic and Protestant contributions and brings out their similarities and connections.[31]

Arabic, the language of the Qur'an, was also the language of most highbrow intellectual output in Muslim lands, from the religious disciplines to scientific treatises. Yet it was just one of the three languages educated Muslims were expected to know, at least in the Ottoman lands. Persian was the idiom of courtliness, poetry, and many mystical writings. Ottoman Turkish served for everyday conversation, and was also the language of administration and the law. Both Persian and Turkish shared an alphabet with Arabic, and contained copious Arabic loanwords, but these were in all other respects three distinct languages for different intellectual activities. Europeans studied Persian and Turkish in the wake of Arabic, albeit not to the same extent.[32] This book focuses on Arabic. A history told through Persian would be slightly different. Most obviously, it would offer a different geography—going all the way to South Asia—and different protagonists, both on the Muslim and on the Christian side.

Geographically the narrative marches from Rome and Padua north to Paris, Oxford, London, Cambridge, and Utrecht, and east to Leipzig. If such peregrinations prevent in-depth study of one location, they bring into view the parallels and connections between scholars of different languages, Christian sects, and affiliations. Spain, which to some degree was isolated from the European Republic of Letters, does not sit in the foreground of this study, yet it is nonetheless a subtle but insistent presence. Spain played a role in seventeenth- and eighteenth-century European Arabic studies, and books written by European scholars, including Protestant ones, circulated there. Indeed, the translation of the Qur'an by Lodovico Marracci, which, as Chapter 2 will show, was crucial to the modern Western understanding of the Qur'an, began with a Qur'an commentary that had been collected in Spain by the papal nuncio Cardinal Camillo Massimo.[33]

This book is not the history of the formation of a field or the emergence of a discipline; disciplines in the modern sense are not to be sought in an era in which scholars could and did pursue broad and eclectic interests. The present work focuses on a single area of inquiry, but its subjects did not. To take but one example: Adriaan Reland, whose work on Islam is discussed in Chapter 3, was also interested in Persian, Hebrew, Malay, Urdu, Hindi, Chinese, Japanese, and the native American languages, and published maps of Persia, Japan, Java, and Palestine. (Nor was he a mere dabbler; his geographical study of the Holy Land was deemed, in the nineteenth century, "next to the Bible . . . the most important book for travellers in the Holy Land.")[34]

Although the Arabists of seventeenth- and eighteenth-century Europe pursued very different career paths, and did not necessarily hold university posts in Arabic, they recognized a common set of problems and were able to tackle these across national, linguistic, and even confessional boundaries. At the same time as they competed, Catholics and Protestants used each other's scholarship and pursued common goals. Occasional direct Catholic–Protestant exchanges, if not outright collaborations, are recorded. The new European knowledge of Islam was formed through this competition and cooperation among scholars—the Republic of Arabic Letters.

ONE

THE ORIENTAL LIBRARY

In 1685, years before his translation of *The Thousand and One Nights* would win him enduring fame, the French scholar Antoine Galland was living in Istanbul. Trained in Arabic, Persian, and Turkish, he was nearing the end of his nearly five-year mission in the city to collect books and ancient coins on behalf of the French crown; he also collected them for himself, and for the French ambassador, the Count of Guilleragues. In his role as interpreter and professional book buyer, as well as in his private capacity as a scholar, he had come to know the city's book markets intimately. The number of works it was possible to find in the Ottoman capital delighted him: "The ease of buying [books] is greater than in any other place, as there is a considerable number of shops where they are sold and where every day new ones are brought to be sold to the highest bidder."[1]

Galland, on whom more below, was no anomaly in his interest in Islamic books or in his deliberate and royally ordained quest to acquire them. Arabic, Persian, and Turkish manuscripts were collected across Europe in the seventeenth and eighteenth centuries. This chapter travels from the book markets of Istanbul via traveling collectors like Galland to the great libraries of Europe, their patrons and their motivations, and, finally, to the ideas that governed these Oriental repositories. Manuscript collecting has been studied in many local contexts, but the comparative angle taken here reveals that the same process unfolded all over the continent, with many of the same aims, challenges, and outcomes, whether in France, the Netherlands, England, or Italy.[2]

In the sixteenth century, great libraries were founded all over Europe—the French Royal Library, initially located in Blois and Fontainebleau, and later in Paris; the Escorial, near Madrid; the Hapsburg Imperial Library, in Vienna; the Leiden University Library; the Bodleian, in Oxford—but it was in the seventeenth century that they gained Oriental collections.[3] (The Vatican

Library was founded in 1475, though the collection was begun earlier in the century.) At this time, thousands of Arabic, Persian, and Turkish manuscripts entered European collections, transforming them and making possible the in-depth study of Islamic literary and intellectual traditions. Oxford, Leiden, Paris, the Escorial, and Rome had the greatest Islamic manuscript collections in Europe, but they were far from the only ones. The Biblioteca Ambrosiana of Milan, founded in 1609, built an Arabic collection, and in Florence's Palazzo Pitti, the grand dukes of Tuscany held an Oriental collection brought from Rome by Grand Duke Ferdinando de' Medici.[4] Moreover, many smaller libraries gathered Islamic manuscripts. In Paris alone, these included, besides the Royal Library, the library of the Sorbonne, the library of the Maurist (Benedictine) abbey of Saint Germain-des-Prés, and the library of the Jesuit school of Louis-le-Grand, as well as the private libraries of Cardinal Mazarin, the sometime finance minister Nicolas Fouquet, and the minister Jean-Baptiste Colbert. All opened their doors to scholars.

Europeans in search of manuscripts were obsessed with great Islamic libraries: the collection of the sultan of Morocco, the library of the imperial seraglio in Istanbul, and the library of al-Azhar mosque in Cairo. In the end, though, European collectors drew their Islamic riches from other sources. When they could, they bought directly from monasteries and other such depositories, but marketplaces and their commercial booksellers proved to be their most valuable suppliers—once European envoys learned what books to seek and how to go about obtaining them.

Istanbul, the Ottoman capital, was one of several locations for acquiring manuscripts. The Ottoman Empire played a sizable role in the formation of European collections and in shaping European collectors' taste—what they considered to be worth acquiring—but the Arabic manuscripts that informed the Western study of Islam came from three continents. What collectors in Spain, Morocco, Persia, and even Indonesia brought back to Europe deter-mined what scholars at home could access and study. The assembly of collec-tions owed much to the displacement to distant locations of intellectually minded Europeans. Oriental scholarship would have been much impoverished without the Dutch East India Company in Batavia, the English East India Company in Fort St. George, the English Levant Company in Aleppo, and the Chamber of Commerce of Marseille in Izmir and Istanbul. Indeed, it is doubtful whether it would have flowered at all. The collecting of foreign books was just one of the ways in which the trading companies affected European culture at this time, shaping consumer tastes and knowledge production.[5]

What made its way to Europe depended both on what Islamic readers and copyists cultivated, and on what, from among that variety, Europeans decided to acquire. Manuscripts obtained for European collections reflected the priorities of Islamic intellectual life and book culture in the seventeenth and eighteenth centuries. The latter, therefore, inevitably shaped what Europeans came to know.

Libraries are fragile entities. Collections must be amassed and then organized and safeguarded. A book unlisted in a catalog or placed on the wrong shelf is as good as lost. And above all, books need readers—an ambitious proposition in the case of ancient or foreign languages. It was not enough to bring Islamic manuscripts from faraway lands; their languages had to be cultivated. The creation of Oriental collections was, therefore, a necessary but not a sufficient step in the understanding of Islamic intellectual traditions. As the following pages show, it should not be understood simply as means to higher scholarly ends, but instead as a cultural phenomenon in its own right. Possessing foreign books seemed valuable even when there was no one on hand to study them. Patrons, collectors, and scholars believed in the ideal of the Oriental library, and they each contributed to its creation. Like all libraries, the Oriental library was an act of faith in the capabilities and interests of future readers.

Istanbul

The largest city in seventeenth-century Europe, Istanbul teemed with intellectual activity. The great mosque complexes housed schools for religious study.[6] Students from the city and provinces attended these schools in order to enter the *ulema,* the class of religious scholars sponsored by the state. The members of the *ulema* were active as teachers, judges, and jurists; they were the ones who interpreted *şeriat* (sharia) law, especially jurisprudence and Qur'anic commentary. Students copied out the classics in these genres for their own use; their teachers wrote commentaries on or abridged them. Religious scholars also produced poetry, biography, and chronicles.[7] Some translated the great works of Arabic literature, such as Ibn Khaldun's *Muqaddima,* into Turkish; many wrote histories. The chief jurisconsult (*şeykhülislam*)

Zekeriyāzāde Yaḥyā (d. 1644) made his mark as much through his verse as through his expertise in the law.[8]

Poetry was an especially prominent art form in Ottoman Istanbul: as one visiting Bosnian author remarked, there was a poet under every paving stone.[9] Poems described local life and love on the Bosporus, depicted or satirized notable men, and celebrated Ottoman cities and court festivities. The numerous biographical dictionaries of poets open windows onto the literary life of Istanbul, and especially of its court, where ambitious men seeking the favor of the sultan sent their literary productions.[10]

The court was not the only locus of literary life. The wooden houses clustered tightly on the hillsides of the city, and the grander *yalıs*, or villas, on the Bosporus waterfront, hosted gatherings of poets in their *selamlık*s (reception rooms). In these salons, organized by the poets themselves or by important officials, writers established their reputations and found patrons.[11] Besides the refined poetry composed in these elevated environments, popular verse, composed to be accompanied by music on the *sāz,* a lute, was performed at coffeehouses and fairs. Coffeehouses mixed conversation with entertainments like poetry recitation, puppet theater, and storytelling.[12] Practicing Sufis composed religious poetry, which was often didactic, and commemorative verse recounting the lives of famous dervishes. Poetry permeated life in Istanbul for everyone from the educated elites to the popular classes, who heard verses recited in the streets and cafés. Inscribed on fountains, gravestones, and public monuments, poetry—and calligraphy itself—was part of daily life.[13]

From the classroom to the salon, intellectual and literary activity spilled forth. Divans, or collections of poems, circulated among coteries of writers and lovers of poetry; Sufi verses were composed, copied, and commented upon by Sufi writers; and the schools generated a large industry of copyists and secondhand booksellers, as in the Fatih mosque complex. In addition, wealthy patrons commissioned and collected albums of miniatures, an art form inspired by Persian models and perfected in the course of the seventeenth century.[14] Secondhand booksellers worked in the Grand Bazaar, the covered market near the Bayezid mosque, where they shared the same enclosed area, known as the *bedestan* or *bezistan,* with the jewelers.[15] On a festival day, the shops "were all covered with beautiful brocade and each Turk had in his shop silver perfume-burners and vials full of perfumed water to sprinkle on the passersby and a great silver candelabrum, which supported a large white lit candle. Since this place is rather narrow, the crowd of people seemed even bigger than it was."[16] The city also had a great number of book-binders, serving those who copied their own manuscripts or who employed others to copy for them.[17] Istanbul possessed commercial lending libraries before these were common in Christian Europe.[18] In the *bezistan,* some secondhand booksellers served mainly as lending libraries, giving out books for 4 or 5 akçes (small silver coins).[19] They were especially popular in winter, when the residents of the city spent the long nights gathered together in groups to read stories aloud.[20] At the end of the seventeenth century, the powerful Köprülü family founded a library on Divanyolu, the street leading to the imperial palace. This was the first independent library building in Istanbul.[21] Thanks to all of these institutions, the shelves of the Ottoman capital brimmed with books both old and new. Persian literary classics and the mainstays of Qur'anic exegesis vied for space with the latest novelties by local literati.

The intellectual life of Ottoman Istanbul was trilingual; most members of the educated elite spoke Arabic, Persian, and Ottoman Turkish. Arabic and Persian had longer literary traditions and greater prestige, but over the course of the seventeenth century Ottoman Turkish rose in respectability for literary composition.[22] Many books were translated from Arabic and Persian into Turkish because readers preferred them in their native language.[23] European outsiders who wished to gain entry into the intellectual circles of Istanbul had to pursue literacy in three distinct tongues.

Printing was marginal to Islamic book culture, including in the Ottoman Empire. Books, even very long ones, existed only as manuscripts until the early eighteenth century, when the first commercial Ottoman printing press—founded in 1727 by the Hungarian renegade Ibrāhīm Müteferriqa in Istanbul and closed in 1729—produced its first printed book, an Arabic-Turkish dictionary.[24] The Müteferriqa press, which had permission to publish secular books, failed commercially and did not inaugurate a wider shift to print. Printing was known to Muslims, of course: medieval Arab traders in China would have been exposed to block printing, and, closer by, Sephardic Jews and Arab Christians ran their own printing presses in Istanbul in the six-teenth century, producing two Polyglot Bibles and other ambitious books.[25] Even though the Ottoman and other Muslim states readily embraced many foreign technical advances, such as military technology, they rejected printing for most of the period before 1800—on account, it is thought, of the power of scribal guilds; the value ascribed to writing by hand, especially for the Qur'an; the respect for person-to-person transmission; and the threat that printing seemed to pose to the authority of the *ulema*.[26]

In our own age, which has equated books with printed works for so long, it is possible to forget that manuscripts are books, too, and that the European predecessor of print was not the spoken word but the manuscript. Manuscript cultures have their own workings: books are written, distributed, and evaluated differently than where commercial printing presses predominate. In Ottoman Istanbul, for instance, "popularity was judged from the frequency with which the manuscripts of a given author circulated among knowledgeable people."[27]

The manuscript books that Europeans sought to collect in the Ottoman Empire would have been eminently recognizable to them. Just like European books in the age of print, they were made of paper, rather than vellum, and they were codices (bound stacks of sheets), not scrolls.[28] They were far more familiar than, say, the pictographs used by the Mexica to record their histories on calendar wheels, yet late sixteenth-century Jesuits had been able to recognize those symbols as a form of writing and had attempted to study them.[29] Indeed, Spanish scholars even identified and described the system of "cotton ropes, that the Indians called *Quippos*"—the knotted ropes that the Inca used for information storage and retrieval.[30] In comparison, Islamic books posed nary a conceptual challenge.

The features of seventeenth-century literary life in Istanbul were also found in major Muslim cities throughout the Levant, North Africa, Central and South Asia, Safavid Persia, and Mughal India.[31] What differed from city to city were books of legal interpretation and exegesis, which reflected local schools and traditions, and histories of local cities and dynasties. Aleppo's rich markets were frequented not only by European book buyers but also by Kātib Çelebi, the Ottoman scholar who was inspired to begin the most important Islamic bibliography of all time while posted there.[32] Cairo and Damascus maintained institutions of higher learning even after they became provincial centers of the Ottoman Empire. Appointments in the heart of the Ottoman bureaucratic machinery in Istanbul were out of the reach of scholars in these cities, but men of learning held local appointments and continued to teach and to write.[33]

A Collector at Large

In order to draw scholarly profit from his visit, a European had to find his way around the elaborately organized intellectual life of a city like Istanbul. Antoine Galland would dedicate many years to the task. Born in 1646 to a family of extremely modest means, Galland was encouraged by his parents, acquaintances, and religious institutions to pursue his studies in Paris, where he was trained in Latin and Greek and also in Hebrew and Arabic. His professional career began to take shape when he was first sent to Istanbul, from 1670 to 1673, to accompany the French ambassador, the Marquis de Nointel. Nointel had been tasked with (and succeeded in) renegotiating on more favorable terms the capitulations, or trade agreements, that had formalized French trade in the Ottoman Empire since the first one was signed by Süleyman the Magnificent and Francis I, in 1536.[34] Galland's assignment, meanwhile, was to collect Greek Orthodox statements of belief regarding transubstantiation, the Catholic doctrine that the bread and wine offered during the Mass become the flesh and blood of Christ. The French theologians Antoine Arnauld and Pierre Nicole hoped that Galland's findings would buttress the Catholic doctrine by proving that the ancient Churches of the East had believed in it.[35]

Thus, diplomatic ties, commercial ambitions, religious politics, and Christian interconfessional rivalry all enabled Galland to pursue his training as a scholar of Oriental matters. While in Istanbul, he worked on his Turkish and on his Arabic, Persian, and modern Greek. The diary he wrote while there offers many insights into the intellectual life of the city.[36] In 1677–1678 he spent almost a year in Izmir, on Anatolia's Aegean coast, collecting medals for the French king's cabinet. In October 1680 he returned to Istanbul, where he served the new ambassador, the Count of Guilleragues, for more than five years.[37]

Looking back over his years in Istanbul in his 1685 manuscript, Galland argued that the city was not just an imperial capital, but also a capital of intellectual life and a major center of Islamic book culture. Books from newly conquered territories found their way to the capital, as did provincial scholars who hoped to gain recognition and employment. For European collectors like Galland, Istanbul was the place to be:

> There is no place more convenient for making progress [in the acquisition of books] in a short time than the city of Constantinople, which, since it is the capital of the Empire, must be considered the gathering place of all men of learning who aspire to receive compensation for their works by accepting an appointment [there]. Moreover, as the Empire has grown, men of letters have found a refuge there, abandoning conquered lands both to avoid witnessing the change of government in their countries, and so that their merit might be known. Then they transported their libraries with them. But the capture of cities has contributed most to multiplying books in Istanbul. They were brought in unbelievable quantity, as much from Egypt, from Syria, from Arabia and Mesopotamia as from Persia itself, where the Turkish armies once advanced considerably.[38]

Galland noted that Arabic and Persian books were readily available in Istanbul and could be had even more cheaply than in the cities where they had been produced: "It often happens that Persian merchants buy books in their language there, finding it advantageous to take them back to sell them upon their return."[39] Although Istanbul was not an ancient Islamic city—unlike Cairo, Baghdad, Damascus, or Aleppo, it had no Islamic life at all until the conquest of 1453—its position at the center of a flourishing empire compensated for its parvenu status. By the late seventeenth century, the capital had boasted teeming bookshops for some time. Almost a century earlier, the Moroccan ambassador had reported that "lots of books could be found in Istanbul, libraries and the bazaar were full to the brim, and books were brought to Istanbul from all around the world."[40]

The capital housed a sophisticated market in which rare books, when they surfaced, were reserved for regular customers, whose interests the booksellers carefully tracked: "These books are often more expensive than others, because they belong to people who recognize their rarity and value."[41] Islamic manuscripts, Galland wrote, varied in price according to content and quality. There were "Alcorans worth two shields [a silver coin], six shields, ten shields, twenty shields, and there are even ones worth one hundred, three hundred, five hundred, and a thousand shields."[42] By paying cash one could gain a competitive advantage over local collectors.[43] But Europeans did not always get what they wanted: on Sunday, February 14, 1672, the French ambassador was outbid by a local by half a piastre (a piastre was worth 120 akçes) for a history of Süleyman's conquests in Turkish.[44] Equally, one could engage a bookseller to seek books that one required, thus "extracting many [books] from their places." Galland himself had found, via this stratagem, "four or five copies of the complete history by Mirkhond [the Persian historian Mīrkhwānd] that is considered so rare in Paris, and that is not at all complete in His Majesty's Library [the Royal Library]."[45] Galland's diary from the years 1672–1673 reveals his dependence on local agents: most of his entries about books he has seen begin with the words "I was brought . . ." He also kept an ear open for news of important private libraries that might be going up for sale.[46]

Different collectors looked at the market in different ways. Galland's priorities diverged from those of the Marquis de Nointel, the French ambassador who was his employer from 1670 to 1673. The marquis admired prestigious, decorated books, such as an almanac he bought for two piastres on February 9, 1672, "whose workmanship was so beautiful, so fine and delicate, that many excellent artisans in France would not accept to do as much for ten piastres."[47] On another occasion, "a Turkish bookseller named Mahamoud Bacha showed [Galland] several figures made in Persia, embellished in their margins by several attractive gilt grotesques, marvelously well applied. My lord the Ambassador did not take them, because [Mahamoud Bacha] wanted to sell them for too great a price."[48] Nointel, in other words, partook in the tradition of collecting Islamic books as objects of prestige, or as art objects.

Galland himself was interested in the classics of the Islamic literary tradition, whether Persian literature or history books, as well as in expensive dictionaries.[49] His goal was to build a scholarly library for himself. Yet he saw an even wider variety of books, such as one that "treated vile and lascivious things."[50] His diary also describes his visits and exchanges with local scholars, including two Ottoman Arabic scholars and astrologers to whom he showed his copy of Johannes Hevelius's 1647 drawings of the moon.[51] Beside books, he bought items like agate gemstones and a painted chessboard.

The delights of the bazaar were hard to resist, yet Galland was hardly an aimless shopper. On his third stay in the Levant, from 1679 to 1688, he had to follow the detailed advice and instructions outlined in a nearly twenty-page closely written letter he received from Jean-Baptiste Colbert, the French minister.[52] This letter, which most likely dates from 1679, reveals the painstaking level of detail at which royally sponsored travel was organized.[53]

Colbert's letter begins by summarizing the three categories under which all investigations during travel fall: "the nature of the country, the customs of the inhabitants, and that which regards the arts and the sciences."[54] Galland was to focus on the last of these without neglecting the first two. "[It will be necessary] while in the country to make sure to seek good ancient manuscripts in Greek, in Arabic, in Persian, and in other Oriental tongues, except in Hebrew, because we have those in great number here. The caloyers [Orthodox monks] and other Greek monks, as well as the Maronites [Arab Christians] of Mount Lebanon will suggest many Greek and Arabic ones; as for the Persian ones, they will only be found in Persia. [It will be necessary] to make sure that they are complete and perfect; the most ancient ones are usually the best."[55] Colbert thought that Galland's first port of call should be native monasteries in Greece or in the Lebanon.

> The most sought-after subjects of these manuscripts are those of religion, the treatises of the Greek Fathers, the ancient councils or synods, ecclesiastical history, secular history, geography, philosophy, medicine, and that which regards all branches of mathematics. One finds several authors of these sciences, in both Arabic and Greek. The same quantity of ancient books, which were written originally in Greek and in Latin and which are no longer found in their original language, can be found translated into Arabic, because this people, having made itself the master of the sciences, even as it chased the Greeks from their country, appropriated their works. An illustrious traveler assures that he saw in the Levant the books of Livy that we are missing, those of Apollonius of Perga, of Diophantes of Alexandria, and a quantity of others translated into Arabic. There is a quantity of these manuscripts in the famous library of the king of Morocco.[56]

Colbert prioritized books that shed light on early Church history, in whatever language they might be found. He went on in the letter to name the Samaritan Pentateuch, "our entire Bible in Arabic, Persian, Syriac, and Coptic," as well as "all that will be found about the councils among the Melchites, Nestorians, Jacobites and Eutychians."[57] His interests extended to secular subjects, many of which he still hoped, at this late date of 1679, to learn about from Arabic manuscripts, especially ancient scientific texts, directing Galland to seek out "what can be found in Arabic by Galen, that is not printed," as well as "the fifth, sixth, seventh, eighth book of Apollonius, in Arabic or Persian."[58] He had high hopes that Galland would find translations into Arabic of Greek writings and works of philosophy as well as the missing books of the Augustan historian Livy's history of Rome, whose masterpiece was (and is) preserved only in fragmentary form. Of prime importance to Colbert were books useful to European intellectual inquiry, whether religious, political, philosophical, or scientific. Colbert's suggestions, while varied and broad, were not especially arcane: his list expressed a recognizable set of intellectual interests. Nor was it particularly cutting edge: the later books of Apollonius had been translated and edited from the Arabic in 1661 by the Maronite scholar Abraham Ecchellensis and the Neapolitan mathematician Giovanni Alfonso Borelli.[59]

In addition to works in Arabic and Greek, Colbert sought manuscripts in other languages, particularly that of the Sabians, a mysterious pagan sect mentioned by Maimonides and in the Qur'an; the Zoroastrian scripture; "all that will be found of books in ancient Syriac"; "all the ancient Armenian books that will be found"; and even "a dictionary in the language of the Malabars or Mazabars [a Tamil dialect spoken in Kerala]."[60] He was as interested in Islamic studies as he was in history of the ancient Jews and Christians. He asked Galland to acquire copies of

Zanmehari [sic; for Zamakhsharī] on the Alcoran.

The *Sunna,* in Turkish: these are the traditions of the mahometan religion; there is a great number of volumes of them.

The works of the four leaders of the mahometan sects: Hanefi, Chafei, Hambali, Maleichi. There is perhaps some difference in the spelling of these names, but they are pretty well known by mullahs and hogias.

Natural histories, of the arts; medical books.

All kinds of histories, in whatever language and of whatever country; especially the history of Mirkhond, in Persian, unabridged. It forms at least seven volumes; of the seven there are two in the Royal Library.

All kinds of geography books; a dictionary, or several, that begin with Turkish, if they are to be found, because those found in the [Royal] Library are well explained by Turkish, but they start with Arabic or Persian.[61]

As this list demonstrates, Colbert sought books that could explain the religion of Islam in greater detail, as well as all Islamic secular histories, geographies, histories of the arts, medical books, and natural histories. But he also specified: "It is not necessary to look for books about the life of Mohamed, or of Aly ['Alī, the cousin of Muhammad who is especially venerated by the Shiites], nor for those that discuss music or the pilgrimage, and even less so [to look for] books of supplications and prayers, nor for Alcorans, and few by poets and novels, there being many of all of these books in the Royal Library."[62] Colbert's list was less an ideal canon of Oriental knowledge than a very practical compilation of desirable books that were missing in Paris.

Colbert did not offer advice and instructions concerning books alone. He ordered Galland to travel with a copy of Pausanias, the Greek geographer, and authorized him to collect coins and medals and to copy inscriptions, the older the better. In "Tchehelminar" (Persepolis) he was to find epigraphs in ancient Persian, and, likewise, in "Bassora" (Bosra, in Syria) he was directed to find inscriptions by the Christians, who, Colbert claimed, were the Sabians "of whom the Arab authors speak so often." These inscriptions were ideally to be collected as casts ("You will have to ask permission"), and if casting was not allowed, they would have to be copied.[63] A learned emissary like Galland had not only to collect books, but also to serve as an all-around antiquarian explorer and collector.[64]

In a letter of 1685 to his government backers in Paris (Colbert had died in 1683), Galland wrote that although the rare books that would be useful to the Royal Library could be found in other cities, "one can do in Constantinople in a year what one would have difficulty doing elsewhere in ten and twenty years."[65] Hidden in Istanbul's markets were resources for a history of most of Asia: "Finally one can presume to find in Constantinople all the histories that were written in Egypt, in Arabia, in Syria, in Anatolia, in Mesopotamia, in Persia, and in the Indies, all the way to Tartary."[66] Only the histories of al-Andalus (Moorish Spain) and of the Eastern Christians could be found more easily elsewhere. If he, Galland, were sent the funds to pursue this collecting scheme, he would be able to improve the Royal Library immensely. His letter, in other words, was a kind of grant application. Galland claimed to labor out of "pure zeal for contributing to the great designs one may entertain of rendering this Treasury [Thresor] the most accomplished of Europe, and, consequently, of the entire Universe."[67]

Colbert and Galland preferred classics in given genres to more recent or less prominent works. Even as European scholars built collections containing the books that mattered most to their Muslim counterparts, they excluded recent material, which may have seemed to them of lesser import. What is more, most European collectors could not obtain the fashionable contemporary poetry that circulated in the salons of Istanbul, because they lacked access to those circles. And they neglected the ample amount of ephemeral literature produced in small pamphlets, which formed an important part of Ottoman book culture.[68]

As we have seen, the French state collected according to a minutely organized program, and no less than the great French minister Colbert was deeply involved in suggesting what should be bought. Colbert believed there was a state interest in the acquisition of a variety of titles in a great number of languages. Yet despite this ambitious goal and the meticulous effort to realize it, some hoped-for works remained unavailable. Some were merely very rare, but others no longer existed or never had (for instance, the hoped-for translations of Livy into Arabic).

Missions

Galland and Colbert's activities were by no means singular. France had dispatched several other collectors before Galland, including Monsieur de Monceaux and Father Wansleben, and later on it sent Paul Lucas, François Sevin, and Michel Fourmont.[69] But these missions were not limited to the French. Indeed, in many respects the French were operating according to a European playbook for systematic collection of knowledge that had largely been codified by their time. To fully understand the scope of the collecting, it is necessary to take a much broader, pan-European view.

Book-finding missions were one part of travel in search of knowledge as theorized and practiced from the late Renaissance onward. Already in the sixteenth century, a series of treatises on the art of travel provided instructions to make such trips useful and educational.[70] A subset of travelers set out in search of new knowledge to bring home, and, increasingly, these men broadened their horizons beyond Europe.[71] For scholars, learning Arabic fluently was a primary motivation for visiting North Africa and the Levant. Others came to make astronomical observations.[72] Antiquarian collectors began prowling the Eastern Mediterranean in the first half of the fifteenth century, beginning with the Italians Cristoforo Buondelmonti and Ciriaco of Ancona.[73]

By the end of the seventeenth century, learned travel was increasingly systematic. Europeans wrote specialized guides for travelers interested in focusing on "literary" or antiquarian explorations or on the natural history or botany of an area. Learned travelers served as data collectors, gathering all manner of information on the lands they visited, including drawing maps and collecting botanical specimens, inscriptions, and even manuscripts.[74] For example, Sir Thomas Roe, the English ambassador to the Ottoman Empire from 1621 to 1628, brought back twenty-nine Greek manuscripts to Oxford.[75] Scientific academies developed questionnaires to help collect, compare, and verify information gathered in countries in Europe and beyond, and they began to dispatch travelers to pursue their aims.[76]

The geographic range of seventeenth-century collectors went beyond the Levant, moreover. Trade in the Indian Ocean and beyond yielded rich scholarly harvests. The Dutch presence in Southeast Asia led to the accumulation of books in Malay, Javanese, Malabar, and Formosan, some of which helped Dutch scholars reinterpret the Qur'an.[77]

Over the course of the 1600s, book collecting became increasingly organized. In France under Louis XIV (r. 1643–1715), royal patronage of Oriental research was but one aspect of the cultural politics of the Sun King's absolutist rule. Manuscript collecting abroad was transformed and greatly expanded during his reign under the management of Colbert (d. 1683) and, during the reign of Louis XV, of Jean-Paul Bignon (d. 1743). These men acted as cultural entrepreneurs, supervising the acquisition and organization of large amounts of new information. Under Colbert, the Royal Library became a state research institute—something along the lines of Solomon's House, the research institute for the arts and sciences featured in Francis Bacon's posthumously published utopian narrative *The New Atlantis* (1626).[78] Bacon's belief that scientific inquiry needed to be supervised by a centrally organized administration was a position Colbert and Bignon shared.[79]

In Istanbul the buying of books by foreigners eventually got so out of hand that in 1715 or 1716 the grand vizir, Şehid Ali Pasha, himself a book collector, "enacted a law . . . banning the sale of books to foreigners."[80] This protectionist measure was designed to prevent the disappearance of valuable intellectual resources from the capital. Referring to secondhand booksellers, the grand vizir wrote: "Because of their crude greed, they send away countless valuable books to different places, perhaps even outside the Ottoman realm."[81] Beyond Istanbul, Europeans collected manuscripts in many locations, including Cairo and Aleppo, where the English ran a factory of the Levant Company. Further afield, manuscripts were to be found in the Indian subcontinent, in Gujarati localities like Ahmedabad, as well as in southern India, where the French Jesuits had a mission, and on the Coromandel Coast.

In the eighteenth century, book buying continued, especially in the major collections of Catholic Paris and Rome. Under Louis XV, whose personal reign lasted from 1723 to 1774, the French royal collection expanded significantly, thanks in large part to these missions.[82] In Rome, Pope Clement XI sent several expeditions to Egypt to collect Coptic and Syriac manuscripts, laying the foundation for modern Syriac studies.[83]

Even the famous exploratory mission to the Yemen, sponsored by the Danish crown in 1761–1767, was intended to be a book-buying opportunity. Despite the death of all but one of the expedition members, as many as 119 Arabic manuscripts, acquired both in Istanbul and in Cairo, made it back to Copenhagen.[84] The philologist in the group, Christian von Haven, who had received instructions about what he was to acquire, recorded the Arabic names of these books in a dedicated section of his diary, noting how much he had spent on buying each one.[85] Literary and historical subjects predominated: of the 119, twenty-six were history books and twenty-seven were poetry collections. There were thirteen books of grammar and rhetoric, twelve anthologies, two books of literary history, and an abridged version of Kātib Çelebi's great bibliography.[86] The expedition also collected botanical samples, spices, and such rare substances as cinnabar and wormwood.[87] In all of these respects, it pursued familiar objectives, if more systematically and on a grander scale.

In France, the abbé Bignon proved no less talented than his predecessor, Colbert, in his judicious meddling with the research agendas of scholars.[88] His nomination, in 1718, as royal librarian inaugurated a new course for the French Royal Library.[89] In 1724 he secured the perpetual right to house the library in the Hôtel de Nevers, a building on the rue de Richelieu much larger than the crowded rooms the library had until then occupied. He donated to the library his personal collection of Chinese, Indian, Tartar, and Islamic manuscripts, oversaw the creation of an inventory in 1719–1720, and arranged a book-buying mission to Istanbul.[90] In addition, he mobilized the French East India Company to acquire printed books and manuscripts about the Far East and enjoined the Jesuits in Pondicherry, Canton, and Bengal to collect South Asian grammars and religious writings.[91] His goal was to create the best library in Europe.

In Rome, as in Paris, an alliance of a sympathetic ruler with a capable librarian created a world-class Oriental collection.[92] Pope Clement XI (Albani) (d. 1721) transformed the manuscript holdings, and the library continued to grow under his successors until 1769. This pope is not usually remembered for his contributions to Oriental studies, yet under his papacy Oriental manuscript collections such as those of the Maronite scholar Abraham Ecchellensis and of the Italian traveler Pietro della Valle entered the Vatican Library.[93] A frontispiece engraving reveals how the pope wished his patronage to be seen (Figure 2).[94] This illustration, from the first volume of the Vatican Library catalog *Bibliotheca Orientalis Clementino-Vaticana,* shows Clement XI seated on his throne, supervising clerics while being presented with a building block inscribed *Bibliotheca Vaticana* and with a case of Oriental books whose spines bear the names of three doctors of the Eastern Church.[95] At Clement's feet kneels an Eastern monk, holding a sheet of paper—perhaps a reference to the communion of the Oriental Churches that Clement XI sought (and which was one of the purposes of his book buying). The title of this image is a quotation from 2 Maccabees, a book of the Bible rejected by Protestants and Jews but accepted by Catholics: "Congregavit de Regionibus Libros" (He collected the books from different regions).

In the long run, a great librarian was, perhaps, even more important than a committed patron. The librarian who can take much credit for the flourishing of the Oriental collection in Rome was the curator Giuseppe Simonio Assemani (1687–1768), a Maronite scholar and priest who began working at the Vatican Library in 1710. He first served Pope Clement XI as a traveling collector, visiting Egypt, Cyprus, and Syria between 1715 and 1717 and returning with several hundred Oriental codices, among which the Syriac ones were a particular prize. He then proceeded to study them, producing the impressive *Bibliotheca Orientalis Clementino-Vaticana,* whose four large folio volumes, which appeared between 1719 and 1730, were focused on the Syriac manuscripts in the library.[96] (This publication, which presented to readers a huge number of texts for the first time, is considered the inception of Syriac studies in the modern West.) But its author's ambition was greater: he aimed to publish a critical bibliography of all of the literatures of the Near East, both Christian and Muslim, that were held in the Vatican Library, of which the *Bibliotheca Orientalis* was only the beginning. In 1739 Assemani was nominated first curator of the Vatican Library, an honor that had never before been bestowed on a Levantine scholar. Among his many projects, he aimed to complete a full, twenty-volume catalog of all manuscripts in the Vatican Library, both Eastern and Western. Together with his nephew Stefano Evodio, he produced the volume on Hebrew and Samaritan books in 1756 and two volumes on Syriac books in 1758 and 1759.[97] He was at work on the Arabic books when he died, in January 1768. A few months later, a fire burned all that had been printed of the Arabic catalog.[98] Even so, by the time of his death Assemani had done more than anyone else to carry on the bibliographic legacy of Pope Clement XI, right through five successive papacies.

Private Collecting

The systematic collection of Oriental manuscripts was initiated by private patronage. Long before institutions and states became involved, private collectors had mobilized Mediterranean networks and book-buying emissaries to build their libraries.[99] When the Bodleian Library, founded in 1598 by Thomas Bodley—who, in Sir Francis Bacon's words, had "built an ark to save learning from deluge"—finally opened, in 1602, it held a single Arabic manuscript, a Qur'an.[100] This was to change at the hands of William Laud, who was chancellor of Oxford from 1630 to June 1641 and archbishop of Canterbury from 1633.[101] The Bodleian began as a repository solely of printed books, but through efforts and donations Laud added a manuscript collection to its holdings. He inspired the first significant accession of these works, the Earl of Pembroke's gift of 240 Greek manuscripts. He himself donated more than a thousand manuscripts (by one count, 1,250) in eighteen languages, including 147 in Arabic.[102] Further private donations, small and large, increased the Bodleian's store.[103]

Elsewhere, too, nascent Oriental collections depended on the riches brought home by private individuals. In Paris, royal Oriental manuscript collecting began in earnest only in the second half of the seventeenth century, when it was transformed by two important acquisitions. First, the scholar Gilbert

Gaulmin's collection was bought by the French crown in 1667, two years after his death. It consisted of 461 books in Arabic, Persian, and Turkish and 127 in Hebrew. A polyglot, Gaulmin had mastered, to varying degrees, Arabic, Hebrew, and Turkish, and by some accounts, Armenian and Persian.[104] The second major acquisition was the collection of Cardinal Mazarin, chief minister of France until his death, in 1661, which was procured through a symbolic sale in 1668 (essentially a bequest). Mazarin's gift totaled 343 books in Arabic, Samaritan, Persian, and Turkish and 102 in Hebrew.[105] Practically overnight the Royal Library became a substantial repository of Oriental manuscripts. From then on, collecting Oriental manuscripts would be an important (and expensive) pursuit of the French crown. The Royal Library continued to acquire further private collections, enriching itself with hundreds more manuscripts.

Mazarin, who could not read his own Oriental books, was a public-minded patron of scholarship. In 1647 he opened the doors of his private library to "all who wished to study there," a first in Paris, and he made a special effort with regard to Oriental manuscripts. In 1644 he wrote to Jean de La Haye, then French ambassador in Istanbul: "You have something else in the country where you are of which I am more curious and for which I have a passion you will not disapprove of. You understand that I mean books, for I have already asked you to have Oriental, Greek, Arabic, manuscripts and other ones collected for me. I am fortifying from every side, insofar as I am able, the library that I have begun, and I wish to leave to the public this monument of good letters as complete as I may."[106] The private collections of scholars, such as Gaulmin, were often less ample than those of wealthy collectors, but they were carefully selected. The scholars could actually read the books in question and valued them for their contents, not just for the beauty of their calligraphy and illuminations.

Some collectors and patrons who, like Mazarin, did not read Arabic but understood its importance, advanced the European acquisition of Islamic books by sponsoring missions and creating libraries. These men, who had to rely on others for selection and purchase, were more oriented toward knowledge production than their Renaissance forebears, who had collected Islamic books for their prestige value. The foreign scripts and the provenance of these manuscripts made them objects of interest even to those who could not decode them. For example, Federigo da Montefeltro, the duke of Urbino, added

Arabic books to his humanist library as a mark of his cosmopolitanism.[107] The French crown, for the same reason, held a handful of Arabic manuscripts at the Château of Blois, in the Loire Valley, in the sixteenth century.[108]

Collecting for the mere pleasure of owning an Arabic book would continue into the eighteenth century, if not necessarily at the same elite level. The most popular bibliographic souvenir for Europeans in Muslim lands was, predictably enough, a copy of the Qur'an.[109] The Austro-Ottoman wars in the Balkans in the late 1600s brought many small Arabic books to Europe, in particular Qur'ans and prayer books that had been seized as booty. A small prayer book, now in Göttingen, contains this inscription, dated October 23, 1683: "[On September 2, 1683] I took this little book as booty from a Turkish officer's tent, since we had defeated the hereditary enemy, praise be to God. Our Christians numbered 100,000 and the Turkish enemies 300,000."[110] These souvenirs continued be valued and to circulate across German lands in subsequent decades, even if they were of little use to scholars.[111] (Of course, Islamic books were not the only books to be treated as objects. For instance, the traveler Pietro della Valle acquired a palm-leaf book in the Kannada language in the city of Ikkeri, in what is now Karnataka. He freely admitted that he did not know what it contained but was "desirous to have one of these Books, to carry as a curiosity to my own Country as an ornament for my Library.")[112]

Even in the eighteenth century, most Europeans regarded Islamic manuscripts as objects to be marveled at rather than texts to be studied. In 1727 the University Library of Cambridge received a large wooden cabinet labeled "Oriental Library." Its upper half contained seventy-six manuscripts that had been collected in India by George Lewis, a former chaplain of the East India Company, and its lower half held curiosities acquired in the Indian subcontinent such as coins, ambergris, chopsticks, and decorative playing cards. Lewis's "Oriental Library" was both a scholarly resource and a cabinet of natural and artificial curiosities. Understandably, most visitors to the cabinet enjoyed the nonmanuscript items the most and experienced the books simply as objects.[113] There were objections to displaying manuscripts this way. When Étienne Le Gac, the superior of the Jesuit mission, was asked to send books in South Indian languages to Paris, he demurred: "These books can only serve for show in a library, for, whatever aptitude one may possess for languages, I do not believe that one could manage to understand them well."[114]

Scholars, or their heirs, were less likely than the great patrons to donate their collections; most of them could not afford to part with their books without recompense. Leiden's Oriental collection began in 1610 with the donation of the scholar Joseph Scaliger's manuscripts.[115] Yet most Dutch Oriental scholars of the subsequent two centuries did not follow Scaliger's lead in donating their manuscripts to Leiden; the collector Levinus Warner, discussed below, who died childless, was very much the exception.[116] In England, the scholar John Selden bequeathed his Oriental manuscripts to the Bodleian.[117] Others who could not or did not do so included the librarian Thomas Hyde, under whose tenure the Bodleian "acquired more oriental manuscripts than under any other librarian before or since"; he sold his own manuscripts to the university in 1692.[118] Upon the death of their owners, great libraries built by scholars for themselves did not necessarily pass unbroken into public repositories, but were often put on the market and dispersed. Their Oriental manuscripts, therefore, had to be acquired in contest with other eager buyers at competitive auctions or in covertly arranged sales. Many collections, like that of the Dutch scholar Jacobus Golius, were broken up and scattered across the continent.[119]

A European Phenomenon

Many aspects of Colbert's and Galland's undertaking mirror those of other European efforts. One example in England is the Bodleian Library's great Oriental collection, the one that had been assembled earlier in the century via agents in the Levant on behalf of Archbishop Laud. Initially Laud attempted to build the collection by going directly through merchants and traders. In 1634 he required that each returning ship of the Levant Company bring with it an Arabic or Persian manuscript:[120] "Euery Shippe of yours at euery Voyage that yt makes should bring home one Arab: or Persian MS. Booke to be delyuered presently to the Master of your Company, and by him carryed or sent to the Lord ArchBishop of Cant."[121] In the interest of expediency, however, Laud soon turned to a person whose interests aligned better with his own: the chaplain of the English Levant Company, the scholar Edward Pococke.[122] Pococke, who would become the most influential Arabist of seventeenth-century England, spent 1630 to 1636 in Aleppo, where the English Levant Company had an outpost. While there, he acquired many of the Arabic manuscripts that Laud then donated to the Bodleian.[123] Upon Pococke's return, Laud arranged to employ him as the first holder of the new chair of Arabic at Oxford, a post that Laud had created. Before Pococke actively assumed that position, Laud convinced him to go East once again, this time with the primary goal of collecting manuscripts. Pococke embarked for Istanbul in July 1637 and stayed until August 1640. Laud also sent John Greaves, professor of geometry at Gresham College, in London, to collect manuscripts in Istanbul and Alexandria.[124] These expert travelers, funded privately, laid the cornerstone of the Bodleian's Oriental holdings.

The Dutch collection of Oriental manuscripts, by many accounts the best in Europe, was also assembled by two learned agents in the field, Jacobus Golius and Levinus Warner. Golius, an Arabic scholar, visited Syria, along with Northern Iraq and Istanbul, in his travels between 1625 to 1629. Using funds he had received from the University of Leiden, he returned home with more than 300 manuscripts in Arabic, Turkish, and Persian, 212 of which ended up in the Leiden University Library. In 1648, the board of governors of the University of Leiden offered the chair of Hebrew to a former student named Levinus Warner who had been living in Istanbul since 1645. Warner, a German from the principality of Lippe, in what is now Nordrhein Westfalen, had studied with Jacobus Golius.[125] Warner accepted the position, but got permission to first visit Syria. With Golius's expedition in mind, the Leiden University board allotted 300 florins to support Warner's journey, just as they had funded Golius. Unlike Golius, Warner never returned to the Netherlands, but spent the rest of his life in Istanbul. He earned a living working for the Dutch embassy in Pera (the Christian enclave across the Golden Horn from Istanbul proper), but his passion was the discovery of the Islamic intellectual and literary traditions. An avid collector of manuscripts, he spent all his money in their pursuit. He died on June 22, 1665, two years before Golius, and made good on his debt by bequeathing his book collection to the Leiden University Library.[126] The books began to arrive in Leiden, via Izmir and Livorno, three and a half years later; further consignments were received in 1669 and 1674. Warner's gift catapulted Leiden to first place among European collections of Islamic manuscripts.[127]

In addition to these sponsored travels, intellectually minded Europeans led abroad by trade or diplomacy contributed to institutional collecting efforts by donating manuscripts they had acquired.[128] Their gifts were not generally as spectacular as Warner's, but they added up. In a unique instance, the

Spanish royal library of the Escorial acquired an outstanding Muslim library practically overnight. In 1612, Christian pirates seized the entire library of a Moroccan prince, which had been loaded onto a ship, and donated it to King Philip II, who handed it over to the Escorial.[129] This tremendous resource remained closed to most researchers until the second half of the eighteenth century, when the Maronite scholar Miguel Casiri, a librarian in the Escorial, published a catalog of its Arabic manuscripts.[130]

Once in Europe, Oriental manuscript collections gradually shifted from private into public hands. As one commentator wrote in 1625 of Erpenius's manuscripts, for which the scholar's widow was then seeking a buyer, "They seem to be a treasure of the Orientall toungs & are not likely to lie long on the boord."[131] Indeed, negotiations for their purchase were competitive. Erpenius's collection ended up enriching the Cambridge University Library, much to the chagrin of the Dutch.[132] Pococke's collection furnished the Bodleian, as did the lion's share of Golius's, which was acquired by the Irish archbishop Narcissus Marsh and then donated.[133] Among other collections that made their way into public libraries was that of the lawyer and Qur'an translator George Sale; his collection was first purchased for Oxford's Radcliffe Camera and then transferred to the Bodleian. Those of Golius's books that the Utrecht scholar Adriaan Reland acquired at auction ended up scattered, on Reland's death, as far apart as Utrecht, Copenhagen, and Rome.[134]

In addition to a high-minded commitment to intellectual life, another, less noble motive for collecting was in operation: European states, already engaged in a competition over the patronage of scholarship and scientific inquiry, viewed knowledge of Eastern languages as an extension and expansion of this contest. The study of the natural world burnished a nation's glory, as is made clear by the patriotic overtones to the founding of the Royal Society for Improving Natural Knowledge, England's official academy of scientific inquiry, formed in 1660.[135] Bacon's interest in knowledge had, after all, been derived from the utility to be drawn from it, and many aspects of Oriental learning seemed useful. National *amour-propre* played its part, as well. In 1695, when Cardinal Barbarigo was in the process of producing Lodovico Marracci's edition of the Qur'an at his Oriental presses in Padua, he remarked that the book "was expected both in Paris and in Holland, and I hope that it will show the ultramontanes [the Protestants] that even in Italy the Oriental tongues are known."[136]

The Idea of a Research Library

European collecting of Oriental manuscripts was informed by new ideas about what a library should be. Ann M. Blair has argued that "more significant than any particular new discovery" in the Renaissance was "a new attitude toward seeking out and stockpiling information."[137] Besides wishing to furnish material in which scholars "might spend theyr paines," Europeans envisioned an ideal library that contained all kinds of books, whether considered good or harmful.[138] The pages of Gabriel Naudé's *Advis pour dresser une bibliothèque* (Advice on establishing a library) of 1627 offer an early articulation of the new conception of the library.[139] Naudé advises the prospective founder of a library to collect all kinds of books, for the harmful ones will "satisfy at least those who want to see them in order to refute them." He remarks that such books "might be among the other books of a Library, like the snakes & vipers among the other animals, like weeds growing in good wheat, like the thorns among the roses, & c. on the model of the world, where such useless & dangerous things complete the masterwork & make of its composition."[140] For Naudé, the pious need to collect heretical books so as to be able to refute them, but on a deeper level, the library must also emulate Creation itself, which contains evil things—the vipers, weeds, and thorns. He drew the most extreme conclusions from his own advice. Catholic libraries, he wrote, must not only make Luther's and Calvin's doctrines available to scholars "so as to refute them," but also "must have no scruple about having a Talmud or an Alcoran that vomits one thousand blasphemies against Jesus-Christ and our Religion."[141] The modern library must safeguard them all, just as the Church Fathers had done with the works of heretical Christian theologians.

Naudé's broad vision stood in stark contrast to the version of an ideal library espoused in the sixteenth century by the Swiss bibliographer Conrad Gessner. Gessner had been motivated to start his famous *Bibliotheca universalis* of 1545—one massive folio volume encompassing all that was worth knowing—by his awareness of the fragility of all learning.[142] This sense was derived from knowing that many works from classical antiquity had been lost; in particular, Gessner bemoaned the recent destruction of the library of King Matthias Corvinus in Buda at the hands of the marauding Ottoman army in 1526.[143] In contrast to Gessner's "universal library," which was limited to only Latin, Greek, and Hebrew manuscripts, Naudé's view was remarkably inclusive:

he believed that Muslims were not a threat to learning and that their litera-ture should be part and parcel of any complete library.

Naudé's cosmopolitanism reflected liberal Catholic views of the Oriental library.[144] Pope Clement XI's interest in Oriental manuscripts did not signal an especial openness to Islamic letters. On the contrary, he promoted a Catholic alliance against the Ottoman sultan after the Ottomans declared war on Venice and reconquered the Peloponnese.[145] His reason for collecting Islamic manuscripts had more to do with acknowledging the thorns of Creation and refuting heresies than it did with building bridges to other faiths. Naudé, Mazarin, and, in later times, Colbert and Bignon all held that knowledge could and should be increased, a viewpoint behind the continuation of acqui-sitions throughout the eighteenth century. The Royal Library and other kin-dred institutions across Europe were regarded as research libraries, not only in the sense that research took place in them, but also because their overseers continued to expand them; they were works in progress.

This expansionist attitude toward knowledge was shaped in part by the humanist revival of ancient letters. Into the eighteenth century, many be-lieved that the recovery of classical literature was still incomplete. The loss of the larger part of ancient literature was keenly felt, and while the monas-teries of Western Europe no longer yielded new wonders as they had during the Renaissance, other routes to antiquity still held promise. In particular, it was thought that Greek Orthodox monasteries in the former lands of Byzan-tium might still contain intact classical Greek manuscripts, a hope that mo-tivated many book-finding expeditions to Ottoman lands. John Greaves reported as much in 1638: "The Greeks would have me believe, that at Mount Athos, where there are some 3000 Monks, that they have store of MSS."[146] In 1728 Bignon received a proposal from a monk of the Benedictine abbey of Saint-Germain-des-Prés, who offered to travel to the Levant. The voyage never took place, but the proposal, "Memoire pour un Voiage Literaire de la Grece et du Levant," which survives in manuscript, reveals much about the expectations early eighteenth-century Europeans had for book-finding mis-sions to the Eastern Mediterranean.[147] As long as the libraries of this part of the world had not been fully explored, the hope that lost Greek masterpieces could be recovered remained alive. Nor was this hope wholly unreasonable, given that searches in libraries from Petrarch's time onward had recovered so much.

In the 1720s in Paris, an ambitious idea took form: to enter the Ottoman sultan's library in Istanbul, in Topkapi Palace, to search for the treasures of the classical past, which it had long been rumored to hold. In 1638, though Greaves doubted that Mount Athos would yield useful manuscripts, he still held out hope for the Ottoman palace, for he had been told by Istanbul's Greek patriarch that the seraglio still held "the Library of the Greek Emperors, in which were also many Latin MSS."[148] In 1720–1721, hope of obtaining access to the library was stoked by the visit to Paris of the Ottoman emissary Yirmisekiz Mehmed Çelebi Efendi.[149] His predecessor, Süleyman Aga, failed to capture the minds and hearts of Paris in 1669, but Mehmed Efendi charmed the city and the court, as did his son, Saïd, who learned French. (Saïd returned to Paris twenty years later, this time as an emissary himself. In an admiring portrait, now in the Musée de Versailles, Jacques Aved painted Saïd as the archetypal "gallant Turk.")[150] After the Ottoman emissaries' return to Istanbul (1721), the friendship of Saïd Efendi raised the hope that French scholars might, through him, gain access to the sultan's library. Indeed, in 1727 Saïd wrote in response to an inquiry that "we have not yet begun to make a list of the Greek and other Frankish books that are found in the Libraries of his Majesty." The letter continued, "Rest assured that as soon as we have found some Interpreters and have had them make a list of these Books, we will send it to you. It seems to us that to do so more rapidly you might consider sending us a Catalogue of Greek Books in general, if you have one. We would be infinitely obliged."[151] Two emissaries, François Sevin and Michel Fourmont, were dispatched to Istanbul the following year to recover Greek literature in the Grand Signior's library. They returned to Paris with Arabic, Persian, and Turkish literary treasures they bought in book markets, but, alas, with nothing from the sultan's library.[152] As hard as lost classical manuscripts were to find, they could, in this as in other cases, be replaced by the acquisition of what was more readily available: Oriental manuscripts.[153] It was far better to return with Islamic manuscripts than with empty hands. Thus the law of unintended consequences helped to strengthen the French royal collection of Islamic manuscripts.

The great libraries of Muslim lands, such as the Ottoman sultan's library, the sultan of Morocco's collection, and the library of the al-Azhar College and Mosque, in Cairo, captivated Europeans not only as potential repositories of lost classical books, but also because they held out the promise of complete collections of Islamic works. These institutions raised such great hopes because they were not only prestigious, but were also reminiscent of ones the collectors knew from home (such as the Royal Library). In 1748 the abbé d'Orvalle, on a mission to Egypt, wrote that he was seeking a copy of the catalog of al-Azhar. He described the library's reputation in breathless tones: "The library of Dgemiaïl Asshar [*Jāmi'at al-Azhar*] ... is recognized by all the learned men of Mahometism, who come there to study from all the parts of the states of the Grand Signior ... [its catalog] contains 50,000 volumes and is recognized by all scholars to represent the total body of their literature."[154] Twelve years later, Christian von Haven, the Danish philologist, would search for (but not obtain) a copy of exactly the same catalog while in Cairo.[155] The hope of gaining a complete overview of the Islamic intellectual tradition in one fell swoop was hard to resist.

Conclusion

During a visit to the Bodleian Library in July 1716, the Cambridge professor of Arabic Simon Ockley contemplated the problems involved in collecting Oriental manuscripts. He was in Oxford to transcribe source material for a history of the Muslim conquests. In a letter, now in Copenhagen, he explained that the most important books for his purposes were missing: "We have enough of their Grammar, Poetry, mahometan Questions and Decisions, but what is of the Greatest Moment, their History and Geography[,] we most want." He believed that the shortcoming was not occasioned by an absence of interest in those subjects, but that it derived from a lack of coordination among the Bodleian's donors: "One Reason is because these Collections being made by Private men for their own use, they buy up what they meet with in the East without any regard to what has been bought before, hence come into our Libraries so many Duplicates of one book, whereas we have not one of another."[156]

The only solution, as he saw it, was to organize a book-buying mission specifically to fill these lacunae. Ockley, who had never been (and never went) to the Levant, even advanced his own candidacy for the mission: "If they have let me have gone with the Constantinopolitan Ambassador ... I could have remedied this inconvenience by making exact Catalogues of what we ha[ve] and supplying what is deficient, which might be done at Constantinople,

Damascus, Aleppo and Alexandria." Much like Galland had before him, he argued that unless the requisite sources were collected, no accurate history of Islam could be written: "Till such a thing is done, in vain do we Expect anything of a Compleat History of these affairs."[157]

As we have seen, Muslim copyists, booksellers, learned European travelers, powerful patrons, and dutiful librarians were all players in the collection of Islamic manuscripts, but the overall process lacked coordination. Collecting was sometimes deliberate, but it also happened at the margins of other ventures, such as diplomatic missions or commercial efforts, and it involved a variety of motivations and private agents. Deliberate book-buying missions did not always yield the desired volumes, and once volumes were in Europe there was no guarantee that they would be accessible for study, because private collectors did not always bequeath their libraries to public institutions. Even then, stockpiling books was not enough; it was necessary to organize them, and to make them available to qualified readers.

As a result of these challenges, books often had to wait decades or longer for someone to read them. In his reminiscences on his tenure in Leiden, which lasted from 1738 to 1746, the German scholar of Arabic Johann Jacob Reiske noted: "I would have collated, inspected, and examined more things, if I had been able to ponder the Oriental treasury, which is incomparable to those who possess it there, with greater freedom. Yet the illustrious overseers of this academy ward off with equal severity both foreigners and locals from use of its Oriental treasury—or at least from the sort of use that really gives it its value."[158] He had especially harsh words for Peter Burmann, under whose directorship of the library "manuscript books are condemned to perpetual imprisonment, and to the teeth of mice."[159]

In spite of these shortcomings, the ideal of the Oriental library not only held firm, it proved to be a remarkably expansive concept. From an initial identification with Semitic languages, and then with Arabic, Persian, and Turkish, in the course of the seventeenth and eighteenth centuries it came to encompass all the Asian literatures that could be collected. In this sense, the ideal that underlay it can be regarded as inclusive rather than exclusive. In simple numerical terms, Arabic literature formed the core of the Oriental library, but—in ambition and in actuality—the library reached far beyond.

TWO

THE QUR'AN IN TRANSLATION

In 1698 the *Alcorani Textus Universus* (Entire text of the Qur'an) was published in Padua. It consisted of two large folio volumes, the first of which, the *Prodromus ad Refutationem Alcorani* (Preliminary to the refutation of the Qur'an), contained a life of Muhammad, a short treatise on the Qur'an, and a four-part refutation of Islam. The second volume, the *Refutatio Alcorani* (Refutation of the Qur'an), included the Arabic text of the Qur'an, its Latin translation, critical notes, and a refutation of each sura.[1] The *Alcorani Textus Universus* was not the first time a printed Arabic Qur'an was published in Europe, but never before had one been accompanied by a full translation, critical notes, and a polemical refutation.[2] The book was the fruit of much perseverance and hard work on the part of Lodovico Marracci, a Roman clergyman (Figure 3). His translation and, especially, his annotations made history as the first philologically sound treatment of the Qur'an in the West, and marked a turning point in the European understanding of Islam. Subsequent French and German translations drew on it, as did the first direct English translation, by the young London solicitor George Sale, whose elegant prose version, published at the end of 1733 (but dated 1734), would remain the standard English translation into the twentieth century.[3] In short, Marracci's scholarly effort in late Counter-Reformation Rome shaped how Islam was understood by readers in Europe, in North America, and across the British Empire in the eighteenth, nineteenth, and twentieth centuries. The following account—the first in English to examine Marracci's entire endeavor—shows that the modern Western understanding of the Qur'an was deeply indebted not only to a work of Christian erudition but, even more remarkably, to a Catholic polemical enterprise undertaken by the confessor to a pope.[4]

Qur'an Translation in the West before Marracci

In 1085, after two and a half centuries of Muslim rule, the Castilians took Toledo, the compact citadel perched above the Tagus River, and turned it into a
Christian city. However, its new governors did not discourage the study of
Arabic, and Toledo soon became an influential international center for Arabic-
to-Latin translation. When the Frenchman Peter the Venerable, the abbot of
Cluny and an energetic reformer of the Benedictine order, came to Toledo in
the middle of the twelfth century, he found a community of scholars skilled
in translating Arabic mathematics and astronomy.[5]

Peter, believing that Christian knowledge of Islam was gravely wanting,
decided to increase it—all for the purpose of inspiring resistance to it. He
feared that Muslim ideas (for instance, about the humanity of Christ) would
persuade Christians.[6] His position was that the refutation of Islam was just as
important as the refutation of any other heresy, and that in pursuing this goal
he was merely following in the footsteps of the Church Fathers: "My intention . . . was to follow the customs of those Fathers, who never passed over in
silence even the mildest heresy."[7] His further aim was, at least in principle, to
win converts to Christianity.

Peter did not know Arabic, nor did he ever learn it. But under his auspices
the Toledan translators of Arabic worked on a number of projects, the most
prominent of which was rendering the entire Qur'an in Latin, a task the Englishman Robert of Ketton finished in June or July of 1143. The first translation of the Qur'an in Western Christendom—and one of the first into any
language—it was accompanied by some other Islamic texts of no great authority; the "Apology" of al-Kindī (*Risālat al-Kindī*), a Christian Arabic
polemic against Islam; and a short summary of Islamic doctrine and a refutation, both written by Peter and based upon his team's translations.[8] Robert of
Ketton's manuscript version marked the opening of the Western scholarly
study of Islam, which at the very outset, therefore, was mediated by anti-Muslim
polemic by a Christian Arabic writer.[9]

Robert's Latin translation of the Qur'an was more a paraphrase than a literal translation. He condensed verses, left out passages, made implicit meanings explicit and vice versa, and rearranged the Qur'an's division into chapters
and verses, turning its 114 chapters into 123.[10] His overall tendency was to
endow the Qur'an with good Latin style—to make it sound eloquent to its

Western readers.[11] His paraphrase has often been criticized as insufficiently rigorous. Yet, as Thomas Burman has shown, Robert went to great lengths to read the Qur'an as Muslims did, even consulting Arabic commentaries on the Qur'an and incorporating their interpretations in his version.[12] The sobriety of his translation contrasts sharply with the hostile marginal annotations that frame it—this visual disjunction of philology and polemic was, as we shall see, also a feature of Marracci's layout.[13]

Despite its flaws, Robert's version, of which only twenty-four manuscript copies survive, remained the principal one for European audiences into the early eighteenth century, when it was eclipsed by the efforts of the scholars discussed in this chapter.[14] It became the first translation of the Qur'an to be printed, but that milestone was not reached until 1543, exactly 400 years after its completion.[15] The printer Johannes Oporinus of Basel and the editor Theodor Buchmann (known as Bibliander) undertook this controversial venture, which succeeded only thanks to the intervention of Martin Luther, who had a long-standing interest in Islam.[16] Luther argued that the Qur'an should be published because it would reveal itself to be a forgery and therefore did not pose a threat to Christian believers. According to him, publishing the translated Qur'an was the most damaging thing that could be done to Islam.[17]

Bibliander's book was a success; a second edition had to be set in 1550.[18] Its Italian translation appeared in Venice in 1547—the Qur'an's first appearance in a European vernacular.[19] That version would be translated into German by a Protestant minister, Salomon Schweigger, in 1616 (with a second edition in 1623), and that German version was translated into Dutch in 1641. By then the text was at four removes from the Arabic original![20] This proliferation of editions bespeaks the lively European interest in the foundational text of Islam during the sixteenth and seventeenth centuries.[21]

Despite the popularity of Robert's translation, humanist scholars gave it decidedly mixed reviews, and several of them attempted to outdo his achievement.[22] An object of attention of Renaissance philology, the Qur'an was translated anew from Arabic into Latin in its entirety twice by the middle of the sixteenth century.[23] These versions were not printed, limiting their circulation and lessening their impact, but they stand as further evidence of the era's reckoning with Islam. Marracci's project may have been undertaken in the spirit of Peter the Venerable, but the tools of Renaissance philology made possible its completion.[24]

In the seventeenth century, many scholars beside Marracci translated the Qur'an in part or in full.[25] For instance, in 1632 the German schoolteacher Johannes Zechendorff copied out the Arabic text of the Qur'an and inserted a word-by-word interlinear Latin translation.[26] This version was never printed, and neither was the edition of the Arabic text and its Latin translation by Germanus of Silesia, which this Franciscan monk, widely traveled in the Levant, completed in the great library of the Escorial in 1670.[27]

On the whole, European writers viewed the Qur'an as a foreign equivalent to their own scripture, at least in the sense of being the central document of a highly successful religion. No other set of writings, even the collections of sayings and deeds of the Prophet (ḥadīth), would ever compete with it in European eyes. The Qur'an's status was also raised by being a legal document, the first source of law of Muslim states.

In spite of all this interest, the published translations of the Qur'an remained a series of increasingly close approximations. They conveyed plenty of information about Islam, but did not provide a precise, line-by-line understanding of the book's intricacies. By the late seventeenth century, no one had yet published a scholarly treatment of the Qur'an.

Rome

Remote even today, the village of Torcigliano clings to the mountainside in the Apuan Alps north of Lucca. Yet, from its streets one glimpses at the end of the valley the Mediterranean Sea—and with it, a wider world. Lodovico Marracci was born there in 1612 to a family that owned two mills in the area.[28] At age fifteen, he joined the Order of the Clerks Regular of the Mother of God, in Lucca, as would three of his brothers and even his father, after his mother's death. The order's Luccan church, Santa Maria Corteorlandini, was dedicated to the Virgin Mary, and its impressive library was one of the intellectual centers of the city.[29] Giovanni Leonardi (1541–1609), who had gained a following preaching the Gospel and teaching the catechism—an instance of the reformist impulses of the Counter-Reformation—founded the order in the late sixteenth century.[30] With the protection of the local bishop, he and his followers were able to gain official recognition. The Order of the Mother of God's distinguishing characteristics were its Marian devotion and its evangelical zeal. The former trait led many members to support the doctrine of the

Immaculate Conception (the notion that the Virgin was exempted at conception from original sin in view of her future role as mother of Christ), which, unlike the virgin birth of Jesus, was a far from universally accepted doctrine within the Catholic Church at that time. The order's evangelism was manifested mainly as a commitment to catechetical education, but Leonardi was also involved in the creation of what, in 1622, after his death, became the Sacra Congregatio de Propaganda Fide (The Sacred Congregation for the Propagation of the Faith), the missionary arm of the Counter-Reformation Roman Church. Lodovico Marracci's translation of the Qur'an, to which he devoted his life, can be understood as a very learned extension of his order's evangelical impulse.[31]

Two years after joining the order, Lodovico moved to Rome to continue his studies of Greek and Hebrew. The Roman chapterhouse of the Order of the Mother of God was located at Santa Maria in Portico, a church dedicated to the cult of an icon of the Virgin. One day, in the course of his studies, the young Lodovico encountered a page written in an unknown alphabet. A Maronite cleric explained that it was Arabic and urged him to study the language.[32]

It is not surprising that when Lodovico was in Rome, he came into contact with an Arab Christian such as this cleric. Today we rarely associate Baroque Rome with Arabic, yet in the seventeenth century the city was the most Arabophone in Christian Europe, largely because of a concerted effort by the Catholic Church starting in the late sixteenth century to strengthen relations with the Christians of the Levant. In 1584 Pope Gregory XIII (he of the Gregorian calendar) set up a Maronite college in Rome to train young Levantine clergymen; in the seventeenth century these students made up just one part of the city's wide cultural diversity.[33] Gregory also authorized the first printing press to produce Arabic books in Christian Europe. In the mid-1600s the Frenchman Barthélemy d'Herbelot traveled to Rome to pursue "conversation with Armenians and other Orientals."[34] Even a hundred years later the Danish scholar Christian von Haven came to Rome to improve his spoken Arabic in preparation for a journey to Egypt and the Arabian peninsula.[35]

Following the Maronite cleric's advice, Lodovico took up Arabic, and proved to be uncommonly skilled at the language. He was assisted at first by Arab Christians, but in the end it was European books about Arabic that helped him master the tongue. It is a sign of the Republic of Arabic Letters at work that some of these volumes were produced in Protestant Northern Europe.[36] For example, among his extant manuscripts are painstaking copies of a grammar and a dictionary published in Leiden, a token at once of the printed books' scarcity and of their importance to him.[37]

His expertise in Arabic would change his life. He returned to Lucca in 1638 but was called back to Rome in 1645 to assist with the translation of the Bible into Arabic. This project, initiated by Gregory XIII as part of the effort to bring Arabophone Christians of the Levant into the Catholic fold, had been languishing for years. When it was taken over by the Propaganda Fide at the beginning of the papacy of Urban VIII, things moved quickly.[38] The Congregation established its own polyglot printing press in 1626, and the translation was completed and printed in 1649.[39]

Although many details concerning the creation of this translation of the Bible into Arabic remain elusive, it is beyond doubt that Marracci played a key role in bringing it to completion. He served as corrector of the proofs in the final phase before the book appeared, in 1671.[40] His contribution was honored by the members of his order in Lucca, who inscribed the following in their copy: "This book, begun by order of Urban VIII, and demanded by the Sacred Congregation for the Propagation of the Faith of several experts in the Oriental Languages, was carried out and completed by Father Lodovico Marracci alone among the other chosen men."[41] The inscription remembers the recent involvement of Pope Urban VIII and not the more distant origins of the project in the time of Gregory XIII.

Upon his return to Rome, Marracci was also charged with helping to investigate the validity of Christian artifacts that had been found near Granada, in Spain. In 1595, just over a century after the fall of Muslim Granada, tablets containing a Christian gospel written in Arabic, along with purported remains of ancient Christian martyrs, had been discovered in the nearby Sacromonte hill. These finds, known as the lead tablets of Granada, inflamed the imaginations of Christian believers and made the Sacromonte into a site of pilgrimage. In 1645 the Holy Office (the Roman Inquisition) had the tablets brought to Rome and ordered that they be translated by six different scholars of Arabic, including Marracci, to determine if they were genuine. The collective verdict, delivered in 1665, was that the tablets were a forgery. The Roman scholars realized that the tablets were written in an Islamic, rather than a Christian, idiom. Indeed, the tablets had been created by a group of recent converts from Islam to Christianity (known as *moriscos*) to enhance the prestige of Arabic among Christians.[42]

Marracci remained in Rome for the rest of his life. In 1656 he received the chair of Arabic at the Collegio della Sapienza, which he would hold until the year before his death, in 1700.[43] He began gathering materials for the Qur'an project as early as the 1650s.[44] Although most of his draft translations bear no date, the sheer abundance of extant materials makes it clear that he had been working on the Qur'an well before 1674, when he wrote that he hoped to "begin" his refutation as soon as possible.[45]

Marracci also served as confessor to members of the nobility at the impressively rebuilt Church of Santa Maria in Campitelli, which in 1662 had become the Roman seat of Marracci's order.[46] Cardinal Benedetto Odescalchi, who happened to live near the church, became Marracci's penitent in 1675 and was elected pope in 1676, as Innocent XI.[47] As a result of Odescalchi's election, Marracci moved into the papal orbit, while continuing to labor on his translation of the Qur'an into Latin.

Sources and Resources

Marracci undertook the massive task of translating the Qur'an because of his belief that it would help to unmask Islam as a heresy and refute its claims. Those few who had previously attempted to reveal Islam as a sham faith were, he wrote, "rare fighters against an immense army."[48] It was his opinion that the false accusations—the exaggerations and misrepresentations—of Christian polemicists had no persuasive power, and that to condemn Islam convincingly first demanded knowing it.[49] To be effective, polemic needed philology.

In the preface to his translation, he asserted: "I attack the enemies with their own weapons"—that is, by relying only on Muslim sources.[50] "Thus far I have tried to fight the Alcoran with the Alcoran and to slaughter Mahomet with his own sword insofar as my forces allow."[51] This principle of exegetical economy had both classical and Islamic precedents: just as Aristarchus used Homer to interpret Homer, medieval Islamic commentators explained the Qur'an with the Qur'an.[52]

Marracci viewed his translation as a polemical instrument, but also as a practical tool for helping to preach the Gospel to Muslims. Many Ottoman provinces had once been Christian, and he hoped that recent Christian military advances in the Ottoman-Hapsburg War meant that some souls might be regained.[53] When he sought permission to publish with the presses of the Propaganda Fide in 1688, he argued that his entire project (which he would publish in full only a decade later) "could do much for the conversion of those [Muslims] in Hungary, and in other parts."[54] Designed to prepare missionaries at home before they set out for disputation with Muslims abroad, the book, he claimed, could be taken to Muslim lands without risk because the Arabic texts were completely orthodox and Ottoman interlocutors would not be able to read the Latin polemic.[55]

Marracci asserted that, in any case, his translation, with its polemical tone, was not meant for Muslim audiences: "I will not deny this and I would disapprove if what I write were to be read by Mahometans. For I am not unaware that a Christian Author, and especially a member of an order, ought to write for strangers to the Christian religion with calm and modest words: for in such a way they are more easily won over to the truth."[56] Whether the hefty, bookish tome could be considered, even in its own time, a useful tool for conversion is questionable. More broadly, Marracci's optimism about its power is a reminder that the project was conceived in the middle of the seventeenth century, in the early decades of the Propaganda Fide, at what was a more confident moment of Catholic missionary striving. By the time it reached publication at the end of the seventeenth century, the expectations of converting non-Catholics were much diminished, and the ambition of Marracci's book had become anachronistic.[57]

By the time of the actual publication, decades after Marracci had begun work on the Qur'an, the geopolitical situation had changed dramatically. In the preface to his full translation, Marracci celebrated the Holy Roman Emperor's victory in 1683 over the Ottomans. By dedicating the book to Leopold I, he reframed it as part of that struggle.[58] Marracci's correspondence, although largely dedicated to scholarly matters, also includes occasional asides to celebrate Christian advances, demonstrating that he had a lively interest in the military campaign.[59] In 1684 he even drew a parallel between the ailing Christian siege of Ottoman Buda and his own difficulty in getting his Qur'an into print: "New obstacles to the publication of my work have emerged, which seems to me to suffer from the same fortune as the conquest of Buda."[60] Yet despite Marracci's interest in the Ottoman-Hapsburg wars of 1683 to 1699, it had been his own understanding of the Qur'an as a tool for delegitimizing Islam that had prompted him to begin the project at a much earlier date.

Although Marracci did not always provide precise bibliographic indications, it is possible to reconstruct the collection of books that he consulted across nine different libraries in Rome and environs.[61] The Vatican Library was not particularly helpful and seems to have supplied only one book (a copy of the Qur'an), in 1671.[62] The library of the Collegio Urbano, the missionary training school of the Propaganda Fide, was apparently much more useful.[63] He also consulted the library of the Maronite College and several libraries of religious orders, both within the city walls (San Lorenzo in Lucina, run by the Caracciolini missionary order, and San Pietro in Montorio on the Janiculum, home of the Reformed Franciscans) and without (San Pancrazio, home to the Discalced Carmelites starting in 1662).[64] The Caracciolini, the Reformed Franciscans, and the Carmelites had all heeded Pope Paul V's call, in 1610, to found Oriental language schools and had collected Arabic manuscripts to support these efforts.[65] The global reach of the Counter-Reformation Roman Church and its intense missionary drive at midcentury had brought to Rome manuscripts that scholars like Marracci could exploit in their research. Marracci also consulted the private collections of the traveler Pietro della Valle (d. 1652), who had visited Persia; the Maronite scholar Abraham Ecchellensis (d. 1664); and the collector and patron Cardinal Camillo Massimo (d. 1677), who had acted as papal nuncio to Spain from 1653 to 1658.[66]

Seeking sources outside of Rome, in 1678 Marracci wrote to Florence, which possessed one of the best Arabic manuscript collections in Italy, to request a list of the Arabic commentaries on the Qur'an that were held in the library of Palazzo Pitti.[67] He could not count on many printed works, because so few Arabic texts had been edited and published in Europe. One he used frequently was the *Specimen Historiæ Arabum* by the Anglican scholar Edward Pococke; this Catholic reliance on an Anglican publication is another example of the Republic of Arabic Letters in action.[68]

The recent discovery of Marracci's own papers allows us to reconstruct how he translated the Qur'an.[69] His first source was a manuscript of a Qur'an commentary, the *Tafsīr* of Ibn Abī Zamanīn, a relatively obscure work that was an epitome, or compendium (*mukhtaṣar*), of an older commentary. Ibn Abī Zamanīn's is a so-called running commentary: it contains the text of the

Qur'an, broken up into short excerpts that are discussed in turn (although it omits certain verses and abridges others).[70] The manuscript Marracci used was produced in 1482 and is still in the Order of the Mother of God in Rome (Figure 4). He made a copy of both Qur'anic text and commentary in his own hand and added his translation of the Qur'anic verses in the margins (Figure 5).[71] Of the five commentaries he used, Ibn Abī Zamanīn's was the least widely distributed among Muslims, and therefore the least representative of mainstream or majority Muslim opinion, which ran counter to Marracci's wish to understand the way the Qur'an was read by most Muslims.[72] The somewhat unfortunate choice would have been dictated partly by what happened to be available. The manuscript, whose Spanish origin is nearly certain, came from Cardinal Camillo Massimo's personal library, to which Marracci had access.[73] Moreover, its concision spoke in its favor; it offered a compact and accessible overview in a single bound volume.

The next source Marracci consulted was the Mamluk-era *Tafsīr al-Jalālayn* (Commentary of the two Jalāls), coauthored by the Egyptian polymath Jalāl al-Dīn al-Suyūṭī. This manuscript had been collected in the early seventeenth century by the Scottish Catholic George Strachan, who spent several decades in the Levant and Persia and bequeathed his books to the Discalced Carmelites of Rome.[74] When dealing with points of interpretation in his own critical notes (*Notae*), and his refutations (*Refutationes*), Marracci relied heavily on the *Tafsīr al-Jalālayn,* along with two other classics of the commentarial tradition: the medieval commentary by al-Zamakhsharī and its one-volume abridgment by al-Bayḍāwī.[75] The al-Bayḍāwī and the *Tafsīr al-Jalālayn* were among the most widely read commentaries in the Ottoman Empire.[76] Reading and comparing multiple commentaries exposed Marracci to a range of native interpretations of the Qur'an, from which he formed his own understandings.[77] Using commentaries may also have served a protective function. In the Rome of Marracci's time, the Qur'an was a controversial book to own; commentaries, even though they contained the Qur'an, did not carry the same stigma as the holy book itself.

Marracci's comparative approach reveals that he respected his Muslim commentators. He knew that he could not produce a reliable translation on his own, much less read the Qur'an better than Muslim readers did. Yet all the while, his work was driven by polemical intent. This combination grounded him in conversation, however adversarial, with Muslim interpretations of the

Qur'an. During his lifetime some claimed that his use of commentators made his work dangerous to Christian belief, because it revealed that "the commentators often give [the Qur'an] a reasonable meaning."[78] Marracci himself believed that his polemical arguments ultimately prevailed over those of the commentators, eliminating the risk that readers would come away persuaded by the Muslim arguments.

Several scholars before Marracci had employed Arabic Qur'an commentaries, but the Italian scholar took a much more systematic approach.[79] He included quotations from commentators, either in Arabic and Latin or only in Latin, in the *Notae* sections of the *Refutatio Alcorani,* turning the book into a veritable anthology of Qur'anic commentary.[80] Among the five sources he studied are three classics of the commentarial tradition: the medieval commentary by al-Zamakhsharī, its one-volume abridgment by al-Bayḍāwī, and the *Tafsīr al-Jalālayn.*[81] The fifth source he used was a lengthy commentary by al-Thaʿlabī of Nishapur, which was influential in the medieval period but fell out of use later.[82] Although Marracci had to rely to a large extent on the serendipity of what was available in Rome, his broad selection ensured the inclusion of several venerable authorities.

Marracci also consulted anthologies of prophetic traditions (*ḥadīth*)— reports of the deeds and sayings of Muhammad. He used the most canonical collection, assembled by the ninth-century Persian scholar al-Bukhārī, and also the anti-Christian Muslim polemic of Ibn Taymiyya.[83] To demonstrate that many Muslim beliefs and rituals were derived from Jewish ones, he examined Talmudic and rabbinic sources.[84]

Inevitably, he made errors. For example, he drew indiscriminately on various legal and theological schools of thought and cited legends from several Shiite books, not realizing that refuting them did nothing to strengthen his argument against mainstream Sunni Islam.[85] All told, however, Marracci's performance was extraordinary, and perhaps matched only by two other seventeenth-century Europeans, Edward Pococke and Barthélemy d'Herbelot, neither of whom concentrated as single-mindedly on the Islamic religious tradition.[86]

In short, Marracci's project brought him into intensive interaction with a remarkable selection of Islamic religious works. Roaming within and outside the field of commentaries, he gained a lively sense of the diversity of Islamic intellectual activity, and his critical notes became an invaluable trove of information for any European studying the Qur'an.

Roman Delays

Publishing the Qur'an in the heart of the Catholic Church was no small endeavor. Not only had the book appeared on many editions of the Index of Prohibited Books, but in the early 1600s the Holy Congregation of Roman Censors had decreed against its publication in any form, and this decree was renewed under Pope Alexander VII (r. 1655–1667).[87] Marracci's project suffered significant delays, mainly due to the skittishness of his Roman contemporaries.[88] In 1677 he was thwarted when he applied for permission to use the printing press of the Propaganda Fide. Then, in 1679, Cardinal Alberizzi, the official in charge of approving his work for publication, was unavailable because of "almost constant ailments."[89] In 1684 Marracci was granted the use of the Arabic types of the Propaganda Fide.[90] Printing was about to begin, but then the pope's theologian (Maestro del Sacro Palazzo) objected, considering "it to be the same thing to print the pure Alcoran, and the refutations of the Alcoran," a conflation Marracci declared erroneous and simplistic.[91] Still without a license for printing, he appealed to the cardinals of the Holy Office, the body in charge of defining orthodoxy. There, more objections were raised, as he reported bitterly: "Among them some said that the Alcoran does not need refutation, being full of so many self-evident errors, some, that this work of mine would serve neither Turks nor Christians, others, that it would more likely harm simple people, and others that it could do great harm if it were found by anyone in Turkey, and other similar inanities."[92] All these objections suggest that the lack of success in converting Muslims over the preceding decades had lessened the Church's commitment to Marracci's project.[93] In addition, as Marracci noted, there was concern that the book would create difficulties for the many Catholics (both missionaries and local communities, such as the Maronites) living in Ottoman lands.

Marracci was incensed by the Holy Office's arguments. He found them to be "platitudes [*inettie*]" and "extremely frivolous objections."[94] The Holy Office claimed to lack the power to approve the publication and deferred the decision to the pope. As far as Marracci was concerned, the justification for his work could be found in Peter the Venerable's defense of his own study of Islam in the Middle Ages.[95] Therefore, the objections raised by the Holy Office had been taken care of in the twelfth century; the matter was "such an evident thing that, so to speak, it could be decided by a child."[96]

In October 1684, a month after the Holy Office issued its rejection, the pope, influenced by the hostility of some in his circle, decided to deny permission to print the Qur'an in Rome, just as Marracci had feared.[97] Pope Innocent XI, austere, mistrustful, and stubborn, rarely changed his mind once it was made up.[98] The whole project seemed to be at an impasse. This predicament was peculiarly frustrating because it was technically possible to print in Arabic in Rome, unlike most other places. Marracci remarked, "Yet one must overcome all things with patience, as I hope that we will overcome this."[99]

There is no doubt that the Church's reluctance was reinforced by the debacle created by *Considerationes ad Mahomettanos,* published in 1649 and written in Arabic by Marracci's predecessor, Filippo Guadagnoli, a member of the Caracciolini order.[100] A chapter of his treatise entitled "The Qur'an Does Not Contradict the Gospels," an attempt to convince Muslims of the truth of the Christian revelation, upset both the Propaganda Fide and the Holy Office, who saw it as implying that the Qur'an was not the farrago of lies that Christian polemic had held it to be since the Middle Ages. The book was banned, and Guadagnoli was disgraced.[101] The Propaganda Fide had printed the treatise and was then forced to withdraw it. Not daring to risk this problem again, the Holy Office and the pope decided to nip Marracci's project in the bud.[102]

Marracci likely learned that it was more prudent to work with, rather than against, the Roman institutions of censorship by observing the experience of his older brother Ippolito. Ippolito, an avid defender of the then-controversial doctrine of the Immaculate Conception, had been under house arrest for his views, and was later put on trial and found guilty on pain of excommunication for his defiance. Ippolito's books were put on the Index and he was banned from teaching.[103]

Marracci remained steadfast in his commitment to publish the entire Qur'an, but he found a pragmatic interim solution to his troubles: pursuing a more modest enterprise. In 1688 he decided to publish a short work against Islam—the *Prodromus ad Refutationem Alcorani* (Preliminary to the refutation of the Qur'an). After various delays, it was printed by the Propaganda Fide in 1690 and authorized and published the following year.[104] The *Prodromus,* essentially the preface to Marracci's translation, contained a life of Muhammad, a short treatise on the Qur'an, and a four-part refutation of its doctrines. The sections of the refutation examined in turn whether Islam found support in Christian scripture, whether any miracles proved the revelation to Muhammad to be true, whether the creeds of Islam conformed with divine truth, and whether Muslim laws bore witness to the truthfulness of Islam. In all cases, of course, Marracci found in favor of Christianity.[105]

The second step in breaking the Roman stalemate came from outside the Eternal City. To Marracci's great fortune, a savior emerged who was willing to take on the venture of publishing the Qur'an.

Printing the Qur'an in Padua

In 1670 the bishop of Padua, Cardinal Gregorio Barbarigo, reestablished the city's seminary. Barbarigo, Venetian by birth, found his vocation as a clergyman in 1655 after an early career as a diplomat had taken him all over Europe. Padua, an important post for a bishop, was assigned to him in 1664. Since the early fifteenth century the city had been part of the Republic of Venice, but its university, the second oldest in Italy, dated back to 1222. Barbarigo created his seminary to improve the quality of the clergy, who would in turn ensure the orthodox education of the members of his diocese. Because he also aimed to train missionaries, the curriculum included not just Latin, Greek, and Hebrew but also Arabic, Persian, and Turkish. Barbarigo was interested both in the conversion of Muslims and in the possibility of the Eastern Churches rejoining the Catholic Church.[106] Ten years after founding the seminary, he established a printing press, despite the vocal opposition of local printers concerned that the new press would steal their business. (The eventual publication of Marracci's Qur'an was funded by the profitable sale of breviaries and missals published by the seminary's press, the so-called red and black liturgical books.)[107]

Barbarigo immediately faced the problem of how to print in Arabic, a significant challenge in seventeenth-century Europe. Arabic letters connect to one another and change shape depending upon their position within a word, requiring an expensively high number of types. Moreover, most attempts at printing did not compare favorably with the beauty and precision that a professional Arabic scribe could produce. Some early printers attempted to use woodblock type to set Arabic, but eventually several movable alternatives were created. The first books produced by this method were published in Fano and in Genoa in 1514 and 1516, respectively.[108] In the late sixteenth century an extensive Arabic printing enterprise was undertaken at the Typographia Medicea, founded in Rome at the time of Pope Gregory XIII.[109] Its products were distinguished by their refinement and beauty, but, sadly, the methods to achieve them died with their talented printer, Giovanni Raimondi, whose work set the gold standard for Arabic typography in Europe. Other cities—Leiden, Oxford, Paris, London—created their own Arabic presses, but because of the expense and complexity of the endeavor, Arabic printing in Europe advanced in fits and starts. For instance, although Paris possessed a set of Arabic types in the middle of the seventeenth century, these fell out of use and were believed lost until 1785.[110]

In September 1683 Barbarigo began gathering materials for printing Arabic. He contacted the director of the Ambrosiana Library in Milan to ask for Arabic matrices (the copper devices used to cast type), which he soon received. In November 1684 he successfully petitioned Grand Duke Cosimo III of Tuscany to ask for the types of the Typographia Medicea (which had been transferred from Rome to Florence earlier in the century).[111] Soon enough, the Paduan typesetters began to set in Arabic type, for which they were paid more than when they set Latin script. In addition, the cardinal arranged for them to have fifteen minutes of instruction in the Oriental languages daily.[112] Things moved along quickly. In 1685 the seminary began to put out books with Arabic text.[113] These would come to include Arabic grammars, anthologies of proverbs in Arabic, Persian, and Turkish, and Christian writings translated into Arabic.[114] Some were slender productions, but others were quite ambitious, albeit nowhere near the scale of Marracci's Qur'an.

Unfortunately, Barbarigo's correspondence with Marracci is not currently available to scholars, if it has survived, which means that we do not know the exact date on which Barbarigo decided to publish the Qur'an in Padua, nor the details of how the two men agreed to bring about the edition. What we do know is that Barbarigo had been introduced to Marracci's Arabic expertise in late 1684, when the Florentine librarian Antonio Magliabechi sent him Marracci's translation of the inscription on a Turkish battle standard.[115] When

Pope Alexander VIII died in February 1691, Barbarigo came to Rome for the conclave to elect his successor. Marracci hoped to see him, but Barbarigo was initially too busy: he was not merely one of the cardinals voting, but a front-runner for the papacy in what, at five months' duration, would become the longest conclave of the seventeenth century.[116] In the end, Barbarigo lost the election; had he been made pope, it is possible that the Qur'an would have been published in Rome rather than Padua.[117]

Marracci and Barbarigo must have agreed on the Paduan Qur'an project by the end of the conclave at the latest. The *Prodromus* was published that year, but a greater objective already beckoned. That autumn Barbarigo set to work persuading the cardinals to approve the endeavor of publishing the Qur'an both in Arabic and in Latin. (The passing of Innocent XI, who had died in 1689, facilitated matters.) In Rome he needed the approval of the Holy Office and the Master of the Sacred Palace, the pope's theologian.[118] He pursued these goals in the autumn of 1691, receiving the authorization he required on November 7.

In addition to the permission to publish the Qur'an, Barbarigo also had to get permission to reprint Marracci's 1691 *Prodromus ad Refutationem Alcorani*. At issue was the protection of printers and their rights. Allowing the work to be reprinted outside of Rome would be an exemption from the protectionist regulation "that books composed in Rome cannot be printed elsewhere."[119]

In the Venetian Republic, the bureaucracy was no less intricate. Barbarigo needed the approval of the Paduan censors as well as of the Venetian state. (Initially he even sent the *Prodromus* to the Paduan Inquistor, but this turned out to be unnecessary, because the content had already been approved in Rome. Steering through this labyrinth was tricky, even for a bishop.)[120] However, permission for the *Prodomus* was granted by the Paduan censors on March 24, 1692.[121] Permission for the *Refutatio Alcorani* would follow on January 31, 1695.[122]

In terms of both the intellectual and the practical effort involved, the refutation of the Qur'an would be a major undertaking for the Paduan seminary. In December 1692 the typesetters began laying out the Arabic type for the full *Alcorani Textus Universus,* which did not appear for six more years.[123] (The other great project of the press in the 1690s was the *Summa Theologica* of Saint Thomas Aquinas. Perhaps incongruously, in the course of that decade the Qur'an and the works of Aquinas were set and printed side by side.)[124]

Why did Barbarigo go to all this trouble? The boundlessly energetic bishop was an emulator of the great Milanese cardinal Federico Borromeo (1564–1631), a militantly active patron of scholarship, the founder in 1607 of the Ambrosiana Library, which was one of the first public libraries in European history, and a sponsor of the study of Arabic. (The first major Arabic dictionary to be published in the West appeared in Milan in 1632.)[125] Barbarigo sought to reactivate Borromeo's legacy.[126] He explained, "Regarding Arabic matters I followed the example of Cardinal Borromeo, and I am sorry that his Successors [in Milan] have not followed it."[127]

The lack of the Barbarigo-Marracci correspondence prevents us from solving the central remaining puzzle of the *Alcorani Textus Universus*: in preparation for the printing of the *Alcorani Textus Universus,* Marracci sent to Padua his translation and its critical notes and refutation, but not the Arabic text of the Qur'an.[128] The reason for this remains unclear, but what is certain is that the Arabic text had instead to be put together at the seminary. In Venice, the great cosmopolitan trading port, many religious orders held Arabic manuscripts in their libraries, but in Padua, an inland university town, neither the seminary nor the University of Padua library possessed a Qur'an.[129] The provenance of the Qur'ans used by the seminary is not known (using multiple copies was a way of detecting scribal error in a given copy, as well as of discovering variants). It is possible that they came from a private collection, but, if so, it was not Barbarigo's, whose books were donated to the seminary at his death.[130] It is likely that the Qur'ans were borrowed from one or several religious orders in Venice, including from the libraries of three churches: the Dominican Santi Giovanni e Paolo, which had a particularly good collection of Arabic manuscripts; Santa Maria del Rosario, formerly of the Gesuati order, on the Giudecca Canal; and Santa Maria della Salute of the Padri Somaschi.[131] It seems a reasonable surmise that Barbarigo leveraged his power and connections in Venice to have Arabic Qur'an manuscripts conveyed to Padua. He sometimes employed a traveling fishmonger to ferry books from Venice to Padua along the Brenta Canal, so it is not inconceivable that the Arabic Qur'ans traveled the same way.[132]

Barbarigo did not read Arabic, so he needed someone to correct the printed pages. Marracci, by then in his early eighties, remained in Rome and could not be of assistance. The man he hired, Timoteo Agnellini (originally Ḥumaylī b. Daʿfi Karnūsh), was a Syriac Orthodox Christian from Diyarbakır, in southeastern Anatolia, who had been converted to Catholicism by Capuchin missionaries and had come to Italy with one of them in the early 1670s. Before his departure, Agnellini had been elected bishop of the city of Mardin, now in Turkey. In spite of this designation, his chances of returning to Eastern Christendom, in accordance with the program of the Catholic Church, were low: like many Eastern Christians before and after, he preferred to try his luck in Catholic Europe.[133] Sometime around 1688 Agnellini was called to the Paduan seminary from Venice to teach Oriental languages and work at the press, where he was responsible for about a dozen of its first printed Arabic texts.[134] (It seems probable that Marracci himself had recommended Agnellini to Barbarigo, as he had examined him at the end of his studies in Rome.)[135] For reasons that remain unclear, Agnellini departed in 1693 for Naples, then a dominion of the Spanish crown, where he served the Archbishopric of Salerno.[136] His absence left Barbarigo without anyone capable of correcting the proofs of the Qur'an that were just then issuing from the press. In a letter from 1693, Agnellini wrote, "I confess that I am sorry not to be able to find the hour, nor the day to fly back to Padua in order to conclude those few efforts of mine, and in particular those of the refutations of the Alcoran, which were left incomplete, as your Excellency knows."[137] Six months later he reported that business was holding him up in Naples, but he could "not wait to fly back to my study in Padua, day and night I desire nothing else."[138] In April 1695 Agnellini told a correspondent that Barbarigo had "suspended the Oriental press on account of my absence."[139] In early June 1695 Barbarigo lamented, "We have the Alcoran in the press. It ought to be completed, but as we lack correctors we cannot really dig into it," adding that he had heard of an Ottoman renegade (a Muslim convert to Christianity) in Venice who was "well-acquainted with the Arabic language," and might be persuaded to come to Padua for a fair price. If not, he continued, "I do not see the end of it."[140] The Venetian convert did not come, and Agnellini was roaming across Sicily and Calabria, "spreading the word of God."[141] In August 1696, now back in Naples, Agnellini wrote, "Yesterday I received a letter from His Eminence Lord Barbarigo, who insistently desires my speedy return there to finish the coran."[142] He finally did return to Padua, and the Qur'an was published in 1698. Alas, Barbarigo had died the year before, when his great task was still uncompleted.[143]

. . .

Translating—and even printing—the Qur'an involved some difficult editorial decisions, and there was no clear path to follow. Some consonants differed from one tradition of transmitting the Qur'an to another, giving certain words correspondingly different meanings (known as *qirā'āt,* or readings).[144] In addition, there are various ways of dividing the Qur'an into verses, and a single manuscript might even record several parallel systems of subdivision. (Besides the organization into chapters, the whole text could also be divided into thirty equal sections, or even into new sections every five or ten verses. These divisions were normally signaled by brief marginal notations.)[145] The running commentaries, which broke up the Qur'an into shorter fragments, did not necessarily record the verse divisions. How authoritative the different schools of verse division were was contested among Muslims (discussed under the rubric of *'adad āy al-Qur'ān*), offering little guidance for a translator.

Given all these choices, Marracci's response was, by necessity, idiosyncratic. For instance, he gave a verse number to the mysterious combinations of letters that open twenty-nine suras (chapters); these letters are counted as a verse in one Qur'anic tradition but not in others. However, he did not go along with that particular tradition in other respects.[146] His system of numeration differed from that of Abraham Hinckelmann, his competitor who had published an Arabic Qur'an (without a translation or notes) in Hamburg just a few years before.[147] By the eighteenth century Marracci's numeration system was already regarded as superior to Hinckelmann's, though even Marracci's approach was far from definitive.[148]

On the printing front, the typesetters in Padua had to come up with a way to reconcile their Qur'anic text with Marracci's Latin translation. Their solution was to break up the text of their Qur'an according to the divisions established in the translation, in effect creating a hybrid product. Unfortunately, the Arabic text and the Latin version did not always follow the same variants of the Qur'anic text, leading to discrepancies that would have bothered the attentive reader. For instance, at Q81:24, a passage with variant readings, Marracci went with *bi-ḍanīn,* as his translation of the passage indicates: "He *is* not niggardly concerning the secrets" (Mahomet does not conceal the secrets revealed to him).[149] The Arabic text on the preceding page reads *bi-ẓanīn,* a change of a single letter that transforms the meaning of the passage to "[Muhammad] suspected not the secrets revealed to him."[150]

The final, two-volume product, the *Alcorani Textus Universus,* included an apology from Agnellini, the corrector, for its errors. They were inevitable, he asserted, because Marracci was not in Padua when the book was set; the Arabic manuscripts of the Qur'an that were consulted were defective and offered variant readings; and he himself had lacked the time to gather and compare the variants.[151] These excuses, which were appended to the end of the second volume, infuriated Marracci. In 1700, in his final published book, he protested that the Paduan Qur'an had been "extremely mangled, through the Printers' and correctors' fault, to my infinite mortification."[152] In a private letter he waxed even more caustic: "My trifles [*inettie*] against the Alcoran, so notable for the weakness of the Author, have been made even more so by the striking ignorance of the Typographers and Correctors of Padua, who, not at all versed in the Arabic tongue, and little in the Latin one, have committed a thousand errors. They have even had the daring to change my original in some places . . . Moreover, they perverted the order of the entire first part of the *Prodromus,* they twisted some things, and added others of their own invention, all erroneous—except for that passage at the end of the work, in which they declare themselves to be a mass of dunces."[153] Marracci added that he had tried to no avail to get some pages reprinted.[154] He requested that his correspondent spread the word that the errors in the book were not his fault.[155] He had waited half a lifetime for his masterpiece to be published. Now he was left with bitterness about the outcome.

The Qur'an Speaks Latin

The *Refutatio Alcorani* follows a strict order: The Arabic text comes first, followed in sequence by translation, notes, and refutations, each clearly marked off from the others (Figure 6). The translation itself is divided into numbered verses, and that numeration is also marked in the Arabic text, which makes comparison straightforward.

Biblical texts—especially multilingual ones—often had a complex *mise-en-page.* The *Refutatio Alcorani*'s layout stands in sharp contrast to the multicolumn Renaissance scholarly editions, such as those of the Polyglot Bibles, which encouraged comparison between the different languages in each column.[156] In Marracci's book, the Arabic has been surrounded by Latin commentary as if to neutralize it, reflecting its conception as a refutation.

A striking feature of the *Refutatio Alcorani* is how many aspects of an Arabic Qur'an it manages to preserve. The Arabic text is decorated with small rosettes that recall the decorations of manuscript Qur'ans. These were not custom-made; they had been used in such earlier publications of the Paduan press as a 1688 edition of Arabic, Persian, and Turkish proverbs.[157] The word *sūra* is not translated into Latin and is preserved throughout. The traditional names of the suras (for instance, "The Cow," "The Women") are retained, as are the traditional ascriptions of the place of revelation (Mecca or Medina) and the number of verses (*āyāt*, translated as *commatum*), albeit with the idiosyncrasies mentioned above. The suras open with the traditional blessing *bismillāh al-raḥmān al-raḥīm* ("in the name of God, the merciful, the compassionate"). The mysterious letters that begin some suras are likewise rendered in Latin as letters (for example, "A. L. M."), and the Arabic text is fully marked up with short vowel sounds.[158] To offer the reader something of the experience of the Arabic text, the editors even included in the margins of the first sura the numeration of the *ajzāʾ*, the thirty equal parts into which the Qur'an is divided.[159] At the same time, they did not want the *Refutatio Alcorani* to appear to be an Arabic Qur'an, so they exercised restraint on the press's proven capacity to achieve such feats as imitating the frontispiece of an Arabic book with remarkable artistry.[160]

The Latin translation was meant to elucidate the Arabic text rather than to be a freestanding literary achievement. Marracci aimed for precision and apologized for sacrificing stylistic beauty, noting, "I have striven not for elegance, but for specificity [*proprietas*]."[161] The German theologian Siegmund Jakob Baumgarten remarked: "How much more comprehensible the translation would be, if it were more Latinate and not so literal." At the same time, he recognized that Marracci's style would help readers who wished to learn Arabic, because they could compare original and translation.[162] As the annotations of a copy now in Madrid suggest, some readers put the book to precisely this use, copying out individual Arabic words and their Latin translations in the margins.[163]

Marracci translated as literally as possible while maintaining Latin intelligibility. His drafts reveal that he began with a freer, more fluid translation, yet worked his way toward something closer to a word-for-word version, albeit without sacrificing syntactic coherence.[164] He was very careful to indicate to the reader, via italics, when he was expanding the original text of the Qur'an with interpolations from commentators that he deemed useful for elucidating the often elliptical sentences. In addition, he included brief definitions or circumlocutions in parentheses to make sure that the meaning of Qur'anic periphrastic phrasing or the referents of ambiguous pronouns were clear. He strove for consistency, rendering the same Arabic word with the same Latin word throughout the work, a challenge for translators when there is no identical equivalent in the target language. But Marracci privileged consistency over the clarity of an individual passage.[165]

For an example of Marracci's techniques at work, we can turn to Q112, one of the shortest suras, which states the Qur'an's central theological tenet, the unity of God (Figure 6).[166] As Marracci's quotation from the commentator al-Baydāwī notes, this sura is so important that reading it affords a spiritual value equivalent to reading a third of the Qur'an.[167] Here it is in Arabic transliteration, Marracci's Latin, and a close English version of his Latin:

1. Qul huwa Allāhu aḥadun. 2. Allāhu al-ṣamadu. 3. Lam yalid wa lam yūlad. 4. Wa lam yakun lahu kufuwan aḥadun.
1. Dic. Est Deus Unus. 2. Deus Sempiternus. 3. Non genuit, et non est genitus. 4. Et non fuit illi par ullus.
1. Say. God is One. 2. God the Everlasting. 3. He does not beget, and is not begotten. 4. And there is not any equal to him.

The Latin version is precise and hews close to the original. It contains the same numeration as the Arabic text, allowing for quick study and comparison. Strikingly, although stylistic effects were not the goal, the translation manages to reproduce the rhyme scheme of the original (*aḥad / as-ṣamad / yūlad / aḥad; unus / Sempiternus / genitus / ullus*). At least in part, this reflects the qualities of Latin, which is a particularly flexible medium for translation because word order is fluid; the same effect would be much harder to achieve in English. Another advantage of Latin for translating Arabic lies in the number of verb forms that the same stem can render: line 3 depends on two forms of the verb *walada,* which Marracci could turn into Latin with two forms of the verb *gigno*.[168] The noun *al-ṣamad,* an attribute of God, appears only this once in the Qur'an. Marracci's interpretation of "everlasting" ("Sempiternus") follows the meaning of Golius's dictionary translation of "perpetuus, permanens."[169] In fact, he had first translated it as "perpetuus" in the margins of the copy he made of Ibn Abī Zamanīn before settling for "Sempiternus."[170]

If this rendition does not capture the complexity of the term and its variety of native interpretations, this is likely because Marracci's attention here was held not by *as-ṣamad,* but by the sura's denial of the Trinity, and of the divinity of Christ in particular, as his polemical refutation on the same page reveals. Marracci refers to Q6:101 (96 in his verse division), where God's fatherhood of Jesus is denied on the grounds that "He has no consort." Marracci remarks that to believe that human procreation is only possible via intercourse is "too stupid, and even beast-like, as plenty of animals are begotten without the intercourse of the male and the female."[171] He then refers to the reader to the second part of his *Prodromus,* in which he treats the matter at greater length.

Although the translation was produced as an instrument of polemic, it represented the fulfillment of the effort, begun in the Renaissance, to approach the Qur'an with philological rigor. Common to such preceding attempts had been the clear distinction between polemic and philology, combined with the wish to reproduce the Arabic text of the Qur'an. Marracci's translation was conceived as a tool for studying the Qur'an and did not claim to take its place. Instead, it was something close to an interlinear paraphrase. Publishing the Arabic text of the Qur'an was an immensely prestigious feat of print technology, but it was undertaken in the conviction that the Qur'an could not be replaced by a text in another language. Polemic had to work at the source.[172]

The Refutatio's *Reception*

In 1695 Cardinal Barbarigo expressed the hope that the publication of the Qur'an "will show the ultramontanes [the Protestants] that even in Italy, the Oriental languages are known" (as was discussed in Chapter 1).[173] The project did indeed have an effect outside Italy. In 1681, long before publication, rumors of Marracci's undertaking had reached Protestant lands.[174] When the *Prodromus* of 1691 was published in Rome, it served as an advertisement for both author and forthcoming translation. Even the philosopher Gottfried Wilhelm Leibniz was impressed with the venture.[175] News of the prospective work launched something of an arms race to translate the Qur'an, though as it turned out, no Lutheran scholar was able to produce a complete version.[176]

The *Alcorani Textus Universus* was collected all over the Italian peninsula by institutional libraries, both secular and religious, where it can still be found today.[177] Members of the clergy especially found it appealing. A copy in the library of Alessandria, in Piedmont, bears owners' marks of the Capuchins Antonio da Mombaruzzo and Gabriele da Villafori.[178] The copy now in Houghton Library at Harvard contains the owner's mark of the bibliophilic Carmelite Father Cirillo Tipaldi (1628–1700) of Naples.[179]

The book was also sought after in Protestant lands, though readers agreed with the Catholic Richard Simon's assessment that the translation and the philological research were more compelling than the polemic.[180] Baumgarten wrote that the "best and most usable part of this *Prodromus* is the frequent quotation of remarkable passages and pieces of information [*Nachrichten*] from unpublished Oriental manuscripts."[181] A second reviewer concurred, noting that in spite of the shortcomings of the refutation, "each buyer must gladly pay for it, since sometimes passages from Arabic manuscripts are quoted, which serve to elucidate Muslim doctrines."[182] Quoting and agreeing with Simon's judgment, Baumgarten praised the translation but criticized the exegesis, "diligently arranged in such a way as to make the statements of the Koran seem either obscure or inconsistent and ridiculous."[183] An English biographical dictionary of the 1760s canonized Simon's view of Marracci as scholar and theologian: "This work of Marracci hath great merit: it shews vast application, and vast knowledge of the Arabic tongue, although the learned have discovered, as may reasonably be expected, several faults in the translation. The notes are very learned, but the refutations are not always solid; they shew him to have been rather versed in Mahometan writers, than skilled in philosophical or theological reasonings."[184] Even so, the polemical sections were no obstacle to readers, who could easily skip over them, because Marracci had so helpfully kept his refutations separate from his editorial work.

The book was not to be reprinted in Padua, but it was translated into German in Nuremberg in 1703 and edited in Latin a second time in Leipzig in 1721.[185] The *Prodromus* was even translated into Arabic in 1724 by the Maronite Yaʿqūb Arūtīn.[186] What is more, Marracci's scholarly achievement would be the foundation of all German translations until the early nineteenth century, when Friedrich Rückert finally produced a translation entirely independently of the Italian scholar's work.[187] Something similar held true in early eighteenth-century France. Antoine Galland, whose career as a collector of Arabic manuscripts was outlined in Chapter 1, translated the Qur'an into a

French version (now lost) using Marracci's excerpts and translations.[188] The later French translation by Claude-Étienne Savary relied heavily on Marracci, though Savary did not acknowledge that debt.[189]

Marracci's thoughts about Islam—in particular, the idea he expressed in the following passage—caught the attention of many Protestant and free-thinking readers: "Without doubt, that Superstition [Islam] contains whatever is credible and probable about the Christian Religion, and that which seems to be in agreement with the laws and lights of Nature. It completely excludes those Mysteries of our Faith, which at first blush seem incredible and impossible, and which especially are considered too difficult by human nature. Thus modern worshippers of Idols more easily and promptly embrace Saracenic Law than the Evangelical Law."[190] Marracci concedes that Islam appeals to reason better than does Christianity because it excludes those mysteries, particularly the Trinity, that Christians are asked to believe without understanding them. The fact that Islam was a more reasonable religion did not make it any more true for him, because true religion required faith. On the contrary, its rational appearance made Islam a more treacherous heresy.

Shorn of its context, the above quotation appeared as an epigraph on the frontispiece of a 1712 English-language *Life of Mahomet,* which had been compiled in part out of Marracci's book.[191] It also caught the eye of the Dutch scholar Adriaan Reland, who quoted it approvingly in the second, 1717, edition of his influential treatise *De Religione Mohammedica.*[192] The unitarian thinker John Toland likewise quoted the passage in a publication in 1720.[193] The multiple quotation of Marracci's words reveals a widespread European consensus that Islam was in agreement with natural law—the question Catholic, Protestant, and freethinking critics differed on was how to evaluate it as a religion.[194]

Not everyone admired Marracci's book. The Lutheran scholar Andreas Acoluthus reasoned that his own translation, a sample of which he published in 1701, was superior because he had consulted Persian and Turkish translations, as well as a large number of Qur'an manuscripts that had come to him as spoils of war (yet the published sample was all that Acoluthus ever produced).[195] In 1754 the Göttingen professor Johann David Michaelis criticized Marracci's translation on two grounds: that the Latin was too literal, and therefore ugly, and that it relied too heavily on Muslim commentators. Both of these purported faults were, of course, the very goals that Marracci had consciously pursued.[196] Michaelis's viewpoint was in line with the mid-eighteenth-century notion that, because the challenge of the philological treatment of the Qur'an had been solved, it was time for a successful literary translation.[197] There was one that Michaelis did admire: George Sale's English *Koran,* published in 1734.

The Qur'an in London

George Sale's translation presented the Qur'an to an English audience formed not solely of scholars but also of general readers. In the dedication of his *Koran,* Sale (ca. 1696–1736) laid out the motive behind his project: "To be acquainted with the various laws and constitutions of civilized nations, especially of those who flourish in our own time, is, perhaps, the most useful part of knowledge."[198] He went on to say that it was especially important to study the religion of such an impressive polity as the early Muslim state: "If the religious and civil Institutions of foreign nations are worth our knowledge, those of *Mohammed,* the lawgiver of the *Arabians,* and founder of an empire which in less than a century spread itself over a greater part of the world than the *Romans* were ever masters of, must needs be so."[199] To this manifestly secular perspective, he added an argument that Marracci had also made: "an impartial version of the *Korân*" was necessary "to enable us effectually to expose the imposture."[200] The contrast with Marracci, while indeed significant, should not be overdrawn.

We know little about Sale or how he got involved in Arabic studies.[201] A practicing solicitor in London, he attended neither Cambridge nor Oxford, the two English universities of his day. He was a minor player on the lively commercial publishing scene of early Georgian London, and made part or perhaps most of his income from writing on commission for various editorial ventures.[202] The earliest mentions of him in sources that survive relate to his work as the corrector of the 1726 Arabic New Testament.[203] There has been speculation that he was taught Arabic by Christian Arabs, but no evidence supports that hypothesis. It seems likely that he taught himself the language, as others did at the time.[204] Sale acknowledged his own deficits: "I am but too sensible of the Disadvantages, one who is neither a Native, nor ever was in the Country must lie under, in playing the Critic in so difficult a Language as the Arabick."[205]

Sale completed his *Koran* without access to the treasures of the Bodleian Library, using what he could acquire or consult in London.[206] His personal collection, while impressive, contained few books that could have assisted him, and not a single Qur'an commentary.[207] He had to find help elsewhere, and nothing could have been more useful to him than Marracci's colossal labor of gathering and organizing the opinions of Qur'an commentators.[208] With one important exception, he relied entirely on the Qur'anic authorities that Marracci used.[209] Sale's appropriation of Marracci's impressive critical apparatus is one of the reasons his translation is so widely respected and has remained useful to scholars into our own time.[210] He repeated quotations from Marracci's commentators and referred to a number of Marracci's other Islamic sources.[211] While he dutifully cites other published Arabic sources, he never directs readers to the relevant Arabic excerpts found in Marracci, an unambiguous sign that he intentionally concealed his reliance on his Italian predecessor. No one in the eighteenth century appears to have detected the extent of this dependence. Sale likely occulted his use of Marracci to conceal that he lacked the scholarly tools to tackle the Qur'an himself. Possibly he preferred not to reveal that he leaned so heavily on a Catholic polemicist.

To be fair to Sale, he improved philologically on Marracci's translation and enriched it with new source material. He had firsthand access, via a loan from the Dutch Church in Austin Friars, to a Qur'an commentary by the medieval Persian scholar al-Bayḍāwī, a commentary that Marracci had also used. With access to the whole book, Sale did not need to rely merely on Marracci's quotations. The manuscript, copied in late sixteenth-century Istanbul, had entered the possession of the church in 1633 as the donation of a merchant, Guiliam Vercruicen (or vander Cruicen).[212] Al-Bayḍāwī's commentary was one of the most popular in the Ottoman Empire, as it contained the full Qur'an explained in a concise, single-volume treatment.

The convenience of al-Bayḍāwī's book recommended it to Sale as well as to the Ottoman readers (and Marracci). He did more than consult it: in his translation, the textual variants of the Qur'an are those of al-Bayḍāwī, rather than the standard ones of the Ottoman period that one might have expected him to use, and which indeed are found in his only personal copy of the Qur'an.[213] This preference for al-Bayḍāwī's Qur'anic text suggests that Sale worked not from his own copy of the Qur'an, nor from Marracci's Arabic text, but directly from the Dutch Church al-Bayḍāwī, which, in the course of discussing each passage, excerpted the full holy book of Islam. In other words, the Austin Friars copy of al-Bayḍāwī was the main source of the first direct English translation of the Qur'an.

In a major deviation from Marracci's book, not a single word in Arabic script appears in the Sale *Koran,* turning it into a translation that stands in for the original. Another difference is that Sale acknowledged the Qur'an's literary qualities: "This book was really admired for the beauty of its composure by those who must be allowed to have been competent judges."[214] This view was controversial in Europe, as Muslims saw in the Qur'an's beauty and inimitability proof that the text was revealed.[215] Even though his publication was meant for a broad audience, Sale gathered his authorities in footnotes on every page, ensuring the book's utility as a tool for scholars.

Sale translated the Qur'an into prose, making no attempt to imitate the lyric effects of the original, and he abolished the verse numeration that Marracci had scrupulously preserved. The transformation of the Qur'an into continuous prose followed the model of the King James Bible (KJV); this English translation, completed in 1611, was approved by the Church of England and did not distinguish between prose and poetry.[216] Here is Sale's version of sura Q112, the one discussed above:

> SAY, GOD is one GOD ; the eternal GOD : he begetteth not, neither is he begotten : and there is not any one like unto him.[217]

Following the example of Marracci, Sale italicized his interjections, preserving a pristine distinction between Qur'anic text and the commentarial elucidations he inserted to clarify the meaning. He also added a brief note to the sura, explaining, "This chapter is held in particular veneration by the *Mohammedans,* and declared, by a tradition of their prophet, to be equal in value to a third part of the whole *Korân.*"[218] (Like Marracci, he cited al-Bayḍāwī as his source for this information.)

The Qur'an is difficult to translate for many reasons: its allusive references, its frequent changes of voice, its nonlinear narration. Particularly challenging for European translators is its prosody—its rhythm and metrics. Traditionally the Qur'an is not called poetry, even though it is composed in a form of rhymed and rhythmic verse known as *sajʿ.* This meter is based on stress rather than on syllabic count, meaning that individual verse lengths can vary considerably. (It is often characterized as being written in "rhymed prose," an obvious oxymoron.)[219] Europeans of the seventeenth and eighteenth centuries had some awareness of *saj'*, but they nevertheless found it hard to make sense of it or to define it precisely.[220] Of course, translators did not have the luxury of claiming ignorance; they had to take a stance.

Both Marracci and Sale sought to replicate some of the Qur'an's stylistic effects, in particular its repetitions and its paratactical sentence structures, features easier to render than others like rhyme.[221] Sale gave his translation the dignified, resonant tone of the KJV by using falling meter and other devices.[222] The KJV reproduced Hebrew poetry's use of parallelism and repetition, so this style (also found in the Qur'an) was familiar to Anglophone audiences. In contrast, Marracci had not sought to produce a literary version of the Qur'an; the notion of making his translation sound like the Latin Vulgate would have appalled him.

Overall, Sale showed his independence and his careful judgment, neither uncharitable, as Marracci could be, nor unduly infatuated with his object of study, as other European writers about Islam had been.[223] His translation was an enormous commercial success, and was reprinted many times in the course of the eighteenth century. Through it, such luminaries as Thomas Jefferson and Voltaire became acquainted with the holy text of Islam.[224] Sale's *Koran* remained the standard English translation throughout the nineteenth century and well into the twentieth. Although it was supplanted by other English versions starting in the 1950s, it remains the most influential English translation of all time.

Conclusion

In the seventeenth century a Catholic translator, working in a city whose Levantine associations we have forgotten, produced a scholarly instrument that retains its uses in our own day. His reasons for wanting to do so, as we have seen, were deeply traditional. To his mind, Peter the Venerable had sufficiently articulated why a Christian should study Islam. That Marracci was able to publish the Qur'an in Arabic and in translation depended in the first instance on the rich availability of relevant Arabic manuscripts in and around

Rome. It required a serious commitment and perseverance, as well as an understanding of Roman politics. The long view was definitely called for, and serendipity counted, too: Marracci found something of a *deus ex machina* in Cardinal Barbarigo, who was willing to publish the Qur'an at the printing press he had founded in Padua. In doing so, Barbarigo was himself reactivating a Counter-Reformation tradition of Arabic study that had flourished in Rome, Florence, and Milan at the beginning of the century.

More than three decades later the first English translation of the Qur'an directly from Arabic would appear and immediately establish itself as a classic. The reason was in no small part the literary skill of the translator, who found a felicitous way of rendering the Qur'an in English prose. If, in the quest for readability, Sale compromised on not separating the verses (*āyāt*), his translation was nevertheless built on a detailed understanding of the Qur'an and its native exegesis, which in large part he owed to the work of Marracci. To consider their respective contributions as a division of labor, one might say that Marracci solved the scholarly challenge of translating the Qur'an, and Sale met the literary challenge, at least for the English language.[225]

In spite of their differences, the two translations offer the same lesson about native mediation in the decades on either side of 1700: the interpretations of the Islamic tradition were at the heart of these groundbreaking "modern" Western translations of the Qur'an. That neither man left his native country, and yet each was able to translate with seriousness and integrity, is proof of the level of maturity of Arabic studies in Europe.[226] These two scholars—with utterly different backgrounds, and working decades and a thousand miles apart from one another—relied, however, on the same basic strategy for approaching the Qur'an: translating it not directly, but from a running commentary. This was the mediation not of living intermediaries but of the written classics of the *tafsīr* genre, procured in the book markets of the Eastern Mediterranean and Iberia. In both cases the commentarial interpretations were not relegated to the bottom of the page, but were intercalated (in italics) throughout the Qur'anic text itself.

There is no one "right" way of rendering the Qur'an in a foreign language. Whether one prefers Marracci's version or Sale's depends on what one expects of a translation. Marracci gives a nearer experience of the Arabic Qur'an, but Sale offers a more fully elaborated literary achievement. One reason Sale has enjoyed more fame is that the absence of polemical packaging has made his *Koran* seem more modern. Another is that Sale's looks the way we expect a translation to look, whereas Marracci's Arabic and Latin texts resemble a scholarly tool more than a literary work. All things told, George Sale's gift to his native literature, the canonical English translation of the Qur'an, is a true product of its time: a joint Catholic and Protestant effort to revise the European understanding of Islam and of its primary text.

THREE

A NEW VIEW OF ISLAM

In the seventeenth and eighteenth centuries, Catholic and Protestant scholars dramatically reconfigured the European perception of Islam. The lengthy "Preliminary Discourse" to George Sale's English translation of the Qur'an (*Koran*, 1734; see Chapter 2) presents Sale's encompassing vision of the religion of Islam and its history. This learned yet accessible essay would provide an overview of Islamic history and beliefs to European and North American readers for a remarkably long time. Balancing measured judgment with deep learning, the "Preliminary Discourse" is one of the most prominent products of a process of study and reevaluation of Islam that stretched back many decades across Catholic and Protestant Europe.

This reconfiguration had two distinct strands. On the one hand, it became increasingly possible to write neutrally about Islam and its rise, to represent Muhammad not as a hoary impostor but rather as an able politician, and to acknowledge that his religion contained moral and spiritual insights. At the same time, discussion of Islam came to be informed empirically by newly translated materials, which added detail and depth to a portrayal that had often relied on a set of recycled tropes. These two distinct processes—the attainment of a nonpolemical point of view, and of an increase in empirical knowledge—were concurrent, and often overlapped.

The reconfiguration of thought about Islam was enacted by scholars and thinkers from entirely different alignments, some who considered their activity to be religious polemic against Islam, and others who instead pleaded for a warmly sympathetic understanding of the religion. This chapter's diverse set of protagonists represents a variety of positions and shows that the reinterpretation of Islam was the result of more than the act of any single interpreter or of a single interpretation. It was a dual process of normative reevaluation and knowledge production, whose eventual outcomes no single individual could have fully anticipated.[1]

What set this reinterpretation in motion? According to a frequently mooted hypothesis, this more sober view of Islam reflected normalized relations between the Ottomans and the Christian powers after the failed siege of Vienna in 1683, the military defeat that stopped the advance of the Ottoman Empire into Europe. Indeed, for most of the following century, the Ottomans posed no immediate threat to European states, and the European study of Islam was in this respect less fraught. Yet this elegant explanation ignores the fact that the reevaluation of Islam was well under way before 1683—it already had deep roots in European intellectual life.

At the same time, Islam, unlike Judaism, was the faith of powerful and vast empires. Even Islam's harshest critics conceded its importance: Humphrey Prideaux (1648–1724), the Dean of Norwich, noted that Muhammad had risen "to make one of the greatest *Revolutions* that ever happened in the World, which immediately gave Birth to an *Empire,* which in Eighty years time extended its Dominions over more Kingdoms and Countries, than ever the *Roman* could in Eight hundred."[2] Interpretations that took Islam's early political success seriously helped make sense of contemporary geopolitics.

Another explanation that has been advanced for the reevaluation of Islam is the rise across Europe of the freethinking movement.[3] This hypothesis assumes that it would have been impossible for Christian scholars, whether Catholic or Protestant, to investigate Islam in a neutral fashion while remaining true to the tenets of their own faith. According to this line of reasoning, only those who held a secular, even an aversive, understanding of Christianity would have been capable of attaining a newly charitable vision of a foreign religion.[4]

In fact, none of the key insights that allowed Islam to be studied with new eyes required unbelief about Christianity. Irreligious writers were not the first to recognize that Islam could be studied as part of a comparative investigation of religions, including Christianity itself. These unbelieving writers did not invent the strategy that made the study of Islam permissible—the analogy between Islam and ancient paganism. As this chapter will demonstrate, orthodox scholars before them had already leveraged the comparison between Islam and pagan Greece and Rome in order to justify their new object of study. The reinterpretation of Islam originated within the culture of Christian learning in both Catholic and Protestant lands.[5]

This chapter covers some of the intellectual responses to Islam during the period bookended by Edward Pococke's *Specimen Historiæ Arabum* of 1650 and George Sale's *Koran* of 1734. Apart from Pococke and Sale, it focuses on the French priest Richard Simon and the Dutch professor Adriaan Reland— with cameo appearances by Humphrey Prideaux, Friedrich Spanheim the Younger, Henry Stubbe, John Toland, and the Count of Boulainvilliers. All these men—even the polemicists and radicals among them—were students and readers of the new European scholarship of Arabic. If they were not active citizens of the Republic of Arabic Letters, they were at least corresponding members. Overall, this chapter skews Dutch and English, but the work of the Catholic scholar Simon, a member of the French Oratorian order until his expulsion in 1678, shows that the reevaluation of Islam was not limited to Protestant Europe. (A complete genealogy of the reconfiguration lies outside the scope of this book, but participants included scholars of Arabic, Church of England and Roman Catholic polemicists, deists, and freethinkers.)

Recent research has made it clearer than ever that the reappraisal of Islam was part of a wider transformation in the understanding and comparative study of religions, one in which both Catholic and Protestant scholars participated. On a macroscopic, European scale, what permitted the reconsideration of Islam was not only the new shared standards of truth but also the breakdown of the religious unity of Western Christendom that occurred after the Reformation. A confessionally divided Europe gave occasion to a long-running dispute between Catholics and Protestants, with Islam as one of the fields of battle.[6] Research into the history of Christianity, spurred by this interconfessional rivalry, could not help but include Islam, with its genetic connections to Judaism and Christianity. In this process, some observers came to see similarities between Islam and Christianity, whose own shifting grounds and (eventual) institutionalized pluralism forced a rethinking of what it meant to be a Christian and of what it meant to be a Muslim. These changes were wrought not by a move away from religion, but rather from the live struggle within religious communities to make sense of the new confessional order that had settled on late seventeenth-century Europe.

A Sample of the History of the Arabs

Sometimes a single book really does transform a field of study and inaugurate a new way of thinking and writing. It is hard to underestimate the impact of the *Specimen Historiæ Arabum* (A sample of the history of the Arabs) by

Edward Pococke (1604–1691), which was published in 1650.[7] The ambitious and learned *Specimen* initiated a new phase in the European study of Arabic. It offered an entry point into Islamic history and letters and brought into view an intellectual tradition comparable to that of Greece and Rome.[8] Pococke's followers recognized their debt: Sale would celebrate him as "for eminency of goodness as well as learning the greatest Ornament of the age in which he lived," and the eighteenth-century German scholar Johann Jacob Reiske would write: "I doubt that Arabic letters owe more to any other man than to this one."[9]

In 1619 Pococke arrived at Oxford, where he studied Greek and Hebrew. In 1626 he discovered Arabic, which became his lifelong passion, and began taking lessons from William Bedwell, the first English Arabist of note.[10] In 1630 he was ordained and appointed chaplain to the English Levant Company in Aleppo, where he studied with a number of local Muslim scholars (and one Jewish scholar), all the while collecting manuscripts. Archbishop Laud created Oxford's Arabic chair (the Laudian Professorship of Arabic) for him.[11] Pococke survived Laud, who was executed in 1645, and spent the years of the Civil War as a parish priest in a Berkshire village. His productivity was undiminished by the surrounding chaos: aside from completing the *Specimen Historiæ Arabum,* he published a partial edition and translation of Maimonides's commentary on the Mishnah, the collection of Jewish oral traditions, which Maimonides wrote in Arabic with Hebrew characters.[12] At the Restoration, in 1660, Pococke returned to Oxford, where he translated the complete Arabic text of the history by the Christian historian Gregorius Bar Hebraeus that he had excerpted in the *Specimen.* Pococke had acquired the manuscript of this medieval history of the Arabs during his stay in Aleppo. The work appeared in 1663 as *Historia Compendiosa Dynastiarum* (The compendious history of the dynasties), the first full history of the Arabs written in Arabic to appear in the West.[13]

The *Specimen*'s modest title and small format belie its novelty, erudition, and impact. It contained an edition and translation of, and commentary on, two short excerpts from Bar Hebraeus's history. The excerpts run for thirty pages (fifteen of Arabic text, and fifteen of Latin translation), under the title "Of the Arab Peoples and of Their Customs," with two subheadings: "Of the Customs of the Arabs before Mohammed" and "Of the Customs of the Arabs after Mohammed."[14] That text, which offers a basic outline of the history and religion of the Arabs and of the rise of Islam, is followed by a much lengthier commentary, "Notes Containing Several Things Illustrating Especially Part of the History of the Orientals, Extracted from the Authors of the Best Reputation Among Them with Labor and Effort by Edward Pococke."[15] These notes run for over 300 pages (Figure 7).[16] They are the heart of the *Specimen,* and go far beyond the limitations of the excerpts that they ostensibly elucidate. The choice to write a commentary was traditional, the content (and the specially made Arabic types) anything but.[17]

The commentary, which draws on many authors, makes up for any shortcomings in Bar Hebraeus. Pococke cited and often quoted at length dozens of Arabic writers, most of whose work was unknown or barely known in the West: the medieval theologian Ibn Taymiyya; the historian and geographer Abū'l-Fidāʾ; the historian al-Shahrastānī; a great number of poets, including pre-Islamic ones; philosophers like al-Fārābī, Avicenna, and Maimonides; Qurʾan commentators including al-Suyūṭī, al-Zamakhsharī, al-Bayḍāwī, and many others.[18]

The *Specimen* endows the history of the Arabs and of Islam with the same dignity traditionally afforded to that of the Greeks and Romans.[19] It achieves this result both through the sheer quantity and quality of source material that it employs and through the effective analogies Pococke makes between the classical past and Arab and Muslim culture and history.[20] Although most European scholars of the next generation did not achieve his erudition in matters Islamic (the two greatest exceptions—Lodovico Marracci and Barthélemy d'Herbelot—are treated elsewhere in this book), Pococke made a profound impact on seventeenth- and eighteenth-century European descriptions of Islamic belief and history.

More Pure Than the Pagans

The French Catholic scholar Richard Simon (1638–1712), one of the great Hebraists and biblical authorities of his era, is best known for his *Histoire critique du Vieux Testament* (1678), his contribution to the study of the Old Testament as a product of history.[21] Simon, a lifelong provocateur, expressed opinions about the historical constitution of the Old Testament that the orthodox majority did not welcome. Among his enemies was the influential French bishop Jacques-Bénigne Bossuet, and in 1678 Simon was expelled from the Society of the Oratory, a French Counter-Reformation order (he had been ordained a priest in 1670).[22] His remarks on Islam help us appreciate what it was possible to think and to say in print about Islam in late seventeenth-century Catholic Europe.

This contrarian Catholic intellectual achieved a new understanding of Islam. His original treatment took written shape in the early 1670s in the form of commentaries on books about the religions of the Near East. His translation of and commentary on the travel account of the Jesuit Girolamo Dandini's mission to the Maronites of Mount Lebanon was published in 1675.[23] (His proposed additions and revisions to the first French edition of the Oxford scholar Edward Brerewood's *Enquiries Touching the Diversity of Languages and Religions through the Chief Parts of the World* were published posthumously, in 1983).[24] Eventually his remarks on Muslims there would appear as "De la créance et des coûtumes des Mahométans" (On the beliefs and customs of the Mahometans), chapter 15 of his *Histoire critique de la créance et des coûtumes des nations du Levant* (Critical history of the beliefs and customs of the nations of the Levant), published in Frankfurt in 1684.[25] The *Histoire critique* was a more encompassing version of the various remarks he had published in 1675 on the peoples of the Levant, now expanded to consider all the Eastern Churches.

Simon studied Oriental languages in Paris from 1659 to 1662, but his level of proficiency in Arabic is hard to ascertain. He approached language learning by reading and translating as much as he could, rather than by spending a lot of time with grammar books.[26] He corrected Dandini's Arabic errors, and claimed to have made use of at least one Islamic work.[27] In any case, he was well read in the new scholarship by Pococke and others and in European travel writing.[28]

Simon's contribution was interpretive rather than empirical. As he wrote in 1675, Islam owed a debt to Christianity and especially to Judaism: "As Mahommetanism is a mixture of Judaism and Christianity, one should not be surprised to find among the Turks many things that can also be observed among us. Those who have a perfect knowledge of these two religions can easily show the origin of most Mahommetan ceremonies."[29] That Islam contained elements of Judaism and Christianity was a traditional polemical argument, but Simon invested it with new meaning.[30] He did not dwell on the implication that Islam was a forgery but focused instead on how and why the same customs and beliefs existed across religious boundaries.[31] This comparative assessment identified analogies that were grounded in common genealogy. Simon argued strenuously that Islam's rituals and its theology were both rooted in Judaism, citing as evidence the Jewish and Muslim habit of constantly praising and blessing God, the restriction on eating pork, ritual ablution and its concomitant blessings, and the prayer ritual.[32] To him, these overlaps demonstrated that Islam had emulated Judaism in its forms and practices. He found Islamic theology to be rife with principles that originated in Judaism, with the obvious exception of the importance ascribed to Muhammad. He traced even the central creed of Islam, the unity of God, back to a passage in Deuteronomy 6:4, "Hear, O Israel: The Lord our God is one Lord."[33] A reference to custom bolstered this assertion: just as Jews swayed when reciting their key prayer based on this verse, *Sh'ma Yisrael Adonai Eloheinu Adonai Ehad,* Muslims swayed when repeating theirs, *lā ilāha illā Allāh* (There is no God but God).[34]

Simon also explored analogies between Islam and Christianity. In the picture he painted, both theologies faced similar intellectual predicaments. Finding that the two groups of Muslim theologians—the "scholastic" and the "positive"—debated the same problems as Christian theologians, he wrote: "Indeed their theology is similar to that which is taught in our schools," adding, "They fall into the same arguments as we do concerning the attributes or perfections of God."[35] Simon traced this kinship to the common Aristotelian root of Christian and Islamic metaphysics and to the influence of Arab philosophers on their Christian counterparts, "who owe [to them] all the greatest subtlety they possess today."[36]

Simon's analysis might appear at first glance to be a more nuanced version of the traditional "imposture" argument, an attempt to unmask Islam as nothing more than a confection of other religions. Instead, what he achieved was a fair-minded judgment of Islamic religion. He argued that one had to give ideas worthy of respect their due in whatever context they were found, making his case on the basis of the Christian assimilation of pre-Christian Greek and Roman thought. To justify incorporating pagan thought into the Christian intellectual tradition, the Church Fathers had acknowledged the virtue and wisdom of ancient pagans like Plato and Cicero.[37] This acknowledgment of "good paganism" was Simon's key to presenting Islam not as a heresy but as a religious tradition with worthwhile insights. He argued that admiring the good qualities of Islam was not breaking with Christian tradition: "Is one pre-vented from having an unfavorable opinion of the religion of the Maho-metans when one simply praises in them that which is indeed praiseworthy? When the gentlemen of [the convent of] Port-Royal admired the morality that is found in Cicero's *On Duties* and in some other famous pagan writers, they did not do so to support paganism."[38] Cicero's moral treatise *De Officiis* (*On Duties*), one of the Roman orator's most popular works, examined con-flicts of duty and personal advantage.[39] The "gentlemen of [the convent of] Port-Royal" were the exponents of Jansenism, a theological movement within the seventeenth-century Catholic Church. Simon chose this example deliber-ately; he frequently targeted the Jansenists in his polemic, and they returned the favor in kind.[40] His point, however, was serious: it was inconsistent to admire the morality of pagans, who had known nothing of the true God, and yet to refuse to extend the same treatment to Muslims.

Simon underpinned his claim on behalf of Muslim morality with the ge-nealogical argument that there is a direct connection between the philosoph-ical virtue of the pagans and that of the Muslims: "The Mahometan doctors have read that which was best in the ancient philosophers who were trans-lated into Arabic."[41] Through this line of argument he bolstered the authority of Islamic thought and encouraged Christian readers to acknowledge it.

The relentlessly probing Simon did not stop there. He followed his com-parison of pagan and Muslim morality with a judgment in favor of the latter: "I have claimed that their morality is even more pure than that of the pagan philosophers, for they have also drawn a good part of it from the books of the Jews and the Christians. One finds nothing in the writings of the most learned pagans that might be compared with what the Arab writers say about the unity of God, of his perfections, of the worship which is his due, and of the charity that one must cultivate for one's neighbor."[42] Consequently, the fair-mindedness that the Church Fathers had extended to pagan authors should be even more justifiably applied to the Muslims, as monotheists—making the study of Islam not only permissible but also relevant and urgent. Simon pro-posed that, given that Islam's excellent theological and moral insights derived from Jewish and Christian writings, the religion be read as a florilegium (anthology) of Judeo-Christian wisdom.

The tradition of Christian appropriations of extra-Christian thought offered Simon the key to a new approach to Islam. Other writers before him had seen a similar potential in the classical heritage: for example, in the six-teenth century the Dominican friar Bartolomé de las Casas had undertaken a lengthy comparison between Greco-Roman paganism and the paganism of New World peoples to show that the latter in fact came closer to worshipping the true God.[43] Simon applied this same comparison to Islam, and found in its favor. What he offered was no less than a reclassification of Islam from the domain of heresy and polemic to the neutral ground of what was appropriate for a Christian scholar to study.[44]

A Manifesto

Scholars can tuck away powerful revisionist statements in their footnotes and their commentaries, but sometimes it takes a manifesto to get the world's at-tention. In 1705 Adriaan Reland (1676–1718), a professor of Oriental languages at the university of Utrecht, sent to the presses a compact octavo that would resonate across Europe out of all proportion to its modest size.[45] *De Religione Mohammedica Libri Duo* (Two books about the Mohammedan religion) was translated into English, German, Dutch, and French; both the original Latin and the German version ran to second editions.[46] The handsome second Latin edition of 1717 reflects this publishing success: the illustrations, newly commissioned, include a visual explanation of how Muslims pray, in eight steps (Figure 8), along with the first detailed representation published in Eu-rope of the mosque of Mecca—a folio-sized foldout that showed the Kaʿba at the mosque's center and pilgrims gathering around to pray (Figure 9).[47]

The various editions of *De Religione Mohammedica* circulated widely. Into Lessing and Gibbon's day, the book served as a useful overview of Islamic creeds—a great success for a little work by a scholar who was not exclusively or even primarily occupied with the study of Arabic or Islam.[48] Reland him-self rarely left Utrecht and never the Netherlands, but his curiosity was global. His manuscript collection included books not only in Arabic but also in the languages of Southeast Asia.[49] What is more, Reland used these Southeast Asian books in his study of Islam. For example, in his second, revised edition of 1717, Reland dismissed the notion that Muslims believed in a plurality of worlds, an idea that had come from Marracci's showpiece refutation of the opening sura of the Qur'an, the *Fātiḥa*. Marracci used the verse that describes God as *rabb al-ʿālamīn* (literally, lord of the worlds) to claim that "Mahomet namely believed with his Arabs that there were plural worlds."[50] One of the arguments Reland used to rebut this notion was that translations of the Qur'an into Malay and Javanese rendered the relevant verse in the Qur'an as "Glory to God, lord of the entire world" (Figure 10).[51] Reland privileged the translations of Southeast Asian Muslims over Marracci's version, using them to determine how an ambiguous Qur'anic phrase should be taken. Thus the global reach of the Dutch Republic and the manuscript collecting that it enabled were brought to bear on a polemical disagreement about how to read the Qur'an.

Why did Reland bother to set the record about Islam straight? He recollected that he had often discussed the topic with his brother Pieter, a lawyer in Amsterdam; making sense of the vast spread of Islam seemed worthwhile to scholar and lawyer alike.[52] The Relands' interest in Islam was stimulated by living in the Dutch Republic, whose citizens had, since its founding in 1581, spread across the world in quest for profit. While Marracci's geopolitical worldview reflected the Mediterranean clash of competing Abrahamic religions, the increasingly global cultural interactions prompted by commerce formed Adriaan Reland's: "Is it not true that much exchange connects us with the Mohammedans, in Constantinople, on the border of Hungary and the Turkish Empire, on the coasts of Africa, in Syria, Persia and the West Indies, where both our colonies, and the places that we frequent in quest of profit, contain many Mohammedans?"[53] Along with this argument for the contemporary importance of the study of Islam—one that would be reiterated decades later by Voltaire—Reland underscored a more traditional one: Arabic could help illuminate obscure passages in the Hebrew Bible, especially those that contain words used only once. Throughout the seventeenth century, scholars had exploited Arabic cognates to understand, or least attempt to understand, biblical Hebrew; Reland believed that Arabic continued to be useful even as the study of the Bible had advanced.[54]

Reland, like Simon, was certain that Islam expressed many truths about the nature of God: "And are [the beliefs of the Mohammedans] bad, merely because they are Mohammedan? Therefore what they write in agreement with truth about the attributes of God ought to be denied by us. What sane man would argue this?"[55] Reland believed the best approach was not to demonize Muslims but to emphasize the common ground between the two religions— a strategy he hoped would ultimately lead to conversions to Christianity.

De Religione Mohammedica has two sections. The first consists of a full reproduction of a concise Arabic statement of faith that describes the basic creeds and ritual obligations of Muslims, along with a facing Latin translation by Reland.[56] The second section is a treatise in forty articles, each of which disputes an erroneous Christian proposition about Islam. The articles follow a format: a claim is presented, the authorities from which it is drawn are cited, and then the claim is debunked. The outcome is to introduce, step by step, a more fair-minded and favorable depiction of Islam. Reland's revisionism drew on a remarkably slender source base—the University of Utrecht had only a very small number of Arabic manuscripts, and Reland did not use the collection at the University of Leiden, the best in the land and one of the best in Europe—yet even those meager resources sufficed to unseat a lengthy European tradition.[57]

Lack of Arabic proficiency, Reland explained, was the culprit that had tainted most European writings about Islam. He turned to the original sources to prove that the vast majority of false European claims about Islam, rather than being pure fabrications, were based on errors in translation.[58] The list of writers whom he corrected or reprimanded is notably long. His greatest scorn was reserved for Robert of Ketton, whose translation of the Qur'an he found to be the fount of most of the European errors.[59] To correct misrepresentations, he consulted the Qur'an itself and other Arabic sources, as well as trustworthy European ones. Among the few European authorities he respected were recent scholars deeply immersed in Arabic scholarship, such as Pococke, d'Herbelot, and Marracci, and a couple of travelers.[60] Occasionally he reached back to earlier sources for information or arguments.[61] Overall, though, the citations of what he considered reliable trace the contours of the interconfessional Republic of Arabic Letters.

Preliminary Discourse

George Sale's *Koran* (1734) opens with an 187-page essay entitled "Preliminary Discourse," his guide to the sacred text that follows. After describing the geography of Arabia, the history and customs of the Arabs, and the state of Judaism and Christianity before the advent of Muhammad, the essay moves on to the Qur'an. Sale tackled its structure, style, and major doctrines, with particular emphasis on its descriptions of the Apocalypse and Paradise. Then, as the lawyer that he was, he examined Qur'anic legal precepts; he also went into the sectarian history of Islam.[62] Each section cites the major English, French, Latin, and Spanish authorities he used, documentation that allows a glimpse of the state of the art of European Islamic studies at the time. The text is complemented by several fold-out illustrations: a map of Arabia; genealogical charts that explain the relationships among the Arab tribes, their descent from Abraham's son Ishmael, the place of the Quraysh tribe among the other Arab tribes, and Muhammad's place within Quraysh; and a view and a plan of the Temple of Mecca, based on the engraving found in Reland's second (1717) edition of *De Religione Mohammedica* (Figure 9).

The "Preliminary Discourse" was so popular that it was published as a stand-alone book in Dutch, French, Swedish, and Arabic.[63] In 1738 Voltaire, who made extensive use of it, called it "more beautiful than all the Alcorans of the world."[64] In 1754 the German philosopher Gotthold Ephraim Lessing wrote: "We possessed no genuine knowledge [of Muhammad and his teachings] before the works of a Reland or a Sale, from which we learned above all that Muhammad is no senseless fraud and that his religion is not merely a poorly constructed web of inconsistencies and forgeries."[65]

Like the other authors discussed here, Sale used comparison to normalize Islam. Finding that a significant number of Muslim doctrines, precepts, and customs resembled Jewish ones, he argued, as Simon had, that Islam emulated Judaism in doctrine, customs, and precepts.[66] For example, believing that the Qur'an derived its histories of the prophets from the Old and New Testaments and "from the apocryphal books and traditions of the *Jews* and *Christians* of those ages," he concluded that Muhammad drew on a vast body of works but had invented little or nothing in this respect.[67] The Jews were "*Mohammed*'s chief guides," but another was Magianism (Zoroastrianism), a religion Sale knew from the recently published *Historia Religionis Veterum Persarum* (The history of the religion of the ancient Persians) by Thomas Hyde, a professor at Oxford and librarian of the Bodleian.[68] Sale reasoned that because the ancient Persians had inspired some Jewish beliefs, Jews and Muslims were both indebted to them.[69] The Zoroastrian Paradise, with its "black-eyed nymphs," offered the "first hint" of the Qur'an's "paradisiacal ladies," the virgins who await blessed men (more on whom below).[70] (Sale imagined that "good women will go into a separate place of happiness, where they will enjoy all sorts of delights," though he did not claim to know whether these would include "the enjoyment of agreeable paramours created for them, to compleat the œconomy of the Mohammedan system.")[71]

Sale pursued his wide-ranging comparativism to an ambitious end: in order to reconstruct the complex chain of religious influence and emulation that had taken place across the ancient Near East. Viewed through that lens, Islam was not exceptional in leaning on preceding traditions—it was only the latest instance of that dynamic process. That Muslims drew on conceptions, such as Paradise, that were already widely shared among Jews, Christians, and Magians, revealed Islam's historical origins and allowed it to be judged in a more equitable way.[72] Islam was not exceptional, an alien heresy, but the product of secular history. For instance, on Islam's concept of holy war and the rewards promised to those who wage it, Sale remarked: "Nor have the Jews and Christians, how much soever they detest such principles in others, been ignorant of the force of enthusiastic heroism, or omitted to spirit up their respective partisans by the like arguments and promises."[73] Even the ostensibly Islamic concept of holy war was akin to Christian and Jewish attitudes, with the difference that Christianity, unlike Islam, did not endorse such attitudes in Scripture.[74]

Sale claimed that the Qur'an has "many excellent things intermixed not unworthy even a Christian's perusal."[75] Indeed, the *Koran*'s frontispiece is inscribed with a hermeneutic maxim from Augustine: "There is no false doctrine, in which something true is not mixed."[76] Some Muslim customs earned Sale's absolute approbation: that "the Mohammedans never address themselves to GOD in sumptuous apparel" and "that they admit not their women to pray with them in public . . . for the Moslems are of the opinion that their presence inspires a different kind of devotion from that which is requisite in a place dedicated to the worship of GOD."[77] He urged Christians to learn from this sobriety.

In the Christian polemical tradition, Islam was most often a Christian heresy, which made it a religion dedicated to the same God of the Gospels; however, that same tradition also emphasized the differences between the two religions, distinctions that Marracci had lately underscored.[78] Drawing analogies between Christianity and Islam always ran the risk of blurring the boundary between true faith and false belief, but to Sale the proximity was undeniable: "That both Mohammed and those among his followers who are reckoned orthodox, had and continue to have just and true notions of GOD and his attributes (always excepting their obstinate and impious rejecting of the Trinity), appears so plain from the Korân itself and all the Mohammedan divines, that it would be loss of time to refute those who suppose the GOD of Mohammed to be different from the true GOD, and only a fictitious deity or idol of his own creation."[79] Instead of emphasizing the foreignness of Islam, Sale viewed it as a kindred religion that recognized and worshipped the same God as Christians did.

Reland and Sale were inspired by recent Christian efforts to study Islam. Both acknowledged Friedrich Spanheim the Younger (1632–1701), a German theology professor and church historian, as a model.[80] In 1670 Spanheim had begun teaching in Leiden, where Reland studied with him (Reland later referred to him as "my venerable former teacher").[81] Spanheim tackled the emergence of Islam in a brief but richly informed section of his *Historia Ecclesiastica,* which covers the history of the Christian church from the birth of Christ to the early Protestant Reformation.[82] (In the edition published at Spanheim's death, the subject of Muhammad and the origins of Islam occupies only 13 of the book's 1,412 columns.)[83] Sale praised Spanheim for his evenhandedness, a quality he emulated in his own stance toward Islam. Sale wrote that he could not help but "applaud the candour of the pious and learned *Spanhemius,* who, th' he owned [Muhammad] to have been a wicked impostor, yet acknowledged him to have been *richly furnished with natural endowments, beautiful in his person, of a subtle wit, agreeable behaviour, shewing liberality to the poor, courtesy to every one, fortitude against his enemies, and above all a high reverence for the name of God; severe against the perjured, adulterers, murtherers, slanderers, prodigals, covetous, false witnesses, & c. a great preacher of patience, charity, mercy, beneficence, gratitude, honouring of parents and superiors, and a frequent celebrator of the divine praises.*"[84] Indeed, Spanheim's discussion toggles between total condemnations of Muhammad (the section is entitled *Antichristi Orientalis ... Historia* [The history of the eastern Antichrist]) and measured, well-informed interpretations.

Sale resisted misrepresenting Islam to make it seem more appealing in the way that both Simon and Reland had done to some extent, especially when it came to Islam's strange and inassimilable aspects. As we will see, Simon and Reland revealed the priority of their allegiance to a sympathetic attitude over the mere dictates of intellectual charity. Sale, offering synthesis rather than original knowledge, arbitrated between similarity and difference more fair-mindedly than any of his polemical or scholarly predecessors. His careful balancing of the available evidence holds up well to this day.

The Death of a Dove

The new standard of truth that the Republic of Arabic Letters established affected everyone writing about Islamic matters, regardless of religious or political commitments. A case in point is the evolution of the legend that Muhammad had trained a dove to feed at his ear. Shakespeare's *Henry VI, Part 1*, refers to that tale when Charles, the dauphin of France, says to Joan of Arc: "Was Mahomet inspired with a dove? Thou with an eagle art inspired then."[85] According to the legend, Muhammad tricked his followers into believing that the obedient dove was an embodiment of the Holy Spirit. Sir Walter Ralegh's *History of the World* (1614) popularized the tale, and among the learned men who repeated it were the classical scholar Joseph Scaliger (1540–1609) and the jurist Hugo Grotius (1583–1645), the sixth book of whose *De Veritate Religionis Christianae* (On the truth of the Christian religion) argued against Islam.[86]

Edward Pococke concluded that the dove story had no Arabic or Muslim source and upbraided Grotius for having repeated it.[87] The Holy Spirit, although mentioned in the Qur'an (where it is named *rūḥ al-qudus,* Q16:102), does not have the same theological salience in Islam as it does in Trinitarian Christianity, and Muslim commentators have often taken the term to refer to the angel Gabriel.[88] Most importantly, in the Qur'an the *rūḥ al-qudus* never takes the shape of a dove as the Holy Spirit does in the Gospels (for example, Luke 3:22). Other kindred tales had been rehashed in the Christian polemical literature: that Muhammad's coffin was suspended with loadstones, that Muhammad suffered from epilepsy, and others.[89] To the European scholars of Arabic, the inaccuracy of these unsourced tales came to seem problematic. For one thing, it undermined efforts at proselytizing. As Maracci remarked, attacking straw men would only inspire laughter among Muslims and allow them to persist in their ways.[90] When Pococke translated Grotius's tract into Arabic, he made sure to omit the passage on Muhammad's dove.[91] His source-based approach was soon adopted by others, including Simon, who did not waste breath on the tale but did report other miracles that were ascribed to Muhammad in the Arabic text that Pococke had edited.[92]

Even those disposed less favorably toward Islam than Pococke had to follow the standard he set. Humphrey Prideaux published *The True Nature of Imposture Fully Displayed in the Life of Mahomet* (London, 1697) to oppose the suggestion of "Christianity as an Imposture," with his particular target "that kind of Infidelity, which is called *Deism*."[93] Instead of relying on medieval and Renaissance polemics about Muhammad, however, Prideaux waged his argument on the higher ground of recent Arabic scholarship: "That I may not be thought to draw this Life of *Mahomet* with design to set forth his Imposture in the foulest Colours I am able, the better to make it serve my present purpose; I have been careful to set down all my Authorities in the Margin, and at the end of the Book have given an Account of all the Authors from whom I collected them."[94] *The True Nature of Imposture* advanced a thoroughly modern polemical attack on Islam and its founder. Prideaux's bibliography includes books by the Catholic Francesco Guadagnoli and the Protestant Johann Heinrich Hottinger, as well as those Arabic works that had been edited and published in Europe, such as Pococke's Bar Hebraeus. Among the lively polemical anecdotes from the European tradition that Prideaux rejected was that Muhammad "bred up *Pigeons* to come to his Ears, to make show thereby, as if the *Holy Ghost* conversed with him." Following Pococke, and like all the authors discussed in this chapter, Prideaux considered these legends unworthy of a valid polemic ("I pass them over as idle Fables, not to be credited"), and he criticized those among his recent predecessors, including Scaliger, Gabriel Sionita, and Grotius, who had been "too easy to swallow them."[95] The foolish stories told about Islam in the West "serve only to the exposing of us to the laughter of the *Mahometans,* when related among them."[96] A serious polemic, Prideaux held, required a higher standard of truth. The bar for evidence had been raised: whatever one's argument, it had to find support in native sources.

Later writers followed the same tack. Reland dedicated an article of the second edition of his work to dismissing the dove story, largely by quoting previous writers.[97] Sale could take the work of his predecessors for granted and refer offhandedly to the inauthenticity of the tale of the "imaginary pigeon" feeding from Muhammad's ear; those authors who had propounded this myth, he wrote, "should have known better."[98] Here and throughout, Sale criticized fellow Christians who had attributed exaggerated or false vices to the prophet; he would condemn Islam only when he could find no charitable explanation for its customs or beliefs. (However, stories that are good in the telling are hard to fully eradicate—the legend of the dove was republished as late as 1759, in Moréri's *Grand dictionnaire historique.*)[99]

Pococke's work not only exploded fictions that had been handed down in Western Christendom in service of the missionary struggle, but also encouraged the intellectual charity that marked all new Islamic scholarship, whatever its specific affiliations. Reland was struck by the contrast between Islam's popularity and the "silly fictions" Europeans attributed to Muhammad and his followers.[100] If the accusations were true, "one would have trouble understanding how so many diverse nations could embrace such an absurd religion, at least short of regarding all Mahometans as imbeciles [*fungos,* lit. mushrooms]."[101] He wrote, "When I reexamined it, not all of it, but some of it for the sake of example, I saw a wholly other face of the Mohammedan religion, and I thought it worth my while to explain it from the Arabic sources themselves."[102]

Reland's intellectual charity stemmed from a philosophical conviction: "Good sense [*bona mens*] is evenly distributed" across the world, a reference to the opening of Descartes's *Discourse on the Method* of 1637 ("Good sense is what is best distributed in the world") that aligns Reland with a current of Cartesian scholars in the Dutch universities.[103] Yet interest in Islam was not new in the Netherlands, and it did not require Cartesianism.[104] Reland's reason for seeking to improve the European study of Islam was the same as that of Marracci, who wrote that it was necessary to reveal Islam "such as it is taught in the Mohammedan temples and schools, so that, by certain blows, we may attack it and convince at least our minds, if not those of the Turks themselves, of its vanity."[105] Christians would then stand on firmer ground when trying to convince Muslims.

Much later, Jean-Jacques Rousseau in *The Social Contract* (1762) agreed that it was necessary to be realistic about the founding of a religion. "It is not up to just anyone to make the Gods speak or to have [vulgar men] believe him when he proclaims himself their interpreter," he wrote, just as it was not enough to "carve tablets of stone, bribe an oracle, feign secret dealings with some divinity, train a bird to speak in his ear, or find other crude ways to impress the people." The founder must be a "great soul . . . the true miracle which must prove [the] mission" of the lawgiver.[106] In Rousseau, the story of the dove does not exemplify religious imposture; instead, it stands for the simplistic ways in which religious inspiration had been explained away.

It seemed impossible to the new European scholars of Islam that Muslims could be as credulous or foolish as traditional Christian polemic claimed. This novel perspective underpinned the intellectual transformation described here: from not being able to describe members of a foreign confession neutrally to no longer being able to regard them as profoundly alien.

Trouble in Paradise

Certain aspects of genuine Islamic belief posed a greater interpretive challenge than hoary legends. What happened when even intellectual charity—the effort to provide the most generous interpretation of the available facts—could not explain away the peculiar or troubling? The desire to offer an appealing portrait of Islam sometimes led to a less precise and empirically informed account. At these junctures, moral reevaluation and scholarly study sometimes parted ways.

One of the most puzzling issues facing Christian commentators was the Islamic conception of Paradise, which features prominently throughout the Qur'an. The Qur'an frequently draws a contrast between Paradise, the reward of the virtuous, and the Hellfire (*al-nār*) that awaits sinners. Although it does not go into much detail about the terrestrial Paradise (the Garden of Eden), the Qur'an paints a vivid picture of the transcendent one (*al-janna*, lit. "the garden")—its lush vegetation, ample waterways, and luxurious furnishings, as well as the pleasures of its food, fragrance, wine (whose sublunary proscription does not extend to the afterworld), and companionship.[107] The Qur'an offers only a succinct vision of God at Q75:22–23, yet it abounds with visions of physical delight such as this:

> Surely the godfearing shall be in gardens and bliss,
> rejoicing in that their Lord has given them;
> and their Lord shall guard them against the chastisement of Hell.
> "Eat and drink, with wholesome appetite, for
> that you were working."
> Reclining upon couches ranged in rows;
> And We shall espouse [wed] them to wide-eyed houris. (Q52:17–20)

The enjoyment referred to in the last line, and in other verses, is the company of the virgins, the "wide-eyed houris / as the likeness of hidden pearls, a recompense for that they laboured" (Q56:22–24). Aside from endowing them with becoming modesty, the Qur'an is short on depictions of the houris; prurient imaginations elaborated on these elliptical descriptions, especially in the *ḥadīth* tradition (the deeds and sayings attributed to Muhammad).[108]

European scholars had to find their way through the thicket of differing positions on Paradise that were taken by Muslim commentators, theologians, and philosophers. Qur'anic commentary (*tafsīr*) was the first and most obvious place to seek explanations of these evocative visions. Overall, native commentators accepted that the Qur'anic Paradise was real, and that the Qur'an's descriptions were to be taken literally. Even the more rationalist commentaries contained plenty of material that not only supported a literal understanding of Paradise, but also included details that enriched the Qur'an account.[109]

Writers in the theological tradition (*kalām*) undertook an explicit exploration of the theoretical issues raised by a sensual Paradise. Even the rationalist Mu'tazilite school of theology did not interpret it to be purely spiritual and allegorical. Their reading was restrained and literal and conceded that Paradise had corporeal qualities. The Ash'arītes stressed that the incomparable and ineffable qualities of Paradise have to be accepted by the believer *bilā kayf* (without asking how).[110] From the tenth century onward, Muslim philosophers had expressed embarrassment at the conception of Paradise as a place of physical pleasure. For example, Avicenna (980–1037) contended that its literal meaning was directed only at the most simple-minded, those who could not comprehend spiritual pleasures. Avicenna's alternative theory of Paradise, however, found few takers and remained marginal to the mainstream Islamic tradition.[111] At the other extreme, the theologically naive popular preachers and many *ḥadīth* embroidered the Qur'an's brief descriptions of Paradise. For instance, the *ḥadīth* tradition elaborates on the virgins, as on other aspects of the Qur'anic Paradise, stipulating variously that 2, 72, or 8,000 will be available to each believer.[112]

In Christian Europe, the Muslim Paradise was something of a lightning rod. Differing from the Christian Paradise in its emphasis on physical pleasures, it caused apoplexy in medieval polemicists, who viewed it as the lurid promise of an impostor—Muhammad—who sought to gain followers in any way he could, no matter how base.[113] In the seventeenth century, explicitly polemical writers continued to find much to aggrieve them in the Qur'anic Paradise.[114] Prideaux argued that it was designed to manipulate followers:

"The main Arguments he made use of to delude men into this Imposture, were his Promises and his Threats, as being those which easiest work on the Affections of the Vulgar. His *Promises* were chiefly of *Paradise,* which he so cunningly framed to the gust [taste] of the *Arabians,* as to make it totally consist in those Pleasures which they were most delighted with."[115] Prideaux was making the traditional argument—that Muhammad's carrot-and-stick approach involved a lewd vision of the hereafter. Marracci made a similar case: "Almost nothing exhibits the vanity and imposture in the Alcoran more than those places where the greatest happiness of men is discussed."[116] The sexual pleasure promised to men was especially distasteful to him. His deep knowledge of *ḥadīth* provided grist for his mill: "Further, that which we reported above from the Sunna [the *ḥadīth*] they understand and take not metaphorically (although even so it would offend honesty and decency) but entirely literally: almost as if the greatest happiness and bliss of men did not reside in the working of his most noble part, namely of the soul (just as not only the Christian faith teaches, but also Philosophy, and the light of nature itself), but in bodily pleasures and lusts."[117]

In fact, Prideaux's and Marracci's work followed in the footsteps of Pococke's detailed and informed study of the Qur'anic Paradise and its many Muslim interpretations, which offered an unprecedented wealth of new information and set European knowledge on an entirely new footing.[118] In an essay first published in 1654, Pococke discussed Muslim doctrines of the resurrection, the apocalypse, the final judgment, and Hell, and elucidated what the Qur'an had to say about Paradise. His descriptions, in Latin with extensive Arabic quotations (published with the same Arabic typeface that had been used to set his *Specimen Historiæ Arabum* just a few years earlier), detail physical features of the Qur'anic Paradise, from its rivers to the paradise virgins, and, thanks to his extensive reading, report what many different groups of Muslims had to say on the subject. He drew on resources ranging from Qur'an commentaries (including those by al-Bayḍāwī and al-Suyūṭī) to theological treatises (such as the work of the Ashʿarite al-Ījī), to philosophical works (Avicenna and al-Maʿarrī). Summing up his findings, he wrote: "Truly, as far as I know, I did not add a word to this that was not taken from their writings."[119] But Pococke could not bring himself to countenance the emphasis on physical pleasures. His judgment was that Qur'anic Paradise was "as different as can be from that which Christians believe," as well as "wholly ridiculous and beyond absurd."[120]

After Pococke, then, the question of Paradise was no longer one of advancing empirical knowledge, but of interpretation. Given its notoriety, the Qur'anic Paradise posed a major challenge to those seventeenth- and eighteenth-century Europeans who wished to give Islam a better name. For example, Richard Simon found echoes of Judaic and Christian descriptions in the Qur'anic Paradise: "This credence of Mahometans concerning Paradise and Hell resembles that of the Jews and Christians, especially the Eastern ones."[121] He employed comparison to blunt the force of polemic, because it made the foreign—in this case, the Qur'an's vision of the afterlife—less alien.

Simon's perception was correct: to this day scholars study the eschatology of late antiquity as a context for the Qur'anic Paradise.[122] Broadly speaking, the Qur'an's many allusions to biblical stories do seem to assume an audience familiar with Judeo-Christian traditions, and Judaism and early Christianity do contain images of a sensual paradise.[123] (Some of the details of the courtly setting of Paradise in the Qur'an, including how wine is mixed and scented with musk, appear to have been inspired by pre-Islamic poetry.) If the Qur'an adopts elements from the Judeo-Christian tradition, it reassembles them in its own way, laying more stress on the corporeality of the hereafter and developing its details as a way of emphasizing God's gift of salvation.[124]

In another conciliatory technique, Simon argued that the Muslim vision of the afterlife should be understood as a metaphor, instead of being taken literally: "There is indeed the appearance that all of those things are rather parables, than actual histories . . . it is indeed in this sense that one ought to explain a great part of what they say about Paradise and Hell."[125] To support this statement, Simon proceeded to evoke the Muslim Paradise, as if to suggest that its descriptive flourishes were so excessive that they could only be read metaphorically: "For example in the description they make of Paradise, they assure that it is all filled with musk, that buildings are made of gold and silver bricks . . . that there are all sorts of delicious meats . . . that in that place one is not subject to [needing to] sleep nor the other necessities of the body, that there are divine and celestial girls and women who are exempted from their menses. This is how they describe their Paradise."[126] An allegorical reading had some Muslim proponents, including Avicenna, whose views

Pococke had put into circulation. Yet Simon does not cite them. His alle-gorical reading was based more on assumptions about what was a reasonable belief than on a deep knowledge of Islam. Turning inconvenient particulars into "parables" (allegories) was an attempt, in a sense, to save the Muslims from themselves—that is, from appearing credulous and unsophisticated in their beliefs. In short, Simon advanced sympathy at the expense of accurate description.

Contemporaries bristled at Simon's interpretation. Antoine Arnauld, a Catholic Jansenist theologian, was appalled by his generous depiction of Islam: "[Simon] only represents what is most plausible in it: he dissimulates the proofs that must make it abhorrent, as the work of an impious and false prophet. That which he has not been able to conceal entirely for being too well known, such as the infamy of its Paradise, he excuses by saying that it appears that these are parables."[127] Arnauld perceived an apologetic intention in Simon's treatment of Islam, and regarded Simon's sympathy as suspect.

On the subject of Paradise, Reland, even though he claimed to attack Islam with precision, also explained away that which he found perplexing. To do so put him through elaborate contortions. He acknowledged that Christians claimed that "Mahommedans expect to exercise nothing but bodily enjoy-ment and libidinous pleasures in [Paradise], and place all their future happi-ness in intercourse with very shapely girls and in contemplation of gardens and rivers of most lovely appearance."[128] However, he noted that Muhammad also "assigned the soul its pleasure," with the contemplation of God's visage being the highest honor and offering the greatest delight, and he quoted d'Herbelot and Pococke to buttress this point.[129] He then proceeded to say that the sen-sual pleasures could be and had been read allegorically, remarking that Plato's discussion of the sensual pleasures that would be offered to warriors had been read as allegory, and that, therefore, the Qur'an deserved the same treat-ment.[130] Like Simon, Reland in this instance was less interested in discovering how Muslims read the Qur'an than in saving the Qur'an from itself. His po-sition aroused some opposition. His otherwise supportive French translator, David Durand, thought that the language of the Qur'an, even if figurative, was still reprehensible: "It seems to me that it would be better to give up all these licentious allegories, which just stir the passions of young people . . . the ill effect of such allegories is very certain, while the good effect is far to seek."[131]

It is more than likely that Simon, Reland, and others who nurtured sympathetic feeling toward Islam were willing to risk misrepresentations in order to advance their cause. As a result, their warm feelings produced what we might term an assimilative bias—a tendency to overstate the resemblance of Islamic beliefs to Christian ones.

Sale tackled the problem of the Qur'anic Paradise by comparing it with passages of the Bible that used concrete images to describe the spiritual: "As it is scarce possible to convey, especially to the apprehensions of the generality of mankind, an idea of spiritual pleasures without introducing sensible objects, the scriptures have been obliged to represent the celestial enjoyments by corporeal images."[132] Like Simon, he used comparison to offer a more sympathetic reading, and he repeated Reland's comment that physical pleasures did not preclude an even greater, purely spiritual, joy.[133] The Qur'an's description of contemplating God's face, "which will give such exquisite delight, that in respect thereof all the other pleasures of paradise will be forgotten and lightly esteemed" offered "a full confutation of those who pretend that the *Mohammedans* admit of no spiritual pleasure in the next life, but make the happiness of the blessed to consist wholly in corporeal enjoyments."[134]

In Sale's case, however, his critical judgment outweighed his desire to offer a sympathetic interpretation. The Qur'anic Paradise, he concluded, contained many "puerile imaginations" and "sensual delights,"[135] but no evidence that Muhammad had meant his words "to be taken, not literally, but in a metaphorical sense . . . the contrary is so evident from the whole tenour of the *Korân,* that although some *Mohammedans,* whose understandings are too refined to admit such gross conceptions, look on their prophet's descriptions as parabolical, and are willing to receive them in an allegorical or spiritual acceptation, yet the general and orthodox doctrine is, that the whole is to be strictly believed in the obvious and literal acceptation."[136] Sale found no allegorical reading that could efface what to him was a coarse and theologically naive element of Islam. Like many Christian critics before him, he believed that Muhammad had developed the religion "to enhance the value of paradise with his Arabians."[137]

Simon, Reland, and other partisan writers (such as the English polemicist Henry Stubbe and the French writer the Count of Boulainvilliers) all, in their different ways, idealized Islam or at the very least glossed over some of its quirkier aspects.[138] The significance of their bias, however, can be grasped only when one considers the full force of the traditional European interpretation of Islam, which so heavily emphasized the differences between Muslims and Christians that it endowed Islam with inaccurate traits. Some of these new writers reacted so strongly against the traditional view that they too paid the price of distorting Islam. By contrast, Sale, closer to Pococke than any of his other predecessors, portrayed the religion in all its strangeness, from the angels and genies to the signs of the Day of Judgment.[139] Sale was stricter on the Qur'anic Paradise than Simon and Reland; he could not explain away the parts of it that he found unappealing. Far from a shortcoming, his attitude is proof of his integrity.

Impostor and Legislator

In the Middle Ages and the Renaissance, most European Christians dismissed Muhammad as one of the impostors Jesus warned against in the Sermon on the Mount: "Beware of false prophets, who come to you in sheep's clothing, but inwardly they are ravenous wolves" (Matthew 7:15). Muhammad seemed to exemplify the category of "false prophet": he promised his followers sensual pleasure in the next world, permitted polygamy in this one, and advanced his cause by waging war.[140] With its encouragement of sensuality and violence, Islam was regarded as antithetical to Christianity. Why God would concede worldly success to this imposture was indeed puzzling, but part of the blame was placed on the corruption of Christianity at the time of Muhammad's birth.

In the Italian Renaissance, above the din of sixteenth-century religious polemic, some interpreters of Islam began to treat its origins as worthy of historical analysis.[141] Instead of focusing on refuting Muhammad's claims, they attempted to explain his rise to power. Their tools were provided by Niccolò Machiavelli, who—in *The Prince* (published posthumously in 1532) and *Discourses on Livy* (published posthumously in 1531)—presented new insights about rulers and the art of gaining and maintaining power. With characteristic freedom of thought, he proposed that the actions and laws of pagan rulers like Cyrus were not different (*discrepanti*) from those of Moses, who was divinely guided; that prophets were superior to secular legislators, because what they founded was more durable; and that religion, whether true or false, helped to preserve the state.[142] He observed that unarmed prophets are destined to fail, whereas "all armed prophets win . . . A prophet must be ready, when [the people] no longer believe, to make them believe by force."[143] This reasoning, if applied to Muhammad, would appear to condone the feature of Islam most reprehensible to Christians: its expansion by means of the sword.

Although he was an avowed admirer of the Ottoman Empire, Machiavelli did not discuss Muhammad at any length and never directly named him an armed prophet. However, Machiavelli's analysis of legislators and prophets offered explicit and implicit suggestions for interpreting Muhammad. As Pier Mattia Tommasino has recently shown, these ideas were picked up remarkably quickly by Italian readers. In 1547 an Italian translation of Robert of Ketton's Latin Qur'an appeared in Venice; Tommasino has identified the translator as the local scholar Giovanni Battista Castrodardo.[144] In addition to the translation, the prefatory materials of this edition contain an original analysis of the reasons for Muhammad's success, expressed in particular through an oration attributed to Sergius, the monk who supposedly collaborated with Muhammad on his forgery.[145] Castrodardo, reworking a recent humanist imagining of this oration, goes beyond his source material. Using Machiavelli's terminology, he portrays Muhammad as exercising his *virtù* to take advantage of the occasions offered by *fortuna* for capturing and maintaining political power.[146] This shrewd analysis attracted the attention of seventeenth-century Italian readers such as the naturalist Francesco Redi, who wrote in a manuscript that Muhammad was "not just equal to all other *heathen legislators* but greatly *superior* to them."[147]

In the course of the seventeenth century, northern European writers, too, applied Machiavelli's analysis to Muhammad. For instance, the seventeenth-century freethinker Henry Stubbe described the prophet as "the wisest Legislator that ever was."[148] (Some scholars have believed that the transvaluation of Muhammad from impostor to legislator originated with Stubbe, but it had already taken place in sixteenth-century Italy. The notion of Muhammad as a prudent legislator would have an impressive career in the course of the eighteenth century.)[149]

Sale, deriving his view of Muhammad from Machiavelli, took the position that Muhammad created a false but powerful belief system: "As *Mohammed* gave his *Arabs* the best religion he could, as well as the best laws, preferable, at least, to those of the ancient pagan lawgivers, I confess I cannot see why he deserves not equal respect, tho' not with *Moses* or *Jesus Christ,* whose laws really came from heaven, yet with *Minos* or *Numa*."[150] Minos was the legendary founder of Crete. According to Livy and Machiavelli, Numa Pompilius, the legendary second king of Rome, was the model of a good legislator who created a false but politically effective religion.

Muhammad adopted force, Sale explained, at first to defend himself from his enemies and later to attack them: "From whence, the politician [Machiavelli] observes, it follows, that all the armed prophets have succeeded, and the unarmed ones have failed. *Moses, Cyrus, Theseus,* and *Romulus* would not have been able to establish the observance of their institutions for any length of time, had they not been armed."[151] Sale's citation of Machiavelli—"the politician"—makes explicit the genealogy of the point of view that informed his appraisal of Muhammad.[152] He classified some of the prophet's actions and beliefs, including the Muslim imitation of the Jews, as strategic maneuvers. The prominence of the Jews of Arabia "made Mohammed at first shew great regard to them, adopting many of their opinions, doctrines, and customs; thereby to draw them, if possible, into his interest."[153] Likewise, Muhammad retained certain pre-Islamic customs—circumcision, ablutions before prayer, and pilgrimage (specifically, the hajj, or mandatory pilgrimage to Mecca)—because of their pragmatic value.[154] These "relics of idolatrous superstition" were too powerful for Muhammad to abolish them.[155] Sale especially scorned the hajj: "It is also acknowledged that the greater part of these rites [pertaining to the hajj] are of no intrinsic worth . . . but . . . commanded merely to try the obedience of mankind, without any further view."[156] Yet he conceded that one "must excuse Muhammad's yielding some points of less moment, to gain the principal."[157]

In Sale's eyes, Muhammad held a position higher than that of the pagan legislators Machiavelli analyzed: "His original design of bringing the pagan Arabs to the knowledge of the true GOD, was certainly noble, and highly to be commended."[158] Building on his belief that Muslims worshipped the same God as the Christians, Sale concluded that Muhammad had raised the polytheists of Arabia to a higher plane of belief: "For I cannot possibly subscribe to the assertion of a late learned writer [Prideaux, the Church of England polemicist], that [Muhammad] made that nation exchange their idolatry for another religion altogether as bad."[159] Sale's Muhammad sought to raise the moral standards of pagan Arabs, often by introducing them to Jewish customs or precepts: "The laws of the Korân concerning inheritances are also in several respects conformable to those of the Jews, though principally designed to abolish certain practices of the pagan Arabs."[160] Sale, admiring Muhammad for reforms such as prohibiting female infanticide and placing limits on polygamy, rejected the idea that Islam was nothing more than an equivalent of paganism.

Muhammad's balancing act—between maintaining customs for pragmatic reasons and instilling new moral precepts—left open the question of whether he was a sincere visionary or a wily fraud (in the period terminology, an "enthusiast" or an "impostor"). Sale deemed that unknowable: "Whether this was the effect of enthusiasm, or only a design to raise himself to the supreme government of his country, I will not pretend to determine."[161] Some fifty years later, Edward Gibbon adopted this same detached stance in *The Decline and Fall of the Roman Empire*. Gibbon, who admired Sale, declined to "decide whether the title of enthusiast or impostor more properly belongs to that extraordinary man."[162] Further, he argued that sincerity ("the unity of God is an idea most congenial to nature and reason") and *raison d'état* could coexist: "From enthusiasm to imposture, the step is perilous and slippery."[163] It was not possible to say to what extent Muhammad had been persuaded by his own vision, nor was it necessary. The imposture debate had been set aside.

Freethinking Readers

Between the sixteenth and the eighteenth centuries, many aspects of Christian belief and ritual were called into question. One of the most controversial was the doctrine of the Trinity—that God is both three and one—a belief that remained a pillar even of mainstream Reformation churches across Protestant Europe. Yet in many quarters the belief spread that the Trinity was a late accretion rather than an original teaching of the early Church.[164] Such a position was both politically and theologically radical. It undermined not only the theology of the official churches but also the political theology that underpinned the legitimacy of the Christian states.

Making an argument against the Trinity meant turning to history for material. The only explicit mention in the Latin Vulgate of the Trinity, the so-called Johannine Comma, had poor textual support in surviving manuscripts of the Greek original, as Erasmus had realized when he produced an edition in 1516.[165] Some critics found further evidence against the Trinity in other texts of the early Christians. Challenging the canonicity of revealed religion through the use of noncanonical ancient (or purportedly ancient) writings such as pseudepigrapha (falsely attributed ancient writings), whether Jewish or Christian, was a common strategy in the period.[166] In this context, certain critics of both the Church of England and the Roman Catholic Church saw in Islam a faith that had remained closer to original Christianity, and enrolled the Qur'an in the effort to buttress their arguments against Christian doctrines.

These imaginative critics of institutional Christianity enlisted the new Arabic scholarship in their cause, although the scholars of Arabic themselves would not necessarily have anticipated or subscribed to these new interpretations. Rather than a neat divide, there is a continuum from the arguments of the scholars to those of the critics of institutional Christianity.[167] Many of the critics had been students of members of the Republic of Arabic Letters: the Englishman Henry Stubbe (1632–1676) studied with Edward Pococke, at Oxford; the French Count of Boulainvilliers (1658–1722) was a protégé of Richard Simon at the Oratorian college in Juilly; John Toland (1670–1722) had delved into biblical criticism in Leiden with Friedrich Spanheim the Younger, who also taught Adriaan Reland.

Stubbe believed that Islam, because it was self-consciously part of the history of Jewish and Christian religion, could be used to question the trajectory of Western Christianity.[168] Taking advantage of the proven falsity of European claims about Islam, he redrew its portrait, describing it as a faith that is recognizably human and rational. His manuscript, of which copies exist under different titles, such as "An Account of the Rise and Progress of Mahometanism" and "The Originall and Progress of Mahometanism," uses Islam to rewrite the history of early Christianity.[169] First published only in the twentieth century, it regards the emergence of Islam as a response to the decline of Christianity in Muhammad's time and casts Islam as a return to early Christianity's unitarian roots, rather than as a new faith. Islam is a purified religion: "No people are more remote from Idolatry then the Saracens, and whatever name you give to their 'errors and follies!'"[170] Moreover, Stubbe welcomed Islam into the fold of the Judeo-Christian history of salvation: "It must be avowed, after all, that they adore no other then the true God, and if they err it is rather in the manner then in the object of their Devotion."[171] Stubbe believed that the Muslim God was same as the Christian God, that Muhammad learned about Judaism and Christianity from the many people of those faiths living in Arabia, and that Muhammad created Islam in consultation with Christians.[172]

None of Stubbe's empirical material was original. He based his life of Muhammad on Arabic sources, but because he did not read Arabic, he relied on Latin editions and translations: those by "Doctor [Edward] Pocock[e]," the Swiss scholar Johann Heinrich Hottinger, the earlier work of the Dutch scholar of Arabic Thomas Erpenius, and Pococke's Oxford colleague John Selden, whose *De Diis Syris* is a comparative treatise from 1617 that detects connections between the ancient world's religions.[173] Stubbe was not coy about his reliance on these works. A manuscript of his work now in the British Library reveals what even the recent edition of the "Progress of Mahometanism" obscures: the extent of Stubbe's reliance on what he read and his practice of methodically citing his sources.[174] This manuscript, unlike other versions of Stubbe's text, preserves in the margins Stubbe's many references (most often several to a page), each recording the author on which he drew, the name of the work, and the relevant page numbers. Stubbe's reading is impressive, spanning all of European erudition since the late Renaissance. It ranged from the great polymaths Joseph Scaliger and John Selden to Hebraists like Johannes Buxtorf, and from ambassadors and travelers like Ogier Ghiselin de Busbecq and Paul Rycaut to scholars who focused on Arabic topics such as Hottinger and Pococke.[175]

Reland's work, like Pococke's, was read and appropriated by those much more radical than he. The English freethinker John Toland, the author of *Christianity Not Mysterious* (1695), an argument against the mysteries of the Christian faith, argued in his later *Nazarenus* (1718) that the Gospels are not prescriptive, and that salvation does not depend upon adherence to one confession or another.[176] *Nazarenus,* which proposes that the three Abrahamic faiths are part of the same religious tradition, uses the (apocryphal) Gospel of Barnabas and Reland's Arabic scholarship to make its point. Toland, who, as we saw, had studied under Reland in Utrecht and Friedrich Spanheim the Younger in Leiden, was steeped in Richard Simon's recent biblical scholarship and in the work of Pierre Bayle and Baruch Spinoza.[177] He credited European scholars of Arabic for being the first to introduce a less distorted perception of Islam: "'Tis but very lately that we begun to be undeceiv'd about MAHOMET's pigeon, his pretending to work miracles, and his tomb's being suspended in the air: pious frauds and fables, to which the Musulmans are utter strangers. The truly learned and candid Mr. RELAND, the celebrated professor of the Oriental languages at Utrecht, has exploded not a few vulgar errors relating to the Al-coranists; as others in other articles have, with that moderate Divine and finish'd Scholar, Dr. PRIDEAUX, Dean of *Norwich,* done 'em the like jus-tice."[178] Reland and Prideaux may strike us as being on opposite sides, with Reland a proponent of a fairer view of Islam and Prideaux a hostile critic. But as we saw, both of them incorporated the new scholarship on Islam. The aim of Prideaux's book was to undermine deism, but its contents were open to re-interpretation by a freethinker like Toland. And Reland's unmasking of many fables and misconceptions bolstered Toland's argument that Islam could le-gitimately be seen as a form of Christianity, and that it was in certain respects closer to early Christianity than to the way the religion was practiced in con-temporary society. Toland wrote: "There is a sense, [wherein] the Mahometans may not improperly be reckon'd and call'd a sort or sect of Christians, as Christianity was at first esteem'd a branch of Judaism."[179] In explaining Muslim belief, he cited Reland: "I cou'd allege for this formulary many undeniable authorities; but shall content my self at present to referr [*sic*] you to the third chapter of *The compendious Mahometan Theology,* translated, illustrated with *Notes,* and published five or six years ago by the eminent Professor ADRIAN RELAND, before mention'd."[180]

The French Count of Boulainvilliers wrote a manuscript entitled *The Life of Mahomet,* which was published in Holland in 1730, almost a decade after the count's death.[181] Like Stubbe, Boulainvilliers knew no Arabic. His account draws extensively on the writings of Pococke, Marracci, d'Herbelot, Reland, and the English historian Simon Ockley (see Chapter 5). Boulainvilliers's cen-tral argument was that Islam was based on Christianity but that it rejected many of Christianity's problematic contentions, including original sin, the incarnation of God, and the Trinity: "That is how Mahomed conceived the design and system of a religion stripped of all controversies, and that, by advancing no mystery that strains reason, makes men satisfied with a simple and invariable cult."[182] Once again, as in the cases of Stubbe and Toland, the material of the scholars of Arabic was mobilized to critique mainstream Christianity.

The new Arabic scholarship of Pococke and his followers, which normal-ized Islam, gave Stubbe, Toland, and Boulainvilliers the opportunity to look at Christianity differently. By the final third of the seventeenth century, the comparative study of religion and its key insights into the interrelations in the history of Levantine monotheism, from Judaism to Islam, offered a new perspective on religion in general. Though it had not been Pococke's goal to give a partisan account of Islam, much less to provide ammunition for an assault on the traditions of the Church of England, his readers adapted his insights for that very purpose. Islam was seen as an alternative tradition, one tied to the same roots as Christianity but manifestly different from it.

Some scholars of our time have claimed that Sale was a freethinker or even an unbeliever, imagining that such a stance would be a prerequisite for his neutrality.[183] However, it is clear from his *Koran* that he developed a fair-minded interpretation of Islam without forsaking an orthodox Church of England position. One of his hermeneutic maxims was "not to quit any article of the Christian faith to gain the Mohammedans." This was a barb aimed at Christian unitarians, who believed that by forsaking the doctrine of the Trinity they would "be most like to prevail upon the Mohammedans."[184] Moreover, he upheld the distinction between Christianity and all other historical religions. His aim was the scientific and secularized study of Islam, but nothing in his *Koran* indicates a similar approach to Christianity. His references to radical atheist and deist writings are notably rare.[185] If he had not been religious, what would explain his participation in the Church of England missionary Society for Promoting Christian Knowledge?[186] Lastly, his manuscript notebook, which dates to 1734–1736, expresses admiration for such scholars as Friedrich Spanheim, John Selden, Thomas Hyde, and Edward Pococke, whose *Specimen* is called "a most accurate and judicious collection out of the best Arab writers relating to the subject which he handles."[187] In short, he was not a radical—he was simply following in the tradition of the comparative study of religion.

Conclusion

All the authors involved in the reinterpretation of Islam, whatever their qualifications and commitments, agreed that claims about the religion founded by Muhammad had to be grounded in fact, and that these facts had preferably to be drawn from Arabic sources. They all understood Islam comparatively, paying especial attention to its similarities to Judaism and Christianity, and saw it in purely secular, or human, terms: even those who were the most ardent admirers of Muhammad thought of him as a secular legislator rather than as an authentic prophet. They explained the genesis of Islam and of the Qur'an dispassionately, without reference to miracles or revelation.

Each author contributed to the halting, but nonetheless decisive, process by which new sources were brought to light and inherited understandings revised. Several of them were far less proficient in Arabic than Pococke and had to hew their interpretations of Islam out of available materials, but many nevertheless managed to articulate new understandings of Islam's foundation and rise. This reinterpretation of Islam was advanced in a collaborative fashion by readers of European Arabic scholarship, whose radical and heterodox thought fed on the new knowledge but did not generate it. Stubbe's sympathy for Islam was matched by that of Simon, who had no irreligious intent. Sympathy, in any case, was not the surest guide for articulating the complexity of Islamic beliefs and customs. Increasingly, sympathetic and unsympathetic impulses had to be justified by reference to a new order of factual knowledge, one that could not be denied or rolled back.

The normative evaluation of Islam underwent significant change, and relied upon the European concept of "legislator," a more neutral category than "impostor." Unlike "false prophet," the concept of legislator drew on the secular analysis developed by Machiavelli and his Italian readers, which allowed, at the very least, for neutral appraisal of Muhammad's achievement. This change was mainly normative, because there was general agreement that Muhammad was a secular leader who had not performed miracles. By Sale's time, one could praise Muhammad for bringing monotheism to Arabia, as well as for founding a remarkably successful state.

The use of comparison was key to this evolution. A powerful tool for legitimizing the study of Islam was to compare it with ancient paganism. Good pagans like Virgil or Cicero resembled wise Muslims: one could admire everything about them except their religious beliefs.[188] Comparing Muhammad with pagan legislators like Numa served a similar function. Comparing Islam with other Near Eastern religions not only explained Islam genealogically— as Islam's Christian critics had done for centuries—but also helped to normalize it.

Gradually the effort at humanistic study yielded a perspective unbounded by partisan commitment and independent of anti-Islamic polemic, which are what we might consider to be the requirements of the comparative study of religion. Improvements in information and knowledge proceeded independently of specific motivations, because knowledge served many arguments and points of view, including anti-Islamic polemical ones. At the same time, the comparative study of religious traditions could exist independently of anti-Islamic polemic. Over time, this comparative approach had an unintended consequence: freethinking writers applied it to Christianity itself, with the goal of relativizing or undermining the religion's claims to truth and revelation. The new European scholarship on Islam put into circulation knowledge that proved useful to those who wished to describe the religion with greater accuracy, as well as to those to whom Islam was a valuable tool for thinking about religion in general and Christianity in particular.

At a more general level, what was perhaps most remarkable about this period in European intellectual history was the deep and widespread engagement with Islam and its traditions. It was a time when the serious study and interpretation of Islam appeared to offer answers to a broad range of questions about theology and history. Even after Europeans stopped believing that Islam held the answers to those questions—and even after European armies in Muslim lands had entirely transformed the political context of any intellectual exchange—the knowledge produced in this period continued to inform European interpreters of Islam.

FOUR

D'HERBELOT'S ORIENTAL GARDEN

The *Bibliothèque Orientale* (Oriental library) of Barthélemy d'Herbelot de Molainville appeared in Paris in 1697, two years after its author's death. The French scholar had used dozens of sources in Arabic, Persian, and Turkish to create a reference work of Islamic history and letters that opened up its subject matter to Europeans to an unprecedented extent (Figure 11).[1] Writing in place of the *Bibliothèque*'s deceased author, d'Herbelot's former assistant Antoine Galland offered a rationale for the book's expansive vision:

> Can one claim that it is useless to know what many excellent writers have thought, what they have written of their religion, of their histories, of their countries, of their customs, of their laws, of the virtues that they practice, of the vices they abhor? And is this not to acquire, without labor and without leaving one's home, that which one would have to seek among them by traveling, in order to perfect oneself and become an accomplished man, a man who judges wisely of all things, who speaks of them with like judgment, and who conforms his actions to his thoughts and words? [These are] things that one cannot accomplish but in proportion to the knowledge one has acquired, not just of what happens within the horizon of the place where one breathes the vivifying air, but more broadly in the entire universe.

Although the *Bibliothèque* was a uniquely learned feat, it reflected a new interest shared by many European men of letters of the time. In the seventeenth century, scholars of Arabic in the West undertook to study the history and cultural achievements of Muslim peoples for secular purposes. In preceding centuries, Europeans who mastered Arabic had largely studied Islam as a religion, mainly for the purpose of proving it to be heretical, or else they had focused on Arabic scientific and philosophical works. Western readers at large were mainly aware of Arabic translations of classical writings, which formed only a narrow slice of the full breadth of Islamic literary and intellectual history. The secular history of Muslim peoples, and their nonreligious literary traditions, largely lay beyond the purview of European scholarship. For instance, the Swiss writer Christophe Milieu, the modern pioneer of the genre of *historia literaria,* or literary history (perhaps more aptly rendered today as cultural history), dedicated several pages of his *De Scribenda Universitatis Rerum Historia* (Writing the history of the universe of things) (1551) to the Arabic translations from the Greek and their subsequent translation into Latin in the Middle Ages.[2] Milieu's narrative placed the intellectual achievements of Muslim peoples at the very origin of the intellectual recovery of Europe in the High Middle Ages, giving them an importance to the history of the West that would never subsequently be doubted or denied. Yet, at the same time, his was still an extremely limited view.

D'Herbelot's *Bibliothèque Orientale* greatly expanded the Western study of Islamic *historia literaria.* When it appeared, it was the most ambitious and wide-ranging European reference work about Islamic topics that had ever been produced.[3] A single volume, written entirely in French, it presented a sustained and detailed argument in favor of the importance of Islamic literary and intellectual culture and would remain the most ambitious single overview of the subject until the publication of the first edition of the *Encyclopaedia of Islam* (1913–1936).

The *Bibliothèque* made the writings of dozens of Arabic, Persian, and Turkish authors available to European readers for the first time.[4] With 8,158 alphabetically arranged articles on a dizzying array of topics, it was a sure-handed guide to large swaths of Islamic history, letters, arts, and religion. One of d'Herbelot's innovations was to use language, rather than religion, to determine the scope of his work. That is, he did not limit himself to material only from Muslim worshippers. Instead, his domain was all countries in which Arabic, Persian, and Turkish were spoken; his concern, as Galland wrote, was "all the peoples dispersed in the three parts of our continent [Europe, Africa, and Asia] that speak them."[5] This inclusive design was not fully achieved, in part due to the sources available. Islam and Islamic letters are the most heavily represented in the *Bibliothèque,* but the work also covers such topics as Zoroastrianism and the Christians of the Levant.

Although d'Herbelot never left Europe, his contemporaries regarded him as a "wise and learned Ulysses," the roaming traveler par excellence, someone who led the way "across a sea of itinerant studies."[6] The *Bibliothèque Orientale*'s range and extent make d'Herbelot's erudite performance, along with Marracci's Qur'an translation, one of the crowning achievements of European Islamic scholarship at the end of the seventeenth century. Whereas Marracci's specialization was religious scholarship in Arabic, d'Herbelot studied Persian and Turkish sources and a much broader range of nonreligious subjects. His research revealed the great range and diversity of intellectual production in the languages of Islam.

The existence of the *Bibliothèque Orientale* demonstrates that it was possible to investigate in great detail a foreign, even an inimical, lettered culture in the Paris of the famously conservative Bishop Bossuet (1627–1704). Catholic scholarship was central not to one but to two major works that would continue to organize and inspire European scholarship on Islamic topics in the course of the century that followed their publication: the *Refutatio Alcorani* and the *Bibliothèque Orientale*. In spite of the limits on learning and free thought in Counter-Reformation lands, d'Herbelot managed to produce a richly textured account of Islamic history and letters. Drawing on a lifetime of reading in Florence and in Paris, he provided something of a canon that Europeans interested in the cultures of Islam could use to get their bearings. It seemed to contemporaries that its author was no less than a discoverer: his book revealed "a sort of new world—new histories, new politics, new customs, in a word, a new sky, a new earth."[7] For all of these reasons, the *Bibliothèque* persisted as a research tool for a century and a half: manuscript evidence shows that it was in active use in the middle third of the nineteenth century. This chapter takes a close-up look at the *Bibliothèque Orientale,* establishing the sources, boundaries, content, and ideals of the book that shaped Western understandings of Islamic history and literature during the Enlightenment and beyond.[8]

The Work in the Life

Barthélemy d'Herbelot left few autograph papers, and his personal motivations are not expressed in any writings that survive.[9] The best available clues to the creation of the *Bibliothèque Orientale* are to be found in the intellectual context in which d'Herbelot was formed and in the circles he frequented.[10] His intellectual career emerged out of the orthodox but aggressively visionary culture of seventeenth-century European erudition. His unprecedented effort to describe Islamic civilization with informed impartiality was not aimed at challenging Catholic orthodoxy. Instead, as we shall see, his pursuits issued directly from, and were in harmony with, the predominant intellectual commitments of his day. Patronized by the grand duke of Tuscany and the king of France, d'Herbelot was not a countercultural figure like the philosopher Baruch Spinoza or the biblical philologist Richard Simon. The *Bibliothèque* issued directly from the seventeenth-century European tradition of Oriental erudition, even as it proved to be one of its most unprecedented accomplishments.

D'Herbelot, who was descended from the petty nobility of Molainville (now Moulainville), near Verdun, in the Lorraine, was born on December 4, 1625, in Paris, the capital of Oriental studies in France.[11] It was from Paris that in 1627, two years after d'Herbelot's birth, François-Auguste de Thou (son of the scholar and book collector Jacques-Auguste) departed for the Levant; four years later, in 1631, a group of Parisian scholars accompanied a French embassy to the Ottoman capital.[12] Those who wished to learn Hebrew and Arabic without leaving town could find some support from the chairs of Hebrew and Arabic at the Collège Royal, the free institution of higher learning (founded in 1530).[13] In addition, Levantine visitors sometimes passed through Paris.[14] From 1629 to 1645, the printer Antoine Vitré and the editor Guy Michel Le Jay were busy producing the Paris Polyglot Bible, the third of the four great multilingual editions of the Bible published in sixteenth- and seventeenth-century Europe. To the languages of the preceding Polyglots—Hebrew, Aramaic, Syriac, Greek, and Latin—the Paris Polyglot added Samaritan (the script of a textual tradition of the Pentateuch transmitted by adherents of Samaritanism, a religion close to Judaism) and Arabic. The expense, as well as the expertise, required to produce all these typefaces, and to set them correctly, indicates the huge intellectual and financial commitment to Oriental studies in mid-seventeenth-century Paris.[15]

At that period, the study of the Bible set the agenda for Oriental scholarship. One of d'Herbelot's predecessors was the biblical scholar Gilbert Gaulmin, who, according to his contemporaries, had mastered Hebrew, Arabic, Persian, Turkish, and Armenian.[16] Gaulmin interpreted the Gospels through use of "traditional phrases of the Jews, Oriental proverbs, and expressions still in use among Mediterranean peoples."[17] He was interested in as wide a set of languages as d'Herbelot, but his main scholarly activity revolved around

Scripture, even though his personal interests were broader. By contrast, d'Herbelot's efforts led him in new directions; he disentangled the study of Near Eastern cultures from its biblical associations and produced distinctive work quite unlike that of any of his predecessors.

In his youth d'Herbelot briefly joined the Jesuit order in Lyon.[18] His eulogist Louis Cousin tells us that, after humanistic studies, he pursued "the Oriental tongues" and especially Hebrew, "with the design of understanding the original text of the books of the Old Testament."[19] To a certain extent he remained true to this motivation: in the 1660s, he participated in an informal "academy" to discuss scriptural problems, and in the 1670s, he joined a circle around Bishop Bossuet that met to discuss the Bible in order to counter the scriptural claims of freethinkers and Protestants.[20] Even so, d'Herbelot pursued his extrascriptural interests on their own terms, without needing to relate them to Christian or biblical topics.

On the surface, the *Bibliothèque* may seem a modest endeavor. Certainly, next to the massive tomes of the Paris Polyglot, it is the equivalent of a paperback. Moreover, it contains no foreign type, not even a single character of Arabic script. Yet conceptually it is an expansion, not a contradiction, of the milieu of biblical studies out of which it grew. Organized not around the most important book of Christianity but around a set of intellectual traditions foreign and largely unknown to Europeans, it gave Islamic historical, religious, and literary achievements due attention without needing to relate them to the study of Christianity.

According to Cousin's eulogy, d'Herbelot journeyed twice to Italy, the only foreign country in which he ever lived. He took the first voyage in 1655, when he was thirty, to experience "the conversation of Armenians and other Orientals."[21] Indeed, Italy—thanks to its ports, and to the Mediterranean networks of the Catholic Church—had more long-standing ties to the Levant than any Northern European country.[22] This initial visit may also have been inspired by a hope of embarking for the Levant, an ambition he never realized.[23]

Upon his return to Paris, he found a patron in the ill-fated Nicolas Fouquet (1615–1680), the superintendent of finance now best remembered for his precipitous fall from grace, who offered him a pension of 1,500 livres annually.[24] At that time the great collections of Oriental manuscripts in Paris were still largely in private hands, which meant that d'Herbelot had to rely for many years on his own initiative and on private sponsors. He joined the circle of scholars who frequented Fouquet's collection of books and manuscripts, a library bested only by Cardinal Mazarin's in terms of "size, scope, and scholarly content," even though it contained only twenty Arabic manuscripts.[25] D'Herbelot pursued language proficiency with a coterie of other Parisian scholars and patrons, some of whom provided assistance by offering him books to consult or, in the case of Fouquet, by supporting him. On Fouquet's fall, in 1661, d'Herbelot passed for the first time into royal patronage, gaining the office of "royal secretary-interpreter for Oriental languages."[26] (Later in life he was granted a pension, and, in 1692, the position of professor of Syriac in the Collège Royal.)

D'Herbelot returned to Italy in 1666 and stayed in the Grand Duchy of Tuscany until about 1670.[27] It was during this trip that he seems to have conceived the idea of the *Bibliothèque*. While in Livorno, d'Herbelot met Duke Ferdinand II (1610–1670), who, like his grandfather Ferdinand I, had an interest in Oriental scholarship (a portrait by Justus Suttermans, now in the Palazzo Pitti, depicts Ferdinand II in Ottoman garb). The duke succeeded in enlisting d'Herbelot in his recently devised plan to revive the scholarly enterprise that his grandfather had supported.[28] When d'Herbelot arrived in Florence on July 2, 1666, he was received by the secretary of state and given a house with "six rooms on a ground floor, magnificently furnished, a dining table for four bearing all kinds of delicacies, and a carriage with the colors of His Serene Highness."[29]

D'Herbelot's Florentine counterparts were impressed and inspired by his polymathic knowledge. The Roman man of letters Lorenzo Magalotti wrote that in the ten years he had been in Florence he had not seen "a man arrive and stay here for some time with a greater and more universal reputation [*aura*] than the one that [d'Herbelot] acquired in Livorno as soon as he became known to the court, and that he brought to Florence and indeed increases there daily."[30] Magalotti noted that "there is gathered in him all the solidity [*sodezza*], civility, and mature worldly wisdom [*accorgimento*] that many of his fellow [French] nationals lack."[31] He continued, "Our men of letters have known erudite men, yet, in the end, it seems that those men all know the same things; this man alone leads them to a new world, across a sea of itinerant studies [*studi pellegrini*], something which cannot be ventured without a perfect understanding of the most famous Oriental languages, in which he is

most well versed."³² D'Herbelot was immediately inducted into the Accademia della Crusca, the Florentine literary academy created in 1583 to establish the purity of the Italian language (the Académie française, founded in
1635, was modeled on it).³³ Magalotti remarked that among the members of
the Academy "there are a few who would be happy to write in Tuscan [i.e.,
Italian] with forethought in the manner that [d'Herbelot] speaks off the cuff."³⁴
Inspired by his French colleague, in 1666 Magalotti began "to study the Arabic language, in which with great effort I begin to read printed books, to
conjugate verbs, and understand constructions."³⁵ Nor did he stop at Arabic;
there is a record of his borrowing some Turkish manuscripts in 1671 in order
"to study the Turkish language."³⁶

In Florence, d'Herbelot enjoyed the use of two separate collections of
Oriental manuscripts. In an echo of his ancestor Cosimo de' Medici's donation of a manuscript of Plato's works to the philosopher Marsilio Ficino two
centuries earlier, Ferdinand bought the best collection of Oriental manuscripts in Florence and bestowed them on d'Herbelot, who brought them
back to Paris when he left Italy.³⁷ In 1713 the French scholar Eusèbe Renaudot
observed that, just as the Medici and the Florentines had been the first to
bring about the rebirth of classical letters, so too were they at the forefront of
promoting Oriental letters in Europe.³⁸ The *Bibliothèque* would come to sym-
bolize French scholarship and patronage, but its roots lay in d'Herbelot's time
at the Medici court.

The other collection at d'Herbelot's disposal belonged to the Medici themselves and was housed in the Palazzo Pitti, the Medici's chief residence. It had
been amassed in Rome by Ferdinand's grandfather, Grand Duke Ferdinand I
(1549–1609), when he served as a cardinal before his accession to the ducal
title in 1574. Ferdinand I had patronized the so-called Medici Oriental Press
in Rome. When he returned to Florence, he brought his Oriental collection
with him, making the Tuscan capital into a major center of Arabic, Persian,
and other Eastern manuscripts.³⁹

During his time in Florence, d'Herbelot produced a partial catalog of the
Medici collection; copies in his own hand survive in Paris and in Florence.
The catalog says as much about d'Herbelot's curiosity as about the collection
itself, and affords an overall view of him as a reader at that time.⁴⁰ It also contains
foreshadowings of the *Bibliothèque*. Written in Italian, it organizes 437 manuscripts by subject—philosophy, mathematics, astronomy, medicine, "Maho-

metan" law, history, and so on—and draws on works in many languages. For example, the first category, Christian books, contains works in Arabic, Syriac (including Karshuni, or Arabic written in Syriac script), Persian, Aethiopic (Geʿez), Hebrew, and Coptic.[41]

The entries are of uneven length, indicating his biases. Some entries are very brief, whereas others are extremely detailed, offering partial translations (for example, of the preface to Naṣīr al-Dīn al-Ṭūsī's astronomical tables and of a Coptic liturgy).[42] He included among Islamic works his own translation of a chapter from a book on Muslim scholastic theology, and commented that al-Bukhārī's collection of ḥadīth (deeds and sayings of the Prophet Muhammad) "is held in very great esteem among the Mahometans and is like their second Alcoran, just as the Talmud is to the Jews."[43] A few of the Islamic books he discussed make frequent appearances in the *Bibliothèque*.[44] Of the Turkish narrative "Tarich Chatai" (History of China) concerning the 1420 trip to China by the ambassadors of Shāhrukh, the son of Tamerlane, d'Herbelot wrote: "This journey would merit to be translated in its entirety, because there are curious things about the knowledge of a country much mentioned by and equally unknown to our authors."[45] Muslim writers were useful as a way of learning about East Asia.

After he returned to Paris, around 1670, he worked on compiling the *Bibliothèque* as well as cataloguing the manuscripts in the Royal Library and producing a trilingual Arabic, Persian, and Turkish dictionary.[46] Famed for his learning, d'Herbelot received frequent visits from those traveling across the Republic of Letters. In the words of a contemporary report: "As strangers come to see him, he is overburdened by visits, and he rids himself of some of his guests by taking them to Makara's coffeehouse, which serves tea and coffee in the rue Mazarine. There is always at [d'Herbelot's] place a great crowd that assembles in a long gallery."[47]

On August 19, 1690, Louis XIV granted d'Herbelot permission to publish "a book entitled *la Bibliotheque Orientale & c.*"[48] D'Herbelot then made an agreement with the bookseller and publisher Claude Barbin, who had produced the works of almost all the greats of seventeenth-century French literature, from Molière to Jean Racine to Jean de La Fontaine, as well as the books about India by the traveler François Bernier.[49] His bookshop was located on the Île de la Cité, the island in the heart of Paris, in the Galerie of the Palais de Justice, an elegant arcade lined with shops selling fans, gloves, ribbons, lace, and books.[50] In 1691 the *Bibliothèque* was reported as being in press.[51] Three years later, in 1694, the Rotterdam journal *Histoire des ouvrages des savans* announced that the printing had reached the letter "N."[52] Due to delays, the book was not recorded in the register of the Community of Printers and Booksellers until November 22, 1696, almost a full year after d'Herbelot's death.[53] The first printing was completed on February 8, 1697 (Figure 12).

Sometime in 1694, d'Herbelot, who had employed other collaborators in the course of his studies (for instance, for the dictionary project discussed below), made the fortunate choice of hiring the young Antoine Galland.[54] After d'Herbelot died, at the end of 1695, at age seventy, before his book could be completed, Galland took charge, overseeing the printing and enhancing the book with a forceful and broad-minded preface. Without Galland, d'Herbelot's massive opus might have remained unpublished.

A New Map of an Old Continent

The three languages of Islamic high culture—Arabic, Persian, and Turkish—are connected by fate, not origin. Arabic, a Semitic language, descends from Nabatean, the language spoken in ancient Petra.[55] Modern Persian, an Indo-European tongue, traces its origin to the language of the Zoroastrian scripture, the Avesta; its modern form, written in Arabic script and known as New Persian, dates to the ninth century.[56] Turkish, part of the Turkic language family, descends from Old Turkic, which, attested in the eighth century in Mongolia, came to Anatolia with the first waves of Turkish invaders in the eleventh century.[57] When Turkish speakers converted to Islam, they too adopted the Arabic alphabet.[58] In other words, in spite of their common script, nothing intrinsic to these three languages recommends their joint study in the way that it might make sense to study Hebrew, Aramaic, and Arabic as a group. They belong together only if one is interested in the literary culture of Muslim lands.

D'Herbelot's trilingual approach was at the cutting edge of scholarship. At the end of the seventeenth century only a few European scholars were able to cultivate the three languages of Islamic high culture and consider them together. Into d'Herbelot's time, among these three languages Arabic was foremost on the European scholarly agenda, in no small part because of its association with Hebrew.[59] D'Herbelot, however, treated Arabic not as an auxiliary discipline of Old Testament studies but as the idiom of an autonomous civilization worth studying in its own right. From the outset, Persian and Turkish manuscripts were collected alongside Arabic ones, but their languages received a much smaller share of scholarly attention. Some grammars and dictionaries in both languages appeared, as well as some editions of Persian prose and poetry.[60] Meanwhile, in the course of the seventeenth century the study of Ottoman Turkish would be institutionalized as France, Austria, Poland, and other states founded their own language schools in Istanbul to train interpreters. (Colbert also created a language school in Paris for the same purpose.)[61] The interpreters, however, occupied a subordinate position to the humanistically trained scholars; their training was vocational rather than humanistic.

D'Herbelot was not the only person in this period to consider the three languages in a single setting—Franz Meninski published a multilingual grammar in Vienna in 1680 that featured Arabic, Persian, and Turkish—but this was still a fledgling area of research.[62] Given that these languages had intrinsic cultural connections and that none of them—not even Arabic—had achieved independence as a field of study, grouping them together was a logical step. In parallel with the *Bibliothèque,* d'Herbelot (and several collaborators, most of whom remain anonymous) worked on a massive trilingual dictionary that survives in manuscript.[63]

D'Herbelot designed the *Bibliothèque Orientale* to encompass the written culture of West Asia, including its geography, political organization and history, poetry and letters, thought, beliefs, and even legends. The term "Oriental" is now viewed as too imprecise to be useful, but that very looseness allowed d'Herbelot, to the extent that his languages and available books would permit, to regard Christians of the Levant, Zoroastrians, and other inhabitants of the lands of Islam as legitimate objects of inquiry. The limits of "Oriental" were defined by the sources d'Herbelot had managed to read rather than by any preconceived notion. This was not just d'Herbelot's idiosyncrasy; his collaborator Galland likewise defined "Oriental" very loosely: "By the name of Orientals, I do not merely mean the Arabs and the Persians; but also the Turks and Tartars, and almost all of the peoples of Asia up to China, whether Mahometans and pagans or idolaters."[64] The vague contours of the *Bibliothèque*'s remit would not have seemed to its author a symptom of lack of rigor, but merely the inevitably incomplete outcome of a lifelong effort to read and to know.

Sources of Information and of Inspiration

The *Bibliothèque* is a virtual library, stacked with foreign tomes. Deliberately omitted from its shelves are almost all European books about Asian topics that had been published in the sixteenth and seventeenth centuries, including the many travel accounts of this period (with only one or two notable exceptions).[65] The European works that the *Bibliothèque* does cite are bilingual Arabic-Latin editions that afforded access to primary sources, such as Edward Pococke's *Specimen Historiæ Arabum*.[66] In other words, d'Herbelot attempted to offer a vision of Islamic history and letters as unmediated as his powers could afford. He directed readers to Arabic, Persian, and Turkish manuscripts or to Arabic printed editions, rather than to translations or nonscholarly accounts. In his attempt to render foreign culture on its own terms, he resisted generating his own terminology when native terms existed. His was a sustained effort to make himself and his own intellectual categories as invisible as possible. For instance, the entry on religion is found under "din" (*dīn,* the Arabic word for religion).[67] Even though this arrangement made the *Bibliothèque* more difficult to use for a French speaker, d'Herbelot's attentiveness to native terminology expressed his deep reverence for his subject matter and also introduced some lexical innovations into French, most notably the term "Islam" itself.[68]

D'Herbelot's readers had to trust his authority. They could not verify his citations or turn to the works themselves to delve further—with the exception of a handful of Arabic books, his sources were unpublished in Europe and could be viewed in manuscript only by the select few who had access to specialized collections.[69]

The *Bibliothèque*'s most important source was the *Kashf al-ẓunūn ʿan asāmī al-kutub waʾl-funūn* (The clearing of doubts in the names of books and arts), the bibliography compiled by the Ottoman scholar Kātib Çelebi (1609–1657), large parts of which are directly incorporated into the *Bibliothèque* (Figure 13). Kātib Çelebi, whose early death left his ambition to produce an encyclopedia of Islamic literature unrealized, had amassed one of the greatest libraries of the era (the work he did complete remains important to the study of Islamic letters to this day).[70] The *Kashf* gave d'Herbelot a range of material greater than any collection of Islamic manuscripts in the West. Kātib Çelebi's bibliography maintains a strictly alphabetical order, which likely influenced d'Herbelot to adopt that same organizing principle for the *Bibliothèque*. The inclusion of large parts of Kātib Çelebi's bibliography was seen as an explicit merit of the *Bibliothèque* (Galland wrote, "the Library of [Kātib Çelebi] . . . is inserted here almost completely"), but d'Herbelot did not credit all the material he took from it, conveying the impression of having read even more widely than he actually had.[71] (The *Bibliothèque* contains an impressively long list of the works it drew upon, but it reveals neither which ones had been most important to d'Herbelot, nor which ones he had consulted only in abridged or anthologized form.)[72]

Kātib Çelebi's book is a prime example of the kind of source to which d'Herbelot was most drawn: reference works, including geographies, compilations, abridgments, and anthologies. His reliance on compilations reveals his implicit trust in native judgments of what mattered. Broadly speaking, d'Herbelot recognized that Muslim scholars who made excerpts and compilations were engaged in the same basic activity as he was. Their collections, often known as "gardens," contained a preselected offering of the best specimens. The *Bibliothèque,* as a compilation of compilations, could be described, poetically, as a garden of gardens. Trusting the relevant authorities was a mainstream theory and practice during his time, the premise being, in the words of French bibliographer Gabriel Naudé (1600–1653), "Because we cannot by our own industry alone learn and know the qualities of the books that one needs to possess, it is not inappropriate to follow the judgment of the most well-versed and learned in this subject."[73] While choosing to read such books made practical sense, it also betokened a deep trust in the native tradition of scholarship and in its judgments of what to excerpt and compile.

Another compilation d'Herbelot favored was "The Gardens of Virtuous Men" (*Rawḍ al-akhyār*) by the sixteenth-century scholar Ibn Khaṭīb al-Qāsim. The book is an abridgment of a voluminous anthology of literary and historical works (*Rabī al-abrār wa-nuṣūṣ al-akhbār*) compiled by the medieval polymath al-Zamakhsharī, who had written one of the Qur'an commentaries used by Marracci. D'Herbelot did not possess al-Zamakhsharī's work in its entirety, and the abridgment served as an expedient substitute.[74] He found other useful shortcuts in a chronicle by a fifteenth-century Syrian scholar; in a hagiographic book by a fourteenth-century Yemeni writer, which itself excerpted earlier biographical dictionaries (a compilation of compilations); and in Ibn Khallikān's biographical dictionary of notable men, a source that remains in use today.[75] One of the most frequently cited Turkish books was another collection, in this case of playful stories by the Ottoman poet Lāmiʿī (d. 1531 / 1532).[76]

Some of d'Herbelot's sources were already known and regarded as classics by his European peers: works by the renowned medieval geographer Idrīsī; by the geographer and historian Abū'l-Fidā, a thirteenth-century prince from Ḥamāh, Syria; by Naṣīr al-Dīn al-Ṭūsī, the polymathic Persian scholar of the thirteenth century; and by Ulugh Beg, a grandson of Tamerlane, who wrote on astronomy and mathematics in the fifteenth century.

Edward Gibbon remarked of d'Herbelot: "I find him more satisfactory in the Persian than the Arabic history."[77] D'Herbelot's focus on Persian, rather on Arabic, historiography (historical writing) was unusual.[78] Three early Safavid historians particularly shaped his understanding of Islamic history: "Mirkhond," or Mīrkhwānd (d. 1498); "Khondemir," or Khwāndamīr (d. after 1535–1536); and Yaḥyā b. ʿAbd al-Laṭīf Ḥusaynī Qazvini (d. 1555).[79] To take but one of them, Mīrkhwānd wrote a seven-volume universal history in Persian, which was translated into Ottoman Turkish in the sixteenth century and again in the eighteenth and relied upon by Western scholars until the late nineteenth century.[80] D'Herbelot also frequently relied on the "Tar Kozideh" (*Taʾrīkh-i guzīda*) by Ḥamdullāh Mustawfī al-Qazwīnī, a fourteenth-century geographer and historian (d. after 1339–1340).[81] The *Taʾrīkh-i guzīda* (completed in 1330) is a compendium of universal history that draws on earlier sources for its initial sections, and offers information about al-Qazwīnī's own day that is still useful to scholars today.[82]

While in Florence, d'Herbelot acquired many Persian books, which helps explain why the preponderance of the *Bibliothèque*'s sources, whether in Arabic or in Persian, were produced in Persian-speaking lands.[83] He demonstrated a genuine, independent interest in Persian-language culture, but his bias toward Persian sources may also have been influenced by his especial fluency in that language. This fluency is suggested by his transliteration of many Arabic words according to Persian pronunciation.[84] In sum, d'Herbelot's choice of sources prioritized native over European writers, and paid particular attention to the period from the late Middle Ages until the early seventeenth century. An

Ottoman bibliography may have sat at the heart of his virtual library, but many Persian writers filled out its shelves.

D'Herbelot on Poetry, History, and Religion

Reading the labyrinthine *Bibliothèque Orientale* can be overwhelming. To pursue a subject one must page forward and backward, making it easy to miss relevant entries. Yet with time a cohesive picture of a given topic comes into view—as do d'Herbelot's idiosyncrasies as a reader. His choices—what he included on a given subject and what he omitted—can seem arbitrary, determined as they are by what he chose to read, but his enthusiasm never flags. He maintained his biographical and anecdotal approach throughout, with the exception of theological issues, on which he was more abstract. What follows is a look at his approach to poetry, history, and religion.

POETRY

Poetry was a key form of expression in Muslim societies, as it had been to the Arabs before the establishment of Islam. Its memorization and recitation brought together and defined communities, ranging from princely courts to Sufi lodges to the transregional community of the learned.[85] The *Bibliothèque*'s entries on individual poets focus less on their poetry than on information gleaned from biographical dictionaries of poets, such as the Persian *Tadhkirat al-shuʿarā'* by Dawlatshāh Samarqandī (d. 1495 or 1507), who surveyed the poets of the Persian tradition and especially of his own time. Gathered together, the *Bibliothèque*'s vivid stories add up to a who's who of Muslim literary life, in particular of the medieval Tīmūrid period, and to an ethnography of that milieu.[86] For instance, he reported that the poets Anwarī and Rashīdī, finding themselves on opposite sides of a siege fought between Seljuks and Khwarazmians, "waged war in their own manner, sending one another verses attached to the ends of arrows, while the two sultans conducted and repulsed assaults."[87] Of the poems of Ḥāfeẓ of Shiraz, the celebrated Persian mystic, d'Herbelot wrote, "They are greatly esteemed, especially on account of their sublime style, and of the mysteries that Muslims pretend to find in them, so much so that one gives this poet the title and accolade of 'lessan gaib' [*lisān al-ghayb,* tongue of the unseen] which means the mysterious tongue."[88] The entry continues with some indication of Ḥāfeẓ's religious sensibility and suggests (surely a touch too hopefully) that there are contact points between Christianity and the poet's mysticism: "Hafiz of Shiraz was suspected during his lifetime of not being too good a Muslim: indeed, whatever hidden and mysterious meaning one might give his verse, it seems to express a great indifference toward Musulmanism, and in several places in his works one might even believe that he refers to JESUS-CHRIST in the manner of the Christians."[89]

Poems appear throughout the *Bibliothèque Orientale,* often without attribution. D'Herbelot's translations of dozens of verses from Arabic, Persian, and Turkish are impressive. For instance, the entry on Ibn al-Rūmī, a Baghdadi poet who died in 896 CE, includes an Arabic couplet, both transliterated into the Roman alphabet and translated into French:

> Lam ar scheïan hadheran nefâho. Lelmarr kelderhem v alseïf.
> Iacdha laho alderhem hagiataho. Valseif iohmiho men al-haïf.
> There is nothing more useful and necessary to man, than a good purse
> and a good sword.
> For the former provides him with all he needs, and the latter protects
> him from all insults.[90]

Although d'Herbelot translated the couplet correctly, he made several mistakes in vocalizing the words (for example, "nefâho" for *nafʿuhū,* "iacdha" for *yaqḍī,* "hagiataho" for *ḥājātihī,* "iohmiho" for *yaḥmihi*), and he omitted the final vowels (for instance, "ar" for *ʾara*), which Arabic meter requires for correct scansion, indicating a weak grasp of Arabic prosody.[91] Perhaps because of these shortcomings, the German scholar Johann Jacob Reiske entered the original Arabic into the margin of his copy of the *Bibliothèque.*[92]

The poet quoted most frequently is Saʿdī of Shiraz, one of the greatest Persian poets, and perhaps with Rūmī the most widely known today, especially for his *Gulistān (Rose Garden)* and *Bustān (Orchard).*[93] Saʿdī's manuscripts were well represented in Paris, and especially in Colbert's library; they had also been published. The *Gulistān* held classic status among Persians, to whom it was also a classic for learning their language. In seventeenth-century Europe, it would serve a similar role both as an entry point and as a model of the literary language.[94]

Of the freethinking poet Abū'l-ʿAlāʾ al-Maʿarrī, one of the first Arabic poets to be published in Europe, d'Herbelot remarked: "He is the most able of the Arab poets according to the judgment of the learned in this language."[95]

A biographical overview is followed by translated excerpts from his poetry. Here are two:

> Jesus came and abolished the Law of Moses.
> Muhammad followed him, and introduced his five daily prayers.
> His sectarians say that there is no other Prophet to come after him, and
>   thus they are fruitlessly engaged from morning to night:
> Tell me now, since you have lived under one of these Dispensations,
> Do you enjoy the Sun or the Moon any more or less?
> If you answer impertinently, I will raise my voice against you:
> But if you speak to me in good faith, I will continue to speak softly.[96]

> The Christians err here and there in their path, and the Mahometans are
>   entirely off the right path.
> The Jews have become nothing but mummies, and the Magi [Zoroas-
>   trians] of Persia dreamers.
> The world is divided into two kinds of people, of which one has wit, and
>   no religion
> And the other has religion and little wit.[97]

Emphatically irreligious quotations like these, and ones from Ḥāfeẓ that revealed his ecumenical tendencies, demonstrated the heterogeneity of Islamic religious and poetic traditions. In addition, including them allowed d'Herbelot to voice, albeit by quotation, some rather liberal thoughts. Whatever his own religious beliefs, he was open-minded enough to quote these passages. Buried in the depths of the labyrinth he had built, they likely escaped the notice of any censor.

After d'Herbelot's death, Galland continued to collect materials for a future expansion of the *Bibliothèque*—either a supplement or a second edition—by making hundreds of manuscript additions in the margins of his personal copy of the *Bibliothèque*. These additional entries were never published, but Galland's copy is preserved in Vienna.[98] At his death in 1715, the handwritten entries numbered around 2,000. Virtually all biographical, they are drawn from four biographical dictionaries of poets of the fifteenth and sixteenth centuries, one in Persian and three in Turkish.[99] These works stand in the same tradition of the biographical dictionary by Dawlatshāh Samarqandī that d'Herbelot had extensively employed. Galland's additions confirm that in the eyes of its creators, the *Bibliothèque* was especially a repository of literary biography, with a focus on the Timurid, early Safavid, and Ottoman periods, and a particular interest in the poetic output of the Persian- and Turkish-speaking Muslim courts of West and Central Asia.

HISTORY

The *Bibliothèque* expanded the range of humanist historical analysis to the lands of Islam, opening a previously untapped wellspring of moral exemplarity and admonitions. In his preface Galland explains that "in speaking of each Prince, [d'Herbelot] has observed the name of his predecessor, and who has succeeded him."[100] Thanks to these cross-references, readers could start with a given ruler and reconstruct an entire dynasty back to its founder and forward to its final representative. Galland also promised that in the *Bibliothèque,* "History is neither dry nor tedious, as would be a simple account of battles won, cities taken, or provinces conquered." By applying a biographical approach, the *Bibliothèque* delivers history by example:

> Princes appear in it, some with their magnificence, their radiance, and their splendor; others with a pure vanity, or a sordid avarice, and an overall parsimony unworthy of their character and of their grandeur, and yet others commendable for their liberality and their mildness. Other princes display a praiseworthy balance between avarice and poorly regulated prodigality, and yet others are detestable and loathsome because of their excessive severity, their tyranny, their impiety, their hypocrisy, their cruelties, their debaucheries, and because of all the other vices that can make one detest them. And all this is accompanied by examples that will generate love and admiration for the ones, and horror about the others.[101]

Some entries reach back before recorded history to the mythical early dynasties and monarchs recounted in Firdawsī's *Shahnameh,* the foundational epic poem of the Persian people.[102] In recounting episodes from that poem as history, d'Herbelot drew not so much on Firdawsī's epic itself as on later renarrations of the same material.[103] At the same time, he noted that "these fabulous histories of Asfendiar [Esfandiyār], and of Rostam were rejected and condemned by Mahomet, on account of the comparison that the Arabs drew between them and what he told them. For his listeners often told him that the stories that Nasser [al-Naḍr b. al-Ḥārith] had brought from Persia were much more beautiful [than the Qur'an]."[104] In his preface Galland remarked that the inclusion of fabulous history was essential because so much later literature drew on it.[105] The truth of these histories was not as important as their wide cultural resonance, or, as d'Herbelot put it: "The valor and courage of Rostam and of Asfendiar are still today the example and model of military virtue among Oriental people, and the greatest kings of the Orient do not disdain to be compared to these two heroes, just as among us the names of Alexander and Caesar are not at all forgotten when one praises the military virtues of our princes."[106]

The first four caliphs—Abū Bakr, ʿUmar, ʿUthmān, and ʿAlī—are known as the "rightly guided" caliphs (al-rāshidūn), the "orthodox" caliphs of the Islamic tradition. Even so, ʿAlī's actions remain controversial among Muslims, and differing evaluations of this caliph defined theological and political allegiances for centuries. D'Herbelot's treatment reflected these native judgments. The biographical entries on the first three caliphs followed canonical Muslim opinion in treating them as worthy of the highest praise, both militarily and personally.[107] D'Herbelot noted succession disputes as well as the titles and styles these men accrued (like caliph and amīr al-muʾminīn, or commander of the faithful), and he narrated the violent coup against Caliph ʿUthmān with depth of feeling and an eye for evocative details, such as ʿUthmān's blood seeping into the copy of the Qur'an that he carried on him.[108]

The fourth caliph, ʿAlī b. Abī Ṭālib, cousin and son-in-law of Muhammad, has one of the longer entries in the Bibliothèque (almost fifteen columns of text, compared to ten dedicated to Muhammad). D'Herbelot offers detailed descriptions of some of ʿAlī's battles to consolidate his reign, and he records where historical sources disagree.[109] ʿAlī governed at a time of great unrest, with many forces resisting his authority, and d'Herbelot writes with relish about the negotiations, battle strategies, and errors of judgment. What is more, the reader learns of ʿAlī's uneven reception among Muslims: disliked by certain Umayyad and even Abbasid caliphs, but admired by the Fatimids (the Shiite dynasty of medieval Egypt).[110] And, at the conclusion of ʿAlī's succession narrative, the reader is reminded of the parallels between these ancient disputes and those of the present day: "The disagreement that Othman had with Ali has been the source of an infinity of wars and of particular disputes within

Musulmanism. They have not calmed down even today, and it is just as dangerous to speak well of Othman the Caliph in Persia as it is to praise Ali too strongly in the states of the Sunnites, such as the Turks are."[111] The *Bibliothèque* followed mainstream opinion in its judgment of the Umayyads—the dynasty that followed immediately after the first four caliphs—who had left a much more ambivalent legacy. D'Herbelot took a dark view of the second Umayyad caliph, the infamous Yazīd: "He did not emulate the virtues of his father, which were clemency and liberality; for he was cruel, avaricious and, what is more, impious in religion."[112] D'Herbelot explained that Persian hatred of Yazīd was based not only on his personal vices but also on his murder of the son of ʿAlī, Husayn, and of Husayn's whole family, on the plain of Karbala, the massacre commemorated by Shiites on the day of Ashura.[113]

Even so, and in spite of the Persian origin of much of his source material, d'Herbelot never adopted a Shiite perspective. He called the "Schiites . . . [those] who have provoked from time to time some very great troubles."[114] His overall emphasis was Sunni, even as he kept track of the Shiite contestations. Of the election of Abū Bakr to succeed Muhammad, he noted: "The sectarians of Ali's party nevertheless hold stubbornly that Ali never gave his consent to this election, nor to the later ones of Omar and Othman."[115] He was particularly scathing about smaller Shiite confessions, such as the Ismailis, which he called "that detestable sect."[116] In this, as in many other respects, he took the point of view of mainstream, Sunni sources.

D'Herbelot's own ideals are often revealed in his accounts of the lives of Muslim princes. For example, his portrayal of al-Maʾmūn, the seventh Abbasid caliph (786–833)—whose death, he wrote, was occasioned by eating too many fresh dates and drinking too much water—includes praise of the ruler's learning and his religious tolerance:

Khondemir [the Persian historian Khwāndamīr] portrayed this prince invested with all the great royal virtues, for he was full of gentleness, liberal, a great captain, and a lover of letters, as well as highly learned. He had particularly pursued speculative sciences, and he incurred extraordinary expenses to assemble learned people from all over and to find the most curious books in Hebrew, in Syriac, and in Greek, all of which he had translated into Arabic.

Plates

Map 1. Europe in 1700.

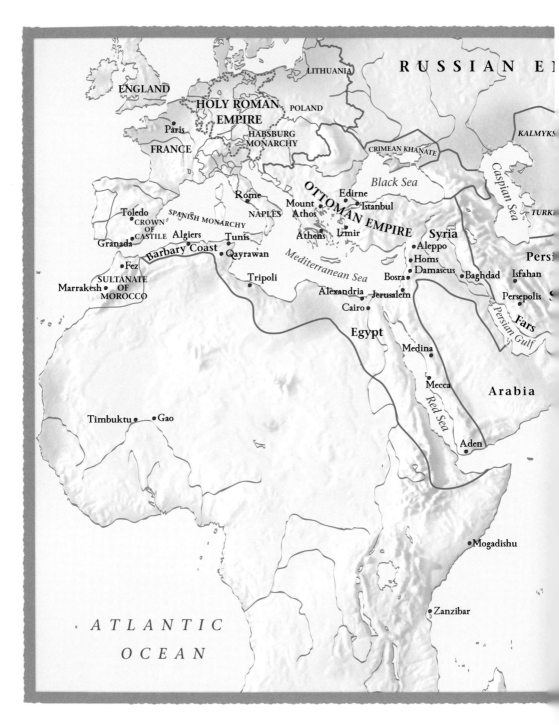

Map 2. Africa and Eurasia in 1700.

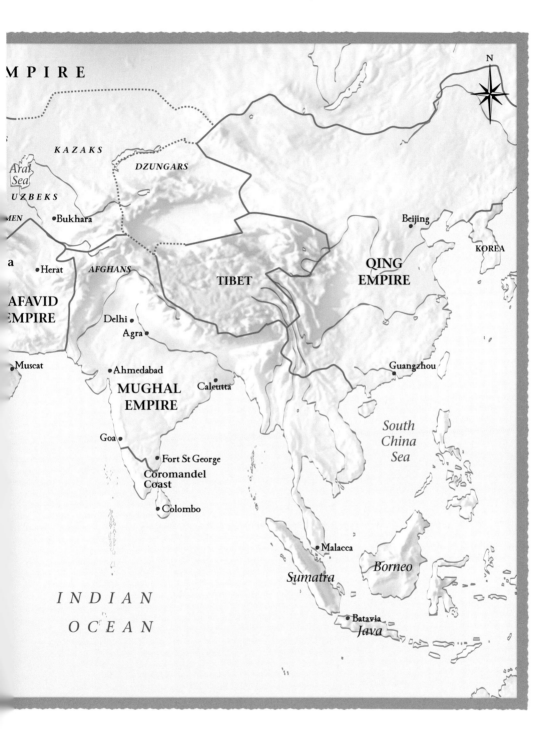

FIG. I. "Students in Pursuit of the Doctorate" (*Lettori del Studio in via del Dotorato*). An Ottoman scholar from a hand-painted costume album. European scholars perceived an analogy between themselves and their Muslim counterparts. This European album closely imitates models created by Ottoman artists; the Italian captions explain who is represented. 1630 or after. The album was collected by François Roger de Gaignères (d. 1715). Paris, Bibliothèque nationale de France, Cabinet des Estampes, Od. 5–4, FOL 86r.

FIG. 2. "He Assembled the Books from Different Regions" (*Congregavit de Regioni-bus Libros*). This allegory represents Pope Clement XI (Albani) ordering the collection of Oriental manuscripts in the Eastern Mediterranean. The spines of the books name doctors of the Eastern Church. Giuseppe Simonio Assemani, *Bibliotheca Orientalis Clementino-Vaticana* (Rome, 1719), vol. 1, frontispiece. Widener Library, Harvard University, OL 85.240 F t. 1.

FIG. 3. Lodovico Marracci's portrait. This anonymous painting hangs to this day in the Roman chapterhouse of the Order of the Mother of God, Santa Maria in Campitelli. Credit: Photograph by Stefano Paradiso.

FIG. 4. Ibn Abī Zamanīn, *Tafsīr*. This Qur'an commentary contains the entire text of the Qur'an (bold lettering), which it excerpts and discusses passage by passage. This page contains Sura 112, known as *al-Ikhlāṣ* or *al-Tawḥīd*. Rome, Church of Santa Maria in Campitelli, MS OMD Marracci I (B78 ML XV), fol. 173r. Copyright Ordine della Madre di Dio (Order of the Mother of God); Photograph by Roberto Tottoli.

FIG. 5. Lodovico Marracci's transcription of Ibn Abī Zamanīn. Marracci copied out Ibn Abī Zamanīn's text, underlining the Qur'anic words (as at the top of the page) to distinguish them from the commentary. He left space for his own draft translation in the margin. This page displays Sura 112. Rome, Church of Santa Maria in Campitelli, MS OMD Marracci III (B70 ML V), fol. 441r. Copyright Ordine della Madre di Dio (Order of the Mother of God); Photograph by Roberto Tottoli.

FIG. 6. Lodovico Marracci, *Refutatio Alcorani* (Padua, 1698), 831. This page, which contains Sura 112, showcases the four parts of Marracci's work: the Arabic edition, Latin translation, critical notes based on Arabic commentaries (*Notæ*), and polemical refutation (*Refutationes*). Each section is neatly divided from the others. Andover-Harvard Theological Library, Harvard University, 163 Marracci.

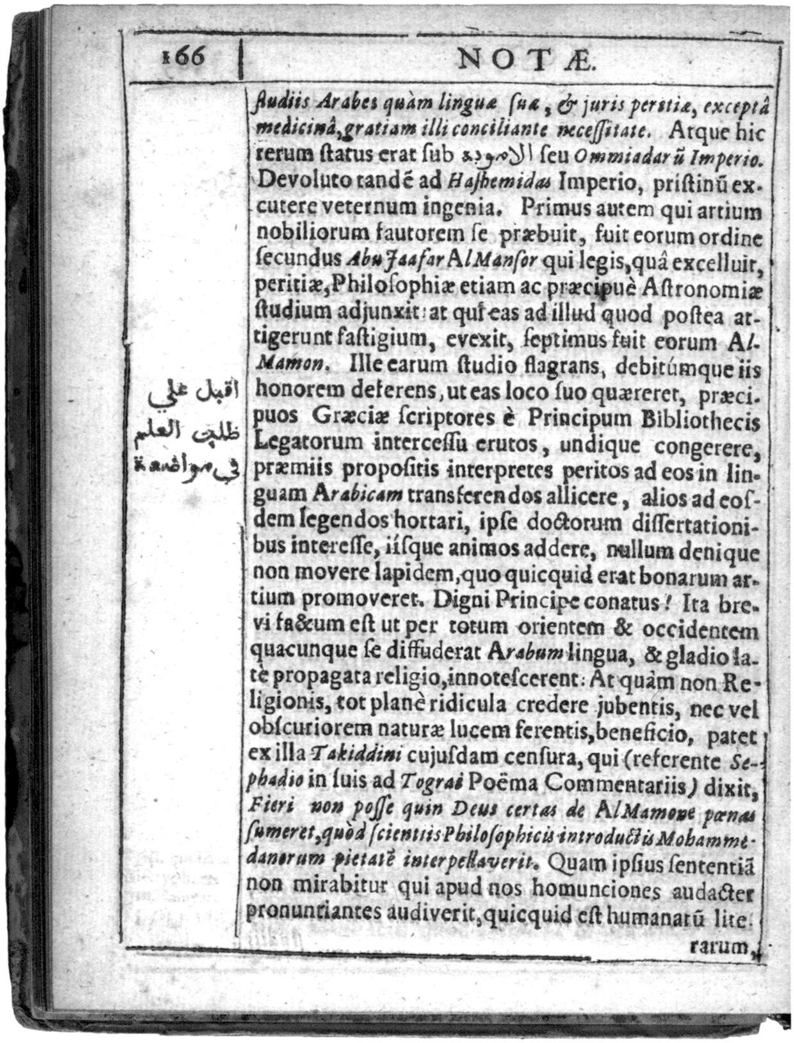

ſtudiis Arabes quàm linguæ ſuæ, & juris peritiæ, exceptâ
medicinâ, gratiam illi conciliante neceſſitate. Atque hic
rerum ſtatus erat ſub ﺍﻟﺍﻣﻴﺔ seu Ommiadarū Imperio.
Devoluto tandē ad Haſhemidas Imperio, priſtinū ex-
cutere veternum ingenia. Primus autem qui artium
nobiliorum fautorem ſe præbuit, fuit eorum ordine
ſecundus Abu Jaafar AlManſor qui legis, quâ excelluit,
peritiæ, Philoſophiæ etiam ac præcipuè Aſtronomiæ
ſtudium adjunxit: at quſ eas ad illud quod poſtea at-
tigerunt faſtigium, evexit, ſeptimus fuit eorum Al-
Mamon. Ille earum ſtudio flagrans, debitúmque iis
honorem deferens, ut eas loco ſuo quæreret, præci-
puos Græciæ ſcriptores è Principum Bibliothecis
Legatorum interceſſu erutos, undique congerere,
præmiis propoſitis interpretes peritos ad eos in linguam Arabicam transferendos allicere, alios ad eoſ-
dem legendos hortari, ipſe doctorum diſſertationi-
bus intereſſe, iiſque animos addere, nullum denique
non movere lapidem, quo quicquid erat bonarum artium promoveret. Digni Principe conatus! Ita bre-
vi factum eſt ut per totum orientem & occidentem
quacunque ſe diffuderat Arabum lingua, & gladio la-
tè propagata religio, innoteſcerent: At quàm non Religionis, tot planè ridicula credere jubentis, nec vel
obſcuriorem naturæ lucem ferentis, beneficio, patet
ex illa Takiddini cujuſdam cenſura, qui (referente Se-
phadio in ſuis ad Tograi Poëma Commentariis) dixit,
Fieri non poſſe quin Deus certas de AlMamone pœnas
ſumeret, quòd ſcientiis Philoſophicis introductis Mohammedanorum pietatè interpellaverit. Quam ipſius ſententiâ
non mirabitur qui apud nos homunciones audacter
pronuntiantes audiverit, quicquid eſt humanatū literarum.

اقبل علي
ظلبي العلم
في مواقسه

FIG. 7. Edward Pococke, *Specimen Historiæ Arabum* (Oxford, 1650), 166. In this
sample page from Pococke's lengthy commentary on his Arabic source, translations
and proper names are italicized. Houghton Library, Harvard University, HD OL
21120.1*.

FIG. 8. "Various Poses of the Mohammedans as They Pray to God" (*Varii gestus Mo-hammedanorum preces ad Deum fundentium*). Foldout plate in Reland, *De Religione Mohammedica,* 2nd ed. (Utrecht, 1717). Rare Book & Manuscript Library, Columbia University, New York, B893.791 R251.

FIG. 9. "The Meccan Temple" (*Templum Meccanum*). Foldout plate in Adriaan Reland, *De Religione Mohammedica,* 2nd ed. (Utrecht, 1717). This, the first Western visual representation of the temple of Mecca, relied on an Ottoman drawing acquired by the Swedish scholar Michael Eneman. Andover-Harvard Theological Library, Harvard University, 161 Reeland.

MECCANVM
...us, et vetustissima religione consecratum.

P. Goeree del.

A. *Porta nuncupata vetus.*
I. *Locus Hanbelitarum, unius e quatuor Sectis praecipuis Mohammedanorum.*
C. *Locus Malekitarum, qui et ipsi unam Sectam constituunt.*
. *Locus Hanifaeorum Schafaci, in loco qui ab Abrahamo nomen habet;*
   congregantur.
. *Fascia aurea adhaerens velo serico nigro operis Damasceni quo Cabae*
   parietes undique Tecti (sic ut nulla pars oculis pateat) nigri apparent.

N. *Tapetes, instrati Solo quibus insident precantes.*
O. *Canalis per quem aqua ex tecto Cabae defluit in Lapidem qui Sepulch-*
   rum Ismaelis habetur.
P. *Locus ubi phialae repletae aqua putei Zemzem dantur peregrinantibus,*
   quas domum reduces secum ferant.
Q. *Septum interius, quod Cabam proxime cingit et noctu accensis lychnis*
   illustretur.

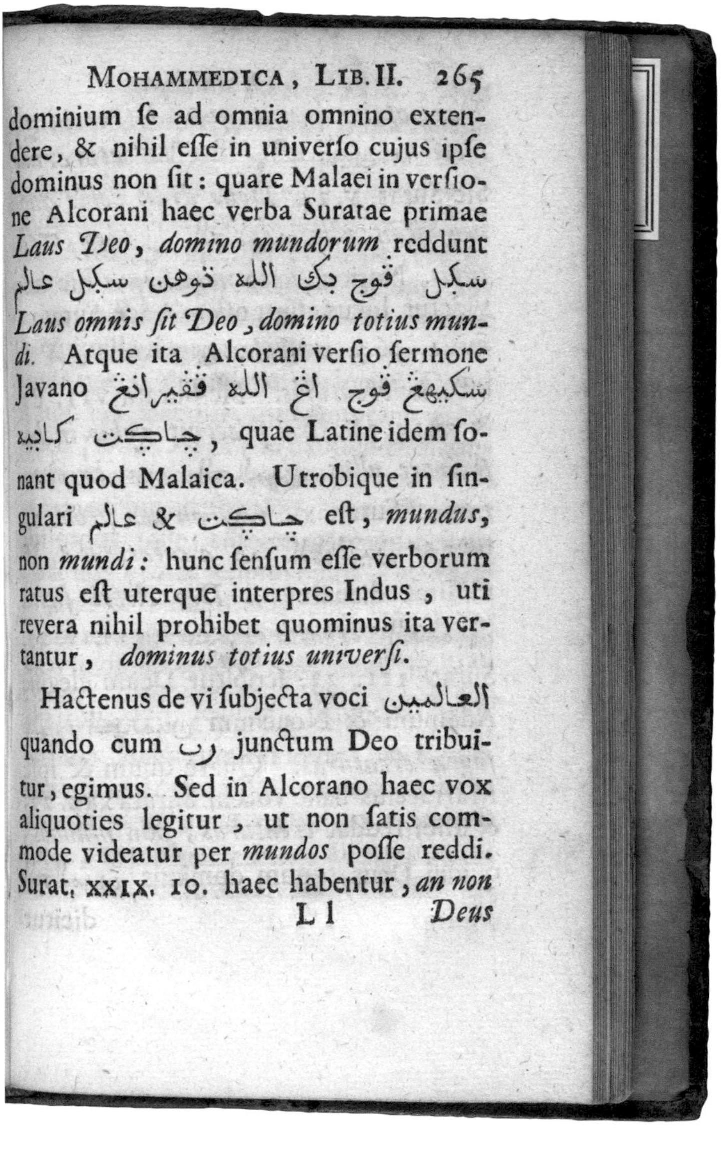

dominium fe ad omnia omnino exten-
dere, & nihil effe in univerfo cujus ipfe
dominus non fit: quare Malaei in verfio-
ne Alcorani haec verba Suratae primae
Laus Deo, domino mundorum reddunt

سكبل قوج بكي الله ذوهن سبكل عالم

*Laus omnis fit Deo, domino totius mun-
di.* Atque ita Alcorani verfio fermone
Javano سكبهغ قوج اغ الله قفير انغ
جابكن كابيه, quae Latine idem fo-
nant quod Malaica. Utrobique in fin-
gulari جابكن & عالم eft, *mundus,*
non *mundi:* hunc fenfum effe verborum
ratus eft uterque interpres Indus, uti
revera nihil prohibet quominus ita ver-
tantur, *dominus totius univerfi.*

Hactenus de vi fubjecta voci العالمين
quando cum رب junctum Deo tribui-
tur, egimus. Sed in Alcorano haec vox
aliquoties legitur, ut non fatis com-
mode videatur per *mundos* poffe reddi.
Surat. **XXIX.** 10. haec habentur, *an non*

L l   *Deus*

FIG. 10. Adriaan Reland, *De Religione Mohammedica,* 2nd ed. (Utrecht, 1717), 265.
This page of Reland's treatise quotes Javanese and Malay translations of the Qur'an
to determine the meaning of the word ʿālam as it is used in the opening sura of the
Qur'an. The two languages are transcribed in Arabic characters. Andover-Harvard
Theological Library, Harvard University, 161 Reeland.

Barthelemi d'Herbelot
Interprete des Langues Orientales
LP 33-82°
+ 1695·

FIG. 11. Portrait of Barthélemy d'Herbelot, "Interpreter of Oriental Languages" (*Interprete des Langues Orientales*). Engraving by Gérard Edelinck. Château de Versailles et de Trianon, Versailles, France, INV.GRAV 3348. Photo © RMN-Grand Palais / Art Resource, NY.

BIBLIOTHEQUE
ORIENTALE

MA.   MA.

ABAMONDI & Mapamondi en Ar. Perf. & Turc, est un mot pris de l'Italien Mappamondo, Chatte de Geographie. Les mêmes Orientaux l'appellent aussi Kharthi & Kharthas, & tous ces mots se prennent souvent pour l'art, & pour un livre de Geographie. Le mot de Kharthi est le plus souvent employé pour signifier une Charte Marine. *Voyez* Kharthi & Kharthas.

MA'BAR. Pays des Indes situé au troisiéme Climat, selon les Geographes Arabes. Ce mot signifie en Arabe, Passage, comme si c'étoit le passage des Indes à la Chine. On pourroit soupçonner que c'est le Malabar; mais nos Geographes le placent entre le huitiéme & le douziéme degré de latitude Septentrionale. *V.* Mibar.

Edrissi a marqué dans le premier climat de sa Geographie une Isle nommée Mabath, proche de celle de Kalad dans la mer des Indes.

MABED BEN KHALED, surnommé Al Gioni Docteur Arabe, Auteur de la seste des Cadariens, qui admet le franc arbitre & la liberté de l'homme dans toutes ses actions, contre le sentiment le plus commun & le mieux receu parmy les Musulmans qui soûtiennent la premotion ou predetermination physique, qu'ils expliquent en disant que nos actions se doivent absolument rapporter à Dieu, parce que c'est luy qui cree en nous; & Mabed tenoit au contraire que les actions des hommes se devoient rapporter aux hommes mêmes qui en sont les maîtres. Ce Docteur fut poussé par ses collegues & deferé à Hegiage Gouverneur de la Ville & Province de Bassora, qui le fit mourir. *Voyez* Giohni.

MABERDIN. Les Cathaïens appellent ainsi la plante que nos Botaniques nomment Anthora, qui est l'antidote du Napel. Les Arabes & les Persans luy ont donné le nom de Geduar & Zeduar, d'où s'est formé celuy des boutiques Zedoaria. Mais il faut remarquer, que nôtre Zedoaria n'est pas la

veritable, ni celle dont nous parlons; mais une plante differente que les Arabes appellent en leur langue Zurunbad.

MABLUI. Surnom de Josef Ben Hegiage Andalusi, Docteur Arabe, natif d'Espagne, qui a composé un Livre intitulé en Arabe Ulf al Mohadherat, c. a. De la maniere de conferer & de disputer sur les matieres contestées par les Docteurs Musulmans. Cet Autheur est souvent cité sous le nom d'Ebn al Scheikh, c. a. Le fils du Docteur, ou du Vieillard.

MABSUTH. Ouvrage de Bezdavi en onze volumes: Ce mot en Arabe signifie Estendu & s'oppose à Mokhtassar qui signifie un Abbregé. *Voyez* le titre de *Bezdavi.*

MACCABIUN. Les Maccabées. Ketab al Maccabiin. Le Livre des Maccabées. Histoire de Josef BenGorion en Arabe traduite de l'Hebreu qui se trouve sous ce titre dans la Bibliotheque Royale & dans la Bibliotheque du G. D. num. 6. où il est joint à quelques livres de l'ancien Testament qui ont été traduits en Arabe pour l'usage de l'Eglise d'Alexandrie. Ce livre des Maccabées est attribué à Joseph l'Historien, ce qui diminuë beaucoup son authorité, parce qu'ils ne pourroient avoir été compris dans le second Canon des Livres sacrés que l'on croit avoir été fait par Esdras.

La mere des Maccabées Martyrs, selon la tradition des Orientaux rapportée par Abulfarage, se nommoit Aschmunah ou Schamunah. Ce mot a été emprunté de l'Hebreu Khaschmanim ou Khaschmonim, lequel signifiant des Grands ou des Princes, a été donné aux Maccabées Princes & Rois de leur nation, d'où les Grecs & les Latins ont formé celuy d'Asmonéens. Les corps de ces Martyrs furent transportez à Jerusalem en Antioche où les Chrétiens leur ont bâti une Eglise.

MACALAT al fasliat. Methode de guerir ceux qui ont été mordus par des bêtes venimeuses ou qui ont été empoisonnez d'Abû Amran Mûssa, al Israeli; al Corthobi. C'est Moyse, £ de Maimon. B. R. num. 864.

Vuu

FIG. 12. D'Herbelot, *Bibliothèque Orientale* (Paris, 1697), 523. This sample page displays the page layout of d'Herbelot's reference work: alphabetically arranged articles are given titles in Arabic (e.g., "Maccabiun" for Maccabees). Many entries conclude with cross-references to other articles. Houghton Library, Harvard University, F Asia 36.97*.

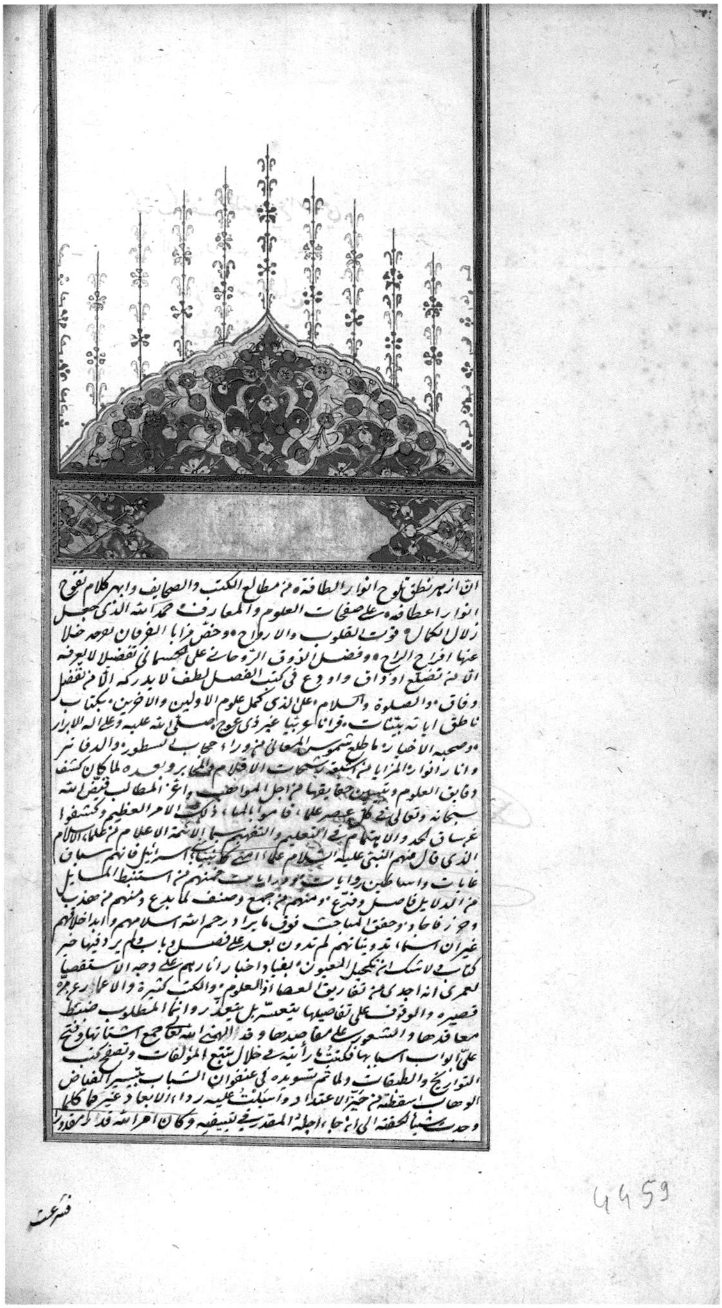

FIG. 13. Kātib Çelebi, "The Clearing of Doubts in the Names of Books and Arts" (*Kashf al-ẓunūn ʿan asāmī'l-kutub wa-l-funūn*), title page. This manuscript of Kātib Çelebi's book was produced in Istanbul in 1680 and acquired for the Royal Library in Paris. D'Herbelot had it copied for his personal use. Paris, Bibliothèque nationale de France, Ms. Arabe 4458, fol. 1v.

IO. IACOBUS REISKE MED. D.
Lingvae Arabicae in Vniv. Lips. Pr.P.
et Scholae urbicae ad D. Nicolai
Rector.
aetatis anno LIV.

J. D. Philippin geb. Sysangin sc. 1770.

FIG. 14. Portrait of Johann Jacob Reiske. Samuel Friedrich Nathanael Morus, *De Vita Ioannis Iacobi Reiskii* (Leipzig, 1777), frontispiece. Engraving by Johanna Dorothea Philipp, 1770. Houghton Library, Harvard University, Tr 484.

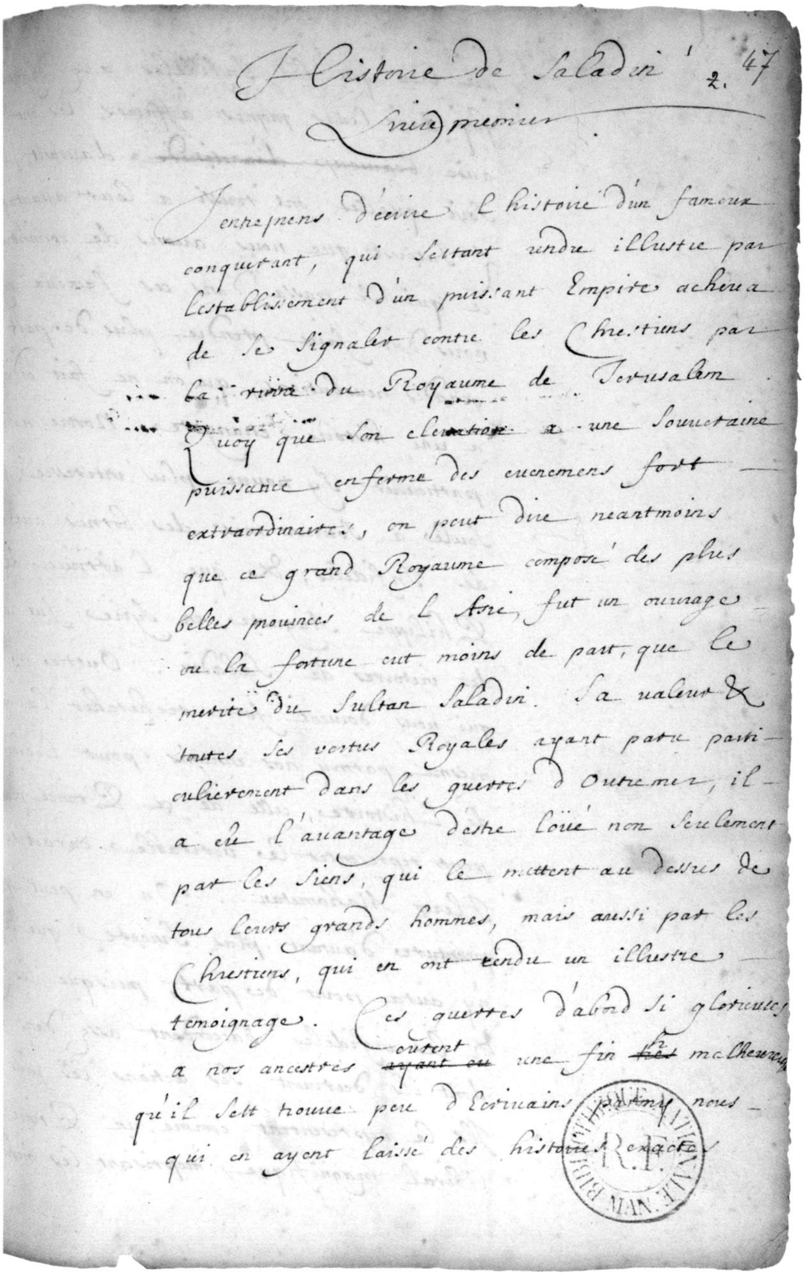

Histoire de Saladin

Livre premier.

J'entreprens d'écrire l'histoire d'un fameux conquerant, qui s'estant rendu illustre par l'establissement d'un puissant Empire acheva de se signaler contre les Chrestiens par la ruïne du Royaume de Jerusalem. Quoy que son elevation a une Souveraine puissance enferme des euenemens fort extraordinaires, on peut dire neantmoins que ce grand Royaume composé des plus belles prouinces de l'Asie fut un ouurage ou la fortune eut moins de part, que le merite du Sultan Saladin. Sa ualeur & toutes ses vertus Royales ayant paru particulierement dans les guerres d'Outremer, il a eu l'auantage d'estre loüé non seulement par les siens, qui le mettent au dessus de tous leurs grands hommes, mais aussi par les Chrestiens, qui en ont rendu un illustre temoignage. Ces guerres d'abord si glorieuses a nos ancestres ayant eu une fin si malheureuse qu'il s'est trouué peu d'ecriuains nous qui en ayent laissé des histoires

FIG. 15. Eusèbe Renaudot, "History of Saladin" (*Histoire de Saladin*). Renaudot's life of Saladin, which was never published, reveals his admiration for the medieval Muslim ruler. Paris, Bibliothèque nationale de France, Ms. Nouvelles Acquisitions Françaises 7477, fol. 47r.

FIG. 16. Pseudo-Wāqidī, "Conquests of Syria" (*Futūḥ al-Shām*). Simon Ockley used this manuscript as the basis for his *The Conquest of Syria, Persia and Ægypt* (London, 1708). Oxford, Bodleian Library, MS. Laud Or. 163, title page.

FIG. 17. Abū'l-Fidā', "Concise History of Mankind" (*Mukhtaṣar fī akhbār al-bashar*). The German scholar Johann Jacob Reiske studied this manuscript of Abū'l-Fidā''s history during his stay in Leiden. Leiden University Library, MS Or. 554, title page.

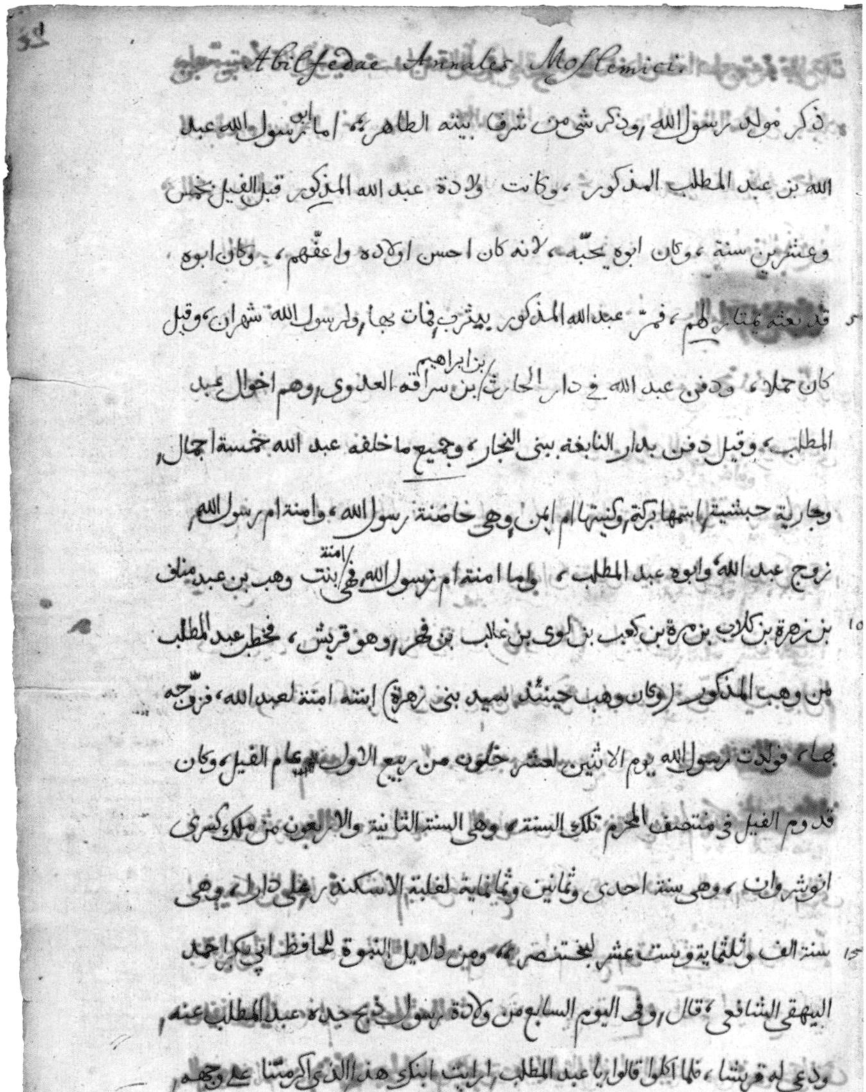

ذكر مولد رسول الله ونذكر شيئاً من شرف بيته الطاهر ﷺ وأمه رسول الله عبد

الله بن عبد المطلب المذكور ، وكانت ولادة عبد الله المذكور قبل الفيل بخمس

وعشرين من سنة ، وكان أبوه يحبّه لأنه كان أحسن أولاده وأعفّهم ، وكان أبوه

قد نعته مطالباً لهم ، فمرّ عبد الله المذكور ببثرب فمات بها وقبر رسول الله شهراً ، وقيل

كان حملاً ، ودفن عبد الله في دار الحارث بن سراقة العدوي وهم أخوال عبد

المطلب ، وقيل دفن بدار النابغة بني النجار ، وجميع ما خلفه عبد الله خمسة أجمال

وجارية حبشية اسمها بركة وكنيتها أم أيمن وهي خاضنة رسول الله ، وآمنة أم رسول الله

زوج عبد الله وأبوه عبد المطلب ، وأمها آمنة أم رسول الله بنت وهب بن عبد مناف

بن زهرة بن كلاب بن مرة بن كعب بن لؤي بن غالب بن فهر وهو قريش ، خطب عبد المطلب

من وهب المذكور ابنته آمنة وهب حينئذٍ سيد بني زهرة إلى أن ماتت آمنة لعبد الله ، فزوّجه

باها فولدت رسول الله يوم الاثنين لاثني عشر خلون من ربيع الأول عام الفيل ، وكان

قدوم الفيل في منتصف المحرم تلك السنة وهي السنة الثانية والأربعين من ملك كسرى

أنوشروان ، وهي سنة إحدى وثمانين وثمانمائة لغلبة الاسكندر على دارا وهي

سنة ألف وثلاثمائة وستة عشر لبختنصر ، ومن دلائل النبوة للحافظ أبي بكر أحمد

البيهقي الشافعي ، قال ، وفي اليوم السابع من ولادة الرسول ذبح جدّه عبد المطلب عنه

ودعى له قريشاً ، فلما أكلوا قالوا يا عبد المطلب أرأيت ابنك هذا الذي جاء أكرمتنا عليه وجههم

FIG. 18. Johann Jacob Reiske's transcription of Abū'l-Fidā''s *Mukhtaṣar*. Reiske's transcription, which he intended to use as the basis for a critical edition, never completed, reveals his elegant Arabic penmanship. Copenhagen, Det Kongelige Bibliotek, uncatalogued, title page.

He supported all learned men equally, whatever their religion. They in turn contributed much to the glory of this monarch through the presents that they gave him of their works, which collected all that was most rare among the Indians, the Magi [Zoroastrians], the Jews, and the Oriental Christians of all sects.[117]

The entry, buried in the pages of a learned tome, and referring to a moment distant in both time and place, quietly affirmed the value of interreligious cooperation in search of knowledge. Religious tolerance was a delicate subject in France after the 1685 Revocation of the Edict of Nantes, which had rescinded the religious and civil rights of Protestants. At the same time, d'Herbelot acknowledged that al-Ma'mūn's policies had been too liberal for his day: the orthodox disapproved of his proximity to the Mu'tazilites, a rationalist Islamic sect, and reacted badly to his introduction of philosophy and the speculative sciences, "for the Arabs then were not yet used to reading books other than those of their own religion."[118]

The *Bibliothèque* pays special attention to the sixth century of the Islamic era (roughly speaking, the thirteenth century CE), during which a series of Mongol invasions from Central Asia overwhelmed medieval Islamic society. If d'Herbelot seems to betray a particular interest in this era, it is likely because it represented the right balance between distance from the present and the availability of information. He considered that information about more recent dynasts such as Aurangzeb or Mehmed IV could be found elsewhere, and that his most distinctive contribution would lie in unearthing knowledge about earlier rulers. As a result of these decisions, Genghis Khan receives seven columns of text and Tamerlane an astonishing twenty-one and a half, more than twice the number dedicated to Muhammad.[119] About half of the Tamerlane entry is taken up by what d'Herbelot acknowledged was his paraphrase of Khwāndamīr; the rest is dedicated to extracts from other sources. Beyond covering Tamerlane's military deeds, the entry records such events as his encounter with theologians in Aleppo. D'Herbelot finally granted the bloodiness of Tamerlane's reign but argued that "this great conqueror was not as savage [*farouche*] as several writers have made him out to be."[120]

D'Herbelot covered the dynasties of his own time—the Safavid (1502–1736), Mughal (1526–1748), and Ottoman (1299–1922)—in less detail.

Contemporaneity did not count for much; in the *Bibliothèque,* it was more important to have been significant than recent. In comparison to the great conqueror Mehmed II, the lesser but more recent Mehmed IV, who ruled for nearly forty years in d'Herbelot's own lifetime, and led the failed siege of Vienna in 1683, rates only the briefest mention.[121] D'Herbelot seems to have decided that more recent history was treated sufficiently in the writings of European travel writers, whom he otherwise scorned. For instance, the Persian ruler Shah 'Abbās (r. 1588–1629) was "pretty well known by Europeans through the reports of those who have written about voyages to Persia in our time."[122] In the entry on Cairo, he wrote that "one can see in the modern accounts of our travelers what is most curious today in this great city: for I had no other design in this work than to report concisely that which I found in the originals of which our [European] authors make no mention."[123] He paid even less attention to the Mughals for the same reason, as well as because of the limitations of his own reading and of what his sources covered.[124] The *Bibliothèque* does provide a basic Mughal chronology, but only because "their lineage is corrupt and confused in most of the accounts of our travelers."[125]

Of these three later dynasties, the Ottomans receive the most notice, and d'Herbelot's stance toward them is one of the book's most distinctive aspects. Traditionally Europeans were dismissive of Ottoman cultural and intellectual achievements. In contrast, the *Bibliothèque* portrays Mehmed the Conqueror, who led the Ottoman capture of Constantinople in 1453, as neither a destroyer of civilization nor an enemy of Christendom. "Sultan Mehmed II was not just a warrior; for the Turks place him among the ranks of the most learned doctors of their religion, and he loved men of letters so much that he attended their conferences and disputes personally, distributing prizes of great value to all those who excelled, whether in eloquence or in poetry. He was not even ignorant of Greek or Latin history, and he had translated into Turkish several of our books, of which we still find versions in the Turkish language that are dedicated to him."[126]

Flattering assessments of the cultural achievements of other Ottoman sovereigns are found in several of the *Bibliothèque*'s biographical entries. To a certain extent d'Herbelot was conforming to a model so dominant in French historiography since the Renaissance that it had become an almost obligatory topos: the celebration of a monarch's patronage of the arts.[127] For example, the entry on Bayezid, Mehmed's immediate successor, concludes with the following evaluation: "He was very magnificent in the construction of mosques, colleges, and hospitals, very liberal toward men of letters, for he himself had cultivated the sciences, and especially those that concern Musulmanism. We even have some Turkish verses from his pen."[128] The brief entry on Süleyman the Magnificent (1494–1566), the most celebrated of all Ottoman sultans, stresses his erudition: "Soliman passes among the Turks for the greatest prince of the Ottoman race who has so far reigned. For, beyond the military virtues that he possessed to a very great degree, he was also very learned in Arabic, Persian, and Turkish. It is even said that he knew Greek, too, and that he had several of our books translated into the Turkish language, among them Caesar's Commentaries."[129] In d'Herbelot's time, Süleyman was the subject of many fictional European accounts, most of them focused on his relationship with Roxelana, his favorite and chief consort.[130] That the *Bibliothèque* did not include even a single tale of Süleyman's romantic entanglements bespeaks its author's high-minded approach to his project and his determination to present a native perspective on its topics.

RELIGION

In a departure from his usual approach, d'Herbelot expressed a point of view on Islam as a religion that did not merely mirror that of his Islamic sources. For example, the *Bibliothèque* calls Muhammad "the famous impostor," rather than using his traditional Islamic title "the seal of prophets" (*khātim al-nabīyīn*), which refers to his place as the last of a sequence of prophets that began with Abraham.[131] This lack of adherence to an Islamic viewpoint on the subject of religion should not be surprising in a book produced in Catholic Paris and dedicated to Louis XIV, one of whose hereditary titles was Roi Très-Chretien or Rex Christianissimus (Most Christian King). Furthermore, no evidence exists that d'Herbelot disagreed with the Catholic polemical assessment of Muhammad, as "the founder of a heresy that has taken the name of religion."[132] D'Herbelot reassured the reader that "you will find in this entire work several other entries in which the ignorance and imposture of this false prophet are uncovered and refuted."[133] Nevertheless, despite such sideswipes, his main goal was to provide an accurate description of Islam, not to attack it. His writings about the religion are primarily scholarly and have a matter-of-fact, temperate tone, and they draw on as many sources as the rest of the *Bibliothèque* does.

Aside from giving an outline of the prophet's life—already covered in depth in the Arabic editions and translations that had been published in Europe—the entry on Muhammad investigates his status among Muslims: the miracles attributed to him, the claim that he enjoyed divine favor in battle, his identification as the Paraclete of the Gospels, and the fact that the Qur'anic Jesus foretells Muhammad's coming (Q61:6, "I am indeed the Messenger of God to you . . . giving good tidings of a Messenger who shall come after me, whose name shall be Aḥmad").[134] D'Herbelot undoubtedly took a polemical interest in taking apart these claims. The entry considers the views of Muslim "scholastic theologians" and the ideas promulgated by the "mystical doctors of the Muslims," which d'Herbelot found even less credible.[135] Overall, he concluded that Muslims endowed Muhammad with almost all of the characteristics of the Messiah.[136]

By citing different authorities in his explanation of salient Qur'anic verses, whether he agreed with them or not, d'Herbelot showcased the plurality of opinions within the Islamic tradition as well as the diversity within the broad community of the Muslim faithful. He also noted that Muslim commentators spent as much time puzzling over and debating the meaning of opaque passages in the Qur'an as Christian scholars did with the Bible.

The topic of Paradise in Islam is treated in a long entry titled "Gennah" (for Arabic *janna,* Paradise). The entry—assembled through commonplacing (gathering excerpts under topical headings), one of d'Herbelot's basic strategies—offers a series of perspectives drawn from a variety of sources, only one of which was the Qur'an.[137] The entry is a characteristic hodgepodge of quotations, each revealing a different Muslim conception. D'Herbelot left the reader to discover Muslim views of Paradise through an accumulation of native quotations and paraphrases, some unattributed (a "Turkish poet," a "Persian author," and "the interpreters" of the Qur'an), and others named (including al-Thaʿlabī, al-Zamakhsharī, al-Rāzī, Sabzavārī Bayhaqī Vāʾiẓ Kāshifī, Jāmī, and Rūmī).

On the question of whether the pleasures of Paradise would be sensual, d'Herbelot wrote: "What several authors who have fought Mahometism have claimed, namely that Muslims do not recognize any other kind of bliss in heaven than the enjoyment of pleasures of the senses, is . . . not true."[138] Muhammad, he explained, had initially promised that the faithful would be sensually rewarded in Paradise, but later altered his message, avowing that the most devout worshippers would be treated to joys beyond sensory ones. According to d'Herbelot, Muhammad "understood that the kind of beatitude that he had [at first] promised his followers would not persuade the most enlightened minds."[139]

D'Herbelot set forth the variety of Muslim responses to the Qur'anic depiction of Paradise with accuracy and complexity while expressing strong disapproval of literalist Muslim doctrine: "The most rigorous Muslims, or, rather, the most superstitious of their scholars, maintain that one must take literally all those bodily delights in Paradise, and they confuse the earthly Paradise, *Paradisum voluptatis,* of which is spoken in the Holy Writ, with the Paradise of glory."[140] An allegorical understanding of Paradise, he noted, agrees with "the manner of the Christians and of the Jews themselves."[141] In passing, he debunked some Western misconceptions—for instance, that Muslim women are not allowed into Paradise, a myth based on a misreading of a *ḥadīth*.[142]

Although d'Herbelot held Muhammad's eschatology to be false, he saw it as part of the conversation about the nature of the divine in which different groups of Christians, including heretics, had been participating since the time of Christ. For instance, he remarked that what is called in Q11:11 *"achar akbar"* (a great reward, or, as A. J. Arberry renders the phrase, "a mighty wage") corresponds to "that view which we call the beatific vision" of God.[143] Incidentally, this reading of the phrase comes from an extra-Qur'anic tradition—it is not self-evident that the phrase refers to the vision of God: d'Herbelot here is following that tradition and canonizing its reading of this passage of the Qur'an.[144] The French scholar thought he could discern some echo of Christian truth in Muslim expressions of the power and grace of God, for "their sentiments [are] quite similar to the sentiments of Christians."[145] He often pointed out such similarities between Muslim and Christian theology. For example, he argued that some Christian contemplatives believed that earthly suffering would be rewarded with sensual pleasures, at least of sight and sound, and asserted that the "Paradise of the Mahometans" was based on that of the heresiarch Cerinthus, an early Christian thinker who defended a physical version of Paradise in which "one would eat, one would drink, and one would exercise the functions of marriage."[146] The ecclesiastical historian Eusebius of Caesarea, whom d'Herbelot would have read, attributed to Cerinthus the notion that the earthly reign of Christ (the Second Coming) would include a "marriage feast lasting a thousand years."[147]

In sum, d'Herbelot drew analogies between Islam and Christianity and made the necessary statements of condemnation, but he was not a virulent anti-Muslim polemicist. His attention was focused on providing a rich description of Islam, which emerges from his pages as a religion equal to Christianity in its diversity, contestations, and multivocalism.

The Purpose of a Library

In his foreword to the *Bibliothèque Orientale,* Galland explained the book's structure, principles, and rationale. He also made explicit some of its implicit arguments. He considered himself to be expressing d'Herbelot's views, not just speaking his own mind, and there is no reason to doubt that he did so to the best of his abilities. The book's wide-ranging look at the history and letters of Muslims proved, in Galland's words, that "general history such as we have it, comprising both sacred and profane history, has been until now defective," and added that Christians did not have to regard Muslim beliefs and customs as true in order to want to learn about them: "Whether their [Muslim] traditions are false, or whether they are true, it is always very enjoyable [*agreable*] to know them."[148] This notion was groundbreaking: Muslim traditions need not be conceived only as the targets of religious polemic, but could be instructive and entertaining subjects in their own right.

One of d'Herbelot's goals, Galland explained, had been to promote admiration for the arts and sciences of Muslim lands: "The reader shall judge whether the Orientals are as barbarous and as ignorant as public opinion would suggest."[149] According to Galland, d'Herbelot had been dedicated to righting that historical wrong. In particular, Galland noted, the *Bibliothèque* makes a strong argument for a reappraisal of Ottoman scholarly and literary achievements, which had been regarded as inferior to those of Arabs and Persians: "We occasionally pay homage to the Arabs, and they pass for having once cultivated the sciences with great exertion. We attribute politeness to the Persians, and we do justice to them. But, by their name alone, the Turks are so decried, that it is normally enough to mention them to mean a barbarous, coarse nation, and of an accomplished ignorance."[150] Yet Galland averred:

"One can say with respect to ignorance, that in the sciences and letters common to these three nations [the Ottomans] are second to none, not to the Arabs, not to the Persians; and that they have cultivated these subjects since the beginning of their empire."[151] The ignorant, he implied, were not the Ottomans, but those Europeans who disparaged their achievements without attempting to learn about them. Galland's own long-standing commitment to Ottoman intellectual life stemmed from his time in Istanbul, Izmir, and elsewhere, where he had witnessed the lively book markets and traded views with local scholars.[152]

Galland noted but did not criticize the overall of lack of Muslim interest in European thought, a situation in marked contrast to the West's growing study of Islamic traditions. "One will cease to be astonished as many people are, that [Muslims] decline to learn our languages, in order to gain instruction by reading our books and fathoming our histories, and by the subject of our thought and our erudition, while they have plenty with which to busy themselves in working on their own stock of materials."[153]

One of Galland's most ambitious assertions was that knowledge of foreign peoples is an essential ingredient for developing good judgment, an idea that echoes Gabriel Naudé: "I certainly believe that there is nothing to be more desired than the fruitful and agreeable occupation and entertainment that a learned man can obtain from such a library . . . since, thanks to it, he can with good cause call himself cosmopolitan or an inhabitant of the entire world, and he can know everything, see everything, and be ignorant of nothing."[154]

D'Herbelot and Galland both believed that the comparative study of customs, laws, and morality was a transformative pursuit, and that the stories in the *Bibliothèque* could contribute to self-understanding and to forming a person to whom nothing human could be foreign. The two commemorative poems that open the *Bibliothèque* underscore this vision of bookish cosmopolitanism, attributing its qualities to the author: Regnier Desmarais's poem celebrates d'Herbelot as one "who knew all the generations of mankind and all ages, and all the regions of the earthly sphere, so that he seemed to have lived in every century, and to have wandered across the entire earthly sphere more often."[155] The Jesuit poet Jean Commire's verse includes the line "For d'Herbelot, who understood the deeds, laws, and languages of all peoples, could be a stranger nowhere."[156] Both poems associate d'Herbelot's broad reading with personal virtue and good manners.

Conclusion

The *Bibliothèque Orientale* owed its sustained reception to d'Herbelot's winning combination of erudition and entertaining edification. The short entry "Megnoun" [*Majnūn*] displays in a nutshell d'Herbelot's trilingual erudition and his inclusive analogical thinking. The entry explains that Majnūn is a literary figure "who is to the Orientals the model of the perfect lover" and that "one finds the loves of Megnoun and of Leïleh [Layla, Majnūn's beloved] written in Arabic, Turkish and Persian."[157] With an analogy to Judaism d'Herbelot elucidates the importance of these lovers in Islamic culture: "All Mahometans equally consider these two lovers, more or less as the Jews consider the bride and groom of the Song of Songs, reading their story allegorically and using it to elevate spiritual readers to the contemplation of divine mysteries."[158] These few lines—in appearance casually tossed off but in fact the fruit of extensive reading—exhibit what can only be described as d'Herbelot's learned cosmopolitanism.

Galland's preface described the *Bibliothèque* enticingly as "a monument for posterity, which would surprise it with its novelty, and would be agreeable both for its utility and for the pleasure it would give."[159] The book went through one reprinting, two translations (one of which was only partial and remained unpublished), and several new editions that updated or expanded its content or made it more accessible by removing the most arcane entries.[160] The *Bibliothèque* formed the basis of what eighteenth-century Europeans knew about Islamic letters and history and was a starting point for such early nineteenth-century scholars as Antoine-Isaac Silvestre de Sacy and Joseph von Hammer-Purgstall. Annotated copies of the *Bibliothèque* show how later European scholars of Arabic put the book to use.[161] Its structure allowed specialists to expand its purview, organizing their own notes and bibliographic references within d'Herbelot's arrangement. Moreover, citations of the *Bibliothèque* in a number of literary, philosophical, and historical writings attest to the work's wide cultural resonance. It succeeded in reaching an audience broader than scholars, becoming a book that educated people, including men of state, had to have.[162] William Jones, Goethe, Lord Byron, Gustave Flaubert, and other literary writers all breathed in its heady attar, giving the book a glamorous second career.

The *Bibliothèque Orientale* offered a more extensive and more eclectic view than anything that had theretofore been available to European readers. Its virtue was its eclecticism, its reliance on a variety of books in different genres and in three languages. But what d'Herbelot gave his sources, above all, was the gift of humanity: he took Muslims seriously as politicians, poets, theologians, lovers—as members of the selfsame community of humankind to which he and his readers likewise belonged.

FIVE

ISLAM IN HISTORY

Sometime before his death in 1720, the French scholar abbé Eusèbe Renaudot conceived an ambitious research project: to write a general history of Islamic lands, "an Oriental history drawn from Arabic, Persian, and Turkish originals."[1] Such a comprehensive overview did not yet exist in Europe. The available information about Islamic history was piecemeal, consisting of no more than selective translations of individual works and sketching out only a limited number of events. Even the *Bibliothèque Orientale* by Renaudot's friend Barthélemy d'Herbelot, which afforded broad coverage of the histories of Muslim peoples, left many aspects unexamined.[2] Renaudot wanted his project to reveal "the history of several large Empires that has been known very imperfectly"—an extensive subject, because "the history of the Mahometans is as vast as the extent of their empire."[3] In his view, Islamic history would enrich understanding of the Western past, which had been shaped by interactions with Muslims. But he went further, arguing that Islamic history was intrinsically interesting, independently of any connections to the West: "One finds in it extraordinary events, several changes of Empire, great men, maxims of politics, wars of religion, princes who love letters and the arts, undertakings and long-distance voyages, and events as curious as they have been thus far entirely unknown."[4] In the seventeenth and eighteenth centuries, European scholars of Arabic not only studied the religious traditions of Islam, but also delved into Arabic poetry, the history of the Muslim conquests, and the lives of medieval Muslim rulers, all to widen European horizons in these fields.[5] This chapter focuses on only one of several domains of the European inquiry into Muslim peoples: their history.

Traditionally Islamic history fell at the very margins of the Western scholarly purview. Europeans were stymied not just by linguistic ignorance but also by conceptual barriers. Studying the history of other peoples has always required a justification, and that is doubly true when they profess an inimical faith. Islamic history was not just non-Christian, however. It was also non-classical. In Europe, history was first and foremost the study of the classical past, in which, as the humanists had taught for centuries, moral and political exemplarity could be found. The subject of modern history was limited to the progress of Christianity and of Christian kingdoms. A place for Islamic history had yet to be found.

Yet Islamic history contained important historical puzzles, such as Islam's rapid expansion, a phenomenon without precedent. Islamic intellectual history also earned the attention of European scholars. For one thing, the transition from empire of the sword to empire of the mind appeared to them very rapid. How had this simple creed become such a fertile soil for the cultivation of the arts and sciences? That Muslims had performed great intellectual feats was beyond question, but the nature of their accomplishments inspired debate. Scholars vacillated between seeking to make Islamic intellectual production correspond to classical models and arguing that it needed to be taken on its own terms.

This European scholarly effort resulted in two major accomplishments. The first was empirical and philological: the translation of previously unknown sources and the refinement of source criticism and of how to read Islamic historians. These were sizable achievements; each decision to locate and edit or translate a new source brought with it many questions about the source's reliability, along with challenges in reading and understanding its content. The second accomplishment of European historians was establishing a neutral space for thinking about the history of Muslim peoples, rejecting what had been a fundamentally unsympathetic approach. To attain a neutral point of view that allowed them to write broad-mindedly about Islamic history, scholars employed a variety of arguments and concepts, from tracing the connections between Christian and Islamic history to establishing analogies between Muslim and classical figures.

Analogies were a powerful tool for validating the Western study of Islamic civilizational achievement, just as they had been for validating the study of the religion itself. They opened the way for European historians of Islam to demonstrate that illustrious Muslims resembled the heroes of antiquity, and that lessons about virtue and eloquence could be drawn from reading their lives. These historians also tried to understand the attainments of Muslim scholars and philosophers, who had made ancient Greek thought available to the medieval Christian West.[6] Their examination of the patronage of Muslim princes gave them clues about the relationship of Islamic government to the cultural and intellectual achievements that had flourished under its auspices. In the process, Western historical scholarship was expanded and the primacy of the classical past as the normative source of moral exemplarity was undermined.

Like those who studied Islam as a religion, the scholars who investigated secular Islamic civilization were a diverse group. Four of them are featured in this chapter: Edward Pococke (1604–1691), whom we encountered in Chapter 3; the French scholar Eusèbe Renaudot (1646–1720); the Cambridge professor Simon Ockley (1678–1720); and the German Arabist Johann Jacob Reiske (1716–1774). With the exception of Pococke, these writers followed in the footsteps of d'Herbelot, who had already pursued many of their goals, from perceiving a likeness between Muslim and Christian heroes to writing about the former as paragons of virtue. Unlike d'Herbelot, Renaudot and Ockley attempted full-length histories, Renaudot of an exemplary ruler and Ockley of the early Arab conquests and of early Umayyad history. These narrative accounts sought to endow Islamic history with the prestige its authors thought it merited and to integrate it into Western historical writing. A generation later, Reiske brought new precision, rigor, and erudition to the European study of Arabic through his editions and translations and through his critical scholarship.

In certain respects these European scholars of Islamic history pursued a more limited agenda than did the polymath d'Herbelot. He had worked in Arabic, Persian, and Turkish, whereas his successors focused mostly on Arabic. Moreover, they did not share d'Herbelot's (and Galland's) interest in the post-Mongol era, but trained their gaze primarily on the medieval period, especially the early centuries of Islam. They tended to think that Ottoman high culture represented a degraded version of Islamic intellectual and literary traditions.

Even so, these European scholars of Arabic made an important contribution to the broader reconfiguration of human history that was being undertaken in the seventeenth and eighteenth centuries.[7] By means of their research into the historical and literary traditions of Muslim peoples, they decentered their own history, raised questions about the undue neglect of non-Western traditions and the place of the West in human history writ large, and challenged their readers to expand their horizons and include the deeds and achievements of Muslims in their historical consciousness.

Why Study Islamic History?

Perhaps more than anyone else in the eighteenth century, Simon Ockley contributed to the wider European assimilation of Islamic history. In 1708 he produced the first narrative history in English to be based on Islamic sources, *The Conquest of Syria, Persia, and Ægypt, by the Saracens,* which draws on Arabic historical accounts to depict the wars of Muslim expansion under the first three caliphs after Muhammad.[8] Ockley's two books on early Islamic history—the second of which was *The History of the Saracens* (1718), completed before his death at age forty-two—are all the more impressive for having been produced in relatively adverse circumstances.[9] Ockley was a Cambridge student of humble background who came to Arabic via Hebrew.[10] Because he was one of a handful of Englishmen able to translate from Arabic, the language ended up determining much of his career. In 1711 he was appointed to Cambridge's Sir Thomas Adams chair of Arabic, founded in 1632.[11] However, the second volume of his history, which focused on the dynastic struggles in the time of ʿAlī, the fourth caliph, and his eventual successor Muʿāwiya, was completed in debtors' prison, of which Ockley wrote: "I have enjoyed more true Liberty, more happy Leisure, and more solid Repose in six Months here, than in thrice the same Number of Years before."[12]

Believing that a history of Muslim expansion would interest a broad audience, Ockley blended vernacular historiography with Arabic scholarship in the tradition of Pococke, and, indeed, his books brought Arab history to the attention of readers outside the scholarly community both in Britain and beyond.[13] He not only made early Islamic history speak English, but also gave it the status of an epic.[14] The books, joined into a single volume, were translated into Dutch in 1741, German in 1745, and French in 1748.[15] They were reprinted in English in 1757 (when a life of Muhammad was added to them), and again in 1847, 1848, 1870, 1873, 1875, 1878, 1890, and 1894.[16]

The Conquest of Syria, Persia and Ægypt made the case that the history of the early Muslims was highly relevant to Europeans. Ockley acknowledged (as Machiavelli already had) that the "Saracen" kingdom was a successor state of the Roman Empire.[17] Yet "Greek and Roman authors" had neglected these events, a state of affairs the Englishman aimed to remedy: "The Arabians . . . have, since the time of Mahomet, [rendered] themselves so very considerable, both by their Arms and Learning, that the understanding of their Affairs seems no less, if not more necessary than the being acquainted with the History of any People whatsoever, who have flourished since the Declension of the Roman Empire."[18] Muslims were, indeed, the "first Ruin of the Eastern Church," that is, the first to weaken the Byzantine (Eastern Christian) Empire, which finally collapsed in 1453 with the fall of Constantinople.[19] It was beyond doubt that Muslims had been great actors in the history of the world: "During [over 1,000 years] Asia and Africa have been the Scene of as great Performances as ever they were in the Time of the Roman Empire, to which that of the Saracens was, in many respects, equal."[20] Like Renaudot, Ockley made it clear that Muslim history intersected with Western history, and that Muslim deeds were equal to those of the Romans and deserved their own *res gestae,* their own narrative account. He expressed "Wonder and Concern" that his predecessors had not seen fit to study the history of the Arabs, a neglect he attributed in part to unwarranted prejudice against them as "meer Barbarians."[21]

To Ockley, the cultural achievements of Muslims were as important as their military deeds. He wished for a "Compleat History of the Affairs of the East" in a Western language, but a *historia literaria* (cultural history) was a particular desideratum: "It would be very well worth observing, how Learning first came in, grew and increas'd among the Saracens; and what Great Men they have had among them; all which would be very well comprehended in a History of the Caliphs or Successors of Mahomet, of which I here present the Reader with a Specimen."[22] Ockley framed his own work as just a small contribution—a specimen, or sample, like Pococke's—to a much larger epic that would trace the progress of learning across the nations; he knew that such an overview could not be accomplished until the details of the dynastic history of Umayyads and Abbasids had been recounted in a European language. What he envisioned was an ambitious program for a new historiography, in which the history of learning would be integrated into broader political and religious contexts—something not so different from the history of manners that Voltaire eventually pursued (see Chapter 6).

The Conquest of Syria and Persia opened the eyes of many readers to a rich and alien history. Ockley's friend J. Hilldrop wrote, "Your Saracenick History is extreamly applauded by the best Judges," and reported that the volume had gained the Archbishop of Canterbury's attention and would surely result in a promotion for Ockley.[23] The author himself recounted some of the reactions to his book: "That it was the strangest Story they ever heard since they were born! They never met with such Folks in their Lives as these Arabians! That they never heard of this Account before, which certainly they must have done of course if any body else had! A Reverend Dignitary asked me, If when I wrote that Book I had not lately been reading the History of Oliver Cromwell!"[24] What exactly the parallel was between the English Civil War and the history of the Muslim conquests is not revealed, but that does not obscure Ockley's main point: the surprise of his contemporaries that the history of the Arabs could be so similar to their own, even if many of the actions of "these Arabians" were remarkable and unlike anything they knew.

Islamic history found its most ardent advocate after Ockley in the German scholar Johann Jacob Reiske, whose career was likewise an improbable one (Figure 14). Born to a tanner in Zörbig, a small town north of Leipzig, Reiske escaped his origins thanks to the teaching of a friendly local pastor and a scholarship to the orphanage school of the Pietist Foundation (Frankesche Stiftung) in Halle. In 1733, at age sixteen, he enrolled at the University of Leipzig, where he developed a passion for Arabic: "A certain unspeakable, ir-resistible lust to learn Arabic, whose origin I myself do not know, took posses-sion of my soul. This burning lust displaced and devoured all other affinities and thoughts. Everything that I could subtract from the essentials of life, and save from my extremely modest assets, I spent on Arabic books."[25] Reiske, who went on to achieve what was then the highest level of Arabic erudition in Eu-rope, was not only a great linguist, he was also a "philosophical" historian: his goal was to recover for European knowledge the history of Muslim peoples and to explain their place in world history. The achievements of this original scholar have been almost completely neglected in English-language scholar-ship.[26] Part of the reason may be that, in spite of his brilliance, Reiske never found a permanent post in a university. After an eight-year stay in Leiden, where he had traveled to work with the famous collection of Arabic manu-scripts, in 1746 he was compelled by financial circumstance to move back to Leipzig, where he once more had to "earn [his] bread with private tutoring, writing books, correcting, translating from other languages into German, and seeking work from scholarly journals."[27] In June 1758 he received the post of headmaster of the Nikolaischule in Leipzig, a famous gymnasium, or grammar school, a position he held until his death.[28] In his final years, however, he soured on Arabic studies, in no small part because they had won him such meager worldly recognition. Of his many intellectual projects, only fragments saw the light of day. Reiske came to believe himself a "martyr of Arabic letters."[29]

His essay "Introduction to Oriental History" (*Prodidagmata*) appeared in 1766, though it was first completed almost twenty years earlier, in August 1747.[30] In the opening sentence he declares that because his topic is the history of Muslims in Asia, Europe, and Africa, it should be called "Muhammedan" history, not "Oriental."[31] He was the first to articulate the need for a designation for Islamic history more specific than the catch-all "Oriental." He felt a responsibility to redress Western ignorance of that history: "Yet the dignity of Muhammedan, or Oriental, history requires that I somewhat praise and commend it, unfairly neglected as it has been by us until now."[32]

Reiske began his vindication of the dignity of "Muhammedan" history by comparing Muslims to the ancient Persians, a people of the classical past who were intimately familiar to Reiske's contemporaries from the Greek historian Herodotus's *Histories,* a founding work of Western historical writing. The Greeks had conceded that the ancient Persians were "great kings," and modern readers of Herodotus "[could] not help but feel admiration" for them, so why did contemporary Europeans not study the Persians of the Muslim period, their successors? In the history of those descendants Reiske perceived "the same dramas enacted on the same stage by the same peoples." When he turned back to Herodotus after his study of modern Persian history, he saw "how much . . . the new Persian empire, the one that [the medieval historian] Abulfeda [Abū'l-Fidā'] shows, agrees with that old one described by Herodotus, how much the peoples are the same until now, in the same provinces, with the same principles of behavior and of civil organization."[33] Reiske used the Persian comparison to make a forceful case that modern Muslims were as classical (or as postclassical) as their Christian counterparts. He argued that adherence to Islam was less influential than their inheritance from antiquity in shaping their "principles of behavior and of civil organization."

To Reiske, the European attitude of immense absorption in the classical past and neglect of other pasts, including the Islamic one, was intellectually inconsistent. His comparisons pointed out that these pasts all belonged to one long history of Eurasian humankind. "We wonder at the rapid progress of the victories of Alexander the Great, greater than anyone might conceive. Yet why do we not wonder at the much greater men than Alexander in the Orient, not just one or another, but several in number, such as Tughril, Gengis Khan, Timur [Tamerlane], two great conquerors of the whole Orient from farthest China to Egypt, of the Pontus and of Russia, or Mehmet the Ottoman (known as al Fateh [Fātiḥ], or the conqueror or Victor)?"[34] The distinction between Alexander the Great and later (Muslim) Eurasian conquerors was untenable. He continued: "We tremble at and boast of the great size of the world of the Romans. Yet we ignore the dynasties of the Orient, which are, if not greater, then certainly not lesser, and which subdued both as many peoples as the Roman dynasty, and the space of as many provinces. Their memory indeed remains obscure until now, because they were victors not as vain as the Greeks and Romans; they were more expert at accomplishing great things worthy of being remembered than at making written records of them, and preferred to strike their contemporaries with the gleam of their weapons, than posterity with the ornament of their words."[35] European interest in Roman history indicated to Reiske that his contemporaries could become equally curious about other significant histories. If Muslims were not as inclined to commemorate their own deeds as the Greeks and Romans had been, they were just as heroic and just as successful at empire building. By implication, Reiske's mediation could compensate for their ostensible lack of vanity.

In sum, Ockley and Reiske advanced forceful and urgent arguments on behalf of the study of the Muslim past. They considered knowing Islamic history to be an imperative for Europeans both because it would enrich Western history and because it was a subject worthy of study for its own sake. Their research programs were largely independent of confessional or even religious concerns. (Indeed, Ockley expressed regret that "so much of the Life of Doctor [Edward] Pocock[e], who could have unlocked to us the Treasuries of the East," had been wasted in the study of theology "out of Compliance to a stupid Generation" and on account of "the Importunity of those perverse Times.")[36] Reiske's suggestion that the subject should be called "Muhammedan history" acknowledged Islamic history's specificity and autonomy. These two historians worked to carve out an intellectual space for the Western study of the history of Muslim Eurasia, a goal that they saw as part of their purview as educated Europeans of the eighteenth century.

Exemplary Princes

In the fourteenth century Petrarch revived the genre of the individual exemplary life, a mainstay of classical historical writing.[37] In antiquity the Greek biographer Plutarch had written the lives of prominent men to offer models for emulation. His *Parallel Lives,* recovered in the late thirteenth century and made available in Latin in the fourteenth and fifteenth, endured as one of the most popular books of the Western tradition.[38] The genre it inspired did not limit itself to lives of political rulers, though they were certainly heavily represented both in Plutarch and in Petrarch and his followers. In posterity's evaluation, what rulers had done to support the arts and sciences—what they encouraged through their patronage—mattered as much as their military exploits, and was indeed a trope of any panegyric.[39]

Biographies of poets, scholars, and princes had formed a major component of d'Herbelot's *Bibliothèque Orientale,* and of its advocacy for Muslim cultural production. Pococke, Renaudot, and Reiske also studied exemplary Muslim rulers and investigated their patronage of the arts and sciences to help explain the cultural flourishing that Muslim societies witnessed just a few centuries after the establishment of Islam.

In his *Specimen Historiæ Arabum* (1650), Pococke reacted against the following comment by the medieval Christian scholar Gregorius Bar Hebraeus, the author of his Arabic source text: "As for the science of Philosophy, God granted those men [the Arabs] nothing at all of it, nor did he make them fit for those studies."[40] Pococke wrote at some length against this slander, arguing that if philosophy was not cultivated until the time of the Abbasid caliphs who ruled from Baghdad, it was not because the minds of the Arabs were unsuited to it: "No one who considered the level at which they cultivated these studies with success thereafter would allow himself to be persuaded of this." The reason for the belated turn to philosophy was the Arab "lifestyle, which was such as not to grant them the time needed for these studies."[41] That is, nomadism was not conducive to the pursuit of the speculative sciences.

Under the Abbasids, the Arabs had shaken off their "former lethargy."[42] If Caliph al-Manṣūr, the second Abbasid caliph, received some credit, al-Maʾmūn, the seventh caliph, was the hero of this development:[43] "Burning to study [philosophy and astronomy], and according them the honor that is their due, he brought together from everywhere major writers of Greece, chosen from the libraries of princes through the intercession of envoys, so as to have them [the writers] on hand. He enticed expert translators to render them into the Arabic tongue by offering rewards, and he exhorted others to read these same writers, and himself was involved in the works of learned men, and cheered them on. Finally, there was no trouble he would not take, if it might contribute to promoting everything to do with the good arts. What worthy endeavors for a prince!"[44] This brief but evocative passage describing the Abbasid translation movement and its particular flowering under Caliph al-Ma'mūn—a famous moment in the history of knowledge—depicts an energetic and passionate *translatio studii*. Pococke's al-Ma'mūn is an ideal prince, enraptured by the pursuit of knowledge and fully involved in shaping its cultivation, whether by mobilizing the resources of his domains or through his own direct input. Pococke saw al-Ma'mūn as an intercultural exemplar, someone who might inspire in modern European readers hopes for their own princes. He recorded a further effect of al-Ma'mūn's patronage: "Thus it came about that throughout all the East and the West, the language of the Arabs spread itself in every direction, and their religion, widely propagated by means of the sword, became known."[45] The spread and endurance of Arabic derived not only from the Muslim conquests, but also from the many scientific and philosophical works that were written in it.

Pococke thought that what had encouraged the Abbasid renaissance of letters was not the religion of Islam, which "sheds not even a dim light on nature"—that is, the Islamic revelation did not offer any scientific insights. He quoted the medieval theologian Ibn Taymiyya's censure of the work of al-Ma'mūn: "God will inflict certain punishment on al-Ma'mūn, who disturbed the piety of the Muhammedans by introducing the Philosophical sciences among them." Recognizing that an opposition to scientific advance was by no means the prerogative of Muslims, or of a particular religious community, he wrote: "This sentence of his will not surprise those who have heard among us little men decreeing audaciously that anything which has to do with the humanities or sciences is inimical to religion, and has to be extirpated from public life by Christians, that to each person his native language suffices, and that any time dedicated to other languages is a complete waste."[46] He argued that Ibn Taymiyya's attitude was equally to be found among Christian "*homunciones*" (little men) and that the progress of learning in any society had to contend with opposition in the name of religion.

To Pococke, the intellectual achievements of the Abbasid renaissance rivaled those of the ancient Greeks. As a result of the patronage of al-Ma'mūn and his successors, "letters advanced by means of zeal and intelligence so that they [the Arabs] showed themselves to be barely inferior to the Greeks." He added, "Of course men excelling in sharpness and diligence did not leave anything in any type of letters unconsidered. Greece had nothing of excellence that they did not make their own, while of what they had not received, they discovered on their own many not less excellent things."[47] While not getting into specifics, Pococke affirmed that the Arabs had recovered all types of ancient letters (a claim perhaps more hyperbolic than empirical, given that Greek poetry and history are not known to have been translated into Arabic).

Pococke sanctioned the notion that more recent Muslim dynasties had been unable to sustain this intellectual tradition, which had ebbed under their guard: "At last these studies declined among them under the barbarous arms of the Turks, and, with their onetime honor, equally they lost their onetime vigor."[48] It is possible that he was not referring solely or primarily to the Ottomans as the cause of a general transformation of Muslim lands and decline of Islamic civilization. He may also have had in mind the Seljuks, who had preceded the Ottomans in invading the Near East, and perhaps even the Mongols.

Half a century later Ockley wrote that the development of Muslim scientific achievements occurred after the early military expansion of Muhammad's successors. Before Muhammad's time, he noted, "Their Learning lay wholly in their Poetry, to which their Genius did chiefly incline them."[49] For the first two centuries after the revelation to Muhammad, "little else [except religion] was minded but War."[50] The reign of Caliph al-Ma'mūn ("Almamôun") had seen the first major efflorescence of intellectual activity: "Learning began to be cultivated to a very great Degree, Mathematicks especially and Astronomy."[51] The lag did not strike Ockley as unusual: "Arms take Place first, and a Government must be well establish'd, before Learning can get room to breath in."[52] He continued: "And in order to promote it, that Noble Caliph spar'd no cost, either to procure such Greek Books as were serviceable to that Purpose, or to encourage Learned Men to the study of them."[53] If these words sound familiar, it is because Pococke had made the same remarks. That Ockley's words are a mere paraphrase of Pococke's Latin is but one sign of the long shadow Pococke's

Specimen Historiæ Arabum had cast; Ockley's vision of the role of the Arabs in the history of letters issued directly from it.[54]

The speed and energy with which the Muslims of Caliph al-Ma'mūn's age had absorbed and outdone the scientific activity of antiquity was remarkable. Ockley wrote: "Their Progress in Learning, after they had once enter'd upon it, seeming no less wonderful than that of their Conquests; for in a few Years time they had Plenty of Translations out of Greek, not only Mathematicians and Astronomers, but Philosophers, Botanists and Physicians. Which Love of Learning was not confin'd to the Eastern Parts, but diffus'd throughout the whole Dominions of the Saracens being first carried into Africa (where they erected a great many Universities) and from then into Spain: so that when Learning was quite lost in these Western Parts, it was restor'd by the Moors, to whom what Philosophy was understood by the Christians was owing."[55] In this depiction, Muslims were as energetic in the pursuit of learning as they had been in the pursuit of military conquest. Their translations of Greek authors had diffused all the way to medieval Spain, where they were absorbed into Latin learning.[56] What had made Western Christians independent of Arabic learning was the revival of Greek learning in the West after the fall of Constantinople.[57]

The Catholic scholar Eusèbe Renaudot is remembered for his research on the Eastern Churches rather than as an Islamic historian, but he, too, tried his hand at writing the life of a Muslim prince, a project that was never published.[58] In his youth Renaudot learned Arabic, Syriac, and Coptic, and toward the end of his life he published a history of the patriarchs of Alexandria and a collection of Eastern liturgies.[59] A well-connected scholar, he was a member of the Académie française and of the Académie des inscriptions et belles-lettres and even served the minister Jean-Baptiste Colbert in a diplomatic capacity. *Ancient Accounts of India and China by Two Muslim Travelers,* published in 1718, provided geographical information from two medieval Arabic sources, showing that his interests ran beyond the confessionally inspired projects that most occupied him.[60]

Among Renaudot's papers now preserved in the Bibliothèque nationale de France are two untitled and unpublished manuscripts on the history of Islam.[61] Their dates are uncertain: they remained in their author's possession until his death in 1720 and may well have continued to be revised until then.

One of them contains a life of Saladin (r. 1174–1193), the valiant Kurdish prince who fought the English king Richard the Lionheart (r. 1189–1199). It is organized by year, like a chronicle (Figure 15).[62] In the introduction Renaudot explained that he was inspired to write about Saladin because of the ruler's merit, "his valor and all his Royal virtues," which were recognized by all parties: "He had the advantage of not being praised solely by his own people, who rank him above all of their great men, but also by the Christians, who have given illustrious testimony of him."[63] This was a traditional historiographical argument: a statement of praise was considered especially creditable if it came from confessional or political enemies.

In Renaudot's opinion, Christian histories provided insufficient detail about the final, inglorious years of the first Christian Kingdom of Jerusalem (1099–1187), gaps he believed he could fill in by consulting Arabic histories. As a Frenchman he had an interest in a history in which a French king, Philip Augustus (r. 1180–1223), had been involved. Above all, however, Saladin represented to him the figure of a "Mahometan Hero."[64] Basing Saladin's history on Islamic sources meant, among other things, finding substantiation of Saladin's setbacks and defeats—which Muslim historians were hardly liable to exaggerate.[65]

Toward the end of his manuscript, Renaudot enumerated Saladin's personal qualities, such as his aversion to luxury: "Often those who came for an audience had trouble recognizing him [as the sultan], so simple were his clothing and manners and without any affectation."[66] Even more impressive were Saladin's forbearance ("It is very difficult to find a more illustrious example of a singular patience and goodness") and his sense of mercy: "His humanity was so great that the Christians themselves give illustrious testimony of it, and if one excepts the inevitable calamities of war, never was a more complaisant enemy seen, nor less harshness in a victorious prince."[67] Renaudot even celebrated Saladin's piety, praising him for being sexually restrained, munificent in his almsgiving, and constant in his prayers, and for inviting "those who passed for best versed in Mahometan theology" to speak on "some point of religion or on the Alcoran" for the spiritual edification of his household.[68]

All in all, Saladin was an exemplary prince: "He performed great deeds of charity, he rewarded virtue, he punished vice, he loved his people and was loved by them like a good father. If one excepts . . . a few . . . things that show that the greatest men living in the darkness of a false religion are not exempt from vices or weaknesses, he must be considered a prince whose history can edify those who seek true greatness."[69] This passage is remarkable in two ways. First, it hews closely to its Islamic sources and repeats its judgments: implicit in "rewarded virtue and punished vice" is the important Islamic precept, "commanding right and forbidding wrong" (al-amr bil-maʿrūf wa'l-nahy ʿan al-munkar).[70] Second, its mention of Saladin's false religion is perfunctory in the extreme. Renaudot's stress falls on Saladin as an exemplar who can instruct Muslims and Christians alike. "A prince controlled in his manners, always occupied with the happiness of his peoples, finally a conqueror whose victories were not like those floods of blood whose dire memory is the praise of the first heroes of antiquity. This history will perhaps offer a more perfect model than do those of those famous pagans whose life has been sullied by all sorts of crimes."[71] Renaudot's treatment of Saladin made explicit what had been implicit in Pococke's portrait of al-Maʾmūn: that a Muslim could be a role model for Christian readers. Using Simon's comparison of Muslims with the pagans of antiquity, Renaudot pointed out that because Islam is closer to Christianity than to ancient paganism, its source materials could provide even more edification than classical ones. On the shifting scales of what it meant to be civilized in France in the early eighteenth century, Saladin's exceptional conduct, less violent than that of the heroes of antiquity, made him a more appropriate model for a modern prince.[72]

In 1747, aiming to gain the patronage of the crown prince of the Electorate of Saxony, Friedrich Christian, Johann Jacob Reiske produced a short survey, the *Dissertatio de Principibus Muhammedanis Qui aut Eruditione aut ab Amore Literarum et Literatorum Claruerunt* (Dissertation on Muhammedan princes who shone for their erudition or for their love of letters and of lettered men).[73] Its point was to show that "oriental history . . . is very worthy of the study of an honest mind, and does not deserve any less than European history to be taught publicly in universities."[74] Befitting a book written for a prince rather than for fellow scholars, the *Dissertatio* was light of touch, so as not to tax its noble recipient.[75]

The first portrait in this gallery of Muslim princes represented ʿAlī, the cousin of Muhammad. Reiske praised him as "a man equal in erudition to Augustus, in mercy and good will to Trajan, in the cultivation of philosophy and piety to Marcus Aurelius the philosopher, and in fortitude and the patronage of just causes, as well as in the sad manner of his end equal to Pompey. He was, moreover, in eloquence superior to all of them; the Orient did not see a prince more illustrious in virtues than he. What a great man he was can be perceived from the encomium spoken by his Julius Caesar himself, that is, his adversary and emulator in matters of sovereignty, Moawijah [Muʿāwiya, who succeeded ʿAlī in the caliphate]."[76] Along with comparing ʿAlī to three Roman emperors and even ranking him above them in eloquence—and, by implication, in his total combination of attributes—Reiske offered a narrative analogy between the fate of Pompey, Julius Caesar's friend and competitor who was murdered in Egypt, and that of ʿAlī, who was praised by Muʿāwiya even though Muʿāwiya, the governor of Syria, did not recognize ʿAlī's authority and his resistance eventually undermined ʿAlī's power.[77] This analogy was meant not only to make the history of the Arabs easier to remember, but also to endow it with the same heroic qualities as the political history of Rome. Reiske's admiration of ʿAlī's oratorical skills was based on the numerous collections of sayings attributed to him, most of which had been composed by Shiite scholars: "I found even his pithy sayings, and his entire speeches, so powerful in their sinews and energy, that they earned him the right to be celebrated as the Demosthenes of the Arabs."[78] Coming from Reiske this praise—Demosthenes was one of the most celebrated Athenian orators—held special weight because he was not only an Arabist but also a scholar of classical Greek who went on to edit many of the Greek orators.[79] He held that it was possible to compare, evaluate, and appreciate oratory across languages and cultures, an assessment few were qualified to dispute. His notion that Arabic or "Oriental" aesthetics were similar to classical ones was far from mainstream, however.[80]

Among the Abbasid princes, Reiske focused especially on the caliph al-Ma'mūn, "he who is famous among our peoples."[81] "This man arranged for the writings of Aristotle, Themistius, Porphyry, Hippocrates, Galen, Dioscorides, Euclid, and others to be turned into the Arabic language, and partly even into Syriac. For Muhammedan writers assert that he was warned by a specter of Aristotle that appeared to him in a dream to make his philosophy familiar to the Saracenic peoples."[82] Reiske did not take al-Ma'mūn's dream of Aristotle—the founding myth of the Abbasid translation movement—at face value. Rather, he saw it as a "pious fraud" that al-Ma'mūn had employed in order to endear classical literature to his people. He added that Caliph ʿUmar had, a century before al-Ma'mūn, introduced a classical work of medicine "recovered by chance in a captured city, by means of a similar pious fraud."[83]

Such tricks were necessary, he concluded, when dealing with "a wild, unpolished people, lacking in culture, and, what is more, superstitious."[84]

Unlike other followers of Pococke, who simply repeated his description of al-Maʾmūn's achievements and patronage, Reiske provided new and substantial information. For example, under the auspices of the caliph, who was "eager to know the true extent of the earth's surface," the "Schakerid [Shākir] brothers set up geometrical observations in the plains of Sengara [Sinjār]."[85] (To be sure, Pococke himself had studied Abū'l-Fidāʾ, Reiske's main source, and incorporated some excerpts into his *Specimen*.)

The *Dissertatio* also introduced dynasties and princes unfamiliar to non-specialists, with a special focus on the Ayyubids (the descendants of Saladin). An Ayyubid whom Reiske particularly celebrated was Abū'l-Fidāʾ, one of his main sources, whose works he planned to translate over the next two years.[86] Concluding the *Dissertatio* with an elegant parallel between the Muslim princes and the local prince whose patronage he hoped to win, Reiske remarked that the history of the Muslims contained much more than his brief sketch could provide—"Saracen history exhibits a great many men excelling in erudition and patrons of the erudite"—but his ability to recover their histories largely hinged on the generosity of the Saxon princes, "under whose auspices and protection happy letters may raise their head, and good temples of the mind may flourish, and this especially in Leipzig."[87] (As it turned out, the court of Saxony, at Dresden, rewarded him with the title of professor and a yearly pension of 100 Taler. This proved insufficient to support him, and neither the medical nor the philosophical faculty ever admitted him to their ranks. His inaugural lecture was also his final one.)[88]

The *Dissertatio* shows how earnestly—one might even say naively—Reiske read his sources. Trusting the chains of oral transmission through which the wise and eloquent sayings of ʿAlī had come down, he attributed them all to ʿAlī himself. This trust extended to Abū'l-Fidāʾ's portrait of the achievements of his Ayyubid ancestors. Moreover, biographies of illustrious men had precedents both in European humanist historiography (the Latin tradition of *De viris illustribus*) and in Islamic historiography (the tradition of biographical dictionaries of scholars), and Reiske exploited this convergence to emphasize the shared cultural and intellectual commitments of good pagans, Christians, and Muslims.

In sum, Pococke, Ockley, Renaudot, and Reiske believed that the eager patronage of Muslim princes, and not the revelation to Muhammad, was responsible for the intellectual achievements of Muslim scholars. Pococke decisively argued that even though Islamic revelation did not prompt the intellectual flowering among Muslim peoples, the religion presented no major hindrance to such a flowering. Although there was opposition to learning among Muslims, that prejudice could be found in all societies. Renaudot's exemplary biography celebrated Saladin's patronage and cast him as a more suitable model for modern rulers than the bloodthirsty rulers of antiquity. For all these scholars, the study of Muslim patronage was essential to the development of a full history of human efforts to advance the arts and sciences.

Both Ockley and Reiske located the heyday of Islamic civilizational achievement in the Middle Ages; in their eyes, modern Muslim dynasties like the Ottomans were not the equal of their predecessors. In this they parted ways with d'Herbelot and Galland, who took a favorable view of more recent Muslim achievement. Overall, however, these historiographic projects emphasized convergences between Christianity and Islam. The goal was to incorporate Islamic history into the history of the revival of learning in the West that had begun in the Middle Ages, and which Europeans understood as the origin of the Renaissance and of their own modernity. At the same time, the study of exemplary Muslim princes also demonstrated that Muslim history contained morally inspiring examples just as much as classical history did.

The emphasis on personal patronage was a child of its time. Modern scholarship on the Greco-Arabic translation movement under the Abbasids has set aside the notion that it arose only because of enlightened rulers such as al-Ma'mūn. Scholars now believe that the movement was an effort too complex and wide-ranging for it to have been the product of the will of a ruler or of a handful of rulers.[89] As for al-Ma'mūn's dream about Aristotle, they agree that it was invented "for the purposes of propaganda," which was, as we saw, how Reiske had understood it.[90]

Reiske and others followed their Arabic sources closely in celebrating princes as the heroes of the translation movement, a view that may have had particular resonance in their own lives. They could hardly avoid perceiving similarities between their world and the one they were studying. In the seventeenth and eighteenth centuries, Europe was home to largely rural and illiterate populations; a clergy overall opposed to the advancement of learning, which it saw as inimical to religion; and princely patrons who shared the ideal of knowledge production with scholars, and who were often the latter's only hope. It is little wonder that European scholars of Arabic read this predicament into their source material and identified so strongly with the quest for knowledge in Islamic history.

Sources of Knowledge

The first task of any would-be historian of the Islamic past was to locate appropriate manuscripts. The University Library at Cambridge offered nothing that could support Simon Ockley's interest in the history of the Muslim conquests, so in 1701, and again in 1706, he traveled to the Bodleian Library at Oxford, the best repository of Arabic manuscripts in England. Each trip lasted only six weeks, "inclusive of the Delays upon the Road"; Ockley worked assiduously (the local scholar Thomas Hearne called him "somewhat crazed").[91] During his time in Oxford, he found and copied what appeared to be an account of the conquest of Syria by the historian al-Wāqidī (d. 823), which would form the basis of his *Conquest* (Figure 16).[92]

The young Reiske had to go even farther afield to find the material he needed. In 1738 he abandoned any prospect of advancement at Leipzig in favor of a mad gamble: traveling to Leiden, in the Netherlands, in hopes of studying the Arabic manuscripts in that university town. As he later put it, he "hungered for the delectable dishes of the legatum Warnerianum [of Leiden]."[93] Reiske had no money and spoke neither Dutch nor French.[94] Once there, he had to overcome many practical and financial obstacles, but eventually managed to pursue scholarship. Under the direction of the Leiden professor of Arabic, Albert Schultens, he published the first European edition and translation of a pre-Islamic Arabic ode.[95] He also copied the manuscripts that would serve as the foundation of his historical research in Leipzig in the following decades.[96]

How did these scholars choose their sources from among all those available in Oxford and Leiden? Islamic historiography includes a variety of genres, from universal history to Prophetic biography (*sīra*), from histories of conquests (*futūḥ*) to histories of specific dynasties and regions (such as Egypt), and collections of biographies of poets, saints, mystics, and martyrs. Researchers looked for sources that had been judged most authoritative by their European predecessors and, especially, for those that held high status within the native historiographical tradition. They also prized material that would give them the most value in terms of coverage, such as universal histories, which offered a broad view, and compilations, reference works, and anthologies like those d'Herbelot had used. And they tended to privilege sources whose forms they recognized; a familiar-seeming genre was more likely to gain attention than one forbiddingly foreign.

Ockley attributed the history he chose, the *Futūḥ al-Shām* (Conquests of Syria), to the early Islamic historian al-Wāqidī ("Abu Abdo'llah Mohammed Ebn Omar Alwakidi"), who, he conceded, lived "above two hundred Years after the Matter of Fact which he relates."[97] (In fact, the historical al-Wāqidī, who lived from about 747 or 748 to 823, was born just over a century after the events that he recounted.)[98] But Ockley noted that "the Particulars relating to the first rise of Kingdoms and Empires are generally obscure."[99] For this reason, in such circumstances one had to make do with later narratives, and "rest satisfied with the best Account we can get."[100] He added that "[al-Wāqidī] is chiefly valuable for this, that we find Materials in him which we have no where else."[101] In spite of these disclaimers, Ockley admired how his author reported evidence, and particularly how he cited the chain of authorities (*isnād*) behind a given piece of information.[102]

As it happens, Ockley's source, the *Futūḥ al-Shām*, was not written by al-Wāqidī, but merely attributed to him. Ockley knew that the manuscript had been copied in the fifteenth century, but he believed the original to be much older.[103] It was eventually established that the *Futūḥ al-Shām* was compiled during the Crusades, making it no older than the Arabic histories that had already been published in Europe in the seventeenth century.[104] If Ockley's achievement turned out to be less significant in this respect than he had believed it to be, the medieval forgery that took him in had also fooled native Arabic readers. A copyist had attributed it to al-Wāqidī to increase its value, and this claim was believed and repeated by many other copyists (the work survives in a number of different European libraries).[105]

Ockley relied mainly on pseudo-Wāqidī, but he also drew on manuscripts he had copied in Oxford from the Laud, Pococke, and Huntington collections. These included Abū'l-Fidā''s history, Ibn Khallikān's biographical dictionary, and a number of other sources.[106] In addition he incorporated a significant amount of material from printed works, especially d'Herbelot's *Bibliothèque Orientale;* he could read neither Persian nor Turkish.[107]

Reiske's broad reading gave him genuine purchase on his source materials and on their merits and demerits, and his critical notes demonstrate an uncommon Arabic erudition. His main authority was the early fourteenth-century Syrian historian and Ayyubid prince Abū'l-Fidāʾ.[108] Born in Damascus in 1273, Abū'l-Fidāʾ governed as prince of Ḥamāh, in Syria, from 1310 until his death in 1331. His scholarly reputation rested on two books, one of which was his universal history, the *Mukhtaṣar fī akhbār al-bashar* (The concise history of mankind; or literally, The abridgment of the accounts of mankind), which goes up to 1329 (Figure 17). It too had its weaknesses. In its earlier sections it draws heavily on a history written by Ibn al-Athīr (d. 1233), who himself had drawn on earlier histories, especially the great tenth-century sixteen-volume *History of the Prophets and Kings,* by al-Ṭabarī, which is written in annalistic form and goes from the creation up to 915. But Ibn al-Athīr had omitted or glossed the difficult passages and eliminated the *isnāds,* or chains of transmission.[109] In short, Abū'l-Fidāʾ was a very indirect source for the early years of Islam, which he could record only at many removes. The *Mukhtaṣar*'s later sections relate the events of Abū'l-Fidāʾ's own time, and there he put his own experience of political life to good use in explaining the corruption, bad management, or weaknesses of leaders that led to military and political failures.[110]

Interestingly, Reiske was not very impressed with Abū'l-Fidāʾ as a historian or even as a source of information, believing there was nothing to learn from him (or from any Arabic writer) about antiquity that was not to be found in classical authors.[111] But then the early history of the Arabs was fraught with difficulty: "The deeds of the Arabs before Muhammad lie utterly buried in deep night, with confused indications of the dates, or none at all."[112] Reiske claimed that Abū'l-Fidāʾ did little to illuminate many domains of history because he was a creature of his own time, when "everyone who considered himself dyed with the color of letters wrote a chronicle." All these histories, which began with the origins of humankind and ended in the time of their authors, had a similar weakness and strength: "As slender as they are in their beginnings, so they are full in their final sections, once their authors reach their own memories and those of their fathers." He valued Abū'l-Fidāʾ most as a historian of more recent times.[113] (A further limitation of the *Mukhtaṣar* is its geographical scope, which is circumscribed to the Near East, the home of Abū'l-Fidāʾ, but Reiske, who shared this bias in favor of the early homeland of Muslims as opposed to the much broader territories they occupied in his time, does not remark on it.)

Given all these weaknesses, why was Reiske drawn to Abū'l-Fidāʾ? For one thing, Abū'l-Fidāʾ was a known and approved authority. Others before Reiske had published excerpts from the *Mukhtaṣar,* including Pococke, d'Herbelot, Marracci, and Ockley.[114] However, "all of these learned men whom I mentioned did nothing more than report single sentences or tiny fragments in Latin or their own vernacular language, and wove these into their own writings."[115] Also, two more of Reiske's predecessors—Gagnier and Albert Schultens—had edited some sections of the *Mukhtaṣar.*[116] Reiske wanted his contribution to be a complete edition of a history that had struck so many as compelling (Figure 18).[117]

In contrast to Ockley and Reiske, Renaudot had the good fortune to live and work in Paris, a city full of resources for readers of Arabic manuscripts. (Moreover, like d'Herbelot he had also visited Florence and seen the Oriental manuscripts there.)[118] He drew on published sources and unpublished ones that his fellow researchers had cited in their work, including the writings of Ibn Khallikān, al-Nuwayrī, and Abū'l-Fidāʾ. He consulted materials that d'Herbelot had used, such as the Persian history *Lubb al-tawārīkh* (Gilbert Gaulmin had already worked on this) and the verse of the tenth-century poet al-Mutanabbī.[119] His turning to these sources was no coincidence; Renaudot was so close to d'Herbelot that he inherited many of the latter's manuscripts upon his death.[120]

To summarize, Reiske and his forebears were deeply dependent on Arabic historians, whom they had to trust if they were to write the history of Muslim peoples. At the same time, these sources seemed unreliable in many ways, and moreover they differed in both form and focus from the classical sources that Europeans considered the gold standard of historiography. In spite of these hindrances, and of grand ambitions to attain a synoptic view of Islamic history, in the end European scholars of Arabic followed their chosen authorities quite closely.

How to Write Islamic History

Arabic and Greek historiography developed independently of one another. The Arabic tradition arose from the custom of collecting first-person testimonies of the sayings and deeds of Muhammad and of his companions, and only

later flourished as large-scale narrative composition.[121] There were undoubtedly some similarities between how Muslims and Greeks wrote history, but
the Greek model was the one that Europeans deliberately revived in the Renaissance. Although Arabic historical writing was kindred in some ways to its
European counterpart, in other ways it was very different, a situation that lent
itself to significant mistranslation.[122]

Ockley lamented that the virtues of classical Greek historiography had
not been transmitted to the Arabs: "Had they, after having taken the Pains to
learn the Greek Tongue, with equal Care applied themselves to the Historians,
as they did to the Philosophers; and studied Herodotus, Thucydides, Xeno-
phon, and such other Masters of correct Writing as that Language could have
afforded them; we might have expected from them a Succession of Historians
worthy to write those great Actions which have been perform'd among them.
But they never turn'd their Thoughts that way, studying Greek only for the
sake of the Sciences, and not valuing either that or any other Language in respect of their own."[123] To Ockley, this failure to emulate the Greek historians
resulted in poor "Propriety of Expression" along with a lack of "Justness and
Exactness (not only with respect to the Choice of Materials, but to the Composition)," characteristics that could have been achieved only by studying
"such Authors as are excellent that way."[124]

Ockley's critique of Arabic historiography helped to justify his own venture
of historical writing: because of the weaknesses that he diagnosed he could not
simply translate an existing Arabic history. In spite of his "great Esteem . . . for
the Eastern learning . . . our Arabick Historians" told "things after a careless
manner," reporting the "trifling" alongside the important, and giving stylistic
virtuosity undue importance: "jingling upon Words, and to show the Copious-
ness of their Language, and Variety of Expression, spinning out a slender Matter
of Fact into a long Story."[125] In his view, the great difference in style—if not in
substance—between Arabic and Western historical writing made the former very
difficult for Western readers to appreciate; hence the usefulness of an interme-
diary such as himself. For example, one stylistic challenge was the chains of oral
transmission (*isnād*) that Arab historians used to evaluate the reliability of a given
item of information. Ockley admired the practice, but decided he had to leave it
out of his history "because it is such a different way from what we are us'd to."[126]

The idea of writing an original narrative history of Islam was not a novelty.
In fact, it was coeval with the desire to translate the Qur'an and to give an

account of Islam's expansion and appeal.[127] Numerous writers had already composed the history of more recent Muslim polities, such as the Ottomans, often writing in vernacular languages.[128] The difference was that writers like Renaudot and Ockley wrote narratively about material drawn from original Arabic source material. In composing their own histories based on these sources, they paralleled a change in how classical history was being written. Beginning in the sixteenth century, the ambition to write original histories of ancient Rome had grown, in part inspired by archaeological and epigraphic finds that offered information independent of literary sources. Eventually the same ambition seized hold of the field of Greek historical scholarship as well.[129]

In his second volume, *The History of the Saracens,* published a decade after the first, Ockley expanded his view of how Arabic source materials should be handled by European scholars. The Arabs' psychological makeup—"the Humour of that Enthusiastick Nation"—had to be reflected in the way their history was written.[130] To write of them "in such a Stile as becomes the Sedateness and Gravity of the Greeks and Romans, would be very unsuitable and most unnatural." This would be tantamount to dressing them up in inappropriate clothes: "In such a Case you put them in a Dress which they would no more thank you for than a Roman Senator would for a long Periwig, or Socrates for a pair of silk stockings." The "Genius and Humour" of the Arabs—their cultural specificity—needed to be preserved in translation: "It is most certain, that the nearer you bring a Man that is singular to the rest of Mankind, the farther you remove him from himself, and destroy the very Being of his Singularity."[131]

Ockley's historicist sense of the cultural specificity of different historical epochs and of the inappropriateness of translating them all into the same terms explained his decision to "let them [that is, 'the Arabians'] tell their own story in their own way." He added that he had "followed them so close that if they themselves were to arise from the dead, they should confess that, according to my poor Ability and small Skill in that copious and difficult Language, I had done them Justice."[132] The classical style of writing history—which, to Ockley, was exemplified by the Roman historian Livy—was too smooth and eloquent to be true to life: "Nothing must be inserted that falls beneath the Dignity of History; whereby it must of Necessity oftentimes happen, that a great deal of Nature is lost."[133] The student of nature was to stick to the facts, as odd, diverse, or disunited as they might be.

Unadorned directness was, in the end, a recommendation of truthfulness: "Let Livy make Speeches for his People, and Tacitus invent Politicks, it is the Glory of our Arabick Historians to represent the naked Truth as handed down from their Ancestors in its native Simplicity. So that as much as we are exceeded by other Authors in their elaborate Expression, and the Strength and Artifice of their Composition, so much at least do we hope to exceed them in the unaffected Plainness and Sincerity of our Relation."[134] In this way Ockley turned a liability—the Arab historians' stylistic otherness—into a virtue.[135] His claim about the simple honesty of the Arab historians cannot but strike a reader of our time as somewhat naive. He placed immense trust in the authority of his sources. Yet there was no reason to assume, as he did, that the Arab historians were narrating the unadorned truth.

Examining the history of the Muslim conquests also raised the question of how to make appropriate judgments across cultures. In the second volume of *The History of the Saracens,* Ockley reflected on his readers' surprise at the behavior of the "Arabians." What seemed extravagant to English eyes, he explained, was the result of the warm climate and the nomadism of the Arabs.[136] He warned against scoffing at customs that might seem "very odd and ridiculous." For it was precisely such strangeness that revealed "the People concerning whom we write," he wrote, begging his readers to account for distance. Laughter at cultural differences was an ignorant reaction: "The reason of our Laughter is the difference of their Manners, which is childish. For this Reason it is that Ignorants laugh at Scholars; Fools at Wise Men; Boys at old Ones; Atheists and Debauchees at Persons of Virtue and Religion."[137] Appealing to his readers' worldliness and humanity, he urged them to accept the medieval Muslims, who differed from them, but not in ways that made them any less dignified or worthy of interest.[138]

Ockley and Renaudot created original narrative accounts, whereas others, including Reiske and his nineteenth-century successors, chose the still-valid option that Pococke had practiced: the edition and Latin translation of Arabic historical texts.[139] Reiske's appraisal of Arabic historiography did not fundamentally differ from Ockley's, but he suspected that readers might be disappointed by Abū'l-Fidā''s history if confronted with it in its entirety. Abū'l-Fidā', after all, was not Livy or Tacitus, but a Muslim chronicler, from whom one could not expect the style of classical writers: "If it [Abū'l-Fidā''s book] seems choppy, which, I for my part, willingly admit, and you can add

laughable, if you wish, the man is to be evaluated not on the basis of our traditions [*moribus*] and the principles of our studies [*studiis*], but on the basis of
his own and those of his compatriots, for whose benefit he wrote."[140] Reiske
argued that Abū'l-Fidā''s work should be read as a source for empirical information that "you seek elsewhere in vain." Not only had Western historians
failed to "discover and record in writing" many things "about the inner provinces of the Orient," they had also failed to do justice to Islamic history, which
"they ought to have shown better, more grandly and splendidly."[141] By implication, the infelicity of style of which Reiske complained was to be tolerated
for the sake of the knowledge that could be gained by reading Arabic histories, as Ockley had also argued.

In sum, Ockley and Reiske trusted their Arabic sources, assuming that
they afforded faithful accounts of the events they described. Just as the European scholars of the Qur'an relied on Islamic commentaries to understand its
meanings, Ockley and Reiske placed great faith in the native sources they
consulted and largely avoided second-guessing them, even though those sources
did not correspond to the aesthetic canons of Western historical writing. Neither Ockley nor Reiske resolved the status of the Arabic histories: they were
treated, in our terminology, both as primary and as secondary sources. The
Arabic historiographic tradition was autochthonous; the highly elaborate
works with complex rhetorical effects produced by Arabic historians were
certainly not naive witness reports, yet at the same time they were unclassical
in a fundamental way. European scholars believed that the Arabs had incurred
a serious deficit by not translating authors like Thucydides and Herodotus, a
loss that not only occasioned stylistic shortcomings but also made them less
rigorous and less attentive to the rules of historical evidence. Generic and stylistic differences seem to have been Ockley's main motivation for penning his
own history of the Arab conquests. However, in the final analysis, this disapproval of style did not extend to the content that he and Reiske derived from
their native sources.

Depending on a single authority, as Ockley did with pseudo-Wāqidī's account of the conquest of Syria, and as Reiske did with Abū'l-Fidā', was not
regarded, however, as the ultimate ideal for historical writing, even by Ockley
and Reiske, who saw this dependence as provisional. (Ockley referred to his
Conquest of Syria as a "small Beginning," hoping it would inspire further work
in the field.)[142] After reading the first volume of the *History of the Saracens,* in

1708, Humphrey Prideaux, author of a life of Muhammad, wrote to Ockley, his mentee: "I received your kind present and have read it over. I do heartily thank you for it but wish you had had a better author to bestow your pains upon. The True way to write the Saracen History is to make a Collection out of all their writers[.] You may continue such a Common place by way of an-nalls [*sic*] where you may insert every thing as it comes in your way and when your Collection is full then you may digest the whole into what method you please and I think there are materialls enough to be gathered together to make a very good History of those people and the Empire which they erected."[143]

In part Prideaux's reproach was influenced by the fact that his protegé Ockley had ignored his advice, which was to combine Byzantine Greek sources along with Arabic ones and make them agree. In Ockley's opinion, the Greek sources were worthless because they did not sufficiently investigate or explain the great transformation of Eurasia wrought by the rise of Islam: "What lame Accounts must we then expect from those who compile Histories of the Saracens out of the Byzantine Historians?"[144]

In his sequel of 1718 Ockley admitted that he had initially intended to integrate Byzantine Greek and Arabic accounts in this second volume, but that the task had proved impossible because of the lack of overlap between the chroniclers writing in each language.[145] "A Man might as well undertake to write the History of France for the time, out of our [English] News-Papers, as to give an account of the Arabians from Christian Historians."[146] He resolved the conundrum by focusing exclusively on the Arabic-language historians, concluding that they "are the most likely to give the best Account of Things performed among themselves."[147] Moreover, he conceded that he had been unable to integrate all the evidence that would have been desirable from such diverse sources as Qur'anic commentary, Arabic poetry and its annotations, dictionaries, coins, and inscriptions.[148] Even so, *The History of the Saracens* relied on multiple sources, including (impressively) a fragment of al-Ṭabari's great history ("the Livy of the Arabians"), as well as some others almost equally venerable: Ibn al-Athīr's *Kāmil*, Yāqūt's geographic *Mu'jam al-buldān*, Jāmī's *Nafaḥāt al-Uns,* along with Abū'l-Fidā' and Ibn Khallikān.[149] (Much of this research had been made possible by a five-month stay in Oxford.)[150]

The idea of a "collection" of histories was not only Prideaux's. In the manuscript cited at the outset of this chapter, Renaudot advocated the same thing, and even recommended starting from Islamic collections. An "epitome of general history" could be translated from Arabic or Persian and followed by a translation of "Cond Emir" (Khwāndamīr), whose history was convenient because it gathered "all that is best in the ancient Arab authors." Once again, European scholars were willing to take the shortcuts that their Muslim predecessors offered. By selecting a few authorities for each century of Islam and for each Muslim empire, and supplementing these with material drawn from such reference works as Ibn Khallikān's biographical dictionary, Renaudot thought that one could constitute "a perfect body of history all the way up to the time of the first Crusades."[151] These shortcuts were all the more useful because Renaudot's interests did not run to the fine grain of the early conquests: "It is difficult in translating authors [of histories focused on the early periods of Islam] to avoid tiresome details about miracles of Prophets, and superstitions whose exact knowledge is not very useful. It will be enough to choose a few that are accurate, as there is a sufficient number of them."[152] In other words, Renaudot envisioned a work that would draw on a variety of Arabic and Persian histories, choosing a few reliable ones for each period and place, and combining them into an interconnected general history. The purpose would be less to get the intricate particulars of each historical episode right than to paint a broad canvas affording a sense of the whole of Islamic history from Muhammad's revelation to the present.

Using multiple authorities to achieve an ideal history would depend on an accurate assessment of each source's virtues. Renaudot cannily weighed the utility of different Muslim historians:

> It will therefore be necessary to employ Turkish books, which are original for this subject, whereas concerning earlier times, one must consider them but poor copies. There are some general histories in each [Oriental] language that contain pretty exactly both ancient and modern histories, such as the works of Abulfeda [Abū'l-Fidāʾ], Nuiri [al-Nuwayrī], Ibn Chekena [Ibn al-Shiḥna] and several others whom one could usefully translate; but it must be noted that Arab historians are ordinarily not very exact about the affairs of Central Asia; that the Persians describe these matters more exactly, but are accordingly less exact than the Arabs concerning the affairs of Syria and Egypt. The history of Africa is very obscure; and few authors have illuminated it, because Africa has almost always been controlled by local princes, who did not have any commerce with the other Mahometan princes.[153]

In this show of expertise, Renaudot advocated consulting Persian and Turkish historians along with Arabic ones. His idea of a "collection" of histories was not to assemble a series of accounts of the same events but instead to gather complementary histories that could sit alongside one another and together offer an overall view of the subject.

Renaudot, who believed that the origins of Islam were not the only valid object of historical inquiry, was more interested in a later period—"This time of the Crusades is a significant epoch in Oriental history"[154]—and recommended for translation some histories that covered the fall of the Crusader Empire of Jerusalem: "The most exact is that of Makrizi, which begins a few years before Saladin, and contains the history of the majority of the sultans of Egypt known as Mamluks. One can add to this history several other particular histories of Egypt and of Syria. Then, with the aid of a few modern histories, one can continue Oriental history until the establishment of the Ottoman house."[155] As Renaudot imagined it, a general Oriental history would contain glosses on details that might be obscure to the general reader: "One will add to each translation some short notes [marques] drawn from Mahometan authors to clarify the main historical facts, customs, manners, and in general all that cannot be known by those who have not made a particular study of this history."[156] Likewise, it would contain material from Greek, Latin, and even medieval European vernacular writers, and would include a glossary of Islamic titles and offices, a geographic index, and chronological conversion tables that would explain the concordance of Islamic and Christian calendars.[157] The work would also draw on coins and inscriptions and would be preceded by a "general preface, which might serve this entire body of history."[158]

Renaudot envisioned the project as a collective enterprise. He had plenty of examples for such initiatives, including the Magdeburg Centuries, an ecclesiastical history produced collectively in late sixteenth-century Magdeburg, Germany, and the work of the Bollandists, the Jesuit hagiographers who began publishing their lives of saints in 1643.[159] As he imagined the project, it would draw on the writings of many Muslim historians, and would require several European scholars to work in concert.

Reiske, too, believed that working from multiple sources was the ideal way to create a history. In his *Annales Moslemici,* he announced his plan to compare Abū'l-Fidā's *Concise History of Mankind* with other historical narratives in order to establish agreements and discrepancies, and promised that he would add material from outside sources. He concluded, "I shall take care, that the commentaries, with God's help, might appear useful and full of material that is still fresh, which might kindle the ardor of souls to study Oriental history (a subject as serious and distinguished, as it is shamefully held in contempt and neglected), if it can be done."[160] The publication of the full Abū'l-Fidā' never got off the ground; the Latin *Annales Moslemici* was the larger part of what Reiske ever printed.[161] Even though there was broad agreement about how such a history should ideally be compiled, doing so posed challenges too significant to be properly overcome.

Conclusion

For all their differences, Pococke, Renaudot, Ockley, and Reiske struck a number of similar notes: they compared Muslims to the pagan subjects of ancient history; they believed that Islamic history was translatable; and they perceived a golden age in Islamic intellectual production that was related to the patronage of enlightened rulers. All of them compared ancient paganism to medieval Islam in order to create a conceptual space for the serious study of Islamic history. Arguing that the Christian assimilation of Greek and Roman history and the rejection of the Muslim past had been more or less arbitrary, Renaudot and Reiske laid out reasons for preferring Saladin to Alexander and ʿAlī to Augustus. Ockley recognized in the heroics of the Muslim conquerors military values of courage and honor similar to those of the ancients. Overall, pagan antiquity's established authority served as the vehicle through which the history of Muslim peoples could be brought into the stronghold of European high culture.

These comparisons breathed life into the heroes of Islamic history. Renaudot's Saladin was as tangible as any protagonist of classical history and possessed even more civility. Reiske humanized men such as ʿAlī and Muʿāwiya by presenting their motives and virtues as fundamentally akin to those of Augustus, Pompey, and Julius Caesar. European scholars recognized that Islamic contributions to the sciences, philosophy, and arts and letters were rooted in the same values as Western ones and were pursued out of a common commitment to the advancement of civilization.

Islamic works that most resembled European ones, such as universal histories, were translated and studied earlier and more fully than those that seemed stranger or more marginal, such as the histories of the killings of holy men. Points of convergence were emphasized at the expense of the peculiarities of Islamic historical writing, although these were not entirely glossed over. Ockley and Reiske both begged their readers' indulgence for the style of Muslim historians, so unlike that of classical writers, explaining that to appreciate another people's history one had to take into consideration differences in place, time, and culture. In addition, Ockley enjoined his readers to appreciate that the manners of the Arabs were necessarily different from their own. Though the project of studying Islamic history relied on analogy, it also led its practitioners to grapple seriously with how to make sense of cultural difference. Should Islamic history be judged by the same standard as Christian history? Or did the actions of Muslims and their way of recording them demand a different standard that was truer to their time and place?

In the effort to make a case for the study of Islamic history, mere resemblance and analogy were arguments not nearly as compelling as genetic connection. As powerful as the comparison with classical antiquity was, it raised the question of what to make of the least classical aspects of the Islamic heritage. The foreignness of Arabic historiography and poetry was perceived to derive from the fact that Greek books in these domains had not been translated into Arabic. For this reason, and perhaps surprisingly to us today, Islam as a civilization was harder to assimilate than Islam as a religion. The religion of Islam had genetic connections to Judaism and Christianity, so the analogies were grounded in those relationships. Islamic scientific contributions were unequivocally heir to Greek science, and for that reason entirely uncontroversial. But Islamic historical writing and poetry could not be connected genealogically to any classical achievement. Thus, studying these genres pushed European scholars into developing forms of historicism and relativism: into arguing, as both Ockley and Reiske did, that what was fitting for the desert Arabs was not fitting for sedentary Europeans, and vice versa.

Another commonality among the European historians profiled here was their focus on the early centuries of Islam. They regretted the (purported) passing of the Muslim commitment to the secular sciences and came up with various theories about what caused its demise: the Mongol invasions that ended the Abbasid era or the hegemony of the Ottomans, forever associated in Europe with the pillaging of Constantinople in 1453. Although d'Herbelot and Galland had praised Ottoman cultural and intellectual life, the general tendency in the generations that followed was to deprecate contemporary Islamic intellectual achievements (even as an Ottoman writer such as Kātib Çelebī was widely exploited).

All analogies break down at some point. Eventually the intellectual achievements of Muslims—and their work as historians and poets—would come to be judged as not classical enough. At a later date, the ways in which Islamic civilization was unclassical would be used as an argument against its civilizational achievements tout court, as we shall see in Chapter 6. But before that happened, Pococke, Ockley, Renaudot, and Reiske argued for the trans-latability of Islamic history, and in doing so, brought to the fore all that Christians and Muslims shared—the great breadth and variety of their histories and their traditions.

SIX

ISLAM AND THE ENLIGHTENMENT

In the entry "Mahométisme" of the *Encyclopédie, ou Dictionnaire raisonné des sciences, des arts et des métiers,* published in 1765, the Chevalier de Jaucourt, the most frequent of the work's more than 130 contributors, explained, "This religion was called *islamism,* which means *resignation* to the will of God. The book that contained it was called *coran,* that is, the *book,* or the writing, or the reading par excellence."[1] This seemingly simple definition actually performed a sensitive learned task: it restored native terminology ("Islamism," although not exactly a native term, was much closer to the Arabic than "Mahometism," and "Coran" was an improvement on "Alcoran," which contracts definite article and noun) and correctly defined these Arabic terms—this in spite of the fact that Jaucourt did not know Arabic and neither did Voltaire, Jaucourt's principal source for the entry. The notion that native Islamic terminology was preferable to the conventional French terms had traveled from the pages of erudite tomes to the *Encyclopédie.* Summarizing the state of human knowledge in the eighteenth-century West, the *Encyclopédie* became one of the symbols of the European Enlightenment.[2]

Recent scholars have acknowledged that the Western understanding of Islam underwent a dramatic change in the eighteenth century. They have largely attributed this shift to the Enlightenment's critical, even skeptical, attitude toward revealed religion and established churches. Although there were different strands to the Enlightenment approach to religion—some writers mounted an attack on all religion, whereas others hoped to rid religion of irrational elements—no one disputes that a more secular stance toward religion was a characteristic of the Enlightenment.[3] It has therefore been assumed that the change in the view of Islam derived from this stance and was an achievement of secular thought.[4] According to this historical narrative, those who threw off the shackles of revealed religion could look at Islam calmly, something Christian thinkers were too prejudiced to do.

The preceding five chapters tell a different story, one of confessional, erudite scholars, both Catholic and Protestant, who, as an outgrowth of their learned interests, laboriously reinterpreted the history and meanings of Islam. The extent to which they understood Islam as complex, multilayered, and akin to Christianity has been underestimated by those who dismiss their work as Christian polemic or Latin erudition. The many perspectives that writers of the Enlightenment adopted from an earlier era included these: the interpretation of Islam not as a loathsome Christian heresy but as a valid unitarian alternative to Western, Trinitarian Christianity; the proposition that Islam was a more rational form of Christianity, closer to natural religion; the idea of Muhammad as a legislator; and the concept of Islam as a civilization whose achievements in philosophy, science, poetry, and the arts were worthy of investigation.[5]

Conventional wisdom might lead us to expect that the secular writers of the Enlightenment would be less dismissive or condemnatory of Islam and less likely to write off its achievements than their Christian predecessors had been, but in general the opposite was true. Certain writers, such as Montesquieu and the Scottish philosophers David Hume, Adam Ferguson, and Adam Smith, relied on knowledge of Islam only when it could be used to support their agendas. These writers were primarily invested in making generalizations and determining patterns across human societies, rather than in pondering, much less investigating, Islam or the history of Muslim peoples—a profound difference from the European scholars of Arabic who, while notably equipped with their own biases, were devoted to establishing empirical information about Islamic history, religion, and culture.

Some Enlightenment writers did develop historical accounts of the rise of Islam. The most prominent and influential were Voltaire and Edward Gibbon, who have been incorrectly credited with first conceiving of the origin of Islam in historical terms and contextualizing it appropriately. That accomplishment had already been achieved by scholars of the Republic of Arabic Letters, from whom Voltaire and Gibbon directly took primary materials and many arguments.

In making their observations, Enlightenment thinkers did not need to rely solely on the output of the European scholars of Arabic. Although the Republic of Arabic Letters provided a qualitatively new kind of information about Islam, supported by the authority of authentic manuscripts and genuine Arabic proficiency, during the Enlightenment it competed with first-person travel accounts as a source of information about Islamic peoples and cultures. Written in the vernacular, these accounts claimed eyewitness knowledge and provided contemporary political and social insights, rather than philological and historical ones.

In this chapter I trace the use of inherited knowledge in the Enlightenment and offer a history of reading and of misreading. Using the cases of Montesquieu, Voltaire, and Gibbon, I reconstruct the visions of Islam that their new perspectives yielded. The writers of the Enlightenment expressed a wider variety of views of Islam, including dismissive or condemnatory ones, than did their scholarly predecessors, who had overall championed Islam as a worthwhile subject of study. Yet even though Enlightenment writers sometimes ignored empirical information, the new knowledge of Islam was an agent in their intellectual debates. Scholarly writing about Islam and its history continued to limit and shape what could be argued and claimed. Although the salience of a given fact or claim altered in response to changing conceptions of religion, politics, and history, nevertheless the information and interpretations of the Republic of Arabic Letters did inform the way the celebrated writers of the Enlightenment understood Islam and Islamic history. Through some of the most powerful authors of the Enlightenment, the legacy of the Republic was passed on to future generations in the West.

From Travel Writers to Philosophes

In 1748, when it was first published, the massive *De l'esprit des lois* (*The Spirit of the Laws*) by the French philosopher Charles-Louis de Secondat, Baron de la Brède et de Montesquieu (1689–1755), afforded the most ambitious and wide-ranging vision of politics of its era. Although informed by its author's broad reading in books both ancient and contemporary, *The Spirit of the Laws* was not in the main a work of erudition. (Voltaire wrote: "Montesquieu is always at fault among the savants, for he himself was not one of them.")[6] For one thing, Montesquieu's aim was not only to study laws—"the necessary relations deriving from the nature of things"—but also to understand their spirit, that is, "the various relations that laws may have with various things." These "things" ranged from a country's physical features to its people's way of life or religion. What he sought, in other words, was to establish general rules that would obtain across political communities. He wrote, "I set down the principles and I saw particular cases conform to them of their own accord," a statement that might ring alarm bells in anyone with less confidence in his methods than the author himself.[7] Indeed, though empirical reality fed Montesquieu's theoretical imagination, when that reality did not entirely suit him he was capable of overlooking it. Data that did not quite fit were modified by a subtle process of misreading, which has been demonstrated in detail regarding his use of the Roman historian Tacitus.[8] This problem troubled readers of *The Spirit of the Laws* even in Montesquieu's time, as we will see.

Some of the themes of *The Spirit of the Laws* were foreshadowed in Montesquieu's first book, *Persian Letters,* which appeared twenty-seven years earlier, in 1721, and was an immediate sensation.[9] Modeled after Gian Paolo Marana's epistolary novel *The Turkish Spy* (1684–1686), it takes what Montesquieu imagined to be a foreign—Muslim—perspective on Europe, and especially on France.[10] In their letters home, the two protagonists, Usbek and Rica, who have traveled from Persia to Europe "for love of knowledge" and "in order to pursue the painstaking search for wisdom," describe, sometimes satirically, French social customs and manners.[11] For example, Rica writes that the French Academy is "the least respected [court of law] in the world" and that its members "have no other purpose except to chat endlessly."[12] He skewers "the caprices of fashion," and the vanity of the French, who "gladly admit that other nations are wiser, as long as you concede that they are better dressed."[13]

Usbek and Rica's displacement gives them the freedom to analyze—and to criticize—both Christians and Muslims. Usbek does not approve of the "ornate style" of the Qur'an or of "a large number of childish matters" that it contains, and he implies that its authorship must be human rather than divine.[14] He finds fault with the hypocrisy and inconstancy of Christian believers, attacks the casuistry of the priests, and declares that, in spite of the greater repression practiced by Muslim rulers, "I do not see that public order, justice, and equity are better upheld in Turkey, Persia, or under the Mogul [the Mughal emperor], than in the republics of Holland, Venice, or even in England."[15]

Persian Letters advances the notion that reason is the path to true religion, and that customs and rituals particular to a given belief system are not its fundamental elements. Usbek writes that "whatever religion one may have, observation of the laws, love of mankind, and filial piety are always the primary acts of religion," and adds that "ritual has no intrinsic goodness in itself."[16] He speculates that the Muslim prohibitions on wine and gambling, and even Muhammad's approval of polygamy, were designed "to deprive us of anything which might disturb our reason" (polygamy preserves reason because "a plurality of wives saves us from being ruled by them; it tempers the violence of our desires").[17] Usbek finds the prohibition on pork to be an example of an arbitrary rule and therefore of doubtful value in the practice of true religion.[18]

This line of thinking leads Usbek to endorse tolerance, the incipient spirit of which he perceives in Europe. He comes to believe that "it would be desirable for Muslims to take as sensible a view on this matter as Christians do" and that Sunni and Shiite Muslims should overcome their enmity and strive to be good Muslims instead of fighting over the correct succession of Muhammad.[19] He concludes that wars of religion are not the inevitable consequence of religious diversity: "These wars were caused not by the multiplicity of religions, but rather by the spirit of intolerance that animated the one that believed itself to be dominant."[20] Therefore, "it is just as well for there to be several religions in a state."[21]

Persian Letters anticipates the much later *Spirit of the Laws* in its negative portrayal of both despotism and absolute monarchy and in the idea of relative freedoms under different systems of government, along with the distinctive emotions and morals to which these political arrangements give rise.[22] For example, Usbek reports a Frenchman's argument that the desire for glory is not present equally in free and in unfree states: when the people are unfree, as in Persia, only fear compels them to act, whereas the French monarchy enables the pursuit of glory and honor. An even better form of government, the Frenchman says, would be a republic, "the sanctuary of honor, reputation, and virtue."[23]

The role of outsiders looking in could perhaps have been played by characters from any non-European culture, though Muslims of high status are seemingly at the right distance—not too familiar, yet also not too foreign. Their Persian origin, moreover, allows for the final plot twist, which takes place in the seraglio Usbek left behind in Ispahan, a place that its "First Eunuch" describes as "a little empire."[24] While he is away, Usbek suffers a rebellion in his harem—his wives disobey his authority—to which he reacts swiftly, inciting his eunuchs to a violent reprisal. For all of the intellectual open-mindedness that his travels have inspired, Usbek remains a despot at home. His hypocrisy, too, is finally exposed—Montesquieu spares no one, Christian or Muslim.

The information about Persia in *Persian Letters* comes from the writings of seventeenth-century French travelers such as Jean Chardin and Jean-Baptiste Tavernier, but the book gives an imprecise portrait of many Persian customs.[25] It is a syncretic depiction, incorporating Ottoman elements along with imaginary ones—for instance, Usbek has five wives, instead of the four that Islamic law permits, and many of the Persian characters' names are not in fact Persian.[26]

In *The Spirit of the Laws* Montesquieu elaborates on the subject of despotism, and particularly on Oriental despotism.[27] Aristotle identified tyranny as a degenerate form of monarchy ("Tyranny is monarchy with a view to the advantage of the monarch"), and then distinguished it from despotism, which he regarded as a legitimate form of government ("based on law and hereditary")—but only for those who are not Greek: "It is because barbarians are more slavish in their characters than Greeks (those in Asia being more so than those in Europe) that they put up with a master's rule without making any difficulties."[28] According to numerous European political philosophers, diplomats, and travelers, including Niccolò Machiavelli and Jean Bodin, the absence of property rights—a purported feature of the Ottoman state—was a sign of despotism.[29]

Montesquieu had a personal interest in the subject of despotism. The term was applied to French politics after Louis XIV (r. 1643–1715) extended royal power by curtailing the political autonomy of the *parlements*—the local courts that served as legislative bodies.[30] Some members of the nobility, which in general opposed Louis's reforms, developed a political theory that emphasized checks on the crown's power as a way of preventing despotic rule.[31] As a baron, and as a former magistrate in the *parlement* of Bordeaux, Montesquieu shared this resistance to centralization, which continued under Louis XV (r. 1715–1774). He feared that France under the Bourbons would come under tyrannical control and saw the nobility and the *parlements* as counterweights to excessive concentration of royal power.[32] By depicting despotism in the worst light possible, he was warning the French of the perils they faced. Montesquieu believed, as he had Usbek say, that monarchy "is an unstable state that always degenerates into despotism, or into republicanism."[33]

One of Montesquieu's insights in *The Spirit of the Laws* is that the despotic state turns on fear, which "must beat down everyone's courage and extinguish even the slightest feeling of ambition" among its subjects. The despotic ruler, who governs through the threat of violence, does not need many laws to govern "timid, ignorant, beaten-down people."[34] Religion also plays a crucial role: "In these [despotic] states, religion has more influence than in any other; it is a fear added to fear." Montesquieu employed Islam as an illustration of this point, writing that it supports Muslim states because "the peoples derive from religion a part of the astonishing respect they have for their prince."[35]

Although Montesquieu cited ancient Rome, Safavid Persia, and Russia under Peter the Great as examples of the despotic state, his primary case in point was the Ottoman Empire. That choice had much to do with his predilection for the work of the seventeenth-century Englishman Paul Rycaut, who had been posted at length to the Ottoman Empire and wrote three books explaining it to his English contemporaries: *The Present State of the Ottoman Empire* (1667 [in fact 1666]), followed by *The History of the Turkish Empire* (1680) and *The History of the Turks* (1700).[36] The latter two are histories, but *The Present State* offers an analysis of the empire's constitution, organization, religion, and army. The book met with enormous success and went through many editions, as well as translations into French, Dutch, German, Italian, Polish, and Russian.[37] Rycaut regarded the Ottoman Empire as a tyrannical form of government whose component parts were held together only by "severity, violence, and cruelty."[38] *The Present State,* although informed by its author's detailed empirical understanding of the workings of the Ottoman Empire, is less a primary source than an essay in comparative political science with a moral for contemporary English politics: the need for checks against the power of a monarch.[39] Rycaut's highly interpreted vision of Muslim political life was ready-made for a writer like Montesquieu.

Rycaut's book found a major following among French political thinkers during and after the Enlightenment. Translated into French in 1670, it enjoyed a considerable readership in France for more than a century.[40] The late eighteenth-century French writer Constantin-François Volney, who relied on it heavily, wrote: "This book is without doubt the best that has been written about Turkey."[41] *The Present State* is part of an alternative tradition of thinking about Muslim states that ran from Rycaut through Montesquieu to Volney;

this tradition of eyewitness observation and political analysis existed in parallel to, and in competition with, the European tradition of Arabic studies.[42]

Montesquieu read the Qur'an as a historical archive rather than as living scripture, occasionally citing it when discussing the customs of the ancient Arabs or the establishment of Islam, but not when he was characterizing more recent forms of Muslim rule.[43] He relied on popularizations of Arabic scholarship—Humphrey Prideaux's *The True Nature of Imposture* (which drew on the work of Edward Pococke and other scholars) and the Count of Boulainvilliers's *Vie de Mahomed* (another pastiche of scholarly work)—but he also used more properly scholarly works, such as the study of the ancient Persians by the Oxford scholar Thomas Hyde and Eusèbe Renaudot's translation of two medieval Arab travel accounts.[44]

Above all, though, Montesquieu leaned on European travel writers. Besides Rycaut, Tavernier, Chardin, and François Bernier made frequent appearances. (Bernier, like Rycaut, produced elaborate works that advanced his own theory of political organization, as Montesquieu would also do.)[45] Other sources were Charles-Jacques Poncet, who wrote the account of Ethiopia in the Jesuit *Lettres édifiantes et curieuses,* and the writers Jacques Philippe Laugier de Tassy and Thomas Shaw.[46]

Because Montesquieu favored sources that supported his arguments and neglected those that did not, he read even his favorite travel writers, such as Chardin and Tavernier, selectively, omitting facts that did not support his own understanding of Oriental despotism.[47] Another instance of Montesquieu ignoring evidence concerns a translation by a French dragoman (professional interpreter) of the *qānūn* (laws) established under Süleyman the Magnificent. These laws had been codified by the famous legal scholar Mehmed Ebū's-suʿūd (1490–1574), the chief jurisconsult of the Ottoman Empire.[48] The translation, published in 1725, received a detailed review with a summary and extracts in the prominent learned periodical *Journal des sçavans* but is absent from *The Spirit of the Laws* in spite of its obvious relevance to Montesquieu's inquiry into the Ottoman Empire and its laws.[49] In addition, given that some of the books from the Republic of Arabic Letters were in his library, it is clear that Montesquieu deliberately chose to omit almost all of that scholarship from his work.[50] In all likelihood, books like d'Herbelot's *Bibliothèque Orientale,* with its rich portrait of Ottoman intellectual life, would have been hard for him to square with his own preconceived concept of Oriental despotism.

In the eighteenth century the empirical tenability of a claim was important, even to the *philosophes* and political thinkers. Montesquieu was taken to task by a serious scholar of Oriental languages, the Frenchman Abraham Hyacinthe Anquetil-Duperron, who went to India to study Brahminical texts but ended up translating the Zoroastrian scripture, the Avesta, which he published in 1771.[51] The programmatic intent of Anquetil-Duperron's 1778 *Législation orientale* was announced on its title page: "By showing what are the basic principles of government in Turkey, in Persia, and Hindoustan, it is proved, that the manner in which despotism, which passes for absolute in those three states, has been represented, affords a completely false idea of them."[52] Anquetil-Duperron directly attacked *The Spirit of the Laws,* attesting that the princes of the Ottoman, Safavid, and Mughal states were constrained by laws and that their people enjoyed the use of private property.

Voltaire, who several times expressed his discomfort with Montesquieu's procedure, argued in a 1778 commentary on *The Spirit of the Laws* that the distinction between monarchies and despotism was more vague and arbitrary than Montesquieu claimed and that his characterization of despotism did not hold up.[53] He also contested the accuracy of the correlations Montesquieu made in his analysis of the relationship between climate and laws, citing information that Montesquieu had disregarded.[54]

Voltaire challenged Montesquieu's assertion that everyone who lives under despotism is equal because they are all slaves. There were, Voltaire insisted, divisions of rank in Istanbul—the grand vizier, provincial governors, and pashas—and in places where the Janissary militia held real power, people in those positions could even appoint and depose sultans.[55] Montesquieu wrote that magnanimity was impossible in despotic states; Voltaire identified three grand viziers of the Köprülü family who had been "just, generous, clement, liberal," along with the grand vizier Ibrahim, who had been sacrificed for his master, Sultan Ahmed III, during the Patrona Halil revolt of 1730.[56] Voltaire turned to the Qur'an for evidence that Montesquieu was mistaken on the subject of Ottoman inheritance law and wrong to state that the sultan did not have to keep his word.[57] Montesquieu claimed that dispute resolution in the Ottoman Empire lacked justice; Voltaire called that "a joke suitable for the *Comédie Italienne.*"[58] If anything, Voltaire wrote, the Ottoman courts, efficient and "founded on common sense, equity and promptitude," could set a good example for reforming the "frightful chaos" of the French system.[59] Voltaire also highlighted Montesquieu's misreadings of Paul Rycaut.[60]

Voltaire's empirical corrections, though they may seem a bit pedantic, were a vehicle for expressing his deep discomfort with Montesquieu's mode of argument and his undiscerning use of sources.[61] Voltaire believed that there was not enough verified knowledge about the Ottoman Empire to justify its use for political philosophy, and that tales of travelers, "or rather of errant men, who have told so many fables, who have taken so many abuses to be laws," were unreliable, a caution also applicable to travelers' reports about China and many other Asian empires.[62] Lack of empirical evidence rendered Montesquieu's view of despotism vague and poorly substantiated. Voltaire wrote: "We are neighbors of the Turks, yet we do not know them. The Count of Marsigli, who lived for so long among them, says that no author has provided true knowledge of their empire, nor of their laws. We did not even have a tolerable translation of the Alcoran before that which the Englishman Sale made in 1734. Almost everything that is said of their religion and of their jurisprudence is false; and the conclusions against them that are drawn therefrom every day have but too little foundation."[63]

The debate between Montesquieu and Voltaire over Oriental despotism can also be read as a debate over political authority in France—with Montesquieu critical of the concentration of power under Louis XIV and Voltaire in favor of it.[64] Rather than engaging that issue directly, their intellectual dispute concerned how well a theoretical claim could hold up under an empirical challenge. Voltaire buttressed his position by employing the scholarly materials that he had mastered and Montesquieu had not.

In spite of the critiques of Anquetil-Duperron and Voltaire, the concept of Oriental despotism that *The Spirit of the Laws* popularized would have a life into the nineteenth century.[65] The change in the overall European perception of Islam from admiring to aversive that took place in the later eighteenth century can, at least in part, be attributed to the influence of Montesquieu's book.[66]

Other eighteenth-century thinkers, such as Jean-Jacques Rousseau, Adam Smith, David Hume, and Adam Ferguson, made occasional references to topics in Islamic history. Rousseau lavished praise on many aspects of Islamic politics and religion but stressed the utter otherness of Muslim customs and manners.[67] Hume used the Qur'an as evidence that there was no universal moral standard, even though moral vocabularies in different languages might seem, misleadingly, to converge.[68] For Smith and Ferguson, the desert Arabs were an example of a primitive state of human civilization and the modern Ottomans of an undesirable modern political arrangement.[69]

In sum, during the Enlightenment the early history of Arabs and of the rise of Islam served many purposes, including as an archive of primitive legislation and as an example of a pastoral society. Some of the discussions, such as Rousseau's, harkened back to the treatment of Muhammad as a legislator that originated in Machiavelli's analysis. The most familiar modern Muslim state, the Ottoman Empire, meanwhile was used in the study of Oriental despotism. Some writers, most notably Montesquieu, reactivated analyses that had been put forth by European travel writers. The impact of the Republic of Arabic Letters is hard to discern in his work. Certain Enlightenment writers, especially those who developed wide-ranging interpretations, were cavalier about facts and opportunistic in their use of Islamic materials. Information about non-European societies was helpful in the development of comparative political thought. Travel writing was relied on more than scholarly accounts, but the most accomplished of these travel accounts were as elaborate and self-conscious as political philosophy. (Moreover, travel writing did not, in any simple way, promote "open-mindedness" about non-European societies.)

With knowledge of what the Republic of Arabic Letters made available to Europeans who did not know Arabic—that is, all the materials presented in the preceding five chapters—we can appraise Enlightenment writings about Islam within a broader context, one that allows us to move away from an anachronistic critique of these writers for not being better informed or for not being interested in Islam for its own sake. Knowing what they did not read and what complexities they ignored permits a more accurate analysis of their intellectual achievements and shortcomings. It also undermines the assumption that the Enlightenment writings are representative, let alone exhaustive, of Western thought on Islam in the eighteenth century. Perhaps it even diminishes their significance.

Voltaire

Voltaire's *Essai sur les mœurs et l'esprit des nations* (literally, Essay on the manners and the spirit of nations, 1756) examines the emergence of modern Europe, starting from the days of Charlemagne, when "the chaos of our Europe begins to take a shape after the fall of the Roman Empire," to the age of King Louis XIV of France, an era that Voltaire (1694–1778, born François-Marie Arouet) believed was on par in greatness with Greece under Pericles and Alexander, Rome under Julius Caesar and Augustus, and Italy in the Renaissance.[70] The *Essai* narrates the gradual rise of a modern, secular European civilization, with *mœurs* (manners) defined as the degree of cultural refinement a nation has achieved.

Voltaire painted the progress of the human spirit in broad strokes, leaving to others the ostensibly tedious details of past dynasties and battles. Though he worked in conversation with primary sources and erudite scholarship, he saw his role as that of selecting facts and events relevant to creating a wide-ranging historical vision.[71] He initially conceived the book for his companion Madame du Châtelet (1706–1749), a brilliant thinker who held a very low opinion of modern history, while she admired antiquity. Its opening pages, addressed to an imaginary reader, begin: "You wish finally to overcome the disgust that modern history since the decline of the Roman empire provokes in you."[72]

Voltaire used non-Western history to show that European civilization did not possess the priority and normativity usually attributed to it. The *Essai* opens in ninth-century Asia, a place more culturally flourishing than ninth-century Europe, and discusses the antiquity, and especially the religions, of China and India, societies more ancient than Europe whose religions were unconnected to Christianity. From there, it moves to a discussion of Persia, Arabia, and the rise of Islam. Voltaire urged his contemporaries to pay attention to Asia: "Why would we neglect to know the *esprit* of these nations, to which the merchants of our Europe have traveled since they were able to find a way there?"[73]

The *Essai* was Voltaire's response to Bishop Bossuet's *Discours sur l'histoire universelle*, which was written for the dauphin and published in 1681. Purporting to be a universal history from the creation to the ninth century, the *Discours* shed no light on the emergence of Islam or Muslim history.[74] The *Essai* begins at the time of Charlemagne, where the *Discours* left off, and greatly enlarges its scope. Voltaire took Bossuet to task for his Eurocentric approach: "This eloquent writer, in a passing mention of the Arabs, who founded such a powerful empire and such a flourishing religion, merely speaks of them as of a flood of barbarians."[75]

Voltaire, who is today most often remembered as a symbol of secularism for his lifelong fight against the French Catholic Church and its abuses, was not, however, an atheist, but a deist.[76] Much of his interest in non-Christian religions derived from a wish to unsettle Christianity and demonstrate that its revelation was not unique or even special. He touched on Islam in a number of publications in the course of his lifetime, allowing us to track the development of his awareness in that sphere.[77] His tragedy *Le fanatisme, ou Mahomet* (1741) which represents Muhammad as a Machiavellian schemer, was written when his knowledge was slight, and it contains some fictional characters and events.[78] Shortly after completing the play, he undertook a serious reading project on the early history of Islam in preparation for the *Essai* and markedly deepened his knowledge.[79]

Chapters 5 through 7 of the *Essai* offer a historical account of the rise of Islam. Voltaire's reading led him to conclude that more reliable information exists about Muhammad than about any other "legislator" or "conqueror."[80] It is true that Muhammad can be read about in several extra-Qur'anic genres, including *ḥadīth* (deeds and sayings) and *sīra nabawiyya* (Prophetic biography), whereas we know Moses only through the Pentateuch and Jesus only through the Gospels. Thus, Voltaire embraced a central tenet of the Republic of Arabic Letters—trust in Arabic sources—and, indeed, he read widely in that tradition. He encountered George Sale's *Koran* (1734) by 1738 at the latest, and perused it during his years at the Château de Cirey, the country estate of Madame du Châtelet in Champagne. He read Sale's "Preliminary Discourse" in English, a language he had learned during his English sojourn (1726 to 1729), and wrote that it was "much more beautiful than all the alcorans of the world," as we saw in Chapter 3.[81] Other sources included d'Herbelot, whose *Bibliothèque Orientale* Voltaire borrowed on December 7, 1742, from the Marquis d'Argenson.[82] He also consulted the biographies of Muhammad by the Count of Boulainvilliers and Jean Gagnier.[83] (However, he was often loath to acknowledge the help he derived from these sources.)[84]

Voltaire, despite all his reading on Islam, considered the Qur'an itself frustrating: "The *Koran* is a disjointed rhapsody without order, without art."[85] The "Preliminary Discourse" put the history of Islam in terms that were immediately useful to him, but he found the translation itself less rewarding. In 1767 he wrote, "The *Koran* is, in truth, a heap of moral sentences, of precepts, of exhortations, prayers, and of features of the Old Testament transmitted according to the Arab tradition. The whole is composed without order, and without connections."[86] The Qur'an does change topic frequently in ways that can be challenging for the reader, yet Voltaire's remarks betray not so much the limitations of reading a translation as a lack of patience for the forms that religious revelation takes. Indeed, the thirty-odd marginal remarks in Voltaire's personal copy of Sale's *Koran* (now held in the National Library of Russia, St. Petersburg) do not bear witness to a profound interaction with the book.[87] Sale, by contrast, assured his readers of the beauty of the Qur'an's Arabic and expressed sorrow at not being able to render its elegance and beauty in English.[88]

In the *Essai sur les mœurs,* Voltaire called the rise of Islam "the greatest and most sudden revolution that we have known on earth," one that led to "a new domination, a religion and customs until then unknown."[89] Like Ockley and others before him, he was impressed with the rapid spread of Islam and its swift remaking of the political contours of Eurasia. He saw this transformation as an extremely rare, if not unique, historical event.

Voltaire viewed Muhammad's revelation along lines similar to the interpretations of Pococke, Simon, Sale, and the other thinkers featured in Chapter 3. Muhammad, he wrote, had been driven by a mixture of "enthusiasm" (sincere belief), self-deceit, and a remarkable ability to deceive others: "Having understood the character of his fellow citizens, their ignorance, their credulity, and their inclination to enthusiasm, he saw that he could raise himself to a prophet."[90] But, Voltaire insisted, Muhammad was not a purely calculating impostor: "It would appear that Mahomet, like all enthusiasts, was violently struck by his own ideas, produced them at first in good faith, fortified them with his daydreams, fooled himself in fooling others, and finally supported with some necessary guile a doctrine that he held to be sound."[91] In this opinion, he elaborated on Sale's dismissal of the question of Muhammad's sincerity: "Whether this was the effect of enthusiasm, or only a design to raise himself to the supreme government of his country, I will not pretend to determine."[92] Voltaire agreed that such a determination could not be made, on the grounds that "enthusiasm" and "guile" were not mutually exclusive traits.

Voltaire followed the new Arabic scholarship in rejecting traditional explanations for the rapid spread of Islam: "It is a common prejudice among us, that mahometism only made such great progress because it furthers voluptuous inclinations."[93] Ever the contrarian, he even defended polygamy on evolutionary grounds and considered the Islamic paradise nothing special: "We declaim daily against Mahomet's sensual paradise; but antiquity knew no other kind."[94] This was the same comparative strategy that Richard Simon had used to normalize the Islamic Paradise.

Voltaire believed that Muhammad's use of military conquest to spread his religion was unique: "Of all the legislators who have founded religions, he [Muhammad] is the sole one to have extended his by means of conquests. Other peoples have brought their cult to foreign nations by means of blade and blaze, but no founder of a sect had ever been a conqueror."[95] While Machiavelli designated several earlier leaders as armed prophets (Moses, Cyrus, Theseus, and Romulus among them), Voltaire held that Muhammad was the first prophet to have also been a conqueror. But he attributed Islam's rapid expansion not simply to military might—Muslims had forced conversions only in the earliest days—for it had also been achieved "through enthusiasm, through persuasion, and above all through the example of the conquerors, which has so much power over the conquered."[96] Voltaire pointed to the rhetorical power of the Qur'an as a persuasive factor (he may not have enjoyed the Qur'an himself, but in this opinion he was Sale's student); the Arabs, devoted to poetry, were convinced of the truth of the Qur'an by its literary qualities. Like Rousseau, Voltaire impressed upon his readers that Arabia was unlike Europe in every way: "Here are manners, customs, facts so different from everything that occurs among us, that they ought to teach us how much we must guard from our habit of judging everything according to our own customs."[97] This passage bears a resemblance to Simon Ockley's admonition in the 1718 preface to his *History of the Saracens*.[98]

Voltaire attributed Islam's success mainly to its message, which was the opposite of mystifying and unfamiliar: "There was nothing new in the law of Mahomet, except that Mahomet was the prophet of God."[99] This simplicity in both theology and morals had drawn large numbers of people to Islam: "All of these laws, polygamy excepted, are so austere, and his doctrine, which is so simple, soon attracted respect and trust to his religion. Above all, the dogma of the unity of God, presented without mysteries, and befitting human intelligence, drew to his law a crowd of nations, including even negroes in Africa, and island-dwellers in the Indian Ocean."[100] In an echo of Machiavelli, Voltaire saw the joint political and religious authority of the caliphs as the source of their might. "If ever a power has threatened the whole earth, it was that of the caliphs; for they had the power of the throne and the altar, of the sword and of enthusiasm."[101] (Rousseau would make the same point in the *Social Contract,* published in 1762.)[102]

Voltaire's focus on the progress of the human spirit brought him squarely up against what he took to be a central paradox of Islamic history: "Already from the second century of the Hegira, the Arabs became the instructors of Europe in the sciences and the arts, even though their law would appear to be the enemy of the arts."[103] This intellectual achievement, he concluded, must have been attained in spite of, rather than because of, the religion's foundational principles. Islam's simple dogma enabled its rapid rise, but that dogma did not constrain the flowering of the arts and sciences, an argument that had been made by the protagonists of Chapter 5. On the way in which these intellectual advances came about, Voltaire said: "To the degree that the mahometans became powerful, they became polished. These caliphs . . . in their new Babylon [that is, Baghdad] . . . soon caused the arts to be reborn there. Aaron al Rachild [*sic;* Hārūn al-Rashīd], a contemporary of Charlemagne, more respected than his predecessors, and who was obeyed from Spain to the Indies, revived the sciences, made the agreeable and useful arts flourish, attracted men of letters, composed poetry, and made civility [*politesse*] succeed barbarism in his vast domains."[104] He went on to list the scientific accomplishments of the Abbasids—Indian numerals, astronomical observations, the translation of Ptolemy from Greek to Arabic, the measuring of one degree of a meridian under al-Ma'mūn, corrections of Ptolemy by "Ben-Honaïn" (Isḥāq b. Ḥunayn), and the cultivation of chemistry, medicine, and algebra—and showed what Europe had gained from each one. He drew most of his information from d'Herbelot's *Bibliothèque;* as we have seen, the celebration of Muslim achievement had been a common theme in the Republic of Arabic Letters. What transpired on Voltaire's reading was a historical irony: Islam had succeeded on account of its intrinsic qualities, but once it was successful, its bearers went beyond its letter and spirit in their pursuit of the arts and sciences.

In the conclusion, he compared the history of Christianity and Islam, drawing a contrast between the unintended outcomes of each founding: "Let us limit ourselves to this historical truth: the legislator of the Muslims, a powerful and terrible man, established his dogmas through his courage and his arms; nevertheless, his religion became indulgent and tolerant. The divine founder of Christianity, living in humility and in peace, preaches forgiveness of affronts, and his holy and gentle religion has become through our fury the most intolerant of all, and the most barbarian."[105]

For Voltaire, it was the national character of the Arabs—their natural generosity, courage, and magnanimity—rather than Islam that explained the early Muslim cultivation of the arts and sciences.[106] He found the Arab "character" more appealing than that of the Jews (Voltaire's anti-Judaic sentiments have been studied at length).[107] Whereas most commentators on Islam in the previous century had emphasized the many beliefs and customs that Islam had adapted from Judaism, Voltaire focused instead on what he believed were the deficits of the Jews in comparison with the Arabs.[108]

He explained the decline of Muslim intellectual achievement by once again finding its cause in national character: the Ottomans had not been worthy successors to the Arabs. "What a difference between the genius of the Arabs, and that of the Turks! The latter have allowed a work to perish whose preservation was worth more than the conquest of a great province."[109] This was an argument that Pococke had already advanced, but it ignored all that d'Herbelot and Galland had done to showcase the intellectual achievements of the Ottomans. Voltaire's point of view reverted to an older European vision of the place of the Ottomans in Islamic intellectual history.

On the question of why Europeans should study Islamic history, Voltaire wrote, "The lovers of antiquity, those who enjoy comparing the genius of nations, will see with pleasure how much the customs, the manners of the time of Mahomet, of Abubeker, of Omar resemble the ancient manners of which Homer was the faithful painter. One sees the military leaders challenge enemy leaders to hand-to-hand combat; one sees them advance in front of their ranks and fight in view of the two immobile armies."[110] Using comparisons between classical and Islamic history and manners and focusing on inspiring examples will strike readers of Chapter 5 as familiar strategies for normalizing Islam. Voltaire went so far as to suggest that in eloquence the Arabs outdid the Greeks: "The speeches of Arab heroes at the head of their armies, or in individual combats, or in swearing a truce, all contain those natural elements that are found in Homer, but they have incomparably more enthusiasm and more sublimity."[111] He believed that manners similar to those of the ancients had abetted Islam's expansion.[112] Observing, moreover, that "an unfailing proof of the superiority of a nation in the humanities [*arts de l'esprit*] is the perfected cultivation of poetry," Voltaire even claimed a connection between Arabic and Latin and French poetry: "that wise and self-assured poetry, such as flourished in the time of Augustus, such as was reborn under Louis XIV—this poetry of image and feeling was known at the time of Aaron al Rachild [Hārūn al-Rashīd]."[113] He was, of course, hardly qualified to make this appraisal, which he supported by utterly reworking a poetic fragment translated by d'Herbelot.[114]

Soon after the *Essai* appeared, an anonymous reader published a vehement critique.[115] This reader, who claimed to have lived "for several years . . . among the Mahometans," argued that Voltaire had made so many factual errors that his authority as a historian was questionable.[116] He excerpted twenty-three passages from Voltaire on the origins of Islam and proceeded to vigorously demolish them. He accused Voltaire of careless errors in chronology, in the sequence of the first four caliphs, and in the five pillars of Islam; he scolded him for not sufficiently making use of the information available in European languages; he rebuked him for consulting "some ancient controversialists"—that is, Western sources that had been discredited by the new Arabic erudition; and he diagnosed him as having been confused when he took the side of the Shiites by saying that Muhammad had appointed ʿAlī his successor: "Until now all Christian refuters of the religion of Mahomet fought it according to the interpretation of the Turks, the Africans, the Arabs, and Mughals, all honorably called *Sonnites,* and the ignominious name of *Rafzis* [rāfiḍī], or Schismatic Sectaries, Heretics, was left to the Persians."[117]

The authority of the anonymous critic came, in fact, from his impressive Arabic erudition rather than from his personal experience in Muslim lands. He cited and quoted Arabic authors, in particular the historians Abū'l-Fidāʾ and al-Jannābī and the Qurʾanic commentators "GelalAddin" [al-Suyūṭī] and "Al-Gazel" [al-Ghazālī]. His familiarity with the plurality of Muslim interpretations of the Qurʾan strengthened his challenge to Voltaire's simplistic notions about Muslim alcohol prohibition; the critic cited three different schools of thought on that subject.[118] He cast doubt on Voltaire's knowledge of the Qurʾan by disputing the *Essai*'s claim that Muhammad "preserved" the Arab custom of circumcision; in fact, the critic noted, this practice is not mentioned in the sacred book.[119] Voltaire, he wrote, was too haughty to "waste his time reading this tedious and enormous morass of foreign controversies: he has employed his talents and his leisure more agreeably, in composing works of all sort."[120] The critique reads as the bitter reproach of the erudite scholar against the spirited man of letters.

On top of all these complaints, the critic accused Voltaire of making a fundamental error of interpretation: because he had not grasped how easy it had been to dupe the Arabs in their ignorance and credulity, he overestimated the greatness of Muhammad's achievement.[121] Along the same lines, the critic disagreed with Voltaire's claim that Muhammad's most significant challenge had been convincing his family of his prophetic status; he countered that Muhammad's household would have simply listened to him and obeyed.[122] In addition, the critic saw no supporting evidence for Voltaire's statement that even the Christians and Jews who thought that Muhammad was an impostor had allowed that he was a "great man."[123] And he rebuked Voltaire for justifying Muhammad's yielding to carnal desire.[124]

Voltaire swiftly fought back. In a pamphlet of his own, he brushed off the criticism, for example by arguing that Muhammad's exact genealogy or his wealth (two of the contested points) mattered little to an understanding of the "Mahometan Religion."[125] He showed off his reading in the Republic of Arabic Letters, citing works by Prideaux, the Count of Boulainvilliers, Sale, and d'Herbelot, pointing out that the disagreements among these scholars proved that many of the critic's definitive statements were actually matters of debate.[126] Voltaire, not easily intimidated, even dared to cite the Qur'an commentator al-Bayḍāwī (heavily featured in the footnotes to George Sale's translation) and to argue with his critic about the correct translation of *al-Qurʾān* as "Coran" rather than "Alcoran."[127]

Wielding his gift for sarcasm, Voltaire dismissed the grievances of his critic as pedantry (among other things, he mockingly called him "our Turkish Scaliger"; Joseph Scaliger had been the greatest humanist scholar of the late Renaissance), and it is true that some of the critic's accusations came from narrow, unsympathetic readings of the *Essai*.[128] Voltaire asserted that he had written not a "universal history, which is but merely a portrait of all the principal forms of foolishness of this world," but a "general history" to which "a thousand details" could have been added, but only at risk of "losing in these little details, the spirit of the nations that I have sought to paint."[129] By treating a philosophical project as a learned compilation, he implied, the critic had made an error of genre.

As far as admiring Muhammad, Voltaire wrote: "It is not my fault that this little man has changed the face of a swath of the world, if he won battles against armies ten times as large as his own, if he made the Roman Empire tremble, and gave the first blows to that colossus that his successors destroyed, and if he was the legislator of Asia, of Africa, and of part of Europe."[130] Muhammad's credentials for being considered a great figure in human history were unimpeachable, Voltaire asserted: "I concede that he is damned, but Caesar and Alexander are too; and is Cicero not as well?"[131] With this normalizing comparison, typical of the Republic of Arabic Letters, Voltaire positioned himself as a less partisan scholar of Islam than his critic, who evaluated Muhammad by Christian standards rather than those of an impartial historian.[132]

The debate between Voltaire and his critic pitted a religiously neutral and sympathetic interpretation of Muhammad against a Christian and unsympathetic one. Associating religious dogma with closed-mindedness and religious neutrality with open-mindedness is common today, but the preceding chapters have shown that a Christian perspective did not necessarily have to be unsympathetic to Islam. These polemical alignments were established only when the discussion about Islam became enmeshed in Voltaire's broader agenda against the Catholic Church and revealed religion. The same phenomenon had arisen in an earlier period when freethinking readers of the new Arabic scholarship had appropriated its arguments; their orthodox critics had responded by vilifying not just their interpretations but Islam itself.[133]

Although Voltaire scored some points against his critic, there is no way around the fact that in his historical work, he was partisan and tendentious. Given his own elastic use of evidence, the mantle of scholarliness that he donned to attack Montesquieu was opportunistic at best. In the second edition of the *Essai,* in 1761, he even knowingly misrepresented the antiquity and authenticity of a Sanskrit text known as the *Ezour-vedam,* which was actually produced by French Jesuits, as part of his quest to undermine the authority and primacy of the Bible.[134]

To summarize, Voltaire's treatment was less grounded in evidence and more daring in argument than the productions of the Republic of Arabic Letters. He thought that a native Arab "spirit," not the religion of Islam, had stimulated the development of the arts and sciences; like his scholarly informants, he promoted similarities between classical Greek and Arab mores. His lack of qualifications did not hinder him from making claims about the kinship of Arabic and Latin and French poetry. In certain respects his originality in interpretation borders on idiosyncrasy, but at the same time he portrayed Muslims as vital and lively historical agents, attracted to Islam by its virtues but able to move beyond it when it did not fit their needs.

Eccentric and weak on evidence as it was, Voltaire's account of Islam enjoyed a serious afterlife in French intellectual history. Its views were absorbed by the *Encyclopédie,* the most prestigious editorial project of the French *philosophes.* The most substantive single treatment of Islam in the *Encyclopédie*—the entry "Mahométisme" by Chevalier de Jaucourt, mentioned at the start of this chapter—consists of a paraphrased summary of Voltaire's views.[135] Jaucourt introduced the entry this way: "The philosopher-historian of our days [that is, Voltaire] has painted its picture so perfectly, that it would betray poor self-knowledge to present readers with another."[136] By reiterating the factual information and opinions of the *Essai sur les mœurs,* "Mahométisme" canonized Voltaire's interpretation.

Edward Gibbon

Edward Gibbon (1737–1794) combined erudite research and highly interpretive narration in a way that has often earned him the title of first "modern" historian.[137] The closest precedent to his great achievement, *The History of the Decline and Fall of the Roman Empire,* is in fact Voltaire's *Essai sur les mœurs,* which, as we have seen, combines a broad empirical sweep with a "philosophical" interest in the progress of manners.[138] Gibbon famously came up with the idea for *The Decline and Fall of the Roman Empire* "on the ruins of the Capitol" in Rome, in 1764, and the first volume appeared in 1776.[139] The six-volume work encompasses both the Western and the Eastern halves of the Roman Empire, relates the empire's history starting with the end of the Flavian dynasty, and charts the rise of Christianity. After completing the third volume, published in 1781—which reached the year 476, the end of the Western Roman Empire—Gibbon moved from Rome to Byzantium and took his account all the way to the fall of Constantinople in 1453. He tackled the rise of Islam in chapters 48–57 of the fifth volume, which he completed on May 1, 1786, and which appeared in print in 1788.[140]

Gibbon first encountered the Islamic Near East in his youth, when he read the English version of *The Thousand and One Nights.* He ranked the work with Alexander Pope's translation of Homer as an enduring classic: "Two books which will always please by the moving picture of human manners and specious miracles."[141] In the summer of 1751, at age fourteen, he discovered late Roman history in a volume of a collectively written *Universal History* (to which George Sale contributed).[142] His interest in the history of the Eastern Roman Empire led him to another collectively written volume, William Howell's *General History of the World*.[143] "Mahomet and his Saracens soon fixed my attention: and some instinct of criticism directed me to the genuine sources. Simon Ockley, an original in every sense, first opened my eyes, and I was led from one book to another till I had ranged round the circle of Oriental history. Before I was sixteen I had exhausted all that could be learned in English, of the Arabs and the Persians, the Tartars and the Turks, and the same ardour urged me to guess at the French of d'Herbelot, and to construe the barbarous Latin of Pocock's *Abulpharagius* [that is, Pococke's translation of Bar Hebraeus]."[144]

Gibbon forever resented Oxford's failure to take advantage of his youthful curiosity and eagerness: he came to consider his time there as "the most idle and unprofitable of my whole life." He knew that "since the days of [Edward Pococke] and [Thomas] Hyde, Oriental learning has always been the pride of Oxford," but the Oxford of his youth was not Pococke's, nor was it the university that would encourage the polymathic William Jones a few decades later. Gibbon wrote witheringly about his Oxford teachers in his memoirs: "From the toil of reading or thinking, or writing they had absolved their conscience."[145] As a result of his tutor's discouragement, Gibbon did not study Arabic and would reckon with Islamic history only decades later, and at second hand.

Gibbon noted in his memoirs that he arrived at the scope of *The Decline and Fall* by following the "judicious precept" of the Abbé de Mably "not to dwell too minutely on the decay of the Eastern [Roman] Empire; but to consider the barbarian conquerors as a more worthy subject of his narrative. *Fas est et ab hoste doceri* [It is right to learn even from an enemy]."[146] Gibbon saw that, as Niccolò Machiavelli had realized in the early sixteenth century, the early Islamic state should be considered one of the successors of the Roman Empire. This gave him license to undertake an extensive consideration of Muslim rule from Muhammad to the Ottoman sultan Mehmed the Conqueror: "The Saracen sect did so many great things and occupied so much of the world after it destroyed the Eastern Roman Empire."[147]

As he would later recollect, Gibbon decided to use "the method of grouping my picture by nations," believing that "the seeming neglect of chronological order is surely compensated by the superior merits of interest and perspicuity."[148] As one commentator has put it, "The volume is like a collection of related historical works dealing (at least in part) with the same period, but with different places or subjects."[149] Gibbon reassured his reader that everything would ultimately connect back to his main subject: "The excursive line may embrace the wilds of Arabia and Tartary, but the circle will be ultimately reduced to the decreasing limit of the Roman monarch."[150]

He continued: "Each [nation] will occupy the space to which it may be entitled by greatness or merit, or the degree of connection with the Roman world and the present age."[151] A narrative of Islamic history fell well within the broad scope of *The Decline and Fall*. Like many of the writers discussed in this book, Gibbon considered the rise and expansion of Islam to be "one of the most memorable revolutions, which have impressed a new and lasting character on the nations of the globe."[152] It deserved, he wrote, three "ample" chapters.[153] His history of Islam begins just like those by George Sale and the Count of Boulainvilliers: with descriptions of Arabia's geography and climate and its transition from hunting to pastoralism and then to agriculture and trade. Some of this information came from recent travel accounts, such as that of Carsten Niebuhr.[154] After establishing this background, he moved on to the life of Muhammad and the origins of Islam.

Gibbon credited his sources and made clear his own limitations: "As in this and the following chapter I shall display much Arabic learning, I must profess my total ignorance of the Oriental tongues, and my gratitude to the learned interpreters, who have transfused their science into the Latin, French, and English languages."[155] The detailed citations that are characteristic of *The Decline and Fall* stand in stark contrast to Voltaire's practice. Gibbon's footnotes to the chapters on Islamic history read as a sort of who's who of the Republic of Arabic Letters, the influence of which is evident throughout. Gibbon aligned himself with seventeenth-century scholars by discussing the differences among Muslim thinkers in their interpretations of Islamic doctrine and in the level of credence they gave to Muhammad's purported miracles—recognizing the polyphony of voices within Islam was a hallmark of European learned scholarship.[156] He based his history of the early dynasties on d'Herbelot, on Arabic chronicles available in Latin translation (including Bar Hebraeus and Abū'l-Fidā'), and especially on Ockley's two-volume history.[157]

Even so, Gibbon did not take the interpretations of the primary sources at face value, arguing, for instance, that "we should weigh with caution the traditions of the hostile [Shiite] sects; a stream which becomes still more muddy as it flows farther from the source."[158] He also felt free to disagree with his European sources. For example, Sale had supposed that Muhammad had preserved many pre-Islamic customs, such as circumcision, ablutions before prayer, and the hajj, in order to ingratiate himself with his pagan audience and to make their conversion to Islam smoother. Gibbon begged to differ: "It has been sagaciously conjectured, that the artful legislator indulged the stubborn prejudices of his countrymen. It is more simple to believe that he adhered to the habits and opinions of his youth, without foreseeing that a practice congenial to the climate of Mecca, might become useless or inconvenient on the banks of the Danube or the Volga."[159] It struck Gibbon as more likely that Muhammad endorsed these customs because he had grown up with them, rather than that he had supported them for cynical purposes.

Though Gibbon had certain arguments with his scholarly predecessors, his depiction of the emergence of Islam mostly comes straight out of their playbook. For example, he repeats many common interpretations of his era. "In the portrait of the modern *Bedoweens,* we may trace the features of their ancestors" he wrote, and he hinged his explanation of their political status on landscape and climate: "The obvious causes of their freedom are inscribed on the character and country of the Arabs."[160] As did many others before him, Gibbon associated eloquence with freedom, because only that condition required the use of persuasive rhetoric (monarchs demanded flattery): "The use and reputation of oratory among the ancient Arabs is the clearest evidence of public freedom."[161] In some cases, Gibbon challenged the received wisdom. Johann Jacob Reiske, among others, had celebrated the equivalence of many aspects of classical and Arabic culture, but Gibbon did not always agree. For instance, in comparing classical and Arabic rhetoric, he contradicted Reiske's judgment that they were analogous: "The sententious Arabs would probably have disdained the simple and sublime logic of Demosthenes."[162] Unlike Reiske and the members of the Republic of Arabic Letters, Gibbon overall perceived Islamic cultural production in contrast to its classical equivalents, rather than as analogous to them.

As brilliant and unprecedented as it was to incorporate the early history of Islam into a history of the Roman Empire, the very possibility of doing so rested entirely on the past century and a half of European scholarship grounded in Arabic sources.[163] Seen from that perspective, Gibbon was the most perceptive and probing eighteenth-century reader of the Republic of Arabic Letters.

This interplay between sources and reader is on view in Gibbon's approach to the figure of Muhammad. His interpretation of the prophet is not very distant from George Sale's, but he writes with particular psychological acuity. His portrait of Muhammad is profoundly human: he imagines a man half pushed by his own motivations and half pulled by the pace of events into the dual role of religious visionary and political and military leader.[164] He evoked vividly Muhammad's many charms and their effect: "[His audiences] applauded his commanding presence, his majestic aspect, his piercing eye, his gracious smile, his flowing beard, his countenance that painted every sensation of the soul, and his gestures that enforced each expression of the tongue."[165] Of Muhammad's religious vision he wrote: "The first idea which he entertained of his divine mission bears the stamp of an original and superior genius."[166] Gibbon sidestepped the imposture debate: "From enthusiasm to imposture the step is perilous and slippery."[167] Like Voltaire, he did not see religious sincerity and tactical opportunism as necessarily in contradiction.

Gibbon's humane approach extended to his discussion of the Qur'an, which he attributed, as Sale did, to the sole authorship of Muhammad: "Conversation enriches the understanding, but solitude is the school of genius; and the uniformity of the work denotes the hand of a single artist."[168] He called the creed of Islam ("There is no God but God and Muhammad is his prophet") "an eternal truth, and a necessary fiction."[169] Conceding that "the mysteries of the Trinity and Incarnation *appear* to contradict the principle of divine unity," he, along with Voltaire, believed that Islam's great attraction was its theological simplicity and coherence: "The creed of Mohammed is free from suspicion or ambiguity; and the Koran is a glorious testimony to the unity of God."[170] He praised Muhammad for declaring "sublime truths" in his description of God, recognizing in the "author of the universe . . . an infinite and eternal being . . . existing by the necessity of his own nature, and deriving from himself all moral and intellectual perfection."[171] He recognized that Muslim theologians grappled with the intellectual challenges that this vision of an omnipotent god raised, from free will and predestination to theodicy, many of which were issues that Christian theologians also had to face: "They struggle with the common difficulties, *how* to reconcile the prescience of God with the freedom and responsibility of man; *how* to explain the permission of evil under the reign of infinite power and infinite goodness."[172] Gibbon wrote Islam into the history of Christianity by observing their genealogical connection and pointing out ways in which they were analogous, an approach characteristic of the Republic of Arabic Letters. His account of the analogies between Christian and Muslim theology, for instance, resembles that of Richard Simon. The differences between Simon, who wrote in the 1670s, and Gibbon, writing a century later, are of tone and context rather than of substance. Simon aimed to provoke, whereas Gibbon, in whose world the threat of Christian conversion to Islam was not a serious prospect, could make evenhanded comments without awakening fear that his readers might be tempted to become Muslims. This context—the lack of any need for religious polemic—gives Gibbon's work the appearance of a profoundly novel, modern attainment, but at bottom his account of Islam was in line with a very traditional European way of reading the religion: as an outgrowth of Christianity and as a Christian heresy.

Gibbon essentially reiterated Pococke's version of the history of Islamic intellectual and artistic achievement: that the pursuit of letters had been restricted to eloquence, poetry, the interpretation of the Qur'an, and medicine during the Umayyad period (which lasted until the year 750), and that the great cultural and scientific achievements began only in the Abbasid period, after the court moved from Damascus to Baghdad.

> After their civil and domestic wars, the subjects of the Abbassides, awakening from this mental lethargy, found leisure and felt curiosity for the acquisiton of profane science. This spirit was first encouraged by the caliph Almansor, who, besides his knowledge of the Mahometan law, had applied himself with success to the study of astronomy. But when the sceptre devolved to Almamon, the seventh of the Abbassides, he completed the designs of his grandfather, and invited the muses from their ancient seats. His ambassadors at Constantinople, his agents in Armenia, Syria, and Egypt, collected the volumes of Grecian science: at his command they were translated by the most skilful interpreters into the Arabic language: his subjects were exhorted assiduously to peruse these instructive writings; and the successor of Mahomet assisted with pleasure and modesty at the assemblies and disputations of the learned.[173]

Gibbon followed this paraphrase of Pococke with a quotation from Ṣāʿid al-Andalusī, qadi of Toledo, that comes from Pococke's main source, Bar

Hebraeus.[174] Although Gibbon did not include in this discussion the additional information found in Reiske, he held Reiske in high esteem, classing him with the best scholars of the modern era, along with Erasmus of Rotterdam, Joseph Scaliger, and Richard Bentley.[175]

In outlining the achievements of the Arabs in various fields of knowledge—he thought they made especially strong contributions in astronomy and medicine—and in describing Arab thinkers' adoption of Aristotelian thought, Gibbon employed "literary anecdotes" from Bar Hebraeus, the *Bibliotheca Arabico-Hispana,* Leo Africanus, and Eusèbe Renaudot.[176] (Curiously, he did not here make use of Reiske's *Dissertatio* and "Prodidagmata," even though they would have suited his purpose, and the latter was certainly known to him.)[177] He believed that the era of Muslim learning had as clear an end as a beginning: "The age of Arabian learning continued about five hundred years, till the great eruption of the Moguls [Mongols], and was coæval with the darkest and most slothful period of European annals; but since the sun of science has arisen in the West, it should seem that the Oriental studies have languished and declined."[178]

Gibbon concluded that the selective translation of Greek writings had done a disservice to Islamic intellectual history: "But the Moslems deprived themselves of the principal benefits of a familiar intercourse with Greece and Rome, the knowledge of antiquity, the purity of taste, and the freedom of thought."[179] He believed that lack of exposure to the full scope of Greek civilization ("the knowledge of antiquity") had stopped Muslims from cultivating their taste and prevented them from attaining intellectual freedom, leaving them captives of their religious and cultural traditions, strictures, and aesthetics.

Unlike Voltaire, Gibbon acknowledged the limits of his ability to judge Arabic poetry, the form most central to Islamic literary culture: "I am not forward to condemn the literature and judgment of nations, of whose language I am ignorant." Yet these limits did not stop him from claiming that Arabic and Persian poetry were inferior to their classical equivalent, whose aesthetics the influential art historian Johann Joachim Winckelmann (1717–1768) had described as "noble simplicity and silent grandeur."[180] "Yet I *know* that the classics have much to teach, and I *believe* that the Orientals have much to learn: the temperate dignity of style, the graceful proportions of art, the forms of visible and intellectual beauty, the just delineation of character and passion, the rhetoric of narrative and argument, the regular fabric of epic and dramatic poetry."[181]

Gibbon argued against Islamic aesthetics on the grounds that classical values had not been transmitted to the Arabs, a position that dismissed the views of his contemporary William Jones (1746–1794), the greatest British scholar of Oriental languages of his day. Jones had studied Persian, Arabic, and Turkish before going to Bengal in 1783 to serve as a judge at the supreme court of British India. There he became deeply involved in the study of Sanskrit literature, introducing it to European readers for the first time.[182] Gibbon wrote off Jones's expert judgment as the enthusiasm of a neophyte, asserting that his treatise on "Oriental [poetry] was composed in the youth of that wonderful linguist" and that "at present, in the maturity of his taste and judgment, he would perhaps abate of the fervent and even partial praise which he has bestowed on the Orientals."[183] Jones's sympathetic and learned treatment of Islamic poetry did not sway Gibbon, who found him too partial to Muslims. Gibbon criticized Jones's translations, including his version of the *Muʿallaqāt,* a famous collection of pre-Islamic Arabic odes, about which he remarked: "[Jones's] honourable mission to India has deprived us of his own notes, far more interesting than the obscure and obsolete text."[184]

Gibbon concluded that the failed transmission of classical writings to Muslim peoples had even more dire consequences for political and moral philosophy than it did for the arts: "The influence of truth and reason is of a less ambiguous complexion. The philosophers of Athens and Rome enjoyed the blessings, and asserted the rights, of civil and religious freedom. Their moral and political writings might have gradually unlocked the spirit of inquiry and toleration, and encouraged the Arabian sages to suspect that their caliph was a tyrant and their prophet an impostor. The instinct of superstition was alarmed by the introduction even of the abstract sciences; and the more rigid doctors of the law condemned the rash and pernicious curiosity of Almamon."[185] To show that political reform would have resulted from a broader study of classical sources, Gibbon cited the "Saracens . . . [whose] sword . . . became less formidable, when their youth was drawn away from the camp to the college, when the armies of the faithful presumed to read and to reflect." This advancement was stymied, he wrote, by the shortcomings of the Muslims and by the pride of the conquered Greeks: "Yet the foolish vanity of the Greeks was jealous of their studies, and reluctantly imparted the sacred fire to the Barbarians of the East."[186]

Gibbon's judgment of Islamic civilization was harsh; the problem was a failed *translatio studii,* a torch whose flame had not been passed on. Not having read the moral and political writings of the ancients, Muslims lacked "the spirit of inquiry and toleration." Al-Ma'mūn's enthusiasm for knowledge had been an exception that was repudiated by his successors. As for Islamic historical writing, Gibbon had submitted his evaluation at the outset of his discussion of Islamic history with a comparison that was unencumbered by modesty, false or otherwise: "The *Oriental library* of a Frenchman [d'Herbelot] would instruct the most learned mufti of the East; and perhaps the Arabs might not find in a single historian so clear and comprehensive a narrative of their own exploits as that which will be deduced in the ensuing sheets."[187]

As an aside, it is worth noting that some of Gibbon's information was not accurate. His claim, for instance, that the moral and political writings of Athens and Rome had not been transmitted to the Muslims is unsustainable: although Aristotle's *Politics* was not translated into Arabic, his *Nicomachean Ethics* was, as was Plato's *Republic*.[188] Gibbon's focus on the failure of transmission derived from his assumption that reading certain works would have necessarily occasioned a particular intellectual and philosophical change. His harsh judgments were his own, and not, as we have seen, those of the European secondary literature on these topics, which strongly emphasized both the intellectual attainments of Muslims and their resemblance to those of classical antiquity.[189] In his deprecation of Islamic intellectual and literary achievement, Gibbon distanced himself from the members of Republic of Arabic Letters and their judgments.

In sum, Voltaire and Gibbon both relied on scholarship from the Republic of Arabic Letters, but each interpreted it differently; Voltaire erred on the side of enthusiasm and idealization and Gibbon on the side of condemnation. Voltaire painted an idealized portrait, both building and embroidering on the arguments of his European scholarly informants. Gibbon discounted the importance of the achievements of al-Ma'mūn's era for understanding Islamic civilization; his work perhaps reflects the moralistic disapproval of Islamic societies that increased in Europe between the 1750s and the 1780s. This attitudinal change derived not from any new research overturning previous accounts of Muslim history, but merely from a different overall appraisal of the place of Islam and of the intellectual achievements it had afforded in the history of humankind.

Conclusion

Reconstructing the views of Voltaire and Gibbon allows us to see, first of all, that these celebrated writers recapitulated the themes of earlier European scholars of Islam and, second, that the most impressive aspects of the Enlightenment interpretations of Islam did not originate with the French *philosophes* or their English and Scottish counterparts. The originality that has been credited to Voltaire and Gibbon for presenting and contextualizing the rise of Islam in historical terms rightly belongs to those from whom Voltaire and Gibbon took primary materials and many of their arguments. What was new about Enlightenment historiography was that the rise of Islam was written into new, "philosophical" histories of the world, a project that was tackled in both Britain and France—a change of context rather than of substance. At the same time, some Enlightenment authors relied primarily on the alternative tradition of travel writing. As we have seen, chief among them was Montesquieu, who, along with others who were invested in comparative political science, paid scant attention to the European scholars of Arabic.

The writers of the Enlightenment were freer to be original than their scholarly counterparts had been. Not having studied Arabic, they did not have to defend the relevance of Arabic literature or Islamic history and letters and could use Islamic materials in any way they pleased; nor were they committed to any particular linguistic, geographic, or regional group.

Montesquieu and Voltaire adopted a global scope—examples from all over the world beckoned, and Islam took its place alongside the other religions of the world. With each decade, more accounts of foreign parts appeared in print and jostled for the attention of Enlightenment thinkers. Persian and Ottoman travel accounts were now supplemented by reports from North and South America, sub-Saharan Africa, South and Southeast Asia, China, and Japan. Voltaire assigned Christianity a more humble place in human history than his predecessors, such as Bossuet, had done, and Islam was likewise demoted to one among many religions worthy of study. Even so, coverage of these other cultures and religions was uneven: Voltaire was nowhere near as accurate about Buddhism as he was about Islam, which is perhaps understandable, given that European study of East Asian religious traditions was more recent and much less developed.[190] Gibbon was much more in the mold of his scholarly predecessors in his focus on Europe, the classical Mediterranean, and the Near East; Islam was the only non-Christian religion he examined in detail.

Considering their freedom of choice, it is remarkable that Voltaire and Gibbon hewed so closely to the discussions of Islamic history and religion by the European scholars of Arabic. Although the scope of their work differed, they drew on the same repertoire of techniques for making sense of Islamic history. Voltaire repeatedly followed in the footsteps of his Arabic-reading informants, for instance confidently stressing the reliability of information about Muhammad. Despite his emphasis on difference Gibbon nevertheless traded in some analogies between classical and Islamic history: by treating them in the context of *The Decline and Fall,* for instance, he made the Rightly Guided Caliphs seem analogous to the virtuous emperors of the Roman Empire.[191]

Voltaire and Gibbon each veered from learned scholarship on the subject of Muslim achievements, with Voltaire insisting that they did not spring from Islam itself, but rather from the national character of the Arabs. Gibbon, in spite of the greater information at his disposal, including the work of Reiske, took the position that the ascendancy of curiosity had been fleeting and that Islamic civilization had condemned itself to a religious captivity. His severe evaluation derived from his view of religion and theology in general and from his understanding of despotism and decline. His greater knowledge of Islamic materials, which he owed to his Arabic-reading predecessors, did not prompt him to reject these interpretations.

In light of how many of their ideas and approaches to Islam derived from the work of an earlier group of writers, the originality of the Enlightenment writers on the subject needs to be reconsidered. The Enlightenment is widely regarded as a formative moment in European intellectual history, one that generated new skepticism about religion. However, the seventeenth-century Catholic and Protestant scholars who committed themselves to reconsidering Islam did not do so because they harbored doubts about their own religion; their work had little to do with their personal beliefs about Christianity or the state. Their reinterpretation of Islam instead arose through the evolution of knowledge production, not from internal developments in European theology and philosophy. As we have seen, knowledge production and normative reinterpretation are closely related processes but not identical ones.

The analysis put forward in this book supports recent research into eighteenth-century intellectual history. This research has changed our view of the Enlightenment, and especially of its most canonical figures, from the Parisian *philosophes* to their Scottish counterparts, by placing them within a wider context of seventeenth- and eighteenth-century traditions of scholarship and erudition.[192] Seen from that broader perspective, it is clear that many ideas traditionally credited to a small set of rather politicized figures were conceived earlier and by a wider range of thinkers.[193] Many of the ideas that the *philosophes* stated in a polemical way were shared by earlier, less incendiary writers. These findings make the intellectual substance of the combative secularism of the *philosophes* both less original and more ideological. As William Bulman puts it, "Proponents of the traditional interpretation [of the Enlightenment] have mistaken an essentially political movement for an intellectual one."[194]

Recent research also shows that a foreign religion could be studied in rich, careful detail, without anger or partiality, and without explicitly rejecting established faiths or institutions. The provocateur Richard Simon, as well as numerous orthodox writers from Adriaan Reland to George Sale, extended intellectual charity to Islam, and understood it in comparison not just with other Near Eastern religions, but with their own. Most of these comparisons were not intended to provoke—sometimes they were buried deep within the pages of an erudite tome, such as the *Bibliothèque Orientale*—but in their substance they do not differ from the content of more political statements that have unhesitatingly been called Enlightened.[195]

It is hard, therefore, to see why the writings of Voltaire and Gibbon qualify as part of the Enlightenment when those of the Republic of Arabic Letters do not. The story of scholars gradually reconfiguring knowledge is perhaps less exciting than that of a band of heroic philosophical warriors remaking their intellectual and political world, but it has the advantage of being truthful. It may well be wise to set less stock in "the Enlightenment" as we have known it. Perhaps our histories of the eighteenth century, not to mention our understanding of the Western tradition, will be shrewder when the famous Enlightenment—a term invested with so much historiographical power—is revealed to be a more humble thing. It is worth acknowledging that many ideas of the period have a Christian heritage and that they issued from the broad intellectual commitments of a long tradition of humanistic scholarship in the wake of the wars of religion and the process of confessionalization. The reconsideration of a foreign religion and its history, including its cultural attainments, did not have to await the development of a secular intellectual culture.

The history of the Republic of Arabic Letters also reveals the intellectual opportunities afforded by the increased Afro-Eurasian circulation of people and objects in the seventeenth and eighteenth centuries. Today historians who talk of a "global Enlightenment" propose that the fundamental ideas of the Enlightenment were elaborated through interaction and engagement with extra-European peoples and cultures.[196] This was certainly true in the case of Islam and Islamic letters. As I have aimed to show, however, this process was neither automatic nor natural, but instead extremely effortful. Most of its intellectual discoveries, moreover, happened in libraries rather than in foreign ports or on the road. They came about because a number of people sought to take intellectual advantage of the increase in global circulation of people and goods. In this respect, the emergence of the Republic of Arabic Letters can be considered an episode in the history of the global Enlightenment. At the very least, it was a significant chapter in the long and painstaking global advance of philological learning and interreligious knowledge.

EPILOGUE

What brought the Republic of Arabic Letters to an end? Eventually the keen sense of analogy, even kinship, felt by several generations of European scholars faded away. The heyday of the Republic, from 1650 to 1750, was an exceptional era in the European evaluation of Islam, a time when the religious, literary, and intellectual traditions of Muslim peoples held so much promise in the eyes of their European students. The distinction this book makes between the creation of knowledge, on the one hand, and normative reevaluation, on the other, can help us understand what happened at midcentury, when the overall perception of Islam changed from one of similarity to its European equivalents to one of difference. In general, the preceding chapters show greater knowledge and greater sympathy proceeding hand in hand. Yet these two interrelated processes could be decoupled. The story of Islam and its reception in the European Enlightenment is not merely about the many ways in which the attainments of European Arabic scholarship were assimilated into the Enlightenment's order of knowledge. It is also a tale of how normative ideas about Islam changed, especially after 1750.

By the second half of the eighteenth century, the sense of kinship with Islam waned both within the broad intellectual culture of Europe and among the community of European scholars of Arabic. Over the course of the century there had been an evolution in the way Europeans understood themselves in regard both to non-Europeans and to their own past. The European economy had changed from primarily agrarian to increasingly commercial, with resultant shifts in manners, architecture, and urban life, transformations that seemed to support the notion of European singularity. Since the Renaissance, numerous observers argued, European civilization had been on a path that might be described as "progress," which marked it off from its own medieval past and from other regions of the world. This path ran from the recovery of classical letters and the invention of the printing press to the "new philosophy" of Descartes and Isaac Newton; over time it led to an increasingly secular European intellectual culture and self-definition, which in turn lowered interest in Islam. No longer considered an equivalent of Christianity (albeit a false one), the religion's status dropped. It came to be regarded as a force holding Muslims back.[1]

Contributing to this reassessment was a diminishment in the geopolitical status of Muslim states. In 1736 the Safavids were deposed by Nadir Shah, who soon threatened the Mughals as well; when he was assassinated in 1747, his empire quickly disintegrated. Meanwhile, the European powers' hold on parts of South Asia, particularly Bengal, expanded during the Seven Years' War (1756–1763). Then, after a major defeat at Russian hands in 1774, the Ottoman Empire seemed to teeter on the brink of collapse. In addition, the European economy significantly outpaced the Ottoman one throughout the eighteenth century, and the balance of trade shifted: in the seventeenth century, French merchants imported coffee from the Ottoman Empire, but by the eighteenth century the Ottoman Empire was importing coffee grown in European colonial plantations.[2] Eventually, as the overland trade with Asia was rendered obsolete by European sea trade, the Mediterranean became a backwater. European observers took the great Muslim states' decline in power as confirmation that luxury brought about moral, cultural, and political corrosion, and they viewed the religion of Islam as complicit in this process. In short, due to new European self-definitions and to global geopolitical transformations, Islam ceased to play the exemplary role in the European imagination that it had done for such a significant season.[3]

By the second half of the eighteenth century, European scholars disagreed as to whether Islam was a kindred tradition or a manifestly inferior one. Reiske thought that Arabic literature was akin, if not superior, to the Western classical tradition, while his contemporary and former classmate Johann David Michaelis believed that, for instance, the Muslim tradition of Qur'anic commentary had few insights to offer; he was persuaded that he could read the Qur'an without its assistance not only perfectly well but also more accurately.[4] A gulf separates Michaelis's sense of superiority from earlier European scholars' indebtedness to Muslim mediation and their willingness to be guided by native judgments. Islam continued to be studied, but not necessarily as a religion endowed with exemplary qualities.

The internal intellectual dynamics of the European study of Islam also transformed over time. At the beginning of the study of Arabic, European scholars had no recourse but to rely on native grammars and dictionaries, and to accept native interpretations of the Qur'an. As time went on, they emancipated themselves from that dependence. For example, after the publication of Marracci's Qur'an, which included notes drawn from five different Qur'anic commentaries, translating further commentaries lost urgency.[5] Michaelis's rejection of the commentarial tradition as obsolete mirrored the earlier course of European Hebrew studies, which by about 1700 rejected the rabbinic tradition that had seemed so full of promise to earlier generations of Christian scholars.[6] The ladder could be kicked away once it had been climbed. In the long run, learning more about the Islamic tradition led to the devaluation of many of its aspects.

To be sure, Arabic philology remained alive in Europe—it did not depend merely or mainly on sympathy—but its forms changed. Difference, rather than analogy, was emphasized. It is worth noting that drawing analogies is not an intrinsically sound strategy. As we have seen, European scholars could overstate similarities, misrepresenting Islam to make it more familiar. Likewise, emphasizing distinctions can lead to specious exaggerations of difference—but it can also bring about more precise knowledge. No longer attempting to reduce Arabic grammar to the rules of Greek and Latin, or Arabic literature to the conventions and categories of classical Greek literature, for example, was an achievement that had eluded earlier generations of European scholars of Arabic.

Eighteenth-century writers, influenced by the heightened sense of European distinctiveness, mined Islamic literary and intellectual traditions for examples of the foreignness of Muslim lands. Traditions of knowledge that are at the margins of the present inquiry, such as travel literature, often served such ends, but even Arabic scholarship could be enrolled to the cause. A case in point is d'Herbelot's *Bibliothèque Orientale,* which served as a storehouse of material for Romantic writers looking for Levantine "color."[7]

Was the Republic of Arabic Letters then a mere flash in the pan, an intellectual cul-de-sac? Jumping to that conclusion would be too hasty. For one thing, it would overlook the movement's later impact. The great achievements of nineteenth-century Islamic studies in the West were built on the work of members of the Republic. When the illustrious French Arabist Isaac-Antoine Silvestre de Sacy (1758–1838) was starting out, he relied on the work of Reiske and his predecessors, and standard works produced in the Republic remained in use and in print throughout the nineteenth century—indeed, Ockley's *History of the Saracens* was published more often in the second half of the nineteenth century than throughout the eighteenth.[8] The greatest success of all was Sale's Qur'an translation, which remained the standard English version into the twentieth century.

Moreover, it is important to recognize that Western interactions with the peoples and religion of Islam did not go directly from Crusades to modern colonialism. The Republic of Arabic Letters stands as a reminder of a moment of intercultural possibility that our historical macronarratives have often overlooked. As a result of continued publication, not to mention continued existence on library shelves across Europe and North America, the knowledge produced in the seventeenth and eighteenth centuries was transmitted to later eras. Even as nineteenth-century Western views of Islam and of Muslims turned increasingly patronizing, the works of the Republic of Arabic Letters offered, at least in principle, a rebuke to any wholly dismissive view of Islam and its religious and intellectual traditions. As imperfect and incomplete as the Republic's intellectual contributions may have been, it seems fair to say that they did justice to Abū'l-Fidā''s maxim: if you cannot know everything, do not for that reason give up, for partial knowledge is always preferable to ignorance.

Abbreviations

APF	Archivio Storico di Propaganda Fide, Rome
ASP	Archivio del Seminario Maggiore di Padova
ASPV	Archivio del Seminario Patriarcale di Venezia
BAV	Biblioteca Apostolica Vaticana
BL	British Library, London
BNCF	Biblioteca Nazionale Centrale di Firenze
BnF	Bibliothèque nationale de France, Paris
BNM	Biblioteca Nazionale Marciana, Venezia
Bod.	Bodleian Library, Oxford
CUL	Cambridge University Library
DBI	*Dizionario Biografico degli Italiani.* 83 vols. Rome: Istituto della Enciclopedia Italiana, 1960–.
DKB	Det Kongelige Bibliotek, Copenhagen
EI2	*Encyclopaedia of Islam.* 2nd edition. Leiden: Brill, 1960–2009.
EI3	*Encylopaedia of Islam.* 3rd edition. Leiden: Brill, 2007–.
EQ	Jane Dammen McAuliffe, ed. *Encyclopaedia of the Qur'ān.* 6 vols. Leiden: Brill, 2001–2006.
KB	Koninklijke Bibliotheek, Den Haag
ODNB	*Oxford Dictionary of National Biography.* Oxford: Oxford University Press, 2004–.
OMD	Santa Maria in Campitelli, Rome
SUB	Göttingen University Library

Notes

INTRODUCTION

1. Edward Gibbon, *Memoirs of My Life,* ed. B. Radice (1795; repr., London, 1984), 82. The conversation with his tutor took place after Gibbon's start at Oxford on April 3 but before the summer vacation of 1752, when his tutor left the university. Gibbon celebrated his fifteenth birthday on May 8, so he may have still been fourteen at the time of the exchange. Chapter 6 offers a more extensive discussion of Gibbon's study of Islamic history.

2. Hans Bots and Françoise Waquet, *La république des lettres* (Paris, 1997). See also Anne Goldgar, *Impolite Learning: Conduct and Community in the Republic of Letters, 1680–1750* (New Haven, Ct., 1995).

3. On the Church Fathers and the good pagans, see John Marenbon, *Pagans and Philosophers: The Problem of Paganism from Augustine to Leibniz* (Princeton, N.J., 2015). Comparison has been criticized as an intellectual tool; see, e.g., Jonathan Z. Smith, *Drudgery Divine: On the Comparison of Early Christianities and the Religions of Late Antiquity* (Chicago, 1990). But see Anthony Grafton, "Christianity's Jewish Origins Rediscovered: The Roles of Comparison in Early Modern Ecclesiastical Scholarship," *Erudition and the Republic of Letters* 1 (2016): 13–42.

4. Thus, this study joins others that have expanded our understanding of the eighteenth-century Enlightenment, directing attention away from the most canonical figures engaged in a fierce struggle with religion and toward an alternative genealogy of the signal accomplishments of the Enlightenment. See Chapter 6 for a fuller discussion and references.

5. This account may be new as a whole, but it emerges from directions indicated by earlier scholarship; see, e.g., Paul Hazard, *La crise de la conscience européenne (1680–1715)* (Paris, 1935), 16–18; Alastair Hamilton, "Lutheran Islamophiles in Eighteenth-Century Germany," in *For the Sake of Learning: Essays in Honor of Anthony Grafton,* 2 vols., ed. A. Blair and A.-S. Goeing (Leiden, 2016), 1:327–343. Jürgen Osterhammel, *Die Entzauberung Asiens: Europa und die asiatischen Reiche im 18. Jahrhundert* (Munich, 1998), was an early inspiration for this study; Osterhammel's focus on scholarship rather than travel literature has, however, occasioned a different chronology and even a different argument about Europeans' changing understandings of Muslim peoples.

6. On medieval views of Islam, see Norman Daniel, *Islam and the West: The Making of an Image* (Edinburgh, 1960); R. W. Southern, *Western Views of Islam in the*

Middle Ages (Cambridge, Mass., 1962); John V. Tolan, *Saracens: Islam in the Medieval European Imagination* (New York, 2002); Tolan, *Sons of Ishmael: Muslims through European Eyes in the Middle Ages* (Gainesville, 2008).

7. Nancy Bisaha, *Creating East and West: Renaissance Humanists and the Ottoman Turks* (Philadelphia, 2004); Margaret Meserve, *Empires of Islam in Renaissance Historical Thought* (Cambridge, Mass., 2008).

8. On the etymology of the term "Saracen," still contested, see *EI2*, s.v. "Saracens."

9. James Kritzeck, *Peter the Venerable and Islam* (Princeton, N.J., 1964); John Tolan, "Peter the Venerable on the 'Diabolical Heresy of the Saracens,'" in *The Devil, Heresy and Witchcraft in the Middle Ages: Essays in Honor of Jeffrey B. Russell,* ed. Alberto Ferreiro (Leiden, 1998), 345–367.

10. Marshall G. S. Hodgson, *The Gunpowder Empires and Modern Times,* vol. 3, *The Venture of Islam: Conscience and History in a World Civilization* (Chicago, 1974).

11. Some recent studies of this influx of material culture include Deborah Howard, *Venice and the East: The Impact of the Islamic World on Venetian Architecture, 1100–1500* (New Haven, Ct., 2000); Lisa Jardine and Jerry Brotton, *Global Interests: Renaissance Art between East and West* (Ithaca, N.Y., 2000); Stefano Carboni, ed., *Venice and the Islamic World, 828–1797* (New Haven, Ct., 2007).

12. Thomas E. Burman, *Reading the Qur'an in Latin Christendom, 1140–1560* (Philadelphia, 2007), 178–197; James Hankins, "Renaissance Crusaders: Humanist Crusade Literature in the Age of Mehmed II," *Dumbarton Oaks Papers* 49 (1995): 111–207; Bisaha, *Creating East and West;* Meserve, *Empires of Islam.*

13. On the increased salience of theology in the sixteenth century, see Carlo Ginzburg, *The Cheese and the Worms: The Cosmos of a Sixteenth-Century Miller* (Baltimore, 1980).

14. Several religious designations for Muslims are first attested in English in the sixteenth century, as recorded in *Oxford English Dictionary,* 2nd ed., s.v. "muslim": "Mahometan" (1504); "Mahometist" (1513); "Turk" (used in religious sense, 1548); "Mahometism" (1584); "Mohammedism" (1614); "Mohammedanism" (1734). "Muslim" or "Moslem" did not enter into widespread usage until the eighteenth century, though the earliest usage reported by the *OED* is a gloss by the Arabist William Bedwell in 1615: "*Muslim,* or *Mussliman,* . . is one that is instructed in the beleefe of the Mohammetanes." The first English use of "Islam" to denote the religion is recorded as 1818, in the title of Shelley's poem *The Revolt of Islam: A Poem in Twelve Cantos* (London, 1818). For French, see *Dictionnaire de l'Académie françoise,* 4th ed. (1762), s.v. "Islamisme" and "mahométisme." On the depiction of Muslims in Renaissance literature, see J. P. Donnelly, "The Moslem Enemy in Renaissance Epic: Ariosto, Tasso and Camoëns," *Yale Italian Studies* 1 (1977): 162–170; Antonio Franceschetti, "On the Saracens in Early

Italian Chivalric Literature," in *Romance Epic: Essays on a Medieval Literary Genre,* ed. Hans-Erich Keller (Kalamazoo, Mich., 1987), 203–211.

15. On unitarianism and Oriental studies, see Martin Mulsow, "Orientalistik im Kontext der sozinianischen und deistischen Debatten um 1700," *Scientia Poetica* 2 (1998): 27–57. Opponents of unitarianism would likewise study the history of Islam on polemical grounds. See, e.g., Jan Loop, *Johann Heinrich Hottinger: Arabic and Islamic Studies in the Seventeenth Century* (Oxford, 2013), chap. 5. Islam could also serve orthodox Christians to reproach their peers—the comparison between Christians and Muslims did not always flatter the former, for example in reference to piety or political organization. See, for instance, Martin Steinmann, *Johannes Oporinus: Ein Basler Buchdrucker um die Mitte des 16. Jahrhunderts* (Basel, 1967), 27–28, on the Basel edition of the Qur'an. On Neuser, see *Allgemeine Deutsche Biographie,* s.v. "Sylvanus, Johann." Ginzburg, *Cheese and the Worms,* suggested that the Qur'an helped the freethinking miller Menocchio to formulate his profoundly heterodox vision of the cosmos. See also Pier Mattia Tommasino, *L'Alcorano di Macometto: Storia di un libro del Cinquecento europeo* (Bologna, 2013). On the Indices, see Jésus Martínez de Bujanda, ed., *Index des livres interdits,* 10 vols. (Geneva, 1984–1996), 3:214; 4:296; 5:218, 307; 8:362–363; 9:665–666.

16. This has been noted by Pierre Martino, *L'Orient dans la littérature française au XVIIème et au XVIIIème siècle* (Paris, 1906); Johann Fück, *Die arabischen Studien in Europa bis in den Anfang des 20. Jahrhunderts* (Leipzig, 1955); Suzanne L. Marchand, *German Orientalism in the Age of Empire: Religion, Race, and Scholarship* (Cambridge, 2009); Guy G. Stroumsa, *A New Science: The Discovery of Religion in the Age of Reason* (Cambridge, Mass., 2010).

17. Justin Stagl, *A History of Curiosity: The Theory of Travel, 1550–1800* (Chur, Switzerland, 1995); Joan-Pau Rubiés, "Instructions for Travellers: Teaching the Eye to See," *History and Anthropology* 9 (1996): 139–190.

18. Clarence Dana Rouillard, *The Turk in French History, Thought and Literature (1520–1660)* (Paris, 1941).

19. On European travel writing, an incomplete list would include, in addition to the titles already cited: Mary Campbell, *The Witness and the Other World: Exotic European Travel Writing, 400–1600* (Ithaca, N.Y., 1988); Amanda Wunder, "Western Travelers, Eastern Antiquities, and the Image of the Turk in Early Modern Europe," *Journal of Early Modern History* 7 (2003): 89–119; Alison Games, *The Web of Empire: English Cosmopolitans in an Age of Expansion, 1560–1660* (Oxford, 2008), chap. 2.

20. On the number of Turkish plays, see Alexander Bevilacqua and Helen Pfeifer, "Turquerie: Culture in Motion, 1650–1750," *Past and Present* 221 (2013): 93n62.

21. On South Asia in European thought, see Ines G. Županov, *Disputed Mission: Jesuit Experiments and Brahmanical Knowledge in Seventeenth-Century India* (Oxford, 1999); Joan-Pau Rubiés, *Travel and Ethnology in the Renaissance: South India through European Eyes, 1250–1625* (Cambridge, 2000); Marie Fourcade and Ines G. Županov, eds., *L'Inde des Lumières: Discours, histoire, savoirs (XVIIe–XIXe siècles)* (Paris, 2013); Sanjay Subrahmanyam, *Europe's India: Words, People, Empires, 1500–1800* (Cambridge, Mass., 2017).

22. On d'Herbelot, see Chapter 4. On Johann Jacob Reiske, see Johann Jacob Reiske, "Prodidagmata ad Hagji Chalifae Librum Memorialem," in Johann Bernhard Köhler, *Abulfedae Tabula Syriae cum Excerpto Geographico ex Ibn ol Wardii* (Leipzig, 1766), 228.

23. Anthony Grafton and Lisa Jardine, *From Humanism to the Humanities: Education and the Liberal Arts in Fifteenth- and Sixteenth-Century Europe* (Cambridge, Mass., 1986); Paul F. Grendler, *Schooling in Renaissance Italy: Literacy and Learning, 1300–1600* (Baltimore, 1989); Robert Black, *Humanism and Education in Medieval and Renaissance Italy: Tradition and Innovation in Latin Schools from the Twelfth to the Fifteenth Century* (Cambridge, 2001).

24. Alastair Hamilton, "Humanists and the Bible," in *The Cambridge Companion to Renaissance Humanism,* ed. Jill Kraye (Cambridge, 1996), 100–117; G. J. Toomer, *Eastern Wisedome and Learning: The Study of Arabic in Seventeenth-Century England* (Oxford, 1995); Stroumsa, *A New Science.*

25. See, among many others, Frank Manuel, *The Broken Staff: Judaism through Christian Eyes* (Cambridge, Mass., 1992); Ilana Zinguer, ed., *L'hébreu au temps de la Renaissance* (Leiden, 1992); Anthony Grafton and Joanna Weinberg, *"I Have Always Loved the Holy Tongue": Isaac Casaubon, the Jews, and a Forgotten Chapter in Renaissance Scholarship* (Cambridge, Mass., 2011); David Nirenberg, *Anti-Judaism: The Western Tradition* (New York, 2013). See also Noel Malcolm's reflection on the difference between European Hebrew and Arabic studies: "The Study of Islam in Early Modern Europe: Obstacles and Missed Opportunities," in *Antiquarianism and Intellectual Life in Europe and China, 1500–1800,* ed. Peter N. Miller and François Louis (Ann Arbor, Mich., 2012), 265–288.

26. Jerry Bentley, *Humanists and Holy Writ: New Testament Scholarship in the Renaissance* (Princeton, N.J., 1983), 70–111; Theodor W. Dunkelgrün, "The Multiplicity of Scripture: The Confluence of Textual Traditions in the Making of the Antwerp Polyglot Bible (1568–1573)" (PhD diss., University of Chicago, 2012); Peter N. Miller, "Making the Paris Polyglot Bible: Humanism and Orientalism in the Early Seventeenth Century," in *Die europäische Gelehrtenrepublik im Zeitalter des Konfessionalismus,* ed. Herbert Jaumann (Wiesbaden, 2001), 59–85; and Miller, "The 'Antiquarianization' of Biblical Scholarship and

the London Polyglot Bible (1653–57)," *Journal of the History of Ideas* 62 (2001): 463–482. On Antwerp's role in seventeenth-century Oriental studies, see Alastair Hamilton, *Arab Culture and Ottoman Magnificence in Antwerp's Golden Age* (Oxford, 2001).

27. Bernard Heyberger, *Les chrétiens du Proche-Orient au temps de la Réforme catholique (Syrie, Liban, Palestine, XVII–XVIIIe siècles)* (Rome, 1994); Aurélien Girard, "Le christianisme oriental (XVIIe–XVIIIe siècles): Essor de l'orientalisme catholique en Europe et construction des identités confessionnelles au Proche-Orient" (PhD diss., École Pratique des Hautes Études, Paris, 2011). On the parallel Catholic efforts on the Greek side (the Greek College was founded in Rome in 1576), see Ingo Herklotz, *Die Academia Basiliana: Griechische Philologie, Kirchengeschichte und Unionsbemühungen im Rom der Barberini* (Rome, 2008).

28. An exemplary study of how a seventeenth-century European scholar of Arabic used his erudition to investigate all of these domains—from Hebrew to Islamic letters to the history of the Christian Church—is Loop, *Johann Heinrich Hottinger.*

29. Arnoud Vrolijk and Richard van Leeuwen, *Arabic Studies in the Netherlands: A Short History in Portraits, 1580–1950,* trans. A. Hamilton (Leiden, 2014), 20.

30. Thomas Erpenius, *Grammatica Arabica: Quinque Libris Methodice Explicata* (Leiden, 1613); Franciscus Raphelengius, *Lexicon Arabicum* (Leiden, 1613); Antonio Giggi, *Thesaurus Linguae Arabicae* (Milan, 1632); Jacobus Golius, *Lexicon Arabico-Latinum Contextum ex Probatioribus Orientis Lexicographis: Accedit Index Latinus Copiosissimus, Qui Lexici Latino-Arabici Vicem Explere Possit* (Leiden, 1653). On the Scaliger bequest, see Arnoud Vrolijk and Kasper van Ommen, *"All My Books in Foreign Tongues": Scaliger's Oriental Legacy in Leiden, 1609–2009: Catalogue of an Exhibition on the Quatercentenary of Scaliger's Death, 21 January 2009* (Leiden, 2009). On Raphelengius, see Alastair Hamilton, " 'Nam Tirones Sumus': Franciscus Raphelengius' Lexicon Arabico-Latinum (Leiden 1613)," in *Ex Officina Plantiniana: Studia in Memoriam Christophori Plantini (ca. 1520–1589),* ed. Marcus de Schepper and Francine de Nave (Antwerp, 1989), 557–589. On Erpenius, see Arnoud Vrolijk, "The Prince of Arabists and His Many Errors: Thomas Erpenius's Image of Joseph Scaliger and the Edition of the *Proverbia Arabica* (1614)," *Journal of the Warburg and Courtauld Institutes* 73 (2010): 297–325. On Bedwell's dictionary, see Alastair Hamilton, *William Bedwell, the Arabist (1563–1632)* (Leiden, 1985). On Arabic in the early modern English university, see Mordechai Feingold, "Oriental Studies," in *Seventeenth-Century Oxford,* vol. 4 of *The History of the University of Oxford,* ed. Nicholas Tyacke (Oxford, 1997), 449–503; and Feingold, "Patrons and Professors: The Origins and Motives for the Endowment of

University Chairs—In Particular the Laudian Professorship of Arabic," in *The "Arabick" Interest of the Natural Philosophers in Seventeenth-Century England,* ed. G. A. Russell (Leiden, 1994), 109–127. For France and Italy, see Aurélien Girard, "L'enseignement de l'arabe à Rome au XVIIIe siècle," in *Maghreb-Italie: Des passeurs médiévaux à l'orientalisme moderne, XIIIe–milieu XXe siècle,* ed. Benoît Grévin (Rome, 2010), 209–234; Girard, "Les manuels d'arabe en usage en France à la fin de l'ancien régime," in *Manuels d'arabe d'hier et d'aujourd'hui: France-Maghreb, XIXe–XXIe siècle,* ed. Sylvette Larzul and Alain Messaoudi (Paris, 2013), 12–26; Girard, "Des manuels de langue entre mission et érudition orientaliste au XVIIe siècle: Les grammaires de l'arabe des *Caracciolini,*" in *L'ordine dei Chierici regolari minori (Caracciolini): Religione e cultura in età postridentina: Atti del convegno (Chieti, 11–12 aprile 2008),* ed. Irene Fosi and Giovanni Pizzorusso [= *Studi medievali e moderni* 14 (2010)]: 279–296. More broadly, see Jan Loop, Alastair Hamilton, and Charles Burnett, eds., *The Teaching and Learning of Arabic in Early Modern Europe* (Leiden, 2017). In spite of all achievements, Arabic instruction continued to set a challenge to those who carried it out, and teachers often sought to produce their own grammatical materials, as archival materials show. See, for instance, BnF, Ms. NAF 8972, fol. 14: "Grammaire de la langue arabe, à l'usage du Collège Royal de France—24 nov. 1715" (Fourmont); Ms. NAF 8943, fols. 27–35 (Leroux-Deshautesrayes).

31. See Bernard Heyberger, ed., *Orientalisme, science et controverse: Abraham Ecchellensis (1605–1664)* (Turnhout, 2010); Heyberger, "L'islam et les arabes chez un érudit maronite au service de l'Église catholique (Abraham Ecchellensis)," *Al-Qantara* 31 (2010): 481–512; Girard, "Le christianisme oriental (XVIIe–XVIIIe siècles)"; Peter N. Miller, *Peiresc's Orient: Antiquarianism as Cultural History in the Seventeenth Century* (Burlington, Vt., 2012); Miller, *Peiresc's Mediterranean World* (Cambridge, Mass., 2015); Daniel Stolzenberg, *Egyptian Oedipus: Athanasius Kircher and the Secrets of Antiquity* (Chicago, 2013); Tommasino, *L'Alcorano di Macometto.*

32. For instance, Franciscus Meninski, *Thesaurus Linguarum Orientalium,* 4 vols. (Vienna, 1680). See also BnF, Mss. Arabe 4844–4849, for a late seventeenth-century European Arabic-Persian-Turkish dictionary in manuscript. On which, see Francis Richard, "Le dictionnaire de d'Herbelot," in *Istanbul et les langues orientales,* ed. Frédéric Hitzel (Paris, 1997), 79–88.

33. On this topic more broadly, see James T. Monroe, *Islam and the Arabs in Spanish Scholarship (Sixteenth Century to the Present)* (Leiden, 1970); Fernando Rodríguez Mediano, "Fragmentos de orientalismo español del S. XVII," *Hispania: Revista Española de Historia* 66 (2006): 243–276; Mercedes García-Arenal and Fernando Rodríguez Mediano, *The Orient in Spain: Converted Muslims, the*

Forged Lead Books of Granada, and the Rise of Orientalism (Leiden, 2013), esp. chaps. 17 and 18; Seth Kimmel, *Parables of Coercion: Conversion and Knowledge at the End of Islamic Spain* (Chicago, 2015); Mercedes García-Arenal, ed., *After Conversion: Iberia and the Emergence of Modernity* (Leiden, 2016).

34. Adriaan Reland, *Palaestina, ex Monumentis Veteribus Illustrata* (Utrecht, 1714); Edward Robinson and Eli Smith, *Biblical Researches in Palestine, Mount Sinai and Arabia Petraea,* 3 vols. (Boston, 1841), 1:47.

1 · THE ORIENTAL LIBRARY

1. BnF, Ms. Français 6130, fols. 4r–4v. The letter is quoted in Henri Omont, *Missions archéologiques françaises en Orient aux XVIIe et XVIIIe siècles,* 2 vols. (Paris, 1902), 1:217. On Galland, see Mohamed Abdel-Halim, *Antoine Galland: Sa vie et son oeuvre* (Paris, 1964).

2. On the collection of Oriental manuscripts, see Omont, *Missions archéologiques;* G. J. Toomer, *Eastern Wisedome and Learning: The Study of Arabic in Seventeenth-Century England* (Oxford, 1995); Alastair Hamilton et al., eds., *The Republic of Letters and the Levant* (Leiden, 2005); Peter N. Miller, *Peiresc's Mediterranean World* (Cambridge, Mass., 2015); John-Paul Ghobrial, "The Archive of Orientalism and Its Keepers: Re-imagining the Histories of Arabic Manuscripts in Early Modern Europe," *Past and Present,* suppl. 11 (2016): 90–111; Simon Mills, *A Commerce of Knowledge: Trade, Religion, and Scholarship between England and the Ottoman Empire* (Oxford, forthcoming). For the collection of information more broadly, see John-Paul Ghobrial, *The Whispers of Cities: Information Flows in Istanbul, London, and Paris in the Age of William Trumbull* (Oxford, 2013).

3. The Bodleian did not officially open until 1602, but the foundation is dated to 1598, when Thomas Bodley offered to fund a refurbished library in Oxford. Ian Philip, *The Bodleian Library in the Seventeenth and Eighteenth Centuries* (Oxford, 1983), 1.

4. On the Ambrosiana's Arabic collection, see Oscar Löfgren and Renato Traini, eds., *Catalogue of the Arabic Manuscripts in the Biblioteca Ambrosiana* (Vicenza, 1975), vol. 1. On the Florentine collection, see Angelo Maria Bandini, "Quando, e per opera di chi fosse da Roma ricondotta a Firenze la Biblioteca Medicea," in *Dei principi e progressi della Real Biblioteca Mediceo Laurenziana: Ms. Laur. Acquisti e Doni 142,* ed. Rosario Pintaudi et al. (Florence, 1990), chap. 9, esp. 79–80; Stefano Evodio Assemani, *Bibliothecae Mediceae Laurentianae et Palatinae Codicum Mss. Orientalium Catalogus* (Florence, 1742). In 1771, 517 shelfmarks (522 items) were transferred from Palazzo Pitti to the Biblioteca Laurenziana, where they are still located.

5. For the Dutch case, see Harold J. Cook, *Matters of Exchange: Commerce, Medicine and Science in the Dutch Golden Age* (New Haven, Ct., 2007); Siegfried

Huigen et al., *The Dutch Trading Companies as Knowledge Networks* (Leiden, 2010).

6. On the centrality of the mosque in Islamic intellectual life, see Johannes Pedersen, *The Arabic Book* (Princeton, N.J., 1984), 20. For a study of madrasas in high medieval times, see Michael Chamberlain, *Knowledge and Social Practice in Medieval Damascus, 1190–1350* (Cambridge, 1994), chap. 2. See also Jonathan Berkey, *The Transmission of Knowledge in Medieval Cairo: A Social History of Islamic Education* (Princeton, N.J., 1992).

7. Madeline C. Zilfi, "The Ottoman *Ulema,*" in *The Cambridge History of Turkey,* vol. 3, *The Later Ottoman Empire, 1603–1839,* ed. Suraiya Faroqhi (Cambridge, 2008), chap. 10.

8. Zilfi, "The Ottoman *Ulema,*" 215.

9. Quoted in Hatice Aynur, "Ottoman Literature," in Faroqhi, *The Later Ottoman Empire,* 481.

10. Seven such dictionaries survive from the seventeenth century alone. See Aynur, "Ottoman Literature," 492–496. For an example of the use of poetry at court, see Cornell H. Fleischer, *Bureaucrat and Intellectual in the Ottoman Empire: The Historian Mustafa Ali (1541–1600)* (Princeton, N.J., 1986), 70–71. Walter Andrews and Mehmet Kalpaklı, *The Age of Beloveds: Love and the Beloved in Early Modern Ottoman and European Culture and Society* (Durham, N.C., 2005), provide a lively portrait of cultural life in Istanbul in the sixteenth century. Such a comprehensive portrait has not been drawn for the seventeenth century, but the present account draws on the various sources cited below.

11. Aynur, "Ottoman Literature," 503. On the Ottoman salons, see Helen Pfeifer, "To Gather Together: Cultural Encounters in Sixteenth-Century Ottoman Literary Salons" (PhD diss., Princeton University, 2014).

12. Alan Mikhail, "The Heart's Desire: Gender, Urban Space and the Ottoman Coffee House," in *Ottoman Tulips, Ottoman Coffee: Leisure and Lifestyle in the Eighteenth Century,* ed. Dana Sajdi (London, 2007), 134–170, at 135.

13. Aynur, "Ottoman Literature," 499.

14. On the Persian album, see David J. Roxburgh, *The Persian Album, 1400–1600: From Dispersal to Collection* (New Haven, Ct., 2005). On the Ottoman album, see Richard Ettinghausen, *Turkish Miniatures from the Thirteenth to the Eighteenth Century* (New York, 1965); Ivan Stchoukine, *La peinture turque d'après les manuscrits illustrés,* vol. 2 (Paris, 1971); Nurhan Atasoy and Filiz Çağman, *Turkish Miniature Painting* (Istanbul, 1974).

15. See the helpful background article (in English and Turkish) by İsmail E. Erünsal, "Osmanlılarda sahhaflık ve sahhaflar: Yeni bazı belge ve bilgiler (Second-hand Bookselling and Booksellers in the Ottoman Period: New Documents

and Information)," in *Türk kitap medeniyeti,* ed. Alper Çeker (Istanbul, 2008), 133–180.

16. See Charles Schefer, ed., *Journal d'Antoine Galland pendant son séjour à Constantinople (1672–1673),* 2 vols. (Paris, 1881), 1:213.

17. Erünsal, "Osmanlılarda sahhaflık," 139.

18. European institutional libraries loaned books to known scholarly patrons, but not to the public at large. In Istanbul, certain institutions were dedicated to lending alone: Galland recorded that in the mosque of Ḥāfeẓ Aḥmed Pasha anyone could borrow the *Gulistān,* the *Bustān,* and the divan (poetry collection) of Ḥāfeẓ, in order to read or copy them, by leaving two piastres as a deposit. Galland, *Journal,* 1:234–235. Meredith Moss Quinn has identified one of the books that the mosque lent. See Quinn, "Books and Their Readers in Seventeenth-Century Istanbul" (PhD diss., Harvard University, 2016), chap. 1.

19. This was a tiny amount; the akçe became so debased over the course of the seventeenth century that it went out of use. See Şevket Pamuk, *A Monetary History of the Ottoman Empire* (Cambridge, 2000), chap. 8. In 1683 it took 300 akçes to buy one Venetian ducat. Pamuk, *Monetary History,* 144.

20. Galland, *Journal,* 1:242. See Quinn, "Books and Their Readers," chap. 3.

21. Dedicated library buildings continued to be built throughout the eighteenth century, especially by sultans. See Zeren Tanındı, ed., *Sakip Sabanci Museum Collection of the Arts of the Book and Calligraphy* (Istanbul, 2012); Quinn, "Books and their Readers," chap. 1.

22. Linda T. Darling, "Ottoman Turkish: Written Language and Scribal Practice, 13th to 20th Centuries," in *Literacy in the Persianate World: Writing and the Social Order,* ed. Brian Spooner and William Hanaway (Philadelphia, 2012), 171–195.

23. Aynur, "Ottoman Literature," 484.

24. On the Müteferriqa press, see *EI2,* s.v. "Ibrāhīm Müteferriḳa"; Franz Babinger, *Stambuler Buchwesen im 18. Jahrhundert* (Leipzig, 1919); Gian Battista Toderini, *Letteratura turchesca,* vol. 3, *Tipografia turca* (Venice, 1787); Aladár v. Simonffy, *Ibrahim Müteferrika: Bahnbrecher des Buchdrucks in der Türkei* (Budapest, 1944); Maurits H. van den Boogert, "The Sultan's Answer to the Medici Press? Ibrahim Müteferrika's Printing House in Istanbul," in Hamilton, *The Republic of Letters,* 265–291; Kathryn A. Schwartz, "Meaningful Mediums: A Material and Intellectual History of Manuscript and Print Production in Nineteenth-Century Ottoman Cairo" (PhD diss., Harvard University, 2015), chap. 2.

25. On the Constantinople Polyglots of 1546 and 1547, see Martine Delaveau and Denise Hillard, eds., *Bibles imprimées du XVe au XVIIIe siècle conservées à Paris* (Paris, 2002), catalog nos. 2011 and 2012. The 1546 Polyglot reproduced the

Pentateuch in Hebrew, Aramaic, Persian, and Arabic, and the 1547 Polyglot in Hebrew, Aramaic, Ladino, and modern Greek. The Arabic translation was that of Saadia Gaon. I thank Theodor Dunkelgrün for sharing his knowledge of the Constantinople Polyglots with me. See also Schwartz, "Meaningful Mediums," chap. 2.

26. Thomas F. Carter, "Islam as a Barrier to Printing," *Muslim World* 23 (1943): 213–216; Francis Robinson, "Technology and Religious Change: Islam and the Impact of Print," *Modern Asian Studies* 27 (1993): 229–251. On the importance of person-to-person transmission, see "Composition and Transmission of Books," in Pedersen, *The Arabic Book,* 20–36.

27. Aynur, "Ottoman Literature," 496–497. There are obvious parallels with coterie literature in Europe in the sixteenth and seventeenth centuries. For the example of England, see Arthur F. Marotti, *John Donne, Coterie Poet* (Madison, Wisc., 1986); Curtis Perry, "Court and Coterie Culture," in *A Companion to English Renaissance Literature and Culture,* ed. Michael Hattaway (Oxford, 2003), chap. 9.

28. On the technology of paper, which came to Muslim lands from China, see *EI2,* s.v. "Kāghad." Muslims adopted paper long before European Christians did.

29. J. H. Elliott, *The Old World and the New: 1492–1650* (Cambridge, 1970), 34–35.

30. Agustin de Zárate, *Historia del descubrimiento y conquista del Perú* (Antwerp, 1555), fol. 7r–v, as translated and quoted by Valeria A. Escauriaza López-Fadul, "Languages, Knowledge, and Empire in the Early Modern Iberian World (1492–1650)" (PhD diss., Princeton University, 2015), 106.

31. Reference to Aleppo and Fez is made in Erünsal, "Osmanlılarda sahhaflık," 152–153; on Damascus, see Jean-Paul Pascual and Colette Establet, "Les livres des gens à Damas vers 1700," *Revue des mondes musulmans et de la Méditerranée* 87–88 (1999): 143–175.

32. On Kātib Çelebi in Aleppo, see Gottfried Hagen, "Kātib Çelebi," in the *Historians of the Ottoman Empire* electronic database, ed. C. Kafadar, H. Karateke, and C. Fleischer, https://ottomanhistorians.uchicago.edu/.

33. Zilfi, "The Ottoman *Ulema,*" 215–216.

34. On trade in this period, see Robert Paris, *Histoire du commerce de Marseille,* vol. 5, *De 1660 à 1789: Le Levant* (Paris, 1957); Edhem Eldem, *French Trade in Istanbul in the Eighteenth Century* (Leiden, 1999); Molly Greene, "Beyond the Northern Invasion: The Mediterranean in the Seventeenth Century," *Past & Present* 174 (2002): 42–71; Maurits H. van den Boogert, *The Capitulations and the Ottoman Legal System: Qadis, Consuls, and Beraths in the 18th Century* (Leiden, 2005).

35. Abdel-Halim, *Galland,* 26–28.

36. The diary was published as Schefer, *Journal d'Antoine Galland*. Reprinted with a preface by Frédéric Bauden (Paris, 2002).

37. Galland's travels are discussed in detail in Abdel-Halim, *Antoine Galland*, 29–97.

38. BnF, Ms. Français 6130, fols. 3v–4r; Omont, *Missions archéologiques*, 216–217. On the process that Galland describes, see Helen Pfeifer, "Encounter after the Conquest: Scholarly Gatherings in 16th-Century Ottoman Damascus," *International Journal of Middle East Studies* 47 (2015): 219–239.

39. BnF, Ms. Français 6130, fol. 4r; Omont, *Missions archéologiques*, 217: "Il arrive souvent, que des Marchands de Perse y achetent les livres écrits en leur Langue, trouvant de l'avantage a les porter & les vendre chez eux a leur retour."

40. Quoted in Erünsal, "Osmanlılarda sahhaflık," 140. See also Frédéric Hitzel, "Manuscrits, livres et culture livresque à Istanbul," in *Livres et lecture dans le monde ottoman*, ed. Hitzel, special issue, *Revue des mondes musulmans et de la Méditerannée* 87–88 (1999): 20. Tamgrūtī's *riḥla*, or travel narrative, was translated into French by Henry de Castries as *Relation d'une ambassade marocaine en Turquie, 1589–1591, par Abou-l-Hasan Ali ben Mohammed et-Tamgrouti* (Paris, 1929).

41. BnF, Ms. Français 6130, fol. 4v; Omont, *Missions archéologiques*, 217.

42. BnF, Ms. Français 6130, fol. 5r; Omont, *Missions archéologiques*, 218.

43. BnF, Ms. Français 6130, fol. 4v; Omont, *Missions archéologiques*, 217.

44. Galland, *Journal*, 1:50; Pamuk, *Monetary History*, 160. In 1690, it took 2 piastres plus 60 akçes (= 300 akçes) to buy one Venetian ducat. Pamuk, *Monetary History*, 163.

45. BnF, Ms. Français 6130, fol. 4v; Omont, *Missions archéologiques*, 217.

46. Galland, *Journal*, 1:225–226.

47. Ibid., 1:45.

48. Ibid., 1:31.

49. For instance, he bought a Turkish-Persian dictionary for 3 piastres on November 5 and an Arabic-Persian dictionary ("Mercat el-loughât") on November 12. See Galland, *Journal*, 1:230, 232.

50. He recorded having seen this book in January 1672. He also saw a collection of erotic poetry on 6 March 1673. Galland, *Journal*, 1:68–69.

51. Ibid., 1:26. This was Hevelius, *Selenographia, sive, Lunæ Descriptio* (Danzig, 1647). See also his *Journal*, 2:57–58, for another such encounter.

52. Galland had traveled to the Levant between 1677 and 1678: Abdel-Halim, *Galland*, 60–61. He departed once more in 1679 for a nine-year voyage that took him via Salonica and Izmir to Istanbul in 1680, where he remained for five years. He was in Egypt and Izmir between 1685 and 1688, at the end of which year he returned to Paris. See Abdel-Halim, *Galland*, pt. 1, chap. 4.

53. BnF, Ms. Supplément grec 932, fols. 190–198. See excerpts quoted in Omont, *Missions archéologiques,* 203–207.

54. BnF, Ms. Supplément grec 932, fol. 190r; Omont, *Missions archéologiques,* 203.

55. BnF, Ms. Supplément grec 932, fol. 194v; Omont, *Missions archéologiques,* 204.

56. BnF, Ms. Supplément grec 932, fols. 194v–195r; Omont, *Missions archéologiques,* 204.

57. BnF, Ms. Supplément grec 932, fol. 197v; Omont, *Missions archéologiques,* 206.

58. BnF, Ms. Supplément grec 932, fols. 197r–v; Omont, *Missions archéologiques,* 206.

59. Abraham Ecchellensis and Giovanni Alfonso Borelli, *Apollonii Pergæi Conicorum lib. V, VI, VII, Paraphraste Abalphato Asphahanensi . . .* (Florence, 1661). See Hélène Bellosta and Bernard Heyberger, "Abraham Ecchellensis et *Les Coniques* d'Apollonius: Les enjeux d'une traduction," in *Orientalisme, science et controverse: Abraham Ecchellensis (1605–1664),* ed. Heyberger (Turnhout, 2010), 191–201. Toomer, *Eastern Wisedome,* 310, suggests that this translation yielded less than had once been expected of it. In that case, Colbert's request was all the less cutting edge. Even so, an edition of Apollonius including a translation from Arabic was published again in 1710 by Edmond Halley, *Apollonii Pergæi Conicorum Libri Octo* (Oxford, 1710). See Michael N. Fried, *Edmond Halley's Reconstruction of the Lost Books of Apollonius's* Conics: *Translation and Commentary* (New York, 2011). For a critical edition and English translation of the Arabic text, see Gerald J. Toomer, *Apollonius: Conics Books V to VII: The Arabic Translation of the Lost Greek Original in the Version of the Banū Mūsā* (New York, 1990).

60. BnF, Ms. Supplément grec 932, fols. 197r–v; Omont, *Missions archéologiques,* 206–207. On European views of the Sabians, see D. Chwolsohn, *Die Ssabier und der Ssabismus* (St. Petersburg, 1856), 23–90; Dmitri Levitin, *Ancient Wisdom in the Age of the New Science: Histories of Philosophy in England, c. 1640–1700* (Cambridge, 2015), 57–60.

61. BnF, Ms. Supplément grec 932, fol. 197v; Omont, *Missions archéologiques,* 207.

62. Ibid.

63. BnF, Ms. Supplément grec 932, fol. 197r; Omont, *Missions archéologiques,* 206.

64. On the numismatic interests of Galland and his colleagues, see Martin Mulsow, "Mobilität und Vigilanz: Zur Informationsgeschichte von Numismatik und Orientreise unter Ludwig XIV," in *Prekäres Wissen: Eine andere Ideengeschichte der Frühen Neuzeit* (Berlin, 2012), 342–366.

65. BnF, Ms. Français 6130, 5r; Omont, *Missions archéologiques,* 219. These words appeared as a preface to Galland's translation of the works of history listed in Kātib Çelebi's bibliography. His translation was originally done in 1683; other versions of it—without this preface—appear in Ms. Français 6131 and 14892.

66. BnF, Ms. Français 6130, 5r; Omont, *Missions archéologiques*, 218.

67. BnF, Ms. Français 6130, 6v: "Le pur zele, que j'ay de contribuer quelque chose aux grands desseins qu'on peut avoir, de rendre ce Thresor le plus accompli de l'Europe, et par consequent, de tout l'Univers."

68. See Nir Shafir, "The Road from Damascus: Circulation and the Redefinition of Islam in the Ottoman Empire, 1620–1720" (PhD diss., University of California Los Angeles, 2016), chap. 3.

69. On these figures, see Omont, *Missions archéologiques*, 27–53 (Monceaux), 54–174 (Wansleben), 317–382 (Lucas), 433–662 (Sevin and Fourmont).

70. Justin Stagl, *The History of Curiosity: The Theory of Travel, 1550–1800* (Chur, Switzerland, 1995). See also Alison Games, *The Web of Empire: English Cosmopolitans in an Age of Expansion, 1560–1660* (Oxford, 2008), chap. 2; Joan-Pau Rubiés, "Instructions for Travellers: Teaching the Eye to See," *History and Anthropology* 9 (1996): 139–190.

71. Stagl, *The History of Curiosity*, 85; Sonja Brentjes, *Travellers from Europe in the Ottoman and Safavid Empires, 16th–17th Centuries* (Burlington, Vt., 2010), chap. 1.

72. Toomer, *Eastern Wisedome*, 130.

73. Ciriaco d'Ancona, *Later Travels*, ed. and trans. E. W. Bodnar with Clive Foss (Cambridge, Mass., 2003). See also Giada Damen, "The Trade in Antiquities between Italy and the Eastern Mediterranean (ca. 1400–1600)" (PhD diss., Princeton University, 2012).

74. Stagl, *The History of Curiosity*, 85.

75. Philip, *The Bodleian Library*, 37–38.

76. Stagl, *The History of Curiosity*, 85–86.

77. See the discussion of Adriaan Reland in Chapter 3.

78. Francis Bacon, *New Atlantis: A Worke unfinished*, published together with *Sylva Sylvarum, or, a Naturall History in ten Centuries* (London, 1626). On which, see Anthony Grafton, "Where Was Salomon's House? Ecclesiastical History and the Intellectual Origins of Bacon's *New Atlantis*," in *Worlds Made by Words: Scholarship and Community in the Modern West* (Cambridge, Mass., 2009), 98–113.

79. For the comparison, see Jacob Soll, *The Information Master: Jean-Baptiste Colbert's Secret State Intelligence System* (Ann Arbor, Mich., 2009), 97–98.

80. Erünsal, "Osmanlılarda sahhaflık," 143. The source is the Ottoman chronicle *Tarih-i Raşid*, which records the ban as taking place in H. 1128; no month is given. I thank Meredith Quinn for uncovering this information.

81. Quoted by Erünsal, "Osmanlılarda sahhaflık," 143.

82. These missions are discussed in Omont, *Missions archéologiques*, 383–851.

83. See William Wright, *Catalogue of the Syriac Manuscripts in the British Museum Acquired since the Year 1838*, vol. 3 (London, 1872). This was the work of Elias

Assemani. Giuseppe Simonio Assemani visited later, in 1715, though he was less successful.

84. See Irmeli Perho, ed., *Catalogue of Arabic Manuscripts: Codices Arabici et Codices Arabici Additamenta,* 3 bks., vol. 5.3 of *Catalogue of Oriental Manuscripts, Xylographs etc. in Danish Collections,* ed. Stig T. Rasmussen (Copenhagen, 2007).

85. The principles for the acquisition of manuscripts were recorded in art. 11 of the royal instructions of 15 December 1760, with which the expedition was dispatched. Von Haven's diary is held in DKB, shelfmark NKS 133 20.

86. These references are drawn from Perho, *Catalogue of Arabic Manuscripts.* The copy of Kātib Çelebi is now DKB, Cod. Arab. 172.

87. See Copenhagen, Danish National Archives (*Rigsarkivet*), Reviderede regnskaber, Videnskabelige Institutioner m.m., Kaptajn C. Niebuhrs rejse 1760–1767.

88. Jack A. Clarke, "Abbé Jean-Paul Bignon 'Moderator of the Academies' and Royal Librarian," *French Historical Studies* 8 (1973): 213–235. On Bignon, see also Nicolas Fréret, "Éloge de M. l'abbé Bignon," *Mémoires de l'Académie des Inscriptions* 16 (1751): 367–380.

89. Clarke, "Abbé Jean-Paul Bignon," 227.

90. During Bignon's tenure the Sanskrit and Indian collection of manuscripts in the French Royal Library was established. See Gérard Colas, "Les manuscrits envoyés de l'Inde par les jésuites français entre 1729 et 1735," in *Scribes et manuscrits du Moyen-Orient,* ed. François Déroche and Francis Richard (Paris, 1997), 345–362.

91. Clarke, "Abbé Jean-Paul Bignon," 232.

92. Giorgio Levi della Vida, *Ricerche sulla formazione del più antico fondo dei manoscritti orientali della Biblioteca Vaticana* (Vatican City, 1939).

93. The following account is based on Ludwig von Pastor, *Storia dei papi,* vol. 15 (1930; trans., Rome, 1933); *DBI,* s.v. "Clemente XI, papa."

94. This image also appears at the front of the first edition of Michele Mercati, *Metallotheca* (Rome, 1717). The identity of the patron may have encouraged the publisher to recycle the image, which seems to have been created for the *Bibliotheca,* as such details as the Oriental figure and the names on the spines of the books suggest.

95. These are *Ephrem Syrus,* or Ephrem the Syrian, a fourth-century Syriac theologian; *Jacobus Sarugensis,* or Jacob of Serugh, a Syriac theologian of the early sixth century; and *Isaac Syrus,* or Isaac of Nineveh, a seventh-century bishop.

96. Giuseppe Simonio Assemani, *Bibliotheca Orientalis Clementino-Vaticana,* 4 vols. (Rome, 1719–1728 [1730]). On Assemani, see *DBI,* s.v. "Assemani, Giuseppe Simonio."

97. Stefano Evodio Assemani and Giuseppe Simonio Assemani, *Bibliothecæ Apostolicæ Vaticanæ Codicum Manuscriptorum Catalogus,* 3 vols. (Rome, 1756–1758 [1759]).

98. The sole surviving copy was published in 1831 by Angelo Mai. See *Scriptorum Veterum Nova Collectio* (Rome, 1831), 4:2.

99. See Miller, *Peiresc's Mediterranean World,* esp. 60–142.

100. Bacon quoted in Philip, *The Bodleian Library,* 3; Colin Wakefield, "The Arabic Collections in the Bodleian Library," in *A New Catalogue of Arabic Manuscripts in the Bodleian Library, University of Oxford,* vol. 1, *Medicine,* ed. Emilie Savage-Smith (Oxford, 2011), xxix–xxxvi.

101. On Laud, see *ODNB,* s.v. "Laud, William (1573–1645)"; Toomer, *Eastern Wisedome,* chap. 4; Hugh Trevor-Roper, *Archbishop Laud,* 2nd ed. (London, 1962), 271–294; and Trevor-Roper, "Laudianism and Political Power: An Intellectual Movement in England and Europe," in *Catholics, Anglicans, and Puritans: Seventeenth-Century Essays* (Chicago, 1987), chap. 2.

102. Philip, *The Bodleian Library,* 37 (Earl of Pembroke donation), 39–40 (Laud's donations). For more detail, see R. W. Hunt, *Laudian Manuscripts,* ed. and intro. H. O. Coxe (1858–1885; repr., Oxford, 1973).

103. Sir Kenelm Digby donated thirty-six Arabic manuscripts in 1640–1642. See *ODNB,* s.v. "Digby, Sir Kenelm (1603–1665)"; Trevor-Roper, *Archbishop Laud,* 273–274. Among the 8,000 volumes of printed books and manuscripts donated by the scholar John Selden were 117 Arabic manuscripts.

104. François Secret, "Gilbert Gaulmin et l'histoire comparée des religions," *Revue de l'histoire des religions* 177 (1970): 35–63. He had learned Arabic from Gabriel Sionita, a Maronite who lived in Paris, as well as from Étienne Hubert, who held one of the first chairs of Arabic at the Collège Royal.

105. On Mazarin's collection, see the exhibition catalog, *Mazarin: Homme d'état et collectionneur, 1602–1661* (Paris, 1961), 177–197. See also BnF: Ms. NAF 5764 (registre); Ms. NAF 5765, fol. 58–59; Ms. Ital. 478. Paris, Bibliothèque Mazarine: Ms. 1587 pièce 85. Whether this predilection for Arabic manuscripts was Naudé's or Mazarin's might be debated. However, in 1630 Naudé did not possess any Arabic books in his already considerable personal collection. Estelle Boeuf, *La bibliothèque parisienne de Gabriel Naudé en 1630: Les lectures d'un "libertin érudit"* (Geneva, 2007), 17.

106. Quoted in Omont, *Missions archéologiques,* 1:3.

107. Thomas E. Burman, *Reading the Qur'an in Latin Christendom, 1140–1560* (Philadelphia, 2007), 143–145.

108. The 1518 inventory of the Blois library by Guillaume Petit mentions only two *libri arabici.* In 1544, with the transfer from Blois to Fontainebleau, six Arabic manuscripts are recorded, four of which are copies of the Qur'an. The accession

in 1599 of Catherine de Médicis's private library brought several more Arabic and Hebrew manuscripts to the collection, though by the end of the sixteenth century the total came at most to several dozen Arabic manuscripts. The 1622 and 1645 catalogs mention only nine Arabic manuscripts.

109. Qur'ans were so frequently collected that European sponsors of systematic collecting tried to ban the acquisition of more, as Laud did in 1634, "because Wee haue choyce of them allready." Toomer, *Eastern Wisedome*, 108n17.

110. SUB, Mich. 294: "Anno 1683 den 2 Septembris auff den Sontag vom getreuen Samaritter habe ich dieses büchlein in einem türkischen Officier-Zelte zur beute mit genommen, da wier dem Erbfeindt geschlagen hatten Gott lob. Unser Christen 100000 undt der Feinde der Türcken 300000 Mann."

111. See the remarks in Johann David Michaelis, "Vorrede zur ersten Ausgabe," in *Arabische Grammatik* (Göttingen, 1781), xiii; Alastair Hamilton, "'To Rescue the Honour of the Germans': Qur'an Translations by Eighteenth- and Early Nineteenth-Century German Protestants," *Journal of the Warburg and Courtauld Institutes* 77 (2014): 174.

112. *The Travels of Pietro della Valle in India from the Old English Translation of 1664*, orig. trans. G. Havers and ed. Edward Grey (Cambridge, 1892), 290–291.

113. CUL, Ms. Add. 3466, fols. 14v–16r (diary of Samuel Dale, 31 May 1730). See also Charles Sayle, *Annals of Cambridge University Library, 1278–1900* (Cambridge, 1916), 96–97; David McKitterick, *Cambridge University Library: A History; The Eighteenth and Nineteenth Centuries* (Cambridge, 1986), 240–241.

114. Quoted in Colas, "Les manuscrits envoyés de l'Inde," 349n7.

115. The printer Franciscus Raphelengius also contributed Arabic manuscripts to the collection. See Alastair Hamilton, "'Nam Tirones Sumus': Franciscus Raphelengius' *Lexicon Arabico-Latinum* (Leiden 1613)," in *Ex Officina Plantiniana: Studia in Memoriam Christophori Plantini (ca. 1520–1589)*, ed. M. de Schepper and F. de Nave (Antwerp, 1989), 557–589.

116. Johann Jacob Schultens: *Bibliotheca Schultensiana, sive Catalogus Librorum Quos Collegit Vir Clarissimus Johannes Jacobus Schultensius* (Leiden, 1780); Henrik Albert Schultens: *Catalogus Bibliothecae Quam Reliquit Henricus Albertus Schultens* (Leiden, 1794). Arnoud Vrolijk notes, "The private collection of a man like Jan Jacob Schultens all but outnumbered the holdings of the University Library itself." See Vrolijk, "'A Sublime Treasure of Pretious Manuscripts': The Schultens's Legacy in the Leiden University Library and the Elusive Purchase of 1806," *Journal of the Royal Asiatic Society of Great Britain and Ireland* 19 (2009): 282. Vrolijk also describes the books that entered the Leiden University collection through the J. J. Schultens auction in 1780.

117. Toomer, *Eastern Wisedome*, 165.

118. Ibid., 249.

119. On the Parisian acquisitions, see N[icolas]-T[homas] Le Prince, *Essai historique sur la Bibliothèque du Roi* (Paris, 1782), 50.

120. Philip, *The Bodleian Library*, 39.

121. Letter issued under the king's name issued on 15 February 1634, as quoted in Toomer, *Eastern Wisedome*, 108.

122. Ibid., 108–111.

123. Laud's donations are detailed in Philip, *The Bodleian Library*, 39–41; and in Toomer, *Eastern Wisedome*, 105–115, esp. 110–111.

124. *ODNB*, s.v. "Greaves, John (1602–1652)."

125. We lack a full-scale biographical study of Levinus Warner. See Jan Just Witkam, "Precious Books and Moments of Friendship in 17th-Century Istanbul," in *Essays in Honour of Ekmeleddin İhsanoğlu*, vol. 1, *Societies, Cultures, Sciences: A Collection of Articles,* ed. Mustafa Kaçar and Zeynep Durukal (Istanbul, 2006), 464–474; and the catalog exhibition, *Levinus Warner and His Legacy: Three Centuries Legatum Warnerianum in the Leiden University Library* (Leiden, 1970). His letters to Leiden have been published in G. N. du Rieu, ed., *Levini Warneri De Rebus Turcicis Epistolae Ineditae* (Leiden, 1883).

126. His will was composed two days earlier. See *Levinus Warner and His Legacy,* 16.

127. On the Leiden collection, see the brief introduction in Jan Just Witkam, "The Middle Eastern Holdings of the Library of the University of Leiden," *Bulletin, British Society for Middle Eastern Studies* 8 (1981): 60–64. The best guide to the Leiden Oriental manuscripts is Witkam's inventory, available online at http://www.islamicmanuscripts.info/. It is chronologically organized, and thus reveals the collection's different phases of expansion.

128. For one example, see J. C. T. Oates, *Cambridge University Library: A History: From the Beginnings to the Copyright Act of Queen Anne* (Cambridge, 1986), 291–293.

129. Daniel Hershenzon, "Traveling Libraries: The Arabic Manuscripts of Muley Zidan and the Escorial Library," *Journal of Early Modern History* 18 (2014): 535–558.

130. Miguel Casiri, *Bibliotheca Arabico-Hispana Escurialensis,* 2 vols. (Madrid, 1760–1770).

131. John Dinley, quoted in Oates, *Cambridge University Library,* 166. Oates discusses the contents of the Erpenius collection on 222–231.

132. The story of why they did not end up in Leiden is told in Oates, *Cambridge University Library,* 164–167.

133. The founder of Marsh's Library in Dublin nevertheless preferred to bequeath his Oriental manuscripts to the Bodleian. See *ODNB,* s.v. "Marsh, Narcissus."

134. They are still held by the Utrecht University Library, the Vatican Library, and the Danish Royal Library. See BAV, Arch. Bibl. 34, fols. 117r–118v; Perho,

Catalogue of Arabic Manuscripts, 1:180–181 (Cod. Arab. 59). Another of Reland's books ended up in Göttingen: SUB, Ms. Pers. 8.

135. Thomas Sprat, *The History of the Royal Society of London, for the Improving of Natural Knowledge* (London, 1667).

136. Letter from Gregorio Barbarigo to Giovanni Pastrizio, Padua, 21 January 1695. Sebastiano Serena, ed., *Quaranta due lettere del Cardinale Beato Gregorio Barbarigo a Giovanni Pastrizio* (Padua, 1938), 46: "Libro atteso in Parigi ed in Olanda, e spero che farà veder agli oltramontani che anco in Italia si sanno le lingue orientali."

137. Ann M. Blair, *Too Much to Know: Managing Scholarly Information before the Modern Age* (New Haven, Ct., 2010), 12.

138. Letter to the Levant Company of 15 February 1634, as quoted in Toomer, *Eastern Wisedome,* 108.

139. A second edition appeared in 1644, a Latin translation in 1658, and an English one in 1661. See the discussion of Naudé and references genres in Blair, *Too Much to Know,* 119–132. On Naudé's life, see James V. Rice, *Gabriel Naudé, 1600–1653* (Baltimore, 1939).

140. Gabriel Naudé, *Advis pour dresser une bibliothèque* (Paris, 1627), 52.

141. Ibid., 52–53.

142. Blair, *Too Much to Know,* 161–164 and passim.

143. Conrad Gessner, *Bibliotheca Universalis* (Zurich, 1545), "Epistola," fol. *2v.

144. For a contrasting view, see Claude Clément, *Musei sive Bibliothecae tam Privatae quam Publicae Extructio, Instructio, Cura, Usus* (Lyons, 1635); Mathilde V. Rovelstad, "Two Seventeenth-Century Library Handbooks, Two Different Library Theories," *Libraries & Culture* 35 (2000): 540–556.

145. The pope was able to free Corfu from an Ottoman siege and sought to support the efforts of Venice and of the Hapsburgs, who reconquered Belgrade in 1717. See *ODNB,* s.v. "Clemente XI."

146. BL, Ms. Add. 34727, fol. 63. As quoted in Toomer, *Eastern Wisedome,* 136.

147. BnF, Ms. NAF 5384, fols. 47r–54v.

148. Quoted in Toomer, *Eastern Wisedome,* 136.

149. Mehmed Efendi, *Le paradis des infidèles: Relation de Yirmisekiz Çelebi Mehmed Efendi, ambassadeur ottoman en France sous la Régence,* trans. J.-C. Galland (Paris, 1981).

150. On this diplomatic mission and its cultural effects, see Perrin Stein, "Exoticism as Metaphor: *Turquerie* in Eighteenth-Century French Art" (PhD diss., New York University, 1997), 129–158.

151. BnF, NAF 5384, fol. 22v: "Soyez assuré qu'aussitost que nous aurons trouvé des Interprettes et que nous leur aurons fait prendre une liste de ces Livres nous vous l'envoyerons il nous paroit meme que pour que cela fut plustost fait il

seroit a propos que vous nous envoyassiez si vous l'avez un Catalogue des Livres grecs en general, nous vous en serions infiniment obligez."

152. See BnF, NAF 5384; Omont, *Missions archéologiques,* 433–536.

153. On which, see "Relation abrégée du voyage litteraire que M. l'Abbé Fourmont a fait dans le Levant par ordre du Roy, dans les années 1719 et 1730," *Histoire de l'Académie royale des Inscriptions et Belles-Lettres* 7 (1738): 344–358.

154. Omont, *Missions archéologiques,* 781–782, quoting a letter by the abbé d'Orvalle dated 1 October 1748.

155. He was instead sold an abridged version of Kātib Çelebi's bibliography, *Kashf al-ẓunūn,* which is now DKB, Cod. Arab 172. See Perho, *Catalogue of Arabic Manuscripts,* 2:637–640. The manuscript was copied in 1762 CE. On December 16, 1761, von Haven recounted the effort that led to its commission and acquisition in his diary, now published as Anne Haslund Hansen and Stig T. Rasmussen, eds., *Min Sundheds Forliis: Frederik Christian von Havens* Rejsejournal *fra Den Arabiske Rejse, 1760–1763* (Copenhagen, 2005), 292–293. See also Stig T. Rasmussen, *Den Arabiske Rejse 1761–1767: En dansk ekspedition set i videnskabshistorisk perspektiv* (Copenhagen, 1992), 330.

156. Ockley, DKB, Bøll. Brevs. U 2° 251 (3 July 1716 letter to the Earl of Oxford).

157. Ibid.

158. Johann Jacob Reiske, "Prodidagmata ad Hagji Chalifae Librum," in *Abulfedae Tabula Syriae cum Excerpto Geographico ex Ibn ol Wardii,* ed. Johann Bernhard Köhler (Leipzig, 1766), 235.

159. Reiske, "Prodidagmata ad Hagji Chalifae Librum," 235.

2 · THE QUR'AN IN TRANSLATION

1. Lodovico Marracci, *Alcorani Textus Universus: Ex Correctioribus Arabum Exemplaribus Summa Fide, atque Pulcherrimis Characteribus Descriptus: Eademque Fide, ac Pari Diligentia ex Arabico Idiomate in Latinum Translatus: Appositis Unicuique Capiti Notis, atque Refutatione: His Omnibus Praemissus Est Prodromus Totum Priorem Tomum Implens, in Quo Contenta Indicantur Pagina Sequenti,* 2 vols. (Padua, 1698). The second volume was independently entitled *Refutatio Alcorani in Qua ad Mahumetanicae Superstitionis Radicem Securis Apponitur, et Mahumetus Ipse Gladio Suo Jugulatur.* Silently, two different versions of the first volume were printed in 1698. See Duncan Brockway, "The Second Edition of Volume I of Marracci's *Alcorani Textus Universus," Muslim World* 64 (1972): 141–144.

2. Europeans had printed the Arabic text twice, both times without translation, first in Venice in 1537–1538 in a rather faulty edition that was virtually lost to posterity, and then in Hamburg in 1694. The Venetian edition was thought perhaps to be a legend until a single copy was recovered in 1987. See Angela

Nuovo, "Il Corano arabo ritrovato," *La Bibliofilia* 89 (1987): 237–271, and the English translation: Nuovo, "A Lost Arabic Koran Rediscovered," *The Library* 6 (1990): 273–292; Maurice Borrmans, "Présentation de la première édition imprimée du Coran à Venise," *Quaderni di Studi Arabi* 9 (1991): 93–126; Edoardo Barbieri, "La tipografia araba a Venezia nel XVI secolo: Una testimonianza d'archivio dimenticata," *Quaderni di Studi Arabi* 9 (1991): 127–31; Arjan van Dijk, "Early Printed Qur'ans: The Dissemination of the Qur'an in the West," *Journal of Qur'anic Studies* 7 (2005): 136–143. The Hamburg edition: Abraham Hinckelmann, *Al-Coranus S. Lex Islamitica Muhammedis, Filii Abdallæ Pseudoprophetæ* (Hamburg, 1694).

3. A. R. Kidwai, *Bibliography of the Translations of the Meanings of the Glorious Qur'an into English, 1949–2002: A Critical Study* (Medina, 2005), 357, counts over 160 editions of the Sale translation and terms it "the most popular and oft-printed translation in both the UK and USA." For the translation's current value, see Michael Cook, *Muhammad* (Oxford, 1983), and Cook, *The Koran* (Oxford, 2000).

4. For other accounts of Marracci in English, see Alexander Bevilacqua, "The Qur'an Translations of Marracci and Sale," *Journal of the Warburg and Courtauld Institutes* 76 (2013): 93–130; Roberto Tottoli, "New Light on the Translation of the Qur'an of Ludovico Marracci from His Manuscripts Recently Discovered at the Order of the Mother of God in Rome," in *Books and Written Culture of the Islamic World: Studies Presented to Claude Gilliot on the Occasion of His 75th Birthday,* ed. Andrew Rippin and Roberto Tottoli (Leiden, 2015), 91–130; Reinhold F. Glei and Roberto Tottoli, *Ludovico Marracci at Work: The Evolution of His Latin Translation of the Qur'an in the Light of His Newly Discovered Manuscripts* (Leipzig, 2016).

5. On Peter the Venerable and Islam, see Virginia Berry, "Peter the Venerable and the Crusades," in *Petrus Venerabilis, 1156–1956: Studies and Texts Commemorating the Eighth Centenary of His Death,* ed. Giles Constable and James Kritzeck (Rome, 1956), 141–162; James Kritzeck, *Peter the Venerable and Islam* (Princeton, N.J., 1964); Maria Teresa Brolis, "La crociata di Pietro il Venerabile: Guerra di armi o guerra di idee?," *Aevum* 61 (1987): 327–354; Benjamin Kedar, *Crusade and Mission: European Approaches toward the Muslims* (Princeton, N.J., 1984), 101; John Tolan, "Peter the Venerable on the 'Diabolical Heresy of the Saracens,'" in *The Devil, Heresy, and Witchcraft in the Middle Ages: Essays in Honor of Jeffrey B. Russell,* ed. Alberto Ferreiro (Leiden, 1998), 345–367; Dominique Iogna-Prat, *Order and Exclusion: Cluny and Christendom Face Heresy, Judaism, and Islam, 1000–1150,* trans. G. R. Edwards (Ithaca, N.Y., 2002), chap. 11; Thomas E. Burman, *Reading the Qur'an in Latin Christendom, 1140–1560* (Philadelphia, 2007), chaps. 3 and 4. See also Norman Daniel, *Islam and the*

West: The Making of an Image (Edinburgh, 1960), passim; Reinhold Glei, ed. and trans., *Petrus Venerabilis Schriften zum Islam* (Altenberge, 1985), Michelina Di Cesare, ed., *The Pseudo-Historical Image of the Prophet Muḥammad in Medieval Latin Literature: A Repertory* (Berlin, 2011).

6. Tolan, " 'Diabolical Heresy,' " 354.

7. Peter the Venerable, "Epistola de Translatione Sua," in *Bibliotheca Cluniacensis,* ed. Martin Marrier and Andreas Quercetanus (1614; repr., Brussels and Paris, 1915), 1109.

8. The very first translation appears to have been a Greek one, authored in the ninth century by Niketas of Byzantium. See Erich Trapp, "Gab es eine byzantinische Koranübersetzung?," *Diptycha* 2 (1981 / 82): 7–17; Kees Versteegh, "Greek Translations of the Qur'an in Christian Polemics (9th Century A.D.)," *Zeitschrift der Deutschen Morgenländischen Gesellschaft* 141 (1991): 52–68; Karl Förstel, ed. and trans., *Schriften zum Islam von Arethas und Euthymios Zigabenos und Fragmente der griechischen Koranübersetzung* (Wiesbaden, 2009); Christian Høgel, "An Early Anonymous Greek Translation of the Qur'an: The Fragments from Niketas Byzantios' *Refutatio* and the Anonymous *Abjuratio*," *Collectanea Christiana Orientalia* 7 (2010): 65–119; and Manolis Ulbricht, "Coranus Graecus: Die älteste überlieferte Koranübersetzung in der «Ἀνατροπὴ τοῦ Κορανίου» des Niketas von Byzanz. Einleitung, Text, Übersetzung, Kommentar" (PhD thesis, Freie Universität Berlin, 2015). In the tenth and the eleventh centuries, numerous Persian translations were produced. See Travis Zadeh, *The Vernacular Qur'an: Translation and the Rise of Persian Exegesis* (Oxford, 2012). The manuscript of the Toledan Collection is held in Paris, Bibliothèque de l'Arsenal, Ms. 1162. It is considered to be the original collection of the various constituent works, assembled either in Spain or at Cluny. See Kritzeck, *Peter the Venerable,* 31–32. On the *Risālat al-Kindī,* see Fernando González-Muñoz, ed. and trans., *Exposición y refutación del Islam: La versión latina de las epístolas de al-Hāšimī y al-Kindī* (A Coruña, 2005). Peter's polemic is not part of the Toledan Collection; the only surviving manuscript is Douai, Bibliothèque municipale, Ms. 381. See Kritzeck, *Peter the Venerable,* 155–199. On the generic differences between al-Kindī's polemic and Peter's, see Tolan, " 'Diabolical Heresy,' " 360–367.

9. On this point, see Tolan, " 'Diabolical Heresy,' " 356–360.

10. Kritzeck, *Peter the Venerable,* 98; Burman, *Reading the Qur'an,* 31.

11. Burman, *Reading the Qur'an,* chap. 1.

12. Ibid., chap. 2.

13. Ibid., 66–67.

14. On the manuscript copies, see Marie-Thérèse d'Alverny, "Deux traductions latines du Coran au moyen age," *Archives d'histoire doctrinale et littéraire du Moyen Age* 16 (1947–1948): 108–112; Burman, *Reading the Qur'an,* 240n1.

15. Theodor Buchmann, ed., *Machumetis Saracenorum Principis, Eiusque Succes-sorum Vitae, ac Doctrina, Ipseque Alcoran* (Basel, 1543).

16. On this edition of the Qur'an, see Hartmut Bobzin, *Der Koran im Zeitalter der Reformation: Studien zur Frühgeschichte der Arabistik und Islamkunde in Europa* (Beirut, 1995), chap. 3, esp. 181–209. For overviews of Qur'an translation from Bibliander onward, see Hartmut Bobzin, "Von Venedig nach Kairo: Zur Geschichte arabischer Korandrucke (16. bis frühes 20. Jarhundert)," in *Sprachen des Nahen Ostens und die Druckrevolution: Eine interkulturelle Begegnung*, ed. E. Hanebutt-Benz et al. (Westhofen, 2002), 151–176; Alastair Hamilton, *The Forbidden Fruit: The Koran in Early Modern Europe* (London, 2008).

17. On this letter, see Bobzin, *Der Koran*, 153–154, 203–205, also 13–157 on Luther and Islam more broadly; Adam Francisco, *Martin Luther and Islam: A Study in Sixteenth-Century Polemics and Apologetics* (Leiden, 2007); Johannes Ehmann, *Luther, Türken und Islam: Eine Untersuchung zum Türken- und Islambild Martin Luthers (1515–1546)* (Gütersloh, 2008). Bibliander's book was more than an edition of the Qur'an: it contained some of Peter the Venerable's writings, other polemical works produced in Toledo, fourteenth- and fifteenth-century refutations of Islam, and a history of the rise of the Arabs. See Bobzin, *Der Koran*, 215–221.

18. Bobzin, *Der Koran*, 262.

19. Although the title page claimed that this book had been translated directly from Arabic into Italian, in fact it was a version of the Latin published by Oporinus. The definitive study of this translation is Pier Mattia Tommasino, *L'Alcorano di Macometto: Storia di un libro del Cinquecento* (Bologna, 2013). See also Tommasino, "Giovanni Battista Castrodardo bellunese traduttore dell'Alcorano di Macometto," *Oriente Moderno* 88 (2008): 15–40.

20. Bobzin, *Der Koran*, 268–270.

21. In addition, in 1647 André du Ryer, a French diplomat, published the first European vernacular translation of the Qur'an to be made directly from Arabic. The definitive work on André du Ryer is Alastair Hamilton and Francis Richard, *André du Ryer and Oriental Studies in Seventeenth-Century France* (Oxford, 2004). On his Qur'an translation, see chap. 4. Soon enough, *L'Alcoran de Mahomet* was translated from the French into English, Dutch, German, and Russian. Alexander Ross, ed., *The Alcoran of Mahomet* (London, 1649); *Mahomets Alkoran*, trans. J. H. Gazemaker (Amsterdam, 1658); *Thesaurus Exoticorum*, ed. Eberhard W. Happel (Hamburg and Frankfurt, 1688); Алкоран о Магомете, или Закон турецкий, trans. Peter V. Postnikov (St. Petersburg, 1716). On the publication history of Du Ryer's translation, see Hamilton and Richard, *André du Ryer*, 108–118. On the authorship of the English translation, see Mordechai Feingold, "'The Turkish Alcoran': New Light on the 1649

English Translation of the Koran," *Huntington Library Quarterly* 75 (2012): 475–501; Noel Malcolm, "The 1649 English Translation of the Koran: Its Origins and Significance," *Journal of the Warburg and Courtauld Institutes* 75 (2012): 261–295.

22. These efforts began at least with the Spanish theologian John of Segovia, who complained about the Toledan translation's quality in the early fifteenth century, and who turned his attention to the Qur'an after the fall of Constantinople. See Burman, *Reading the Qur'an,* 179–181.

23. These other translations were by Mark of Toledo, Flavius Mithridates (a partial translation), and Egidio of Viterbo. See Burman, *Reading the Qur'an,* chaps. 5 and 6. For a listing of further partial translations, see Hamilton and Richard, *André du Ryer,* 92.

24. Burman reads Marracci's translation as the crowning achievement of a tradition of Qur'anic philology going back to Ketton. See Burman, *Reading the Qur'an,* 53–58, 195–196. Although the translators were engaged in parallel tasks, I would stress that Marracci's knowledge of Arabic and his battery of tools—not to mention the manuscripts available to him—were the fruit of late humanism, and in particular of the advances of biblical philology, which also made possible the intensive study of Arabic books.

25. For a listing of some of these partial translations, see Hamilton and Richard, *André du Ryer,* 92; Alastair Hamilton, "'To Rescue the Honour of the Germans': Qur'an Translations by Eighteenth- and Early Nineteenth-Century German Protestants," *Journal of the Warburg and Courtauld Institutes* 77 (2014): 175 and 175n10.

26. Roberto Tottoli, "The Latin Translation of the Qur'ān by Johann Zechendorff (1580–1662) Discovered in Cairo Dār al-Kutub: A Preliminary Description," *Oriente Moderno* 95 (2015): 5–31. On Zechendorff, see Asaph Ben Tov, "Johann Zechendorff (1580–1662) and Arabic Studies at Zwickau's Latin School," in *The Teaching and Learning of Arabic in Early Modern Europe,* ed. Jan Loop, Alastair Hamilton, and Charles Burnett (Leiden, 2017), 57–92.

27. Burman, *Reading the Qur'an,* 53–56.

28. Luca Santini, "Genealogia della famiglia di Ludovico Marracci e i suoi rapporti con Torcigliano, il paese di origine," in *Il Corano e il pontefice: Ludovico Marracci fra cultura islamica e Curia papale,* ed. Gian Luca D'Errico (Rome, 2015), 24. For a full citation of discussions of Marracci's life and works, see Bevilacqua, "Marracci and Sale," 96n16. In addition to the works listed there, see the essays in D'Errico, *Il Corano e il pontefice*; Glei and Tottoli, *Ludovico Marracci at Work.*

29. In the late nineteenth century, the library became the *Biblioteca Statale* of Lucca, but its seventeenth-century reading room remains intact.

30. On Leonardi and the Order of the Mother of God, see Francesco Ferraironi, *Tre secoli di storia dell'Ordine della Madre di Dio* (Rome, 1939); *DBI,* s.v. "Giovanni Leonardi, santo." While the Jesuits are the most widely known new religious order of the Counter-Reformation, a large number of orders were founded. See Michael A. Mullett, *The Catholic Reformation* (London, 1999), chap. 3, and on Leonardi, 102–103; John Patrick Donnelly, "New Religious Orders for Men," in *The Cambridge History of Christianity,* vol. 6, *Reform and Expansion, 1500–1660,* ed. R. Po-Chia Hsia (Cambridge, 2008), chap. 10, and on Leonardi, 168. Mullett describes the Order of the Mother of God as an "archetype" of the new orders: "pastoral, oriented towards devotional provisions for the laity, urban-based, of Italian origin and location, founded by a saintly charismatic, and favoured and directly employed by the papacy," 103.

31. On the foundation of the Propaganda Fide, see the essays in Josef Metzler, ed., *Sacrae Congregationis de Propaganda Fide Memoria Rerum: 350 anni a servizio delle missioni,* vol. 1, 2 tomes (Rome, 1971–1972).

32. Marracci, "Praefatio ad Lectorem," in *Refutatio Alcorani,* 1.

33. Antonella Romano, "Rome, un chantier pour les savoirs de la catholicité post-tridentine," *Revue d'histoire moderne et contemporaine* 55 (2008): 101–120. See also Romano, ed., *Rome et la science moderne: Entre Renaissance et Lumières* (Rome, 2008). On the presence of Arab Christians in Rome at this time, see Bernard Heyberger, "Chrétiens orientaux dans l'Europe catholique (XVIIe–XVIIIe siècles)," in *Hommes de l'entre-deux: Parcours individuels et portraits de groupes sur la frontière de la Méditerranée (XVIe–XXe siècle),* ed. Bernard Heyberger and Chantal Verdeil (Paris, 2009), 61–92; Aurélien Girard, "Le christianisme oriental (XVIIe–XVIIIe siècles): Essor de l'orientalisme catholique en Europe et construction des identités confessionnelles au Proche-Orient" (PhD diss., École Pratique des Hautes Études, Paris, 2011). On the Christians of the Levant in general, see Bernard Heyberger, *Les chrétiens du Proche-Orient au temps de la Réforme catholique: Syrie, Liban, Palestine, XVIIe–XVIIIe siècles* (Rome, 1994).

34. Louis Cousin, "Éloge de Monsieur d'Herbelot, fait par Monsieur Cousin, President a La Cour des Monnoyes," sigs. ũ2v–ũ3r, here sig. ũ2v, in Barthélemy d'Herbelot, *Bibliothèque Orientale* (Paris, 1697).

35. On von Haven's journey to Rome, see Johann David Michaelis, *Lebensbeschreibung von ihm selbst aufgefasst* (Leipzig, 1793), 69. Arguably, by the 1660s the Arab Christians were no longer at the forefront of Oriental knowledge production, and by the late eighteenth century, northern Europeans complained about the quality of Oriental studies conducted in Rome. See Girard, "Christianisme oriental," 339–341.

36. Marracci, "Praefatio ad Lectorem," 1. These were Francesco Martellotto, *Instituti-ones Linguae Arabicae* (Rome, 1620); Antonio Giggi, *Thesaurus Linguae Arabicae*, 4 vols. (Milan, 1632); Filippo Guadagnoli, *Breves Arabicae Linguae Institutiones* (Rome, 1642); Thomas Erpenius, *Grammatica Arabica* (Leiden, 1613); Franciscus Raphelengius, *Lexicon Arabicum* (Leiden, 1613); and Jacobus Golius, *Lexicon Arabico-Latinum* (Leiden, 1653). Manuscript copies of some of these books are still held by the Ordine della Madre di Dio in Rome. See Tottoli, "New Light," 120. On Martellotto and Guadagnoli, see Aurélien Girard, "Des manuels de langue entre mission et érudition orientaliste au XVIIe siècle: Les grammaires de l'arabe des *Caracciolini*," in "L'Ordine dei Chierici Regolari Minori (Caraccio-lini): Religione e cultura in età postridentina," ed. Irene Fosi and Giovanni Piz-zorusso, special issue, *Studi Medievali e Moderni* 14 (2010): 279–296.

37. These copies of Franciscus Raphelengius's Arabic dictionary, based on the printed edition, and of Thomas Erpenius's grammar are in the same hand. OMD, Marracci Mss. XII, XIII. See Tottoli, "New Light," 120–122.

38. Giorgio Levi della Vida, "Ludovico Marracci e la sua opera negli studi islamici," in Levi della Vida, *Aneddoti e svaghi arabi e non arabi* (Milan, 1959), 198–199.

39. See Willy Henkel, "The Polyglot Printing-Office of the Congregation," in *Sacrae Congregationis*, ed. Metzler, tome 1, chap. 9. On the history of the *Biblia Arabica*, see Alberto Vaccari, "Una Bibbia araba per il primo Gesuita venuto al Libano," *Mélanges de l'Université Saint-Joseph* 10 (1925): 90–104; Nikolaus Kowalsky, "Zur Vorgeschichte der arabischen Bibelübersetzung der Propa-ganda von 1671," *Neue Zeitschrift für Missionswissenschaft* 16 (1960): 268–274; Girard, "Christianisme oriental," 435–454; Ronny Vollandt, "Che portono al ritorno quì una Bibbia Arabica integra: A History of the Biblia Sacra Arabica (1671–73)," in *Græco-Latina et Orientalia: Studia in Honorem Angeli Urbani Heptagenarii*, ed. Juan Pedro Monferrer-Sala and Samir Khalil Samir (Cor-doba and Beirut, 2013), 401–418.

40. *Biblia Sacra Arabica, Sacræ Congregationis de Propaganda Fide Iussu Edita ad Usum Ecclesiarum Orientalium*, 3 vols. (Rome, 1671). Some of Marracci's cor-rections are found in Rome, APF, Congressi Stamperia I, fols. 211r–246v. See the discussion in Girard, "Christianisme oriental," 450–452.

41. Lucca, Biblioteca Statale, shelfmark S.M.N. 332.9. *Biblia Sacra Arabica*, title page (handwritten inscription): "Opus hoc incoeptum iussu Urbani VIII. de-mandatumque a S. Congregatione de Propaganda Fide pluribus viris Linguarum Orientalium periti, perfecit, absolvitque P. Ludovicus Marraccius solus ex Lectis superstes."

42. The affair, however, continued until Innocent XI's condemnation of the Tab-lets in 1682. This episode is well studied; see T. D. Kendrick, "An Example of

the Theodicy-Motive in Antiquarian Thought," in *Fritz Saxl, 1890–1948: A Volume of Memorial Essays from His Friends in England,* ed. D. J. Gordon (London, 1957), 309–325; Kendrick, *St. James in Spain* (London, 1960); Manuel Barrios Aguilera and Mercedes García-Arenal, eds., *Los plomos del Sacromonte: Invención y tesoro* (Valencia, 2006); A. Katie Harris, *From Muslim to Christian Granada: Inventing a City's Past in Early Modern Spain* (Baltimore, 2007); Mercedes García-Arenal, "The Religious Identity of the Arabic Language and the Affair of the Lead Books of the Sacromonte of Granada," *Arabica* 56 (2009): 495–528; García-Arenal and Rodríguez Mediano, *Un Oriente español: Los moriscos y el Sacromonte en tiempos de Contrarreforma* (Madrid, 2010), English version, *The Orient in Spain: Converted Muslims, the Forged Lead Books of Granada, and the Rise of Orientalism,* trans. Consuelo Lopez-Morillas (Leiden, 2013), esp. 297–305.

43. Levi della Vida, "Marracci e la sua opera," 200.

44. OMD, Marracci Ms. XI. Various parts of this collection of sources are dated, and record the years 1654, 1657, and 1658. See Tottoli, "New Light," 114–117. Likewise, his copy of the *Tafsīr al-Jalālayn* bears the date 1 July 1651. OMD, Marracci Ms. IV. Tottoli, "New Light," 102–106. Later we find him writing to Pope Clement X (Altieri) to request a copy of the Qur'an, "havendo dato principio a un'opera nella quale confuta i perversi dogmi dell'Alcorano, et havendola già ridotta à buon segno, per perfettionarla havrebbe necessità d'un esemplare Arabico di d[ett]o Alcorano." See Vatican City, BAV, Archivio della Biblioteca 26, fol. 652r (formerly 586r). The date (of when the decision was made to loan a Qur'an) of 20 July 1671 is inscribed on fol. 653v. See also BAV, Archivio della Biblioteca 27, fols. 24r (formerly 21r) and 35v (formerly 32v), where the request is specifically for "qualche Libro Arabico et in specie l'Alcorano e sue glosse." In other words, Marracci continued his search for native elucidations of the Qur'an.

45. In October 1674 he expressed the hope that the Holy Office would soon grant him permission to begin his "work against the Alcoran." Marracci to Magliabechi, 7 October 1674, BNCF, Carteggio Magliabechiano (hereafter Magl.), VIII, 572, fol. 1: "tengo bona speranza di cominciare quanto prima la mia opera contra l'Alcorano."

46. Santa Maria in Campitelli was (and is) located near the Roman ghetto, which inspired the setting of Marracci's final, posthumous work, a polemical disputation against Judaism that takes the form of conversations with the rabbis of Rome: Lodovico Marracci, *L'ebreo preso per le buone, o vero discorsi familiari, et amichevoli fatti con i Rabbini di Roma intorno al Messia* (Rome, 1701).

47. Francesco Bustaffa, "Confessore e 'consigliere': Intorno a padre Marracci e Innocenzo XI," in *Il Corano e il pontefice,* ed. D'Errico, 48–66.

48. Marracci, "Praefatio ad Lectorem," in *Prodromus ad Refutationem Alcorani in Quo per Quatuor Praecipuas Verae Religionis Notas Mahumetanae Sectae Falsitas Ostenditur: Christianae Religionis Veritas Comprobatur,* 4 vols. (Rome, 1691), 1:2; 5 (on the necessity of refuting Islam); 1:1 (on the paucity of refutations of Islam). Because pagination restarts in each section of Marracci's work, I indicate the relevant section.

49. Marracci, "Praefatio," *Prodromus,* 1:1.

50. Ibid., 1:7.

51. Marracci, "Conclusio Totius Operis," *Prodromus,* 4:124. This approach stood in contrast to that of his predecessor Abraham Ecchellensis, who had grounded his anti-Muslim polemic in Christian, rather than Muslim, sources. See Heyberger, "L'islam et les Arabes chez un érudit maronite au service de l'Église catholique," *Al-Qantara* 28 (2010): 481–512; Heyberger, "Abraham Ecchellensis dans la 'République des Lettres,'" in *Orientalisme, science et controverse: Abraham Ecchellensis (1605–1664),* ed. Heyberger (Turnhout, 2010), 9–51.

52. Aristarchus's maxim is elucidated in James I. Porter, "Hermeneutic Lines and Circles: Aristarchus and Crates on the Exegesis of Homer," in *Homer's Ancient Readers: The Hermeneutics of Greek Epic's Earliest Exegetes,* ed. Robert Lamberton and John J. Keaney (Princeton, N.J., 1992), chap. 4, esp. 70–80. Qur'anic commentators adduced external materials, including Prophetic traditions, traditions about the Prophet's companions and their followers, and even Christian and Jewish materials, to interpret the Qur'an. The theologian Ibn Taymiyya's treatise on exegesis stated that the first step in interpretation should be to refer to other relevant verses. In his wake, this method was adopted by many exegetes, including his follower Ibn Kathīr, author of a classical Qur'an commentary. See Jane Dammen McAuliffe, "The Tasks and Traditions of Interpretation," in *The Cambridge Companion to the Qur'an,* ed. McAuliffe (Cambridge, 2006), 196–198.

53. Marracci, "Praefatio," *Prodromus,* 1:5.

54. APF, SOCG (Scritture originali riferite nelle Congregazioni Generali) 502, fol. 338r: "possa giovar molto alla conversione di quelli nell'Ungaria, et altrove." See also the similar argument made in APF, SOCG 504, fol. 52r.

55. Marracci, "Praefatio," *Prodromus,* 1:5–6.

56. Marracci, "Praefatio ad Lectorem," *Refutatio,* 16.

57. On this point, see Giovanni Pizzorusso, "Ludovico Marracci tra ambiente curiale e cultura orientalista a Roma nel XVII secolo," in D'Errico, *Il Corano e il pontefice,* 113. On the difficulties that the Propaganda Fide had in dealing with Oriental Christians alone, see Bernard Heyberger, "'Pro nunc, nihil respondendum': Recherche d'information et prise de décision à la Propagande: L'exemple du Levant (XVIIIe siècle)," *Mélanges de l'École française de Rome: Italie et Méditerranée* 109 (1997): 539–554.

58. Marracci, "Augustissime Caesar" (dedication to Leopold), *Refutatio*. He may have been encouraged to do this by Barbarigo himself, as Pedani Fabris suggests. See Maria Pia Pedani Fabris, "Intorno alla questione della traduzione del Corano," in *Gregorio Barbarigo: Patrizio Veneto, vescovo e cardinale nella Tarda Controriforma (1625–1697): Atti del convegno di studi Padova 7–10 Novembre 1996*, 2 vols., ed. Liliana Billanovich and Pierantonio Gios (Padua, 1999), 364.

59. BNCF, Magl. VIII, 572, letter 19 (29 August 1684): "Qui ogni giorno riceviamo nuove migliore de progressi dell'armi Christiane contra i Turchi, e si stà di giorno in giorno aspettando l'avviso della totale conquista di Buda."

60. BNCF, Magl. VIII, 572, letter 23 (21 October 1684): "Si sono di nuovo suscitate difficoltà contra la stampa della mia opera, la quale mi pare che habbia l'istessa fortuna, che l'espugnazione di Buda."

61. On Marracci's sources, see Carlo Alfonso Nallino, "Le fonti arabe manoscritte," in Nallino, *Raccolta di scritti editi e inediti a cura di Maria Nallino* (Rome, 1940), 2:94–125.

62. See Giorgio Levi della Vida, *Ricerche sulla formazione del più antico fondo dei manoscritti orientali della Biblioteca Vaticana* (Vatican City, 1939), 445 and 445n3. This was BAV, Vaticano Arabo 206, a copy of the Qur'an that, as its title page indicates, once belonged to Lelio Ruini, the bishop of Bagnoregio (d. 1621). See also Glei and Tottoli, *Ludovico Marracci at Work*, 28–29.

63. Levi della Vida, *Ricerche sulla formazione*, 445n2, argued that the copies in the Collegio Urbano of the Propaganda Fide of many works cited by Marracci (transferred to the Biblioteca Apostolica Vaticana in 1902 as Borgiano Arabo) were in all likelihood the ones Marracci had employed.

64. Marracci mentions these collections in "Praefatio ad Lectorem," in *Prodromus* (1698), 7. Their Arabic manuscripts have since been transferred to the Biblioteca Nazionale di Roma (S. Lorenzo in Lucina) and to the Vatican Library (S. Pancrazio).

65. On this topic, see Giovanni Pizzorusso, "Tra cultura e missione: La congregazione *De Propaganda Fide* e le scuole di lingua araba nel XVII secolo," in Romano, *Rome et la science moderne*, 121–152; Pizzorusso, "La preparazione linguistica e controversistica dei missionari per l'Oriente islamico: Scuole, testi, insegnanti a Roma e in Italia," in *L'Islam visto da Occidente: Cultura e religione del Seicento europeo di fronte all'Islam*, ed. Bernard Heyberger et al. (Genoa, 2009), 253–288. On the involvement of the Caracciolini with Arabic, see Girard, "Des manuels de langue," 279–296. On the teaching of Arabic in Rome in the following century, see Aurélien Girard, "L'enseignement de l'arabe à Rome au XVIIIe siècle," in *Maghreb-Italie: Des passeurs médiévaux à l'orientalisme moderne (XIIIe–milieu XXe siècle)*, ed. Benoît Grévin (Rome, 2010), 209–234; see also Girard, "Teaching and Learning of Arabic in Early

Modern Rome: Shaping a Missionary Language," *in* Loop, Hamilton, and Burnett, *The Teaching and Learning of Arabic.*

66. On Camillo Massimo's library, see Roberto Marzocchi, *"Facere bibliothecam in domo": La biblioteca del Cardinale Carlo Camillo II Massimo (1620–1677)* (Verona, 2005), and 109–112 on his Arabic manuscripts; Marzocchi, "Biblioteche cardinalizie: I libri del cardinale Camillo Massimo dallo Studio alla Libraria," in *Biblioteche private in età moderna e contemporanea,* ed. Angela Nuovo (Milan, 2005), 117–128. Marracci dedicated a copy of his life of Giovanni Leonardi to Camillo Massimo: Marzocchi, *"Facere bibliothecam,"* 380. On Ecchellensis, see Heyberger, "L'islam et les Arabes"; Heyberger, ed., *Orientalisme, science et controverse.*

67. BNCF, Magl. VIII, 572, letter 2 (Rome, 14 January 1678).

68. Marracci also cited Johann Heinrich Hottinger's *Historia Orientalis* (Zurich, 1651). But he does not seem to have known Pococke's full version of Bar Hebraeus, only the extract published as the *Specimen.* Nallino, "Le fonti arabe manoscritte," 95. See Tottoli, "New Light," 120–123.

69. Tottoli, "New Light"; Tottoli, "I manoscritti di Ludovico Marracci conservati presso l'Ordine della Madre di Dio in Roma," in D'Errico, *Il Corano e il pontefice,* 119–126; Tottoli and Glei, *Ludovico Marracci at Work.*

70. Tottoli and Glei, *Ludovico Marracci at Work,* 20–21 and 21n32. Marracci soon employed other manuscripts to fill out the lacunae of Ibn Abī Zamanīn's commentary.

71. Tottoli, "New Light," 98–100. Ms. I is a complete copy of the epitome of Ibn Abī Zamanīn by Yaḥyā b. Sallām. OMD, Marracci Mss. II and III are a copy of the original Arabic text with Marracci's translations of the Qur'an in the margins.

72. The commentary is so rare that the recovery of Marracci's own copy constitutes a significant philological discovery. For references to the few surviving manuscripts of Ibn Abī Zamanīn, see Tottoli, "New Light," 100. For the commentary's prominence in the Morisco community, see Nuria Martínez de Castilla, "La transmisión de textos entre los moriscos: Dos copias del tafsīr abreviado de Ibn Abī Zamanīn," *Anaquel de Estudios Árabes* 26 (2015): 147–161.

73. Tottoli, "New Light," 101. Some of the other Arabic manuscripts that Camillo Massimo brought to Rome from Madrid ended up in the Vatican Library. See García-Arenal and Mediano, *Orient in Spain,* 286n69.

74. OMD, Marracci Ms. IV; Tottoli, "New Light," 104, 106. On Strachan, see *ODNB,* s.v. "Strachan, George (*fl.* 1592–1634)." The original is now held in Naples.

75. Glei and Tottoli, *Ludovico Marracci at Work,* 34–35.

76. Susan Gunasti, "Political Patronage and the Writing of Qur'ān Commentaries among the Ottoman Turks," *Journal of Islamic Studies* 24 (2013): 336.

77. Glei and Tottoli, *Ludovico Marracci at Work,* 39–40.

78. Gottfried Wilhelm Leibniz, letter to the abbé Nicaise, 1697. Quoted in Mohamed Abdel-Halim, *Antoine Galland: Sa vie et son œuvre* (Paris, 1964), 167.

79. John Selden, for instance, consulted Suyūṭī. See G. J. Toomer, *John Selden: A Life in Scholarship* (Oxford, 2009), 2:616. And even Robert of Ketton's translation employed commentaries. See Burman, *Reading the Qur'an,* chap. 2. Marracci's increased exploitation of the Islamic commentarial tradition followed in the footsteps of the translation by Christian Hebraists of rabbinic commentaries on the Hebrew Bible, begun already in the latter sixteenth century. See Herman Hailperin, *Rashi and the Christian Scholars* (Pittsburgh, 1963); Frank Manuel, *The Broken Staff: Judaism through Christian Eyes* (Cambridge, Mass., 1992); Ilana Zinguer, ed., *L'Hébreu au temps de la Renaissance* (Leiden, 1992). Even so, this process too had medieval antecedents. See Amos Funkenstein, "Changes in Christian Anti-Jewish Polemics in the Twelfth Century," in Funkenstein, *Perceptions of Jewish History* (Berkeley, 1993), 172–201.

80. Nowadays such work is undertaken collaboratively, yet is no less slow and grinding for that. See Feras Hamza, Sajjad Rizvi, and Farhana Mayer, eds., *An Anthology of Qur'anic Commentaries,* vol. 1 (Oxford, 2010–); Seyyed Hossein Nasr, Caner K. Dagli, Maria Massi Dakake, Joseph E. B. Lumbard, and Mohammed Rustom, eds., *The Study Quran: A New Translation and Commentary* (New York, 2015).

81. Gunasti, "Political Patronage and the Writing of Qur'ān Commentaries," 336.

82. See *EI2,* s.v. "'al-Thaʿlabī."

83. Nallino, "Le fonti arabe manoscritte," 114.

84. The topic of Marracci as a polemicist is complex; in this chapter he is considered as a translator. On his polemic, see Giuseppe Rizzardi, "Il modello controversistico di Ludovico Marracci," in *Il Corano: Traduzioni, traduttori e lettori in Italia,* ed. Maurice Borrmans et al. (Milan, 2000), 81–109, and on his argument that Islam borrows from the Talmud, 95.

85. Nallino, "Le fonti arabe manoscritte," 117, 119. See 117n3 for the passages in which Marracci adduces these texts.

86. Ibid., 128–129. On Pococke, see Chapters 3 and 5. On d'Herbelot, see Chapter 4.

87. The Qur'an was on many editions of the Index, starting with the very general ban in Portugal, in 1547, of "Livros da septa de Mafamede em hebraico [*sic!*] nem en lingoajem." Quoted in Jésus Martínez de Bujanda, ed., *Index des livres interdits,* vol. 4., *Index de l'inquisition portugaise: 1547, 1551, 1561, 1564, 1581* (Geneva, 1995), 296. This was followed by Spain, in 1551 and again in 1559 (Bujanda, *Index de l'inquisition espagnole: 1551, 1554, 1559* [Geneva, 1984], 218, 307), and Venice and Milan (in 1554) (Bujanda, *Index* [1987], 3:214). The Rome Index of 1559 banned the Basel edition of the Qur'an, which was singled out again in the

Rome Index of 1596 (Bujanda, *Index* [1990], 8:362–363; 9:665–666). In addition, in 1603, anything to do with Islam was condemned: see *Index Librorum Prohibitorum Clementis X* (Rome, 1670), 6, 205. Hamilton, *Forbidden Fruit,* 3. For the additional decree under Alexander VII, see Levi della Vida, "Marracci e la sua opera," 202; Pedani Fabris, "La traduzione del Corano," 363; Giovanni Pizzorusso, "Filippo Guadagnoli, i Caracciolini e lo studio delle lingue orientali e della controversia con l'Islam a Roma nel XVII secolo," in Fosi and Pizzorusso, *L'Ordine dei Chierici Regolari Minori,* 268–273.

88. For a more detailed discussion of the intricacies of Marracci's dealings in Rome, see Pizzorusso, "Marracci tra ambiente curiale e cultura orientalista," 91–118.

89. BNCF, Magl. VIII, 572, letter 4: "quasi continue indisposizioni."

90. Ibid., letter 19 (29 August 1684).

91. Ibid., letter 20 (2 September 1684): "Stimando erroneamente, e con troppa simplicità, il Maestro del Sacro Palazzo, che sia una medesima cosa stampare il puro Alcorano, e le confutazioni dell'Alcorano."

92. Ibid.: "Tra questi chi ha detto che l'Alcorano non ha bisogno di confutazione, essendo ripieno di tanti spropositi per se stessi evidenti: chi, che questa mia Opera non servirebbe ne per i Turchi, ne per i Christiani: chi, che potrebbe più tosto portar danno alle persone semplici, chi, che potrebbe far gran danno, se fusse trovato da alcuno in Turchia, e altre simili simplicità."

93. Charles A. Frazee, *Catholics and Sultans: The Church and the Ottoman Empire, 1453–1923* (Cambridge, 1983), chap. 6, discusses the involvement of Propaganda Fide in missions to the Ottoman Empire, and to Istanbul in particular. For Aleppo, see Bruce A. Masters, *Christians and Jews in the Ottoman Arab World: The Roots of Sectarianism* (Cambridge, 2001), 80–88. The Church focused its energies on the Christians of the Empire, not on its Muslims. Not everyone had given up on converting Muslims to Catholicism: see the *Manuductio ad Conversionem Mohametanorum,* 2 vols. (Madrid, 1687) by the Spanish Jesuit Tirso González de Santalla, cited by Marracci in his *Prodromus* and studied by Emanuele Colombo, *Convertire i musulmani: L'esperienza di un gesuita spagnolo del Seicento* (Milan, 2007).

94. BNCF, Magl. VIII, 572, Letter 20: "inettie . . . frivolissime opposizioni."

95. Marracci cited a specific passage of Peter's defense, entitled *Epistola de Translatione Sua:* see *Bibliotheca Cluniacensis* (Paris, 1614), 1010 (in fact, there is a typographic error, and the column is 1110, but Marracci cites it as 1010). See the 1915 reprint, column 1110. When Marracci's translation finally appeared, its preface cited Peter the Venerable and Robert of Ketton. See Marracci, "Praefatio ad Lectorem," *Refutatio Alcorani,* 17.

96. BNCF, Magl. VIII, 572, letter 21 (23 September 1684): "una cosa tanto chiara, e che per dir così, potrebbe giudicarsi da un fanciullo."

97. For Marracci's fear, see ibid., letter 20. He reports the development in letter 24 (28 October 1684).

98. Ludwig Pastor, *The History of the Popes from the Close of the Middle Ages,* vol. 32, *Innocent XI. (1676–1689), Alexander VIII. (1689–1691), Innocent XII. (1691–1700),* trans. Dom Ernest Graf, O.S.B. (1891; repr., London, 1940), 14–17. Marracci produced a biography of Odescalchi, an abridgment of which was published in the late nineteenth century. See Mattia Giuseppe Lippi, *Vita di Papa Innocenzo XI raccolta in tre libri* (Rome, 1889), 240–258. While he awaited the pope's decree in 1684, Marracci remarked that Innocent XI had "a great propensity for denials" ("una gran propensione alle negative"). See BNCF, Magl. VIII, 572, letter 20, fol. 36r.

99. BNCF Magl. VIII, 572, letter 21 (23 September 1684): "Mà conviene con la pazienza vincere tutte le cose, sicome spero, che vinceremo questo." For further mentions of Marracci's travails in this period, see ibid., letters 22, 23.

100. Pizzorusso, "Filippo Guadagnoli," 245–278.

101. Ibid., 266–272.

102. On Marracci's relations with the Holy Office, see Tommasino, *L'Alcorano di Macometto,* 43–44.

103. He was cleared five years later, a few years before his death. See Davide Carbonaro and Francesco Petrillo, eds., *L'Immacolata Madre di Dio nel Seicento: Apporti teologici e spirituali di Ippolito Marracci nel IV centenario della nascita (1604)* (Rome, 2006); *DBI,* s.v. "Ippolito Marracci."

104. Marracci, *Prodromus ad Refutationem Alcorani.* Marracci discusses this publication in letters to Antonio Magliabechi: see BNCF, Ms. Magl., VIII, 572, letters 59–63. See also Pizzorusso, "Marracci tra ambiente curiale e cultura orientalista," 109.

105. For the Protestant reception of the *Prodromus,* see Alastair Hamilton, "A Lutheran Translator for the Quran: A Late Seventeenth-Century Quest," in *The Republic of Letters and the Levant,* ed. Hamilton, Maurits H. van den Boogert, and Bart Westerweel (Leiden, 2005), 197–221.

106. Giorgio Fedalto, "Il Cardinale Gregorio Barbarigo e l'Oriente," in Billanovich and Gios, *Gregorio Barbarigo,* 977–1001, esp. 996 and references there. On Barbarigo, see also Ireneo Daniele, "Gregorio Giovanni Gaspare Barbarigo," *Bibliotheca Sanctorum* 7 (1966): 387–403; *DBI,* s.v. "Gregorio Barbarigo, santo."

107. Marco Callegari, "La tipografia del seminario di Padova fondata dal Barbarigo," in Billanovich and Gios, *Gregorio Barbarigo,* 231–251.

108. Giorgio Vercellin, *Venezia e l'origine della stampa in caratteri arabi* (Padua, 2001).

109. On this tradition, see Robert Jones, "The Medici Oriental Press (Rome 1584–1614) and the Impact of Its Arabic Publications on Northern Europe,"

in *The 'Arabick' Interest of the Natural Philosophers in Seventeenth-Century England,* ed. G. A. Russell (Leiden, 1994), chap. 5, and Jones, "Learning Arabic in Renaissance Europe (1505–1624)" (PhD diss., School of Oriental and African Studies, University of London, 1988). See also G. E. Saltini, "Della Stamperia Orientale Medicea e di Giovan Battista Raimondi," *Giornale Storico degli Archivi Toscani* 4 (1860): 257–308; Alberto Tinto, *La tipografia medicea orientale* (Lucca, 1987); Sara Fani and Margherita Farina, eds., *Le vie delle lettere: La Tipografia Medicea tra Roma e l'Oriente* (Florence, 2012).

110. The punches and matrices were rediscovered by Joseph de Guignes only in 1785. See Joseph de Guignes, *Essai historique sur la typographie orientale et grecque de l'Imprimerie royale* (Paris, 1787). For modern treatments of the Paris Polyglot types, see Gérard Duverdier, "Les débuts de la typographie orientale: Les caractères de Savary de Brèves et la présence française au Levant au 17e siècle," in *L'art du livre à l'Imprimerie nationale: Cinq siècles de typographie,* ed. Julien Cain and Georges Bonnin (Paris, 1973), 68–87; Duverdier, "Les impressions orientales en Europe et le Liban," in *Le livre et le Liban jusqu'à 1900,* ed. Camille Aboussouan (Paris, 1982), 157–279; J. Balagna, *L'imprimerie arabe en Occident: XVIe, XVIIe, et XVIIIe siècles* (Paris, 1984), 55–58.

111. See letter 84 (11 November 1684) from Barbarigo to Cosimo III de' Medici in *Lettere di Gregorio Barbarigo a Cosimo III de' Medici (1680–1697),* ed. Pierantonio Gios (Padua, 2003), 80–81.

112. Callegari, "La tipografia del Seminario," 235. They received ten lire a day for setting Latin text, eleven for Greek, 12 for Hebrew, 13 for Arabic, and 14 for Aramaic and other Oriental languages. On their lessons, see Giuseppe Bellini, *Storia della Tipografia del Seminario di Padova, 1684–1938,* 2nd ed. (Padua, 1938), 57.

113. On these publications, see the list in Bellini, *La Tipografia del Seminario,* 295–445, esp. 296–297 and 312, though a modern list would be desirable.

114. First publication: Pietro Bogdanus, *Cuneus Prophetarum* (Padua, 1685). Grammar: Agapitus a valle Flemmarum, *Flores Grammaticales Arabici Idiomatis Collecti ex Optimis Quibusque Grammaticis* (Padua, 1687). Proverbs: Timoteo Agnellini, *Adagii turcheschi con la parafrase latina e italiana* (Padua, 1688); Agnellini, *Proverbii utili, e virtuosi in lingua araba, persiana, e turca, gran parte in versi, con la loro ispiegatione in Lingua Latina, e Italiana* (Padua, 1688).

115. BNCF, Magl. VIII, 388, letter 1 (9 January 1685). An orthographic hint suggests that this was in all likelihood Barbarigo's (or at least his amanuensis's) first acquaintance with the Roman translator: the letter misspells the latter's name as "Maracci," as it appears, incorrectly, on the translation's title page. The translation was published the preceding year as *Disegno dello Stendardo del*

Primo Visire levato sotto Vienna dal Serenissimo e Invittissimo Giovanni Terzo Rè di Polonia, e da Sua Maestà Mandato alla Santità di nostro Signore Papa Innocenzo Undecimo, Aggiuntavi la vera interpretatione delle parole Arabiche, che in detto Stendardo sono artificiosamente intessute (Rome and Bologna, 1683).

116. BNCF, Magl. VIII, 572, letter 54 (27 August 1689): "Non ho veduto ancora il Sig.re Card. Barbarigo, ne penso poter vederlo se non terminato il Conclave."

117. Pastor, *History of the Popes,* 32, chap. 2.

118. For Barbarigo's efforts to secure permission from the Holy Office, see Pizzorusso, "Marracci tra ambiente curiale e cultura orientalista," 110–111.

119. Pierluigi Giovannucci, ed., *Il decennio finale dell'episcopato padovano: Lettere di Gregorio Barbarigo ai familiari (1688–1697)* (Padua, 2011), letter 542 (16 September 1695), 411: "ci è un ordine particolare in Roma che i libri composti in Roma non si possono stampar fuori." Other letters concerning the matter of the Qur'an are held in ASPV, Ms. 1168, 701–702 (16 September 1695), 705 (17 September 1695); Ms. 1170 (già 586), letters 596 (7 March 1695) and 598 (9 March 1695); Ms. 1171 (già 587), letters 655 (4 June 1695), 747 (15 October 1695) and 788 (8 March 1696); Ms. 1172 (già 588), letter 807 (27 March 1696).

120. ASPV, Ms. 1171, n. 788 (8 March 1696). I thank Hannah Marcus for her clarifications on this subject.

121. The censors' authorization is reproduced at the end of *Prodromus.*

122. The authorization is reproduced at the end of the front matter of *Refutatio Alcorani.*

123. See ASP, vol. 122, p. 274. This is earlier than stated in Callegari, "La tipografia del Seminario," 232, and Giovannucci, *Il decennio finale dell'episcopato padovano,* clvii. On May 17, 1692, Marracci already announced that printing in Padua would begin "quanto prima" (as soon as possible). See BNCF, Magl. VIII, 572, letter 64.

124. As it turned out, the two books would appear in the same year: Thomas Aquinas, *Summæ Theologicæ in Quinque Tomos Distributæ,* 5 vols. (Padua, 1698).

125. On the Biblioteca Ambrosiana, see Angelo Paredi, *A History of the Ambrosiana,* trans. C. McInerny and R. McInerny (Notre Dame, Ind., 1983); for a study of art and religious thought in Borromeo's Ambrosiana, see Pamela M. Jones, *Federico Borromeo and the Ambrosiana: Art Patronage and Reform in Seventeenth-Century Milan* (Cambridge, 1993). The dictionary was Giggi, *Thesaurus Linguae Arabicae.*

126. Sebastiano Serena, "Il Cardinale Gregorio Barbarigo e l'Oriente," in Serena, *S. Gregorio Barbarigo e la vita spirituale e culturale nel suo Seminario di Padova,* 2 vols. (Padua, 1963), 1:137–171.

127. BNCF, Magl. VIII, 388, letter 9 (24 August 1685): "Per le cose arabiche veramente io presi l'esemplare del Sig. Cardinal Borromeo, e mi dispiace, che i suoi Successori non l'habbino seguito."

128. Nallino, "Le fonti arabe manoscritte," 92–94. The experience of producing the Arabic Bible had made Marracci keenly aware of the difficulty of setting Arabic type and of the errors that were liable to be made. For some of his corrections, see APF, Congressi Stamperia I, fols. 211r–246v.

129. The Paduan Seminary Library contains fourteen Arabic, Persian, and Turkish manuscripts, including grammars, prayer books, proverb collections, and other miscellaneous works, none of which seem to have been used for creating *Alcorani Textus Universus*. The Paduan University Library contains only four Arabic manuscripts: three Christian books and a collection of poems by Mutanabbī. See G. Gabrieli, "Documenti orientali nelle biblioteche e negli archivi d'Italia," *Accademie e biblioteche d'Italia* 7 (1933–1934): 295–296.

130. Claudio Bellinati, "La Biblioteca del card. Gregorio Barbarigo in eredità al Seminario di Padova (1697)," *Atti e memorie dell'Accademia Patavina di Scienze, Lettere ed Arti* 108 (1995–1996): 191–197.

131. The famous Biblioteca Marciana did not have a Qur'an. For its holdings, see BNM, Cons. Cat. Mss Marc. (orientali 1 and 2), available online. Most of the nineteen Qur'ans held in the library today come from the collection of the Nani brothers, which entered the library in the early nineteenth century. Because in the Napoleonic period Venice's clerical libraries were seized (over 17,000 books were removed in 1806 alone) and moved out of the city, it remains extremely difficult to reconstruct their holdings in the earlier period. See Marino Zorzi, *La Libreria di San Marco: Libri, lettori, società nella Venezia dei Dogi* (Milan, 1987), 320–332, 349–364; the figure for 1806 is cited at 358. Further libraries were sacked in 1810, including the Dominicans at Ss. Giovanni e Paolo. A few copies in the Marciana come from religious orders: Cod. CLXXVII (= 202) from the Gesuati (S. Maria del Rosario); CLXXVIII (134) from an order merely designated in the bookplate as "Frati"; CLXXXIII (= 160) from the Somaschi (S. Maria della Salute).

132. ASPV, Ms. 1169, letter 290: "Alla barchetta del Pesce di Zelega Pescatore che porta il Pesce a Padova e che torna di mattina si consegnano i Libri ordinati da V. E." I thank Maria Pia Pedani for our exchange about this passage.

133. On Agnellini, see Bernard Heyberger, "La carrière manquée d'un ecclésiastique oriental en Italie: Timothée Karnûsh, archevêque syrien catholique de Mardîn," *Bulletin de la faculté des lettres de Mulhouse* 19 (1995): 31–47.

134. Agnellini himself claimed to have edited twelve books for the Press. See the quotation in Serena, *S. Gregorio Barbarigo*, 1:155–156. The citation is from

Veneta seu Patavina Beatificationis et Canonizationis Ven. Servi Dei Gregorii Card. Barbadici Episcopi Olim Bergomensis, Postea Patavini, Summarium (Rome, 1746), 85.

135. Heyberger, "Timothée Karnûsh," 38, citing Rome, ASPV, *Scritture Originali riferite nelle Congregazioni Generali,* vol. 535, fols. 178r–181v.

136. See the documentation in BNCF, Magl. VIII, ser. 3, vol. 1, letters 5–7, and Magl. VIII, 1356, letter 2.

137. BNCF, Magl. VIII, ser. 3, vol. 1, letter no. 6 (27 August 1693): "con che li confesso mi dispiace di non poter ritrovar l'hora, ne il giorno di poter volare in Padova per poter dar termine a quelle poche mie fatighe et particolarmente quelle del rifiutationi del Alcorano, che gia son rimaste imperfette come V.S. Illma sa."

138. BNCF, Magl. VIII, ser. 3, vol. 1, letter no. 5 (16 March 1694): "non trovo l'ora per volare al mio gabinetto di studio in Padova notte e giorno non desidero altro."

139. BNCF, Magl. VIII, ser. 3, vol. 1, letter no. 7 (28 April 1695): "per haver sospeso le stampe in lingua Orientale per mancanza mia."

140. ASPV, Ms. 1171, n. 655, letter from Barbarigo to Grimani, Borgoricco, 4 June 1695: "Habbiamo in stamparia l'Alcorano che doverebbe esser finito, ma perché ci mancano i correttori non possiamo dargli addosso dadovero; ho pensato se potessimo ritrovare a Venezia qualche d'uno ben prattico della Lingua Araba che facesse questo. Venne già a Venezia un Turco, che si fece cristiano[,] di cui si diceva, che se ne voleva servire anco al publico e insegnare la lingua. Se questi vi fosse e venisse a mediocre conditione forse sarebbe buono. Metteressimo due torchi per finir l'opera, di cui altrimenti non posso vedere il fine."

141. BNCF, Magl. VIII, 1356, letter no. 2 (Naples, 20 February 1696): "per li molti travagli di Viaggi fatti in Calabria e Sicilia seminando la parola di Dio con molta edificatione de Popoli."

142. Ibid.: "Hieri apunto riceveti Lettera dal Eminentissimo mio Signore Barbarigo, il quale con raduplicate istanze vuole presto il mio ritiro colà per finire il corano, non havendosi potuto terminare per la mia assenza."

143. Six days before his death, Barbarigo had visited the typography personally to check on the progress of the *Alcorani Textus Universus.* See Daniele, "Gregorio Giovanni Gaspare Barbarigo," 400. The source is Giuseppe Musoco, an intimate of the cardinal's, who wrote a memoir after the latter's death.

144. For a discussion on the accepted variant readings of the Qur'an, see *EI2,* s.v. "Ḳirāʾa," and references there. See below for an example of the variant readings as they surfaced in the *Alcorani Textus Universus.*

145. On Qur'anic verse division, see Anton Spitaler, *Die Verszählung des Koran nach islamischer Überlieferung,* special issue, *Sitzungsberichte der Bayerischen Akademie der Wissenschaften* 11 (1935); Keith Small, *Textual Criticism and Qur'ān Manuscripts* (Lanham, Md., 2011). I thank Roberto Tottoli for his clarifications on this subject.

146. He followed here, as elsewhere, Ḥafṣ ʿan ʿĀṣim, but differed from Ḥafṣ in other respects, e.g., counting 287 verses in Q2, where Ḥafṣ counts 286, or 110 in Q17, where Ḥafṣ counts 111.

147. Hinckelmann, *Al-Coranus S. Lex Islamitica Muhammedis.*

148. Marracci's division was closer to the Arabic than Hinckelmann's, as Johann Friedrich Hirt remarked in *Anthologia Arabica* (Jena, 1774), 252, 252–253, 256. See also Nallino, "Le fonti arabe manoscritte," 94n1; Glei and Tottoli, *Ludovico Marracci at Work,* 20–31. For example, a reader of a copy now at Columbia University tried to renumber the Qur'an's verses in his copy of Marracci's book, suggesting that this aspect of the work displeased him. See Rare Book & Manuscript Library, Columbia University, shelfmark B893.7K84.J81.

149. Marracci, "Refutationes," *Refutatio,* 784.

150. Ibid., 3.

151. Marracci, "Benigno Lectori," *Refutatio,* n.p.

152. Marracci, "Al Christiano Lettore," *L'Ebreo preso per le buone,* n.p.

153. BNCF, Magl. VIII, 572, letter 65 (2 May 1699): "le mie inettie contra l'Alcorano, le quali assai notabili per la debolezza dell'Autore, sono stati notabilmente accresciuti dall'ignoranza crassissima de' Tipografi, e Correttori di Padova, i quali niente intendetori di lingua Arabica e poco di lingua latina hanno fatto mille spropositi, havendo di più havuto ardire di mutare in alcuni luoghi il mio originale . . . Hanno di più pervertito tutto l'ordine della prima parte del Prodromo; hanno rejerato alcune cose, altre ne hanno aggiunte di propria testa tutte a sproposito fuor che quell'ultimi passi dell'opera, con le quali si dichiarano d'essere una mano di ignoranti."

154. Ibid.: "Io facevo pregar il Sig. Card Cornaro a farmi ristampar alcuni fogli; ma non se n'è fatto niente."

155. Ibid.: "Compatirà V.S. Ill.ma a queste mie disgrazie, e si compiacerà, quando ne venga l'occasione, far conoscere che la stroppiatura dell'opera non è venuta tutta da me."

156. In his MS translation, Egidio da Viterbo had placed Arabic, Latin transliteration, Latin translation, and notes in four parallel columns. See Burman, *Reading the Qur'an,* 149–165.

157. Agnellini, *Proverbii Utili e Virtuosi in Lingua Araba.*

158. See, for instance, "Refutationes," *Refutatio,* 9. On the enduring puzzle of these letters, see *EQ,* s.v. "Mysterious Letters."

159. See "Refutationes," *Refutatio Alcorani*, 1. In the rest of the volume, these divisions are marked in the margin of the translation rather than of the Arabic text. See, e.g., ibid., 91, 128, 171, 407, 472, 509, 676.

160. Timoteo Agnellini, *Libro della Penitenza e Passione di Gesù Christo e di sua santissima madre, in arabo e italiano*, 3 vols. (Padua, 1693).

161. Marracci, "Praefatio," *Prodromus*, 8; Marracci, "Praefatio," *Refutatio*, 16.

162. Siegmund Jakob Baumgarten, [book review], *Nachrichten von einer hallischen Bibliothek* 5 (March 1750): 230–236, at 234.

163. Madrid, Biblioteca Nacional de España, Alcorani Textus Universus, shelfmark 2 / 41438, 265, 320–321, 325–328, 335, 343, 350, 352–353. Other readers also focused their annotations on the Arabic text, rather than on the notes and refutations: see, e.g., BnF, shelfmark Fol-O2G-126 (2); CUL, shelfmark C.1.22.

164. For studies of Marracci's Latin, see Reinhold Glei, "*Arabismus Latine Personatus:* Die Koranübersetzung von Ludovico Marracci (1698) und die Funktion des Lateinischen," *Jahrbuch für Europäische Wissenschaftskultur* 5 (2009 / 10): 93–115; Glei and Tottoli, *Ludovico Marracci at Work*, 41–136, and 41–43 on this point.

165. One example is the Arabic word *ummī*, which he consistently translates as "idiota" or "idiotae"; another is *ḥanīf*, which he renders as "orthodoxus." See Maurice Borrmans, "Marracci et sa traduction latine du Coran," *Islamochristiana* 28 (2002): 80–81.

166. For a more detailed study of Marracci's translation of a much longer sura, see Glei and Tottoli, *Ludovico Marracci at Work*, 93–115.

167. Many *ḥadīth* attribute particular merit to the recitation of certain suras of the Qur'an. According to al-Bukhārī, Muhammad would recite Q112, Q113, and Q114 over his cupped hands each night before going to sleep. On this topic, see *EQ*, s.v. "Recitation of the Qur'ān" and "Popular and Talismanic Uses of the Qur'ān."

168. Similarly, he could translate *bismillāh al-raḥman al-raḥīm* as *In nomine Dei Miseratoris Misericordis,* which in English is more often rendered as "In the name of God, the Compassionate, the Merciful," two words with unrelated origins. Compare Borrmans, "Marracci et sa traduction latine," 78–79.

169. Golius, *Lexicon*, 1380. *The Study Qur'an*, 1579, renders it as "the Eternally Sufficient unto Himself," following al-Zamakhsharī, a source available to Marracci; see the discussion at 1579n2.

170. OMD, Marracci Ms. III, fol. 441r. The pages of this MS are currently unfoliated.

171. Marracci, *Refutatio*, 831.

172. Borrmans, "Marracci et sa traduction latine," 82. See also the positive appraisal in O. A. Sheikh Al-Shabab, "The Place of Marracci's Latin Translation of the

Holy Quran: A Linguistic Investigation," *Journal of King Saud University—Languages & Translation* 13 (2001): 57–74.

173. Letter from Gregorio Barbarigo to Giovanni Pastrizio, Padua, 21 January 1695. Sebastiano Serena, ed., *Quaranta due lettere del Cardinale Beato Gregorio Barbarigo a Giovanni Pastrizio* (Padua, 1938), 46. The original is held in BAV, Borgiano-Latino 738.

174. Hamilton, "A Lutheran Translator for the Quran," 198.

175. Ibid., 198–199.

176. Ibid.

177. See the dozens of entries in the Online Public Access Catalog (OPAC) of the Servizio Bibliotecario Nazionale (SBN).

178. Biblioteca Civica di Alessandria, shelfmark AM.44.B.1. On Mombaruzzo, see Emanuele Cadinini and Crescenzio Milano, *Necrologio dei frati minori Cappuccini della provincia di Alessandria* (Alessandria, 1972), 217. On Villafori, see Fabrizio Quaglia, *I libri ebraici nei fondi storici della Biblioteca Civica di Alessandria* (Alessandria, 2004), 31, 84. I thank Fabrizio Quaglia for drawing my attention to this copy and for these references.

179. Houghton Library, Harvard University, shelfmark OL 2482.2F. On Tipaldi, see Mariano Ventimiglia, *Degli uomini illustri del Regal Convento del Carmine Maggiore di Napoli Libri IV* (Naples, 1756), 180–181.

180. Richard Simon, *Nouvelle Bibliothèque Choisie,* 2 vols. (Amsterdam, 1714), 2:223.

181. Siegmund Jakob Baumgarten, *Nachrichten von einer Hallischen Bibliothek* 5, 233.

182. Jacob Wilhelm Blaufus, *Vermischte Beyträge zur Erweiterung der Kentniß seltener und merkwürdiger Bücher,* 2 vols. (Jena, 1753), 1:258.

183. Baumgarten, *Nachrichten von einer Hallischen Bibliothek* 5, 234–235.

184. John Whiston, *A New and General Biographical Dictionary; containing an Historical and Critical Account of the Lives and Writings of the Most Eminent Persons in every Nation; particularly the British and Irish; from the earliest Accounts of Time to the present Period,* 12 vols. (London, 1761–1767), vol. 8 (1762), 248–250, quotation at 249.

185. David Nerreter, *Neu-eröffnete Mahometanische Moschea* (Nuremberg, 1703); Christian Reineccius, *Mohammedis Filii Abdaliæ Pseudo-Prophetæ Fides Islamitica* (Leipzig, 1721).

186. This translation remained in manuscript. It is in Karshuni (Arabic written in Syriac script). See BAV, Codice vaticano siriaco 446, fols. 279r–505r. On Arūtīn, see Georg Graf, *Geschichte der christlichen arabischen Literatur* (Vatican City, 1949), 3:430–432.

187. Even so, Rückert had first read Marracci's book with care. See Hamilton, " 'To Rescue the Honour,' " 209.

188. Only a draft translation of the first two suras, attributed to Galland, survives, in BnF, Ms Fr. 25280, fols. 1–120. Galland's explanation of his enterprise is found in KB, shelfmark 72 G 6, letter to G. Cuper of 31 October 1710, fols. 6–7. See also KB shelfmark 72 G 5, letter to Cuper, 30 December 1709. See also Mohamed Abdel-Halim, "Correspondance d'Antoine Galland" (thèse complémentaire, University of Paris, 1964; held in Sorbonne University Bibliothèque Georges-Ascoli et Paul-Hazard). Galland's methodology resembles that of the English Bible translators. See David Norton, *The King James Bible: A Short History from Tyndale to Today* (Cambridge, 2011); Nicholas Hardy, "The Septuagint and the Transformation of Biblical Scholarship in England, from the King James Bible (1611) to the London Polyglot (1657)," in *Oxford Handbook of the Bible in Early Modern England, c. 1530–1700,* ed. Kevin Killeen, Helen Smith, and Rachel Willie (Oxford, 2015), 117–130; Jeffrey A. Miller, "Fruit of Good Labours: Discovering the Earliest Known Draft of the King James Bible," *Times Literary Supplement,* 16 October 2015, 14–15.

189. *Dictionnaire des orientalistes de langue française,* s.v. "Savary, Claude-Étienne" and references there.

190. Marracci, "Praefatio ad Lectorem," *Prodromus,* 4. In fact, the passage continues: "nisi a Missionariis nostris, his, quem ego in meo opere pono, argumentis praeveniantur, ac praemuniantur." But this clause was left out of the two quotations of the passage discussed here.

191. "The Life and Actions of Mahomet," in *Four Treatises concerning the Doctrine, Discipline and Worship of the Mahometans* (London, 1712), A2r (frontispiece).

192. Adriaan Reland, *De Religione Mohammedica,* 2nd ed. (Utrecht, 1717), "Praefatio," fols. 2r–v.

193. John Toland, *Mangoneutes* (London, 1720), 161–163.

194. This understanding of Islam as fundamentally rational was largely based on the denial of the Trinity, for many other puzzling aspects of Islamic theology remained, as Marracci was well aware.

195. Andreas Acoluthus, *Tetrapla Alcoranica, sive Specimen Alcorani Quadrilinguis, Arabici, Persici, Turcici, Latini* (Berlin, 1701). On Acoluthus, see Hamilton, " 'To Rescue the Honour,' " 177–180.

196. See Olaus Domey, *Nova Versio Partis Surae II Corani* (Göttingen, 1754). On this discussion in Michaelis, see Hamilton, " 'To Rescue the Honour,' " 181–182.

197. Hamilton, " 'To Rescue the Honour,' " 190.

198. George Sale, *The Koran, Commonly Called the Alcoran of Mohammed, Translated into English immediately from the Original Arabic; with Explanatory Notes, taken from the Most Approved Commentators. To which is prefixed A Preliminary Discourse* (London, 1734 [1733]), "To the Right Honourable John Lord Carteret," n.p.

199. Sale, "To the Reader," *Koran,* iii.

200. Ibid. In addition, Sale likely had economic motivations for undertaking the translation. See Bevilacqua, "Marracci and Sale," 100–101.

201. R. A. Davenport, "A sketch of the life of George Sale," in G. Sale, *The Koran, commonly called the Alcoran of Mohammed,* rev. ed. (1734; repr., London, 1825); *Dictionary of National Biography,* s.v. "Sale, George"; *ODNB,* "Sale, George"; Bevilacqua, "Marracci and Sale."

202. Sale also worked on a general reference work modeled on Pierre Bayle's, and on a universal history. See *A General Dictionary, Historical and Critical,* 10 vols. (London, 1734–1741); *An Universal History, from the Earliest Accounts of Time,* 7 vols. (London, 1736–1744). On the latter, see Giuseppe Ricuperati, "*Universal History:* Storia di un progetto europeo; Impostori, storici ed editori nella *Ancient Part,*" *Studi settecenteschi* 1 (1981): 7–90.

203. In late August 1726 Sale agreed to act as corrector for the Arabic New Testament of the Society for Promoting Christian Knowledge (hereafter SPCK), an Anglican missionary organization founded in 1698. CUL SPCK MS. A1 / 12, 40. The same is reported in CUL SPCK Ms. A32 / 1, 46. See also C. Rose, "The Origins and Ideals of the SPCK, 1699–1716," in *The Church of England, c. 1689–c. 1833: From Toleration to Tractarianism,* ed. J. Walsh, C. Haydon, and S. Taylor (Cambridge, 1993), chap. 7.

204. Take the case of the journeyman tailor of Norwich, Henry Wilde, who, "having a strange inclination to languages," had mastered seven of them in as many years, "by a prodigious industry . . . without any help or assistance from others." Wilde's talents raised high expectations, yet he died abruptly in 1721. See William D. Macray, *Annals of the Bodleian Library, Oxford,* 2nd ed. (Oxford, 1890), 194–195. The quotations are from the diary of Thomas Hearne. On the general subject of learning Arabic at this time, see Loop, Hamilton, and Burnett, *The Teaching and Learning of Arabic.*

205. CUL SPCK Ms. D5 / 4, 43 (letter of 25 August 1729).

206. By his own avowal, in Sale, "To the Reader," *Koran,* vii–viii.

207. William Hamerton, *A Choice Collection of Most Curious and Inestimable Manuscripts, In the Turkish, Arabic and Persian Languages, from the Library of the late Learned and Ingenious Mr. George Sale* (London, [1736]). The collection was acquired in its entirety by Thomas Hunt for the Radcliffe Library at Oxford, and later passed to the Bodleian. Ms. Sale 67 is not the Qur'an that Sale used for the translation; see below. Sale did, however, possess Ibn Khallikān's biographical dictionary *Wafayat al aʿyān* (Mss. Sale 48–49); a selection of Prophetic traditions (Ms. Sale 70); collections of the stories of saints (Ms. Sale 77) and martyrs (Ms. Sale 78); the sayings of ʿAlī (Ms. Sale 82); biographies of famous Shiites (Ms. Sale 68); a book on the use of the Qur'an

for divination (Ms. Sale 69), a treatise on the merits of visiting the Prophet's grave (Ms. Sale 56, fols. 67v–89r), and a selection of mystical treatises (Ms. Sale 41).

208. On the relationship of Sale to his predecessor, see E. Denison Ross, "Ludovico Marracci," *Bulletin of the School of Oriental Studies* 2 (1921): 117–123. See also Ross, introduction to *The Koran*, trans. Sale and intro. Ross (London, 1921), v–x. *Dictionary of National Biography*, s.v. "Sale, George (1697?–1736)"; *ODNB*, s.v. "Sale, George (*b.* in or after 1696, *d.* 1736)." For comparisons of Marracci and Sale, see W. G. Shellabear, "Is Sale's Koran Reliable?," *Muslim World* 21 (1931): 126–142; Bevilacqua, "Marracci and Sale."

209. See Bevilacqua, "Marracci and Sale," 103–106; and further instances in Shellabear, "Sale's Koran."

210. Shellabear, "Sale's Koran."

211. These other sources included the famous collector of Prophetic traditions (*ḥadīth*) al-Bukhārī and a number of others. See Bevilacqua, "Marracci and Sale," 106.

212. Sale acknowledges a Reverend Bolten, responsible for the loan, in his prefatory "To the Reader." The manuscript is now in London, Metropolitan Archive, CLC / 180 Ms. 20185 / 11. It is cataloged, incorrectly, in the inventory published by K. J. Bostoen, "De Handschriften in de Dutch Church Library (Austin Friars) te Londen," *Nederlands Archief voor Kerkgeschiedenis* 60 (1980): 56–89, at 63, which confuses the copyist with the author. The scribe, Aḥmad al-Saʿdī al Khazrajī, copied it in Istanbul in 989 AH / 1581 CE.

213. Bod., Ms Sale. 67. This manuscript follows the reading of Ḥafṣ ʿan ʿĀṣim, standard in the Ottoman Empire.

214. Sale, "Preliminary Discourse," *Koran*, 61.

215. Jan Loop, "Divine Poetry? Early Modern European Orientalists on the Beauty of the Koran," *Church History and Religious Culture* 89 (2009): 477–480, on Sale in particular.

216. On the King James translation, see Norton, *King James Bible;* Hardy, "The Septuagint"; Miller, "Fruit of Good Labours."

217. Sale, "Al Koran," *Koran*, 507.

218. Ibid.

219. For an analysis and definition of *sajʿ* as a form of rhymed poetry, rather than as "rhymed prose," see Devin J. Stewart, "*Sajʿ* in the Qurʾan: Prosody and Structure," *Journal of Arabic Literature* 21 (1990): 101–139.

220. Kristine L. Haugen, "Hebrew Poetry Transformed, or, Scholarship Invincible between Renaissance and Enlightenment," *Journal of the Warburg and Courtauld Institutes* 75 (2012): 1–29.

221. Nallino, "Le fonti arabe manoscritte," 132, compares Marracci's two translations of the *fātiḥa*, the first with stylistic effects in the course of a discussion in
"De Alcorano," *Prodromus*, 35, and the second for literal meaning in the actual
translation, "Refutationes," *Refutatio*, 1.

222. Burman, *Reading the Qur'an*, 29–35.

223. For examples, see Bevilacqua, "Marracci and Sale," 120–128, and Chapter 3.

224. On Jefferson, see Kevin J. Hayes, "How Thomas Jefferson Read the Qur'ān,"
Early American Literature 39 (2004): 247–261; Denise A. Spellberg, *Thomas
Jefferson's Qur'an: Islam and the Founders* (New York, 2013).

225. German translators would pursue an equivalent accomplishment into the early
nineteenth century. Hamilton, " 'To Rescue the Honour,' " describes the era
after Lodovico Marracci and before Friedrich Rückert.

226. Many earlier European scholars of Arabic had had to travel to Arab lands, not
least to assemble a manuscript collection from which to work, although
other predecessors—Thomas Erpenius, William Bedwell, Johann Heinrich
Hottinger—did not.

3 · A NEW VIEW OF ISLAM

1. Earlier accounts of the transition described in this chapter can be found in
Johann Fück, *Die arabischen Studien in Europa bis in den Anfang des 20. Jahrhunderts* (Leipzig, 1955); Bernard Lewis, "Gibbon on Muhammad," *Daedalus*
105 (1976): 89–101; Ahmad Gunny, *Images of Islam in Eighteenth-Century
Writings* (London, 1996); Robert Irwin, *For Lust of Knowing: The Orientalists
and Their Enemies* (London, 2006), chap. 5; Rolando Minuti, *Orientalismo e
idee di tolleranza nella cultura francese del primo '700* (Florence, 2006), chap. 2;
Lynn Hunt, Margaret Jacob, and Wijnand Mijnardt, *The Book That Changed
Europe: Picart and Bernard's Religious Ceremonies of the World* (Cambridge,
Mass., 2010), chap. 10; Guy Stroumsa, *A New Science: The Discovery of Religion
in the Age of Reason* (Cambridge, Mass., 2010), chap. 6; Humberto Garcia,
Islam and the English Enlightenment, 1670–1840 (Baltimore, 2011).

2. Humphrey Prideaux, *The True Nature of Imposture Fully Display'd in the Life of
Mahomet. With a Discourse annex'd, for the Vindicating of Christianity from this
Charge; Offered to the Consideration of the Deists of the present Age* (London,
1697), 135–136.

3. Within a vast literature, see Margaret Jacob, *The Radical Enlightenment: Pan-
theists, Freemasons, and Republicans* (London, 1981); Jonathan Israel, *Radical
Enlightenment: Philosophy and the Making of Modernity, 1650–1750* (Oxford,
2002); Israel, *Enlightenment Contested: Philosophy, Modernity, and the
Emancipation of Man, 1670–1752* (Oxford, 2006); Silvia Berti, *Anticristianesimo*

e libertà: Studi sull'Illuminismo radicale europeo (Bologna, 2012). On Islam and radical thought: Justin A. I. Champion, *The Pillars of Priestcraft Shaken: The Church of England and Its Enemies, 1660–1730* (Cambridge, 1992); Martin Mulsow, "Socinianism, Islam and the Radical Uses of Arabic Scholarship," *Al-Qantara* 31 (2010): 549–586; Israel, *Enlightenment Contested,* 615–639.

4. E.g., Ziad Elmarsafy, *The Enlightenment Qur'an: The Politics of Translation and the Construction of Islam* (Oxford, 2009), 26, 30.

5. The central contention of this chapter is in agreement with William J. Bulman, *Anglican Enlightenment: Orientalism, Religion, and Politics in England and Its Empire, 1648–1715* (Cambridge, 2015). See also Dmitri Levitin, "From Sacred History to the History of Religion: Paganism, Judaism, and Christianity in European Historiography from Reformation to 'Enlightenment,'" *Historical Journal* 55 (2012): 1117–1160; Levitin, "John Spencer's *De Legibus Hebraeorum* (1683–85) and 'Enlightened' Sacred History: A New Interpretation," *Journal of the Warburg and Courtauld Institutes* 76 (2013): 49–92, esp. 88–92; Levitin, *Ancient Wisdom in the Age of the New Science: Histories of Philosophy in England, c. 1640–1700* (Cambridge, 2015).

6. On the role of Islam in Catholic-Protestant interconfessional polemic in the seventeenth century, see Jan Loop, *Johann Heinrich Hottinger: Arabic and Islamic Studies in the Seventeenth Century* (Oxford, 2013). For the perspective of a Christian minority, see Justin J. Meggitt, *Early Quakers and Islam: Slavery, Apocalyptic and Christian-Muslim Encounters in the Seventeenth Century* (Uppsala, 2013).

7. Edward Pococke, *Specimen Historiæ Arabum: Sive, Gregorii Abul Farajii Malatiensis, de Origine & Moribus Arabum Succincta Narratio, in Linguam Latinam Conversa, Notisque è Probatissimis apud Ipsos Authoribus, Fusiùs Illustrat* (Oxford, 1650).

8. On English scholarly achievements in Arabic studies, see P. M. Holt, *Studies in the History of the Near East* (London, 1973), 3–63; Alastair Hamilton, *William Bedwell, the Arabist, 1563–1632* (Leiden, 1985); G. J. Toomer, *Eastern Wisedome and Learning: The Study of Arabic in Seventeenth-Century England* (Oxford: 1995); Mordechai Feingold, "Patrons and Professors: The Origins and Motives for the Endowment of University Chairs, in Particular the Laudian Professorship of Arabic," in *The 'Arabick' Interest of the Natural Philosophers in Seventeenth-Century England,* ed. G. A. Russell (Leiden, 1994), chap. 6; Feingold, "Oriental Studies," in *The History of the University of Oxford,* vol. 4, *Seventeenth-Century Oxford,* ed. Nicholas Tyacke (Oxford, 1997), chap. 8.

9. Bath, Central Library, shelfmark SAL 1/1 (George Sale's Manuscript Notebook entitled "Historiae Verae Analecta"), p. 120 [fol. 63r]; Johann Jacob Reiske, *Abilfedae Annales Moslemici* (Leipzig, 1754), iv.

10. The life of Pococke can be found in Toomer, *Eastern Wisedome,* chaps. 5–8, and in *ODNB,* s.v. "Pococke, Edward (1604–1691)." Hamilton, *William Bedwell,* 53.

11. Pococke held this appointment from 1636, but in 1637 he returned to the Levant to collect further manuscripts for his own research and for the Bodleian. See Toomer, *Eastern Wisedome,* 125–216, 134–136.

12. Edward Pococke, *Porta Mosis* (Oxford, 1655). On this work, see Toomer, *Eastern Wisedome,* 163.

13. Edward Pococke, ed., *Historia Compendiosa Dynastiarum* (Oxford, 1663). Toomer, *Eastern Wisedome,* 212.

14. Pococke, *Specimen,* 1, "De Arabum Populis Eorumque Moribus"; 2–6, "De Arabum Moribus ante Mohammedem"; 6–31, "De Arabum Moribus post Mohammedem."

15. Pococke, *Specimen,* [31a].

16. Ibid., 33–339.

17. On the Oxford types, which were nevertheless not as elegant as the Dutch ones produced under Erpenius, see Toomer, *Eastern Wisedome,* 114–115.

18. See ibid., 160–162, and on the *Specimen*'s sources, 160, and, cited there, appendix 9 of P. M. Holt, "Arabic Studies in Seventeenth-Century England" (B.Phil. thesis, University of Oxford, 1952), which I have not been able to see. See also Pococke, *Specimen,* 359: "Authorum, eo fere ordine quo legenti primum occurrunt, Nomenclatura" (Names of Authors, more or less in the order of first appearance).

19. Toomer, *Eastern Wisedome,* 160.

20. Ibid., 225.

21. Richard Simon, *Histoire critique du Vieux Testament* (Paris, 1678). On Simon, see Jean Steinmann, *Richard Simon et les origines de l'exégèse biblique* (Paris, 1960); Paul Auvray, *Richard Simon, 1638–1712: Étude bio-bibliographique avec des textes inédits* (Paris, 1974); *Dictionnaire de la Bible,* s.v. "Simon (Richard)"; Sascha Müller, *Richard Simon (1638–1712), Exeget, Theologe, Philosoph und Historiker: Eine Biographie* (Würzburg, 2005). In English: William McKane, *Selected Christian Hebraists* (Cambridge, 1989), 111–150; Stroumsa, *A New Science,* 62–66.

22. On Simon's training in the Oratorian order, see Auvray, *Simon,* 9–31. On the French Society of the Oratory, see John Donnelly, "New Religious Orders for Men," in *The Cambridge History of Christianity,* vol. 6, *Reform and Expansion, 1500–1660,* ed. R. Po-Chia Hsia (Cambridge, 2007), chap. 10, esp. 177–178; Yves Krumenacker et al., eds., *L'Oratoire de Jésus: 400 ans d'histoire en France* (Paris, 2013); on French Counter-Reformation Catholicism more broadly, see Michael A. Mullett, *The Catholic Reformation* (New York, 1999), 153–168.

23. *Voyage du Mont Liban traduit de l'italien du R. P. Jérôme Dandini, nonce en ce pais-la, où il est traité tant de la créance & des coûtumes des Maronites que de pleusieurs particularitez touchant les Turcs, et de quelques lieux considérables de l'Orient, avec des remarques sur la théologie des Chrêtiens du Levant et sur celle des Mahométans. Par R.S.P.* (Paris, 1675). Simon's edition of Dandini went through several reeditions (Paris, 1684; Paris, 1685) and an English translation: *A Voyage to Mount Libanus* (London, 1698). On this project, see Steinmann, *Simon,* 77–84.

24. Edward Brerewood, *Recherches cvrievses svr la diversité des langves et religions: Par toutes les principales parties du monde . . . et mises en françois par I. de Montagne* (Paris, 1640). See Steinmann, *Simon,* 157–164; Auvray, *Simon,* 94–95. A manuscript of these remarks, Leiden University Library Ms. Marchand 70, was published as *Additions aux 'Recherches curieuses sur la diversité des langues et religions' d'Edward Brerewood,* ed. Jacques Le Brun and John D. Woodbridge (Paris, 1983), chap. 4, 74–86.

25. Sieur de Moni [i.e., Richard Simon], *Histoire critique de la créance et des coutumes des nations du Levant* (Frankfurt, 1684), 164–183. Steinmann, *Simon,* 157–164, esp. 161. Some of the materials had appeared earlier in his *Histoire critique du Vieux Testament* (Rotterdam, 1685), as well as his *Cérémonies et coutumes qui s'observent aujourd'hui parmi les Juifs* (Paris, 1674), a translation of Leon Modena. See Steinmann, *Simon,* 157–164. For Simon's complete bibliography, see Auvray, *Simon,* 179–189.

26. Steinmann, *Simon,* 25–28.

27. Simon's source on Muslim customs like prayer and ablutions was a Turkish text by an author born in 929 AH / 1522 CE, which reported the "most approved" customs in Istanbul. See Simon, *Additions aux 'Recherches curieuses,'* 84–85. See also Simon, *Histoire de la créance,* 180. The editors of *Additions* were unable to identify this work in Simon's catalog of the Oriental MSS in the Parisian Oratorian library.

28. See, e.g., Simon, *Voyage du Mont Liban,* 278.

29. Ibid., 251. Also discussed in Stroumsa, *A New Science,* 65.

30. See, for instance, R. W. Southern, *Western Views of Islam in the Middle Ages* (Cambridge, Mass., 1962), 92–94, on Nicholas of Cusa, who used this argument. Establishing the non-Muslim sources of the Qur'an was a research project that had also attracted Arabists of the seventeenth century, such as Hottinger. See Jan Loop, "Johann Heinrich Hottinger (1620–1667) and the 'Historia Orientalis,'" *Church History and Religious Culture* 88 (2008): 182.

31. Simon did not, however, deny that it was a false religion. See, e.g., Simon, *Additions,* 74.

32. Simon, *Voyage du Mont Liban,* 253 (pork) and 254 (ablutions), 259–261; *Additions,* 83 (prayer).

33. Simon, *Voyage du Mont Liban,* 258.

34. Ibid., 259–261.

35. Ibid., 264, 265, 267.

36. Ibid., 265.

37. John Marenbon, *Pagans and Philosophers: The Problem of Paganism from Augustine to Leibniz* (Princeton, 2015).

38. Richard Simon, *Lettres choisies,* 3 vols. (Rotterdam, 1705), 3:228–229.

39. Marcus Tullius Cicero, *On Duties,* ed. and intro. M. T. Griffin, and ed. and trans. E. M. Atkins (Cambridge, 1991). On Cicero's reception, see Sabine McCormack, "Cicero in Late Antiquity," and David Marsh, "Cicero in the Renaissance," both in *The Cambridge Companion to Cicero,* ed. Catherine Steel (Cambridge, 2013), chaps. 15 and 16 respectively.

40. Simon's lifelong quarrel with the leading Jansenist theologian Antoine Arnauld, of which an extract is discussed below, is chronicled in Steinmann, *Simon,* 45–49 and passim, and see also 163–164 on Muslims; Auvray, *Simon,* 107–110 and passim.

41. Simon, *Lettres choisies,* 3:229.

42. Ibid.

43. Marenbon, *Pagans and Philosophers,* 252; Carmen Bernard and Serge Gruzinski, *De l'idolâtrie: Une archéologie des sciences religieuses* (Paris, 1988), 41–88.

44. This reclassification was quite radical, and did not immediately gain wide acceptance. For the Catholic theologian Antoine Arnauld's comments, see below. For an equally vehement Protestant reaction, see Jean Le Clerc, *Défense des Sentimens de quelques Théologiens de Hollande sur l'Histoire Critique du Vieux Testament contre la reponse du Prieur de Bolleville* (Amsterdam, 1686), 62: "Il faut bien avoir lû les livres des Mahometans, comme a fait nôtre Auteur, et avoir bien égligé la lecture du Nouveau Testament, pour faire cette horrible comparaison des Livres des Apôtres de Jesus Christ, avec celui de l'imposteur qui a malheureusement trompé tout l'Orient."

45. Adriaan Reland, *De Religione Mohammedica Libri Duo: Quorum Prior Exhibet Compendium Theologiae Mohammedicae . . . Posterior Examinat Nonnulla, Quae Falso Mohammedanis Tribuuntur* (Utrecht, 1705). On Reland's study of Islam, see Alastair Hamilton, "Adrianus Reland (1676–1718): Outstanding Orientalist," in *Zes keer zestig: 360 jaar universitaire geschiedenis in zes biografieën,* ed. Hervé Jamin (Utrecht, 1996), 22–31; Hamilton, "From a 'Closet at Utrecht': Adriaan Reland and Islam," *Nederlands Archief voor Kerkgeschiedenis* 78 (1998): 243–250; Hamilton, "Arabists and Cartesians at Utrecht," in *Leven na Descartes:*

Zeven opstellen over ideeëngeschiedenis in Nederland in de tweede helft van de zeventiende eeuw: Uitgegeven ter gelegenheid van de vijftigste verjaardag van het verschijnen van Nederlands cartesianisme *van dr. C. Louise Thijssen-Schoute,* ed. P. G. Hoftijzer and Theo Verbeek (Hilversum, 2005), 97–105.

46. Two other texts were appended to it for the English edition, which appeared as *Four Treatises Concerning the Doctrine, Discipline and Worship of the Mahometans* (London, 1712). German: *Hn. Adrian Reelands . . . Zwey Bücher von der Türckischen oder Mohammedischen Religion* (Hanover, 1716). Dutch: *Verhandeling van de Godsdienst der Mohametaanen, als mede van het Krygsregt* (Utrecht, 1718). French: *La religion des Mahométans: Exposée par leurs propres docteurs avec des éclaircissemens sur les opinions qu'on leur a faussement attribuées; tiré du Latin,* trans. David Durand (The Hague, 1721). 2nd Latin ed.: *De Religione Mohammedica Libri Duo* (Utrecht, 1717).

47. Its source was an Ottoman drawing that the Swedish scholar Michael Eneman had brought Reland from his travels to the Levant. Reland, *Religione Mohammedica* [1717], 117, n(m). The image was later reproduced in George Sale, *The Koran, Commonly Called the Alcoran of Mohammed, Translated into English immediately from the Original Arabic; with Explanatory Notes, taken from the Most Approved Commentators. To which is prefixed A Preliminary Discourse* (London, 1734 [1733]) and elsewhere. See David Brafman, "Picart, Bernard, Hermes, and Muhammad (Not Necessarily in That Order)," in *Bernard Picart and the First Global Vision of Religion,* ed. Lynn Hunt, Margaret Jacob, and Wijnand Mijnhardt (Los Angeles, 2010), 139–168, esp. 148–150.

48. On Reland's biography, see Joseph Serrurier, *Oratio Funebris in Obitum Viri Celeberrimi Had. Reeland* (Utrecht, 1718); A. J. van der Aa, *Biographisch Woordenboek der Nederlanden,* 21 vols. (Haarlem, 1874), 16:145–151; Jan Nat, "Reeland (Adriaan)," in *Nieuw Nederlandsch biografisch woordenboek,* 10 vols., ed. P. C. Molhuysen (Leiden, 1933), 9:851–852; Jan Nat, *De studie van de oostersche talen in Nederland in de 18e en de 19e eeuw* (Purmerend, 1929), 11–21; J. van Amersfoort and W. J. van Asselt, eds., *Liever Turks dan Paaps? De visies van Johannes Coccejus, Gisbertus Voetius en Adrianus Relandus op de islam* (Zoetermeer, 1997), 103–126; Arnould Vrolijk and Richard van Leeuwen, *Arabic Studies in the Netherlands: A Short History in Portraits, 1580–1960,* trans. Alastair Hamilton (Leiden, 2014), 65–72.

49. See P. A. Tiele, *Catalogus Codicum Manu Scriptorum Bibliothecae Universitatis Rheno-Trajectinae,* vol. 1 (Utrecht, 1887), where Arabic manuscripts are Mss. 1430 to 1465. Upon Reland's death, his manuscripts were scattered, with ten ending up at the library of the University of Utrecht and twenty-two acquired by the Vatican Library in 1763. BAV, Arch. Bibl. 34, fols. 117r–118v [231–234 in more recent pencil numeration].

50. Marracci, *Refutatio,* "Refutationes," 2.

51. Reland, *Religione Mohmammedica* [1717], 265. This refutation of Marracci's claim only appeared in the second edition because Reland does not seem to have been acquainted with Marracci's book at the time of the first, 1705 ed.

52. Reland, *Religione Mohammedica* [1705], dedicatory epistle, fol. *2r. Reland had already written on Islamic topics in 1696, when he defended two dissertations on Muhammad's views of the Trinity, and on the Jewish origins of Islam. See the discussion in Hamilton, "From a 'Closet at Utrecht.'"

53. Reland, *Religione Mohammedica* [1705], "Praefatio," fol. ***3r.

54. Ibid., fols. ****v–****2r.

55. Ibid., fol. **3r.

56. Ibid., "Index Codicum Orientalium Manuscriptorum, quos citavimus, & quibus usi sumus" [Index of Oriental manuscript books cited and consulted] lists at n. 18 a "Compendium Juris Sacri & Civilis" by "Abu Schosjain"—i.e., the compendium of Shāfiʿī law by Abū Shujāʿ Aḥmad b. al-Ḥasan al-Iṣfahānī, of which Reland wrote, "Hoc in plerisque convenit (quod ad priora capita sive jus sacrum attinet) cum *Compendio nostro Theologiae Mohammedicae,* quod hic Arabice & Latine dedimus." Likewise, n. 19, a similar item, "nec id a Compendio nostro multum differt."

57. Ibid., n.p., "Index Codicum Orientalium." He cited twenty-four manuscripts: eighteen in Arabic, four in Persian, one in Turkish, and one in Spanish written in Arabic script. See also Hamilton, "Adrianus Reland," 23.

58. Reland, *Religione Mohammedica,* dedicatory epistle, fol. *3r.

59. See, e.g., ibid., 121.

60. Jean Chardin, *Journal du voyage du Chevalier Chardin en Perse* (London, 1686); Guillaume-Joseph Grelot, *Relation nouvelle d'un voyage de Constantinople* (Paris, 1680).

61. From the Middle Ages: Anna Comnena, Albert of Aix, Matthew Paris, Jacques de Vitry, Gregory IX. From the Renaissance, the diplomats Ogier Ghiselin de Busbecq and Johannes Löwenklau.

62. The sections of the "Preliminary Discourse" are as follows: Arabs before Muhammad (I.1–32); state of Christianity and Judaism (II.33–56); the Qur'an (III.56–69); doctrines and positive precepts of the Qur'an (IV.70–122); negative precepts (V.122–132); civil laws (VI.132–147); holy days (VII.147–151); Muslim sects (VIII.151–187).

63. It appeared in Dutch as *Verhandeling over de historie, stammen, zeden en godsdienst der Arabieren, zo wel voor als na Mahomet* (Amsterdam, 1742); in French as *Observations historiques et critiques sur le mahométisme, ou Traduction du discours préliminaire mis à la tête de la version anglaise de l'Alcoran* (Geneva, 1751); in Swedish as *Inledning till Al Koran* (Stockholm, 1814); and in Arabic as

Maqāla fī al-islām li-Jūrj Ṣāl al-Injilīzī (n.p., 1891). The French translation was reprinted in G. Pauthier, ed., *Les livres sacrés de l'Orient* (Paris, 1875), 463–538.

64. Voltaire quoted in Natalia Elaguina, ed., *Corpus des notes marginales de Voltaire,* vol. 4 (Oxford, 2011), 724n599.

65. See Gotthold Ephraim Lessing, "Rettung des Cardans," in *Gotthold Ephraim Lessings sämtliche Schriften,* vol. 5, ed. K. Lachmann, 3rd ed. (Stuttgart, 1890), 325. On this work, see Michael Multhammer, *Lessings 'Rettungen': Geschichte und Genese eines Denkstils* (Berlin, 2013), 170–200.

66. Sale, *Koran,* "Preliminary Discourse," 56 (name of Qur'an), 73 (jinn), 78 (location of souls of the just), 109 (prayer), 110–114 (alms, fasting).

67. Ibid., 63.

68. Ibid., 126. Thomas Hyde, *Historia Religionis Veterum Persarum, Eorumque Magorum* (Oxford, 1700). E.g., Sale, *Koran,* "Preliminary Discourse," 59 (origins of the bismillah).

69. E.g., Sale, *Koran,* "Preliminary Discourse," 72 (doctrine of the angels).

70. Ibid., 101.

71. Ibid., 103.

72. Ibid., 100–102.

73. Ibid., 142.

74. Ibid., 143. Sale thought Judaism close to Islam in this respect: "The *Jews,* indeed, had a divine commission . . . to attack, subdue, and destroy the enemies of their religion." If all faiths had encouraged a warlike approach to nonbelievers, he found it most disappointing among Christians, given the teachings of their Scripture.

75. Ibid., 63.

76. Sale, *Koran,* title page. See Augustine, *Quaestiones Evangeliorum,* bk. 2, chap. 40, in *Sancti Aurelii Augustini Quaestiones Evangeliorum,* ed. Almut Mutzenbecher (Turnhout, 1980), 98.

77. Sale, *Koran,* "Preliminary Discourse," 108.

78. Norman Daniel, *Islam and the West: The Making of an Image* (Edinburgh, 1960), 192–194; Marracci, *Alcoranus,* 102: "Deum suum fictitium, et chimæricum."

79. Sale, *Koran,* "Preliminary Discourse," 71.

80. On Spanheim's life, see Gustav Adolf Benrath, *Reformierte Kirchengeschichtsschreibung an der Universität Heidelberg im 16. und 17. Jahrhundert* (Speyer, 1963), 105–126. Before his employment at Leiden, Spanheim had taught at Heidelberg, where one of his colleagues was Johann Heinrich Hottinger, a major scholar of Oriental studies, on whose time in Heidelberg see Loop, *Hottinger,* 35–41.

81. Reland, *Religione Mohammedica* [1705], 135.

82. Whose first version he published in 1675, but which he continued to rework and expand until his death. Spanheim's church history served as a textbook in Protestant universities and was reprinted until 1770.

83. Friedrich Spanheim, *Opera Omnia,* 3 vols. (Leiden, 1701–1703), 1: cols. 1206–1218.

84. Sale, *Koran,* "To the Reader," v. The quoted passages are found in Spanheim, *Opera Omnia,* 1:1209, 1213.

85. *Henry VI,* ed. G. Blakemore Evans (Boston, 1997), 1.2.140–141.

86. Sir Walter Ralegh, *History of the World* (London, 1614), pt. 1, bk. 1, chap. 6, 178. Marcus Manilius, *Astronomicon Libri Quinque,* ed. Joseph Scaliger (Leiden, 1600), 438; Hugo Grotius, *De Veritate Religionis Christianae,* 2nd ed. (Leiden, 1629), 221. See also Grotius, *The Truth of the Christian Religion,* ed. Maria Rosa Antognazza (Indianapolis, 2012), 238. Grotius presumably received the story from Scaliger.

87. Pococke, *Specimen,* "Notae," 186–187.

88. *EI3,* s.v. "Gabriel."

89. The legend of Muhammad's epilepsy was particularly widespread. See Daniel, *Islam and the West,* 27–28.

90. Marracci, *Prodromus,* "Praefatio," 1.

91. See Toomer, *Eastern Wisedome,* 145–146, 215–218; Toomer, "Edward Pococke's Arabic Translation of Grotius, *De Veritate,*" *Grotiana* 33 (2012): 100.

92. On miracles attributed to Muhammad, see also Simon, *Lettres choisies* (1705), 3:222; Simon, *Bibliothèque critique* (1708), 3:63–72 (his review of the *Specimen historiæ arabum*), esp. 69–70.

93. Prideaux, *Nature of Imposture,* "To the Reader," ii, iii.

94. Ibid., iv–v.

95. Ibid., 48.

96. Ibid., 39.

97. Reland, *Religione Mohammedica* [1717], proposition 39, 259–262. This is, in fact, an addition to the second edition. Reland largely quotes the English Arabist Simon Ockley, who had settled the matter to Reland's satisfaction in *Introductio ad Linguas Orientales* (Cambridge, 1706), 126–127.

98. Sale, *Koran,* "Preliminary Discourse," 116. The authors chastised here are the two Maronites Gabriel Sionita and Johannes Hesronita.

99. Louis Moréri, *Le grand dictionnaire historique,* 10 vols., 20th ed. (Paris, 1759), 7:54.

100. Reland, *Religione Mohammedica* [1705], dedicatory epistle, fol. *2r.

101. Ibid., fol. *2v.

102. Ibid., fol. *3r.

103. Reland, *Religione Mohammedica* [1705], "Praefatio," fol. ***2v. See also Reland, *Religione Mohammedica* [1705], "Praefatio," fol. **2v.

104. In 1648 Gisbert Voetius (Gijsbert Voet, 1589–1676), professor of theology at Utrecht, had criticized the European "gross ignorance of Muhammedan matters." Far from Cartesian himself, Voetius provided a native precedent for Reland's own interest. See Hamilton, "Arabists and Cartesians at Utrecht," 100.

105. As quoted in Reland, *Religione Mohammedica* [1717], "Praefatio," fols. **2v–**3r.

106. Jean-Jacques Rousseau, *The Social Contract and Other Later Political Writings*, ed. and trans. Victor Gourevitch (Cambridge, 1997), bk. 2, chap. 7, 71.

107. On Qur'anic Paradise, see Christian Lange, *Paradise and Hell in Islamic Traditions* (Cambridge, 2016), chap. 1, esp. 43–48; Sebastian Günther, Todd Lawson, and Christian Mauder, eds., *Roads to Paradise: Eschatology and Concepts of the Hereafter in Islam*, 2 vols. (Leiden, 2017).

108. Lange, *Paradise*, 44–45; *EI3*, s.v. "Afterlife."

109. Andrew J. Lane, " 'Reclining upon Couches in the Shade' (Q35:56): Quranic Imagery in Rationalist Exegesis," in Günther, Lawson, and Mauder, *Roads to Paradise*, 1:221–250.

110. *EI2*, s.v. "Djanna"; Lange, *Paradise*, 179–185.

111. Lange, *Paradise*, 183–186.

112. See *EQ*, s.v. "Houris."

113. For the history of Christian views of Christian Paradise, see Colleen McDannell and Bernhard Lang, *Heaven: A History* (New Haven, Ct., 1988); Alan F. Segal, *Life after Death: A History of the Afterlife in the Religions of the West* (New York, 2004). For medieval Christian views of the Muslim Paradise, see Daniel, *Islam and the West*, 148–152.

114. E.g., Nicholas of Cusa, *Nicolai de Cusa Opera Omnia*, vol. 8, *Cribratio Alkorani* (1460–1461), ed. Louis Hagemann (Hamburg, 1932); Juan Andrès, *Confusion de la secta mahomatica y del alcoran* (Valencia, 1515); Johannes Hoornbeeck, *Summa Controversiarum Religionis cum Infidelibus, Hæreticis, Schismaticis* (Utrecht, 1653).

115. Prideaux, *Nature of Imposture*, 25.

116. Marracci, *Refutatio*, "Refutationes," 18.

117. Ibid., 20.

118. Pococke appended his reflections on Qur'anic Paradise to his *Porta Mosis* of 1655, 235–313. They appeared within an additional work entitled *Appendix Notarum Miscellanea* that was first published in 1654, as its title page records (Oxford, 1654). See Toomer, *Eastern Wisedome*, 163n73. Chap. 7 is entitled "In quo Mohammedanorum etiam de eodem articulo [i.e. of the resurrection] ex autoribus apud ipsos fide dignis profertur." For an assessment of Pococke's achievement, see Lange, *Paradise*, 20–22.

119. Pococke, *Notae,* 305.

120. Ibid., 303. See also Lange, *Paradise,* 22.

121. Simon, *Créance,* 169. Compare Simon, *Additions,* 77.

122. Angelika Neuwirth, *Der Koran als Text der Spätantike: Ein europäischer Zugang* (Berlin, 2010); Lange, *Paradise,* 56–70.

123. Lange, *Paradise,* 65–66; Georg Jacob, *Altarabisches Beduinenleben* (Berlin, 1897), 107; Josef Horovitz, "Das koranische Paradies," *Scripta Universitatis atque Bibliothecae Hierosolymitanarum, Orientalia et Judaica* 1 (1923): 1–16; Wendell, "The Denizens of Paradise," *Humaniora Islamica* 2 (1974): 22–59; Neuwirth, *Der Koran als Text der Spätantike;* Neuwirth, "Paradise as a Quranic Discourse: Late Antique Foundations and Early Quranic Developments," in Günther, Lawson, and Mauder, *Roads to Paradise,* vol. 1, chap. 5; Rüdiger Lohlker and Andrea Nowak, "Das islamische Paradies als Zeichen: Zwischen Märtyrerkult und Garten," *Wiener Zeitschrift für die Kunde des Morgenlandes* 99 (2009): 199–225.

124. Lange, *Paradise,* 67–70; Neuwirth, "Paradise," 89–90.

125. Simon, *Créance,* 171. Compare *Additions,* 79.

126. Ibid. Incidentally, this description betrays Simon's reading of Pococke's characterization of Qur'anic Paradise, including the "aedificia lateribus aureis et argenteis tessellata" (*Notae,* 294).

127. Arnauld, quoted in Simon, *Lettres choisies,* 3:218.

128. Reland, *Religione Mohammedica* [1705], 146.

129. Ibid., 148; 149–150.

130. Ibid., 150. In the 1717 edition, Reland added a passage, p. 205.

131. Adriaan Reland, *La Religion des Mahométans, exposée par leurs propres Docteurs, avec des Eclaircissemens sur les Opinions qu'on leur a faussement attribuées,* trans. D. Durand (The Hague, 1721), 164.

132. Sale, *Koran,* "Preliminary Discourse," 101.

133. Many of his comparisons, such as that between the bridge the faithful must cross in Islam and in Zoroastrianism, are still made by scholars today. See, e.g., Nerina Rustomji, "Early Views of Paradise in Islam," *Religion Compass* 4 (2010): 166.

134. Sale, *Koran,* "Preliminary Discourse," 100.

135. Ibid., 101. Even so, he conceded in a footnote that some Christian authors had indulged in such fantasies, quoting a passage in Irenaeus, *Adversus Haereses,* bk. 5, chap. 33. See Ireneaus, *Libros Quinque adversus Haereses,* 2 vols. (Cambridge, 1857), 2:415–419.

136. Sale, *Koran,* "Preliminary Discourse," 102.

137. Ibid.

138. Henri de Boulainvilliers, *La Vie de Mahomed: Avec des Réflexions sur la Religion Mahometane, et les Coutumes des Musulmans* (London [i.e., Amsterdam], 1731).

139. Sale, *Koran,* "Preliminary Discourse," 79–84.

140. Daniel, *Islam and the West,* 67–73.

141. On Renaissance polemic against Islam: James Hankins, "Renaissance Crusaders: Humanist Crusade Literature in the Age of Mehmed II," *Dumbarton Oaks Papers* 49 (1995): 111–207. On historical inquiry into contemporary Muslim empires: Nancy Bisaha, *Creating East and West: Renaissance Humanists and the Ottoman Turks* (Philadelphia, 2004); Margaret Meserve, *Empires of Islam in Renaissance Historical Thought* (Cambridge, Mass., 2008).

142. Niccolò Machiavelli, *Il Principe,* chap. 6. See Machiavelli, *The Chief Works and Others,* 3 vols., trans. Allan Gilbert (1965; repr., Durham, N.C., 1989), 1:25. For a later case of Italian political thought inspired by the Ottoman Empire, see Noel Malcolm, "The Crescent and the City of the Sun: Islam and the Renaissance Utopia of Tommaso Campanella," *Proceedings of the British Academy* 125 (2004): 41–67.

143. Machiavelli, *The Chief Works,* 1:26.

144. Pier Mattia Tommasino, "Giovanni Battista Castrodardo bellunese traduttore dell'Alcorano di Macometto," *Oriente Moderno* 88 (2008): 15–40.

145. This brief summary does not do justice to Tommasino's rich account in *L'Alcorano,* chap. 7.

146. Tommasino, *L'Alcorano,* 229–230.

147. As quoted in ibid., 249.

148. Two manuscripts of Stubbe's text have been published: Henry Stubbe, *An Account of the Rise and Progress of Mahometanism: With the Life of Mahomet and a Vindication of him and his Religion from the Calumnies of the Christians; from a manuscript copied by Charles Hornby of Pipe Office, in 1705, with some variations and additions,* ed. Mahmud Khan Shairani (London, 1911); Nabil Matar, ed., *Henry Stubbe and the Beginnings of Islam: The Originall & Progress of Mahometanism* (New York, 2014). The 1911 edition was reprinted in Lahore, 1954 and 1975; on the circumstances of its origin, see Garcia, *Islam and the English Enlightenment,* 225–229. Shairani edited Bod., Eng. Misc. c. 309; Matar edited University of London MS 537, the earliest complete version of the text. We still lack a critical edition that integrates these and other MSS, such as BL Harleian MS 1876, discussed below. Publications such as Jacob, *Henry Stubbe,* and Champion, *Pillars of Priestcraft,* rely on Shairani's edition. Moreover, the exact nature of Stubbe's heterodoxy is the subject of disagreement. He has traditionally been viewed as a unitarian, but Matar contests this interpretation. See Matar, *Henry Stubbe,* 12–16. The quoted passage is found in Shairani, 151, and Matar, 192–193.

149. This interpretation had a further life in the writings of Toland and Boulainvilliers. See Israel, *Radical Enlightenment,* 701–703; Israel, *Enlightenment Contested,* 615–639.

150. Sale, *Koran,* "Dedication to Lord John Carteret," fol. A1v.

151. Ibid., "Preliminary Discourse," 49.

152. He stands in the genealogy of the Italian interpreters of the Qur'an; see Tommasino, *L'Alcorano,* 244.

153. Sale, *Koran,* "Preliminary Discourse," 35.

154. Ibid., 104–106.

155. Ibid., 121.

156. Ibid.

157. Ibid., 121–122.

158. Ibid., 39.

159. Ibid. Humphrey Prideaux, who had died in 1724, had claimed in his *Life of Mahomet* that "*Mahomet* [had] forced [the *Arabs*] to exchange their *Idolatry* for another *Religion* altogether as bad." Prideaux, *The Nature of Imposture,* 96–97.

160. Sale, *Koran,* "Preliminary Discourse," 137.

161. Ibid., 39.

162. Edward Gibbon, *The Decline and Fall of the Roman Empire,* 6 vols. (New York, 1994 [1788]), 5:303.

163. Ibid., 5:304.

164. See Champion, *Pillars of Priestcraft,* 99–132.

165. Grantley McDonald, "Erasmus and the Johannine Comma (I John 5.7–8)," *Bible Translator* 67 (2016): 42–55.

166. James H. Charlesworth, "Pseudepigrapha," in Erwin Fahlbusch et al., eds., *Encyclopedia of Christianity Online.* On the example of the Gospel of Barnabas, see Champion, *Pillars of Priestcraft,* 125–130.

167. Islam played a further role not considered in this book: as a symbol of the imposture of all revealed religion, as in the *Traité des trois imposteurs.* See Israel, *Radical Enlightenment,* 684–703; Silvia Berti, Françoise Charles-Daubert, and Richard Popkin, eds., *Heterodoxy, Spinozism, and Free Thought in Early Eighteenth-Century Europe: Studies on the* Traité des trois imposteurs (Dordrecht, 1996).

168. *ODNB,* s.v. "Stubbe, Henry (1632–1676)"; P. M. Holt, *A Seventeenth-Century Defender of Islam: Henry Stubbe (1632–76) and His Book* (London, 1972); James R. Jacob, *Henry Stubbe: Radical Protestantism and the Early Enlightenment* (Cambridge, 1983), chap. 4, 64–77; Champion, *Pillars of Priestcraft Shaken,* 120–132; Champion, "Legislators, Impostors, and the Politic Origins of Religion: English Theories of 'Imposture' from Stubbe to Toland," in Berti et al., *Heterodoxy, Spinozism,* chap. 11; Champion, "'I Remember a Mahometan Story of Ahmed Ben Edris': Freethinking Uses of Islam from Stubbe to Toland," *Al-Qantara* 31 (2010): 443–480; Garcia, *Islam and the English Enlightenment,* chap. 1.

169. For details concerning this text, and problems relating to the lack of a critical edition, see note 148 of this chapter.

170. Stubbe, *Mahometanism,* 155 (Shairani), 196 (Matar).

171. Ibid., 197 (Matar).

172. Ibid., 144 (Shairani), 190 (Matar).

173. Stubbe cited Arabic editions produced by these scholars, such as "Elmacin," the translation of the history by al-Makīn that Erpenius edited and translated in 1625, and the work of "Abulfeda," the medieval Syrian historian and geographer Abū'l-Fidā'.

174. BL, Harleian MS 1876. Although the editor does not include these references in his critical edition, see his remarks in his introduction, p. 14, on Stubbe's sources.

175. See Loop, *Hottinger,* 214–215, for Stubbe's use of Hottinger. Justin A. I. Champion has also recently shown the importance of Stubbe's Arabic sources to the writing of his treatise. See Champion, "'I Remember.'"

176. John Toland, *Nazarenus, or Jewish, Gentile, and Mahometan Christianity* (London, 1718).

177. *ODNB,* s.v. "Toland, John (1670–1722)"; Justin Champion, *Republican Learning: John Toland and the Crisis of Christian Culture, 1696–1722* (Manchester, 2003).

178. Toland, *Nazarenus,* 4.

179. Ibid., 4–5.

180. Ibid., 10.

181. Boulainvilliers, *La Vie de Mahomed.* Diego Venturino, "Un prophète 'philosophe'? Une *Vie de Mahomed* à l'aube des Lumières," *Dix-huitième siècle* 24 (1992): 321–331; Stefano Brogi, *Il cerchio dell'universo: Libertinismo, spinozismo e filosofia della natura in Boulainvilliers* (Florence, 1993).

182. Boulainvilliers, *Vie de Mahomed,* 226.

183. The hypothesis of Sale as a freethinker was developed by Giuseppe Ricuperati, "*Universal History:* Storia di un progetto europeo; Impostori, storici ed editori nella *Ancient Part,*" *Studi settecenteschi* 1 (1981): 7–90, esp. 13–24. But the attribution of the anonymous essay "Mahomet No Impostor" to Sale seems doubtful; in spite of its overlap in argument with the "Preliminary Discourse," there are significant differences. Because the sincerity of Sale's beliefs cannot be investigated, it seems enough merely to determine that the culture of erudition in which he participated was very capacious, enough to sustain comparisons between religions, including Christianity even as the latter's distinctiveness was upheld.

184. Sale, *Koran,* "Preliminary Discourse," vi.

185. Sale cites the Comte de Boulainvilliers a single time as an authority for an interpretation. Ibid., §2, 33. Elsewhere he corrects him: both times in "Preliminary Discourse," §2.

186. Alexander Bevilacqua, "The Qur'an Translations of Marracci and Sale," *Journal of the Warburg and Courtauld Institutes* 76 (2013): 101–102.

187. Bath, Central Library, SAL 1 / 1, p. 120 [fol. 63r].

188. Marenbon, *Pagans and Philosophers.*

4 · D'HERBELOT'S ORIENTAL GARDEN

1. Antoine Galland, "Discours pour servir de Preface à la Bibliotheque Orientale," in Barthélemy d'Herbelot de Molainville, *Bibliothèque Orientale* (Paris, 1697), sig. ī2r. The book's full title was: *Bibliothèque Orientale, Ou, Dictionaire Universel: Contenant Généralement Tout ce qui regarde la connoissance des Peuples de l'Orient. Leurs Histoires et Traditions Véritables Ou Fabuleuses. Leurs Religions, Sectes et Politique. Leurs Gouvernement, Loix, Coûtumes, Mœurs, Guerres, et les Révolutions de leurs Empires. Leurs Sciences, et Leurs Arts. Leurs Théologie, Mythologie, Magie, Physique, Morale, Médecine, Mathématiques, Histoire naturelle, Chronologie, Géographie, Observations Astronomiques, Grammaire, et Réthorique. Les Vies et Actions Remarquables de Tous Leurs Saints, Docteurs, Philosophes, Historiens, Poëtes, Capitaines, et de tous ceux qui se sont rendus illustres parmi eux, par leur Vertu, ou par leur Savoir. Des Jugemens Critiques, et des Extraits de Tous Leurs Ouvrages, De leurs Traitez, Traductions, Commentaires, Abregez, Recüeils de Fables, de Sentences, de Maximes, de Proverbes, de Contes, de bons Mots, et de tous leurs Livres écrits en Arabe, en Persan, ou en Turc, sur toutes sortes de Sciences, d'Arts, et de Professions.*

2. C. Mylaeus, *De Scribenda Universitatis Rerum Historia* (Basel, 1551), 297–300. On historia literaria, see Wilhelm Schmidt-Biggemann, *Topica universalis: Eine Modellgeschichte humanistischer und barocker Wissenschaft* (Hamburg, 1983); Donald R. Kelley, "Writing Cultural History in Early Modern Europe: Christophe Milieu and His Project," *Renaissance Quarterly* 52 (1999): 342–365; and references in Kelley, ed., *History and the Disciplines: The Reclassification of Knowledge in Early Modern Europe* (Rochester, N.Y., 1997); Michael C. Carhart, "Historia Literaria and Cultural History from Mylaeus to Eichhorn," in *Momigliano and Antiquarianism: Foundations of the Modern Cultural Sciences,* ed. Peter N. Miller (Toronto, 2007), chap. 6; Frank Grunert and Friedrich Vollhardt, eds., *Historia literaria: Neuordnungen des Wissens im 17. und 18. Jahrhundert* (Berlin, 2007); Frederic N. Clark, "Dividing Time: The Making of Historical Periodization in Early Modern Europe" (PhD diss., Princeton University, 2014).

3. D'Herbelot's most significant predecessor in this quest was Johann Heinrich Hottinger. See Jan Loop, *Johann Heinrich Hottinger: Arabic and Islamic Studies in the Seventeenth Century* (Oxford, 2013), chap. 4.

4. The bibliography on d'Herbelot and the *Bibliothèque Orientale* is relatively circumscribed: Johann Fück, *Die arabischen Studien in Europa bis in den Anfang des 20. Jahrhunderts* (Leipzig, 1955), 98–101; Jean Gaulmier, "A la découverte du Proche-Orient: Barthélemy d'Herbelot et sa *Bibliothèque Orientale,*" *Bulletin de la Faculté des Lettres de Strasbourg* 48 (1969): 1–6; Henri Laurens, *Aux sources de l'orientalisme: La* Bibliothèque Orientale *de Barthélemi d'Herbelot* (Paris, 1978); Ahmad Gunny, *Images of Islam in Eighteenth-Century Writings* (London, 1996), 45–52; Dominique Carnoy, *Représentations de l'islam dans la France du XVIIe siècle: La ville des tentations* (Paris, 1998), 300–310; Francis Richard, "Le dictionnaire de d'Herbelot," in *Istanbul et les langues orientales,* ed. Frédéric Hitzel (Paris, 1997), 79–88; Raïa Zaïmova, "La *Bibliothèque Orientale* d'Herbelot de Molainville (1697) et ses interprétations," *Études balkaniques* 44 (2008): 143–158; Nicholas Dew, "The Order of Oriental Knowledge: The Making of d'Herbelot's *Bibliothèque Orientale,*" in *Debating World Literature,* ed. Christopher Prendergast (London, 2004), chap. 11; Dew, *Orientalism in Louis XIV's France* (Oxford, 2009), chaps. 1 and 4.

5. Antoine Galland, "Discours pour servir de Preface," in *Bibliothèque Orientale,* sig. āv.

6. Claude Nicaise, *Les sirènes, ou discours sur leur forme et figure* (Paris, 1691), 12; Lorenzo Magalotti, *Quinte della storia,* vol. 3, *Scritti di corte e di mondo,* ed. Enrico Falqui (Rome, 1945), 276. See also the fuller discussion of this passage below.

7. Abbé Lambert, *Histoire littéraire du règne de Louis XIV,* vol. 3 (Paris, 1751), 109.

8. This chapter is a companion essay to Alexander Bevilacqua, "How to Organise the Orient: D'Herbelot and the *Bibliothèque Orientale,*" *Journal of the Warburg and Courtauld Institutes* 79 (2016): 213–261. Whereas that article examines the *Bibliothèque Orientale*'s genre, organization, and relationship to Kātib Çelebi's *Kashf al-zunūn,* this chapter discusses d'Herbelot's intellectual career, the *Bibliothèque Orientale*'s domain, its other sources, its coverage of poetry, history, and religion, and the ambition underlying it.

9. BnF, Ms. Italien 480 (Florence catalog); BnF, Ms. Arabe 4844–4849 (dictionary); BNCF, II, II, 115 (catalog).

10. Dew, *Orientalism,* chap. 1, explores in detail d'Herbelot's career and the patronage he enjoyed.

11. See Alastair Hamilton and Francis Richard, *André du Ryer and Oriental Studies in Seventeenth-Century France* (Oxford, 2004), chap. 1, esp. 40–50.

12. René Pintard, *Le libertinage érudit dans la première moitié du XVIIe siècle* (Paris, 1943), 96; Peter N. Miller, *Peiresc's Mediterranean World* (Cambridge, Mass., 2015). See also Miller, "Peiresc, the Levant and the Mediterranean," and Alastair Hamilton, "'To Divest the East of all Its Manuscripts and All Its Rarities': The Unfortunate Embassy of Henri Gournay de Marcheville," both in *The Republic of Letters and the Levant,* ed. Alastair Hamilton, Maurits H. van den Boogert, and Bart Westerweel (Leiden, 2005), 103–122, 123–150.

13. Hamilton and Richard, *André du Ryer,* 47–49. For the Arabic teaching at the Collège Royal of one of d'Herbelot's contemporaries, see Pierre Ageron and Mustapha Jaouhari, "Le programme pédagogique d'un arabisant du Collège royal, François Pétis de La Croix (1653–1713)," *Arabica* 61 (2014): 396–453.

14. Alastair Hamilton, "An Egyptian Traveller in the Republic of Letters: Josephus Barbatus or Abudacnus the Copt," *Journal of the Warburg and Courtauld Institutes* 57 (1994): 123–150.

15. Peter N. Miller, "Making the Paris Polyglot Bible: Humanism and Orientalism in the Early Seventeenth Century," in *Die europäische Gelehrtenrepublik im Zeitalter des Konfessionalismus,* ed. Herbert Jaumann (Wiesbaden, 2001), 59–85; Auguste Bernard, *Antoine Vitré et les caractères orientaux de la Bible polyglotte de Paris* (Paris, 1857).

16. See François Secret, "Gilbert Gaulmin et l'histoire comparée des religions," *Revue de l'histoire des religions* 177 (1970): 35–63.

17. Pintard, *Libertinage érudit,* 184.

18. Bruno Neveu, "La vie érudite à Paris à la fin du XVIIe siècle d'après les papiers du P. Léonard de Sainte-Catherine (1695–1706)," *Bibliothèque de l'École de Chartes* 124 (1966): 478–480; reprinted in Neveu, *Érudition et religion aux XVIIe et XVIIIe siècles* (Paris, 1994), 25–92.

19. Louis Cousin, "Éloge de Monsieur d'Herbelot, Fait par Monsieur Cousin, President à la Cour des Monnoyes," in *Bibliothèque Orientale,* sigs. ū2v—ū3r.

20. Mohamed Abdel-Halim, *Antoine Galland: Sa vie et son oeuvre* (Paris, 1964), 166–167; Dew, *Orientalism,* 52–61 on the first gathering, and 77 and references in 77n87 on the circle around Bossuet.

21. Cousin, "Éloge de Monsieur d'Herbelot," sig. ū2v.

22. On Catholic Mediterranean networks, see Bernard Heyberger, *Les chrétiens du Proche-Orient au temps de la Réforme catholique: Syrie, Liban, Palestine, XVIIe–XVIIIe siècles* (Rome, 1994).

23. In Rome, he met Jean de Thévenot, with whom he intended to travel East. Thévenot later wrote: "He determined me entirely to travel to the Levant." Jean de Thévenot, *Les voyages aux Indes Orientales,* ed. Françoise de Valence (1689; repr., Paris, 2008), 8. Yet some family business held him back, even as Thévenot

embarked on the journey all the way to India that would make him famous. See Thévenot, *Relation d'un voyage fait au Levant* . . . (Paris, 1664), and discussion in Dew, *Orientalism,* 44.

24. See Cousin, "Éloge de Monsieur d'Herbelot." On Fouquet's patronage of scholars, see E. Stewart Saunders, "Politics and Scholarship in Seventeenth-Century France: The Library of Nicolas Fouquet and the College Royal," *Journal of Library History* 20 (1985): 1–24.

25. Saunders, "Politics and Scholarship," 11. In 1667, well after Fouquet's 1661 fall, the best manuscripts of the collection were brought into the Royal Library, including five Arabic ones. Saunders, "Politics and Scholarship," 1.

26. "Secrétaire-interprète royal pour les langues orientales." The English equivalent title was "His Majesty's Interpreter for the Oriental Languages." European scholars of Arabic performed diplomatic translations at least starting with Joseph Scaliger. See Arnoud Vrolijk, "Scaliger and the Dutch Expansion in Asia: An Arabic Translation for an Early Voyage to the East Indies (1600)," *Journal of the Warburg and Courtauld Institutes* 78 (2015): 277–309.

27. The dates of the journey are difficult to establish with precision; see the discussion in Dew, *Orientalism,* 47, 64–65.

28. Marco Chiarini and Serena Padovani, eds., *La Galleria Palatina e gli Appartamenti Reali di Palazzo Pitti: Catalogo dei dipinti,* 2 vols. (Florence, 2003), 2:425, fig. 702: Justus Suttermans, "Ritratto di Ferdinando II de' Medici vestito alla turca."

29. Cousin, "Éloge de Monsieur d'Herbelot," sig. ū2v.

30. Lorenzo Magalotti, letter to Alessandro Segni, Florence, 24 August 1666. Reproduced in Magalotti, *Scritti di corte e di mondo,* 275. On Magalotti, see Eric Cochrane, *Florence in the Forgotten Centuries, 1527–1800: A History of Florence and the Florentines in the Age of the Grand Dukes* (Chicago, 1973), chap. 4, and, on his relationship with d'Herbelot, 264–265.

31. Magalotti, *Scritti di corte e di mondo,* 276.

32. Ibid.

33. The Accademia della Crusca in the seventeenth century is described in Eric W. Cochrane, *Tradition and Enlightenment in the Tuscan Academies, 1690–1800* (Chicago, 1961), esp. chap. 1. On the intellectual life of Florence in this period, see also Cochrane, *Florence in the Forgotten Centuries, 1527–1800.*

34. Magalotti, *Scritti di corte e di mondo,* 276.

35. Ibid. See also Lorenzo Magalotti, *Relazioni di viaggio in Inghilterra, Francia e Svezia,* ed. Walter Moretti (1668–1674; repr., Bari, 1968), 139–140. Discussed in Dew, *Orientalism,* 69–70.

36. BNCF, II, II, 115, fol. 362r: "per studiare la Lingua Turchesca." A note on this page dated 27 June 1671 records the absence of six volumes that were loaned to

Lorenzo Magalotti. These are nos. 172, 173, 187, 286, 298, 306. The books were two Arabic Qur'ans, a prayer book with Qur'anic excerpts, a volume of Turkish *inshā'* (model letters), a Turkish anthology, and a miscellany.

37. See Cousin's "Éloge de Monsieur d'Herbelot." On the earlier donation, see James Hankins, "Cosimo de' Medici and the 'Platonic Academy,'" *Journal of the Warburg and Courtauld Institutes* 53 (1990): 144–162. The collection had most likely belonged to the Vecchietti brothers, two travelers who had lived in Persia between 1584 and 1608–1609. On the Vecchietti brothers, see Francis Richard, "Les frères Vecchietti, diplomates, érudits et aventuriers," in Alastair Hamilton et al., *The Republic of Letters and the Levant,* and the references there; also Richard, "Les manuscrits persans rapportés par les frères Vecchietti et conservés aujourd'hui à la Bibliothèque Nationale," *Studia Iranica* 9 (1980): 291–300. Upon d'Herbelot's death they were offered to the French Royal Library, which, however did not acquire them. See Neveu, "La vie érudite à Paris," 479–480; Richard, "Le dictionnaire de d'Herbelot," 82; Dew, *Orientalism,* 79.

38. Eusèbe Renaudot, *Historia Patriarcharum Alexandrinorum Jacobitarum* (Paris, 1713), "Cosmo III Magno Duci Etruriæ . . . ," sigs. ā2r–ā4v. See also the eighteenth-century remark by Angelo Maria Bandini, *Dei principi e progressi della Real Biblioteca Mediceo Laurenziana: Ms. Laur. Acquisti e Doni 142,* ed. R. Pintaudi et al. (Florence, 1990), 77.

39. On Ferdinando's patronage of Oriental scholarship, see Chapter 2.

40. Two autograph manuscript copies of this catalog survive: BNCF, II, II, 115, and BnF, Ms. Italien 480. The latter came to the Bibliothèque nationale via the collection of Antoine Galland. The two catalogs differ occasionally in phrasing but offer substantially the same information. The Florence copy is entitled "Registro di Libri Orientali del Serenissimo Gran Duca con una succinta esplicazione del contenuto de' medesimi fatta dal Signor Bartolomeo d'Herbelot, insigne Letterato Francese in Firenze l'Anno 1666." The Oriental manuscripts would be described again, in greater detail and in Latin instead of Italian, by Stefano Evodio Assemani, in a catalog published in 1742. See Stefano Evodio Assemani, *Bibliothecae Mediceae Laurentianae et Palatinae Codicum Mss. Orientalium Catalogus* (Florence, 1742). In 1771, 517 of these books (522 tomes) were transferred from Palazzo Pitti to the Laurenziana Library, where they are still held. The rest passed to the BNCF, formerly known as the Biblioteca Magliabechiana.

41. D'Herbelot even listed two manuscripts that contained "Abyssinian" as opposed to Aethiopic. One of these (Ms. Orientali 70) is listed today as Geʿez.

42. Naṣīr al-Dīn al-Ṭūsī: BnF, Ms. Italien 480, entry no. 82; BNCF, II, II, 115, entry no. 82, fols. 330v–333v. Coptic liturgy: BnF, Ms. Italien 480, entry no. 26; BNCF, II, II, 115, entry no. 26, fols. 317v–321r.

43. Scholastic theology: BnF, Ms. Italien 480, entry no. 203; BNCF, II, II, 115, entry no. 203, fols. 344v–346r. BnF, Ms. Italien 480, entry no. 208; BNCF, II, II, 115, entry no. 208, fol. 346v: "Questo libro è di grandissima stima appresso i mahometani ed è come il loro secondo Alcorano, e appunto qual che è il Talmude agli Ebrei."

44. BnF, Ms. Italien 480, entry no. 247; BNCF, II, II, 115, entry no. 247, fol. 350r. In the Florence copy, a later hand has entered "manca," i.e., missing. This is Ibn al-Shiḥna's "Garden of the spectacles of the history of antiquity and modernity" (*Rawḍat al-manāzir fī ʿilm al-awāʾil waʾl-awākhir*). On which, see discussion below. A copy in the Royal Library in Paris had come from the library of Gilbert Gaulmin, and would have been available to d'Herbelot.

45. BnF, Ms. Italien 480, entry no. 263; BNCF, II, II, 115, entry no. 263, fols. 351r–v: "questo viaggio meriterebbe di essere tradotto tutto perché vi sono cose curiose intorno alla cognitione d'un paese molto nominato et altretanto sconosciuto ai nostri autori." A note in the margin of the Florence copy of the catalog notes: "La Traduzione fu poi fatta da Monsieur d'Herbelot, et arrichitane una parte con illustrazioni Istoriche, e note molto erudite." The *Bibliothèque Orientale*, however, contains only a brief entry on this book: see "Tarikh Khathaï," 864b.

46. Cataloguing the Royal Library's Oriental manuscripts was an ongoing project in which a number of scholars participated. For a brief period description, see Magalotti, "Diario di Francia," *Relazioni di viaggio*, 176–177. See Simone Balayé, *La Bibliothèque nationale des origines à 1800* (Geneva, 1988), 107; Richard, "Le dictionnaire de d'Herbelot," 83; Dew, *Orientalism*, 77, n85. The catalog to which d'Herbelot is supposed to have contributed is BnF, Ms. NAF 5408.

47. Père Léonard de Sainte-Catherine, as quoted in Neveu, "La vie érudite à Paris," 479. Parisian cafés, still a relatively new import from the Ottoman Empire, were often run by expatriate Armenians and Persians at this time. On the emergence of the coffeehouse in England and France, see Brian Cowan, *The Social Life of Coffee: The Emergence of the British Coffeehouse* (New Haven, Ct., 2005); Thierry Rigogne, "Entre histoire et mythes: Le premier siècle des cafés à Paris, 1660–1789," in *Les histoires de Paris: XVIe–XVIIIe siècle*, ed. Thierry Belleguic and Laurent Turcot, 2 vols. (Paris, 2013), 2:161–181.

48. *Bibliothèque Orientale*, "Privilege du Roy."

49. On Barbin, see Gervais E. Reed, *Claude Barbin, libraire de Paris sous le règne de Louis XIV* (Geneva, 1974).

50. An etching by Abraham Bosse from ca. 1683 shows men and women shopping in the Galerie. Metropolitan Museum of Art, accession no. 22.61.16.

51. Nicaise, *Les sirènes*, 12.

52. [Henri Basnage de Beauval], *Histoire des ouvrages des savans* 10 (August 1694): 551.

53. *Bibliothèque Orientale,* "Privilege du Roy," n.p. Moreover, the book was not published by Barbin alone but as the joint venture of a "Compagnie des libraires"—a cooperative of booksellers who split the cost of production. See Neveu, "La vie érudite à Paris," 479.

54. *Bibliothèque Orientale,* "Discours pour servir de Preface," sig. ū2r. Galland writes that he collaborated with d'Herbelot for over a year before the latter's death (in December 1695), placing the start of their collaboration in 1694.

55. On the history of the Arabic language, see Kees Versteegh, *The Arabic Language* (New York, 1997); Jonathan Owens, *A Linguistic History of Arabic* (Oxford, 2006).

56. Gilbert Lazard, "The Rise of the New Persian Language," in *The Cambridge History of Iran,* vol. 4, ed. R. N. Frye (Cambridge, 1975), chap. 19.

57. Lars Johanson and Éva Á. Csató, eds., *The Turkic Languages* (London, 1998).

58. Linda T. Darling, "Ottoman Turkish: Written Language and Scribal Practice, 13th to 20th Centuries," in *Literacy in the Persianate World: Writing and the Social Order,* ed. Brian Spooner and William Hanaway (Philadelphia, 2012), chap. 5.

59. Franz Babinger, "Die türkischen Studien in Europa bis zum Auftreten Josef von Hammer-Purgstalls," *Die Welt des Islams* 7 (1919): 103–129.

60. On Persian studies: Francis Richard, introduction, *Catalogue des manuscrits persans,* vol. 1, *Ancien Fonds* (Paris, 1989), 1–23. The Royal Library began to collect Persian manuscripts at the same time that it acquired its first major Arabic holdings under Colbert. André du Ryer, *Gulistan, ou l'empire des roses, composé par Sadi* (Paris, 1634); George Gentius [Gentz], trans., *Musladini Sadi Rosarium Politicum: Sive Amoenum Sortis Humanae Theatrum* (Amsterdam, 1651); Adam Olearius, *Persianischer Rosenthal: In welchem viel lustige Historien, scharffsinnige Reden und nützliche Regeln vor 400. Jahren von einem sinnreichen Poeten Schich Saadi in Persischer Sprach beschrieben* (Schleswig, 1654). Golius's Persian dictionary was published posthumously as part of Edmund Castell, *Lexicon Heptaglotton Hebraicum, Chaldaicum, Syriacum, Samaritanum, Aethiopicum, Arabicum, conjunctim, et Persicum, Separatim* (London, 1669). On du Ryer, see Hamilton and Richard, *André du Ryer.* On Persian grammars: Lodewijk de Dieu, *Rudimenta Linguae Persicae* (Leiden, 1639); John Greaves, *Elementa Linguae Persicae* (London, 1649). See Francis Richard, "Aux origines de la connaissance de la langue persane en France," *Luqmân: Annales des Presses universitaires d'Iran* 3 (1986–1987): 23–42. On Turkish studies: Giovanni Battista Donado, *Della letteratura de' Turchi. Osservationi fatte da Gio. Battista*

Venezia e i turchi] di Bailo in Costantinopoli (Venice, 1688). On
see Paolo Preto, Venezia e i turchi (Florence, 1975), 310–351.

61. Gustave Dupont-Ferrier, Du Collège de Clermont au Lycée Louis-le-Grand
(1563–1920): La vie quotidienne d'un collège parisien pendant plus de trois
cinquante ans, 3 vols. (Paris, 1921), 1:354–110.

62. Franciscus à Mesgnien Meninski, Linguarum Orientalium Turcicae Arabicae
Persicae Institutiones, seu Grammatica Turcica (Vienna, 1680), Meninski, Thesaurus Linguarum Orientalium Turcicae, Arabicae et Persicae (Vienna, 1680).

63. This dictionary is now BnF, Ms. Arabe 4814 (1–849), but its location was not
known for much of the eighteenth century. It passed from the abbé Renaudot
to the library of the Maurists at Saint-Germain, and thence to the Bibliothèque
nationale (the former Royal Library) during the French Revolution. See Richard,
"Le dictionnaire de d'Herbelot"; Richard, "Une traduction française méconnue
du XVIIème siècle: Celle du Sifāt al ʿāshiqin de Helālī par Claude Bérault,"
Luqmân: Annales des Presses universitaires d'Iran 19 (2002–2003): 147–148.
See also fig. 1 in Bevilacqua, "How to Organise the Orient," 217.

64. Antoine Galland, "Avertissement," in Les paroles remarquables les bons mots et
les maximes des orientaux (Paris, 1694). Discussed in Abdel-Halim, Antoine
Galland, 153–154.

65. He mentioned his friend Jean de Thévenot's Indian travel account. See Bibliothèque Orientale, "Agra," 70a.

66. Bibliothèque Orientale, "Aboulfarage," 25a. Interestingly, d'Herbelot devotes
only the edition and translation of the Arabic source, leaving the Pococke's commentary unmentioned. D'Herbelot also referred to Galland's unpublished
translation of a history of Tamerlane's successors. See Ibid., "Schahrokh," 770a.

67. Ibid., "Wäq," 193b.

68. The Chevalier de Jaucourt credited d'Herbelot with this novel term, yet he also
indicated that it had still not become standard. See Denis Diderot and Jean Le
Rond d'Alembert, eds., Encyclopédie, ou, Dictionnaire raisonné des sciences, des
arts et des métiers, 17 vols. (Paris, 1751–1765), 8:913.

69. For instance, Edward Pococke, Specimen Historiæ Arabum (Oxford, 1650) and
Pococke, ed., Historia Compendiosa Dynastiarum (Oxford, 1663); John Selden
and Edward Pococke, Contextio Gemmarum sive, Eutychii Patriarchae Alexandrini Annales, 2 vols. (Oxford, 1656, 1654).

70. Bevilacqua, "How to Organise the Orient," esp. 226–234, 239–241. See also
Gottfried Hagen, "Katib Çelebi," in the online database Historians of the
Ottoman Empire, ed. Cemal Kafadar, Hakan Karateke, and Cornell Fleischer,
https://ottomanhistorians.uchicago.edu/en/historians/65.

71. Galland, "Discours pour servir de Preface," in Bibliothèque Orientale, sig. ī2v.
Bevilacqua, "How to Organise the Orient," 223.

72. *Bibliothèque Orientale,* sig. ū4r–ū4v: "Auteurs Orientaux, et autres Ouvrages citez dans la Bibliotheque Orientale."

73. Naudé, *Advis,* 24.

74. Laurens, *Aux sources,* 51.

75. *Bibliothèque Orientale,* 773b. The chronicle was by Ibn al-Shiḥna. See *Encyclopedia of the Medieval Chronicle,* s.v. "Ibn al-Shiḥna"; *EI2,* s.v. "Ibn al-Shiḥna." Both of these concern the homonymous son of the author of the *Rawḍat al-manāẓir,* but the former makes reference to the father also. The Yemeni writer was Abū ʿAbd Allāh b. Asʿad ʿAfīf al-Dīn al-Yāfiʿī. Dates: ʿAfīf al-Dīn ʿAbd Allāh ibn Asʿad al-Yāfiʿī, died 767 AH / 1366 CE or in 778 AH. See *EI2,* s.v. "al-Yāfiʿī."

76. Lāmiʿī's *"Dester Lathif"* [Laṭāʾif-nāma]. See N. Hanif, *Biographical Encyclopedia of Sufis: Central Asia and Middle East* (New Delhi, 2000), 254.

77. Edward Gibbon, *The Decline and Fall of the Roman Empire,* 6 vols. (1788; New York, 1994), 5:332n5.

78. Sara Nur Yıldız, "Ottoman Historical Writing in Persian, 1400–1600," in *A History of Persian Literature,* vol. 10, *Persian Historiography,* ed. Charles Melville (London, 2012), chap. 9.

79. D'Herbelot discusses Khwāndamīr himself at *Bibliothèque Orientale,* 994b. See *EI2,* s.v. "Khwāndamīr." On Khwāndamīr, Mīrkhwānd, and their milieu, see Beatrice Forbes Manz, *Power, Politics and Religion in Timurid Iran* (Cambridge, 2007), chap. 2.

80. See Chapter 1 for Colbert and Galland's comments on it. On Mīrkhwānd, see Ali M. Ansari, "Mīrkhwānd and Persian Historiography," *Journal of the Royal Asiatic Society* 26 (2016): 249–259; *EI2,* s.v. "Mīrkhwānd."

81. Laurens, *Aux sources,* 53, counted about ninety citations. D'Herbelot also calls it the "Tarikh Montekheb."

82. See Edward Granville Browne, *A Literary History of Persia,* vol. 3, *A History of Persian Literature under Tartar Dominion, A.D. 1265–1502* (London, 1920), 87–95, and 94 on appraisal of its value. On al-Qazwīnī in general, see *EI2,* s.v. "al-Ḳazwīnī."

83. Several other Persian books made frequent appearances in the *Bibliothèque Orientale:* e.g., the *Nigāristān* (1552) of Aḥmad b. Muḥammad al-Jaʿfarī al-Qazwīnī (1515–1567 / 8 C.E.), and the history of the Prophet, of ʿAlī, Fāṭima, Ḥasan and Ḥusayn in Persian by Sabzavārī Bayhaqī Vāʾiẓ Kāshifī (died 1505), entitled *Rawḍat al-shuhadā* (The garden of martyrs).

84. Gaulmier, "Barthélemy d'Herbelot," 1. For instance, the word *dīwān* is spelled "divan," with a Persian "v" sound, rather than the Arabic "w." Likewise, in *Bibliothèque Orientale,* "Mohammed," 600a, he turns the phrase *ana sayyid walīd Ādam* into "Ana seïd veled Adam," also substituting the short "a" that an Arabic speaker would insert after the first consonant with a short "e." Also, he tends to

transliterate short "i" sounds (represented in Arabic by the *kasra* vowel point) as "e," so that *tadhkirāt* (biographies) becomes "tadhkerat" and *ʿilm* (knowledge) is "elm."

85. For introductions to the role of poetry in premodern Islamic societies, see James Kritzeck, ed., *Anthology of Islamic Literature from the Rise of Islam to Modern Times* (New York, 1964); Abdelfattah Kilito, *The Author and His Doubles: Essays on Classical Arabic Culture,* trans. Michael Cooperson (1985; trans., Syracuse, N.Y., 2001); Robert Irwin, ed., *Night and Horses and the Desert: An Anthology of Classical Arabic Literature* (New York, 1999).

86. See, e.g., *Bibliothèque Orientale:* "Amak," 105b; "Anuari ou Anueri," 118b; "Atsiz," 156a; "Reschidi," 715b.

87. Ibid. "Anuari ou Anueri," 119.

88. Ibid. "Hafedh," 416b.

89. Ibid.

90. Ibid. "Roumi," 722a.

91. The verse is recorded in Ibn al-Rūmī, *Dīwān,* 1:96 and 1:2913. It is quoted also in al-Zamakhsharī, *Rabīʿ al-abrār,* 1:329, and in Rāghib al-Iṣbahānī, *Muḥāḍarat al-udabāʾ,* 1:229 (with *ṣādiqan* for *ḥāḍiran*). The meter is *sarīʿ,* and the correct transliteration of the couplet is: "lam ʾara shayʾan ḥāḍiran nafʿuhū / lil marʾi ka ʾl-dirhami wa ʾl-sayfi / / yaqḍī lahu ʾl-dirhamu ḥājātihī / wa ʾl-sayfi yaḥmihi min al-ḥayfi." I thank Michael Cook for these references and observations.

92. DKB, uncataloged, part of the Reiske papers. *Bibliothèque Orientale,* "Roumi," 722a.

93. See *EI2,* s.v. "Saʿdī."

94. Faramarz Behzad, *Adam Olearius' 'Persianischer Rosenthal': Untersuchungen zur Übersetzung von Saadis 'Golestan' im 17. Jahrhundert* (Göttingen, 1970); Hamilton and Richard, *André du Ryer,* chap. 3. Sir William Jones would recommend study of the Gulistān in his Persian grammar: William Jones, preface, *A Grammar of the Persian Language* (London, 1771), xviii–xix.

95. *Bibliothèque Orientale,* "Aboulola," 26b. Johann Fabricius Dantiscanus published a poem by al-Maʿarrī in his *Specimen Arabicum* (Rostock, 1638), which Golius later reproduced in his edition of Erpenius's grammar, *Arabicae Linguae Tyrocinium* (Leiden, 1656), together with another poem. See Loop, *Johann Heinrich Hottinger,* 173–174.

96. *Bibliothèque Orientale,* "Aboulola," 26b. For a modern translation, see Reynold Alleyne Nicholson, *Studies in Islamic Poetry* (Cambridge, 1921), 178; Nicholson treats al-Maʿarrī's views of religion on 141–207. See also Nicholson, *A Literary History of the Arabs* (London, 1907), 313–324.

97. *Bibliothèque Orientale,* "Aboulola," 26b. For a modern translation, see Nicholson, *Studies in Islamic Poetry,* 167. Both of these excerpts are from al-Maʿarrī's

later collection *Luzūm mā lā yalzam* rather than from the earlier and more
conventional *Saqṭ al-Zand*.

98. Vienna, Österreichische Nationalbibliothek, shelfmark Altprunk 12.C.9.

99. Galland's additions and their sources are discussed in more detail in Bevilacqua,
"How to Organise the Orient," 245–246.

100. Galland, "Discours," in *Bibliothèque Orientale*, sig. ā2r.

101. Ibid., sig. ō r.

102. With entries such as: "Caia'n," 234b; "Caicobad," 239a; "Cai Khosru," 237a; "Cai-
kaus," 235a; "Manougeher," 550a; "Rostam," 719a; and others. On Firdawsī,
see Jan Rypka, *History of Iranian Literature*, ed. Karl Jahn (Dordrecht,
1968), 154–162.

103. The *Lubb al-tawārīkh* and the *Tā'rīkh-i guzīda*. On both of which, see the
discussion and references above.

104. *Bibliothèque Orientale*, "Rostam," 719b.

105. Galland, "Preface," in *Bibliothèque Orientale*, sig. ī2v.

106. *Bibliothèque Orientale*, "Rostam," 719b.

107. Ibid., "Omar," 687a, and "O'thman," 695b.

108. Ibid., "O'thman," 696a.

109. For instance, about his treatment of Muhammad's widow Aisha after the Battle
of the Camel. Ibid., 90b.

110. Ibid., "Ali," 95a. On the following page, 96a, he elucidates the negative conno-
tations of the word "Shi'a."

111. Ibid., "O'thman," 696b.

112. Ibid., "Jezid," 486a.

113. Ibid.

114. Ibid., "Ali," 96a.

115. Ibid., "Abu'Becre," 18a.

116. Ibid., "Holagu," 453a.

117. Ibid., "Mamon," 546b. The historian al-Ṭabarī recounts a version of the story
of the dates and water. See C. E. Bosworth, ed. and trans., *The History of al-
Ṭabarī*, vol. 32, *The Reunification of the 'Abbāsid Caliphate* (Albany, N.Y., 1987),
224–225.

118. *Bibliothèque Orientale*, "Mamon," 546b.

119. Ibid., "Genghiz Khan," 378b, and "Timour," 877b. Tamerlane's successors, the
Timurids and their successor dynasties, earned his attention, too: ibid.: "Schahrokh," 770a; "Ulug Beg," 914a; "Abdallathif," 7a; "Abdallah," 6a; "Abou-Said,"
34b. The material on Gengis Khan continues in other entries, such as that
about his contemporary Muhammad II of Khwarezm: ibid., "Mohammed,"
609a.

120. Ibid., "Timour," 888a–b.

121. Ibid., "Mohammed," 615b.

122. Ibid., "Abbas," 3b.

123. Ibid., "Caherah," 233b.

124. See ibid.: "Babur ou Babor," 160a; Humayun: "Homaioun," 455a; Shah Jahan: "Schahgehan," 768a; Jihangir: "Selim," 302a; Aurangzeb: "Aurenk," 152b and the mention on 163a.

125. Ibid., "Homaioun," 456a.

126. Ibid., "Mohammed," 615b.

127. Orest Ranum, *Artisans of Glory: Writers and Historical Thought in Seventeenth-Century France* (Chapel Hill, N.C., 1980), 41–49 and passim.

128. *Bibliothèque Orientale,* "Baiazid," 177b–178a.

129. Ibid., "Soliman," 824a.

130. Roxelana, known in the Ottoman Empire as Hürrem Sultan, was sometimes reprehended by Ottoman writers for her political influence, but she seems not to have inspired in them the same prurient interest that she awoke in Europeans. See, e.g., Cornell H. Fleischer, *Bureaucrat and Intellectual in the Ottoman Empire: The Historian Mustafa Âli (1541–1600)* (Princeton, N.J., 1986), 258.

131. *Bibliothèque Orientale,* "Mohammed," 598b.

132. Ibid.

133. Ibid., 599a.

134. Ibid., 598b. Aḥmad is traditionally understood here as a name for the Prophet Muhammad, meaning "most worthy of praise." See *EI2,* s.v. "Aḥmad"; Ahmad Pakatchi and Jawad Qasemi, "Aḥmad," in *Encyclopaedia Islamica,* 4 vols., ed. Farhad Daftary and Wilferd Madelung (London, 2008–2013).

135. *Bibliothèque Orientale,* "Mohammed," 600b.

136. Ibid., 602b.

137. Bevilacqua, "How to Organise the Orient," 218–219.

138. *Bibliothèque Orientale,* "Gennah," 376b.

139. Ibid., 377b.

140. Ibid., 377a.

141. Ibid.

142. Ibid., 376b.

143. Ibid., 377b.

144. Ibid. cites "Hussain Vaêz," fol. 403. This was a Persian Qur'an commentary by Sabzavārī Bayhaqī Vāʾiẓ Kāshifī (died 910 / 1505). D'Herbelot possessed a copy that he had acquired in Florence, and which had belonged to the printer Raimondi. It is now BnF, Supplément persan, 54. In his "Discours," sigs. õr–õv, Galland remarked on d'Herbelot's particular reliance on this source.

145. *Bibliothèque Orientale,* "Gennah," 376a.

146. Ibid., 378a–b.

147. Roelof van den Broek, "Cerinthus," in *Dictionary of Gnosis & Western Esotericism*, ed. Wouter J. Hanegraaff, in collaboration with Antoine Faivre, Roelof van den Broek, and Jean-Pierre Brach (Leiden, 2006). See also Matti Myllykoski, "Cerinthus," in *A Companion to Second-Century Christian "Heretics,"* ed. Antti Marjanen and Petri Luomanen (Leiden, 2005), 213–246. Of the several traditions concerning Cerinthus, only one—transmitted by Eusebius—concerns this belief in earthly pleasures in the kingdom of Christ. See Myllykoski, "Cerinthus," 214–215, 236–243.

148. Galland, "Discours pour servir de Preface," in *Bibliothèque Orientale*, sig. ẽv.

149. Ibid., sig. ĩr.

150. Ibid.

151. Ibid.

152. Antoine Galland, *Journal d'Antoine Galland pendant son séjour à Constantinople (1672–1673)*, 2 vols., ed. Charles Schefer (Paris, 1881), 1:26. See also 2:57–58 for another such encounter.

153. Galland, "Discours pour servir de Preface," in *Bibliothèque Orientale*, sig. ĩ2v.

154. Naudé, *Advis*, 17–18. Compare Galland, "Discours pour servir de Preface," in *Bibliothèque Orientale*, sig. ĩ2r.

155. *Bibliotheque Orientale*, sig. ũ3r.

156. Ibid., sig. ũ3v.

157. Ibid., "Megnoun," 573a.

158. Ibid.

159. Galland, "Discours pour servir de Preface," *Bibliothèque Orientale*, sig. ã.

160. *Bibliothèque Orientale* (Maastricht, 1776). *Bibliothèque Orientale*, 4 vols., rev. ed. (The Hague, 1777–1779). *Bibliothèque Orientale*, 6 vols., rev. ed., ed. Nicolas-Toussaint Lemoyne des Essarts (Paris, 1781–1783); *Orientalische Bibliothek: Universalwörterbuch, welches alles enthält, was zur Kenntniss des Orients nothwendig ist*, 4 vols., trans. J. C. F. Schulz (Halle, 1785–1790). The Halle edition was in German translation; a partial English translation is CUL, Ms. Add. 7513.

161. Bevilacqua, "How to Organise the Orient," 245–256.

162. Ibid., 258.

5 · ISLAM IN HISTORY

1. BnF, Ms. NAF 7478, fol. 1r: "Le projet de faire une histoire Orientale tirée des Originaux Arabes, Persiens, et Turcs, est un ouvrage dont l'utilité peut estre comparée à celle des autres recueils d'histoire qui ont paru depuis le retablissement des belles lettres."

2. There was, of course, a vast literature written by Europeans who did not know Arabic. But histories based on Arabic sources were few, and mostly aimed at

other scholars, with the notable exception of the *Bibliothèque Orientale.* The most important was Edward Pococke, *Specimen Historiæ Arabum: Sive, Gregorii Abul Farajii Malatiensis, De Origine & Moribus Arabum Succincta Narratio, in Linguam Latinam Conversa, Notisque è Probatissimis apud Ipsos Authoribus, Fusiùs Illustrat* (Oxford, 1650).

3. Ms. NAF 7478, fol. 1r: "Il comprendra l'histoire de plusieurs grands Empires qui n'a estee connue que d'une maniere tres imparfaite."

4. Ms. NAF 7478, fol. 1r: "On y trouve des evennemens Extraordinaires, plusieurs changmens d'Empire, des grands hommes, des maximes d'Estat, des guerres de religion, des Princes amateurs des belles lettres, et des beaux arts, des entreprises et des voyages de longcours, et des evenemens d'autant plus curieux qu'ils ont esté jusques a present entierement inconnus."

5. The European study of Arabic poetry lies beyond the confines of this book. For some indications of its history, see Jan Loop, "Divine Poetry? Early Modern European Orientalists on the Beauty of the Koran," *Church History and Religious Culture* 89 (2009): 455–488.

6. For an overview of this process, see Charles Burnett, "Arabic into Latin: The Reception of Arabic Philosophy into Western Europe," in *The Cambridge Companion to Arabic Philosophy,* ed. Peter Adamson and Richard Taylor (Cambridge, 2005), 370–404.

7. On historiography in the late seventeenth century, see, among others, Arnaldo Momigliano, "Ancient History and the Antiquarian," *Journal of the Warburg and Courtauld Institutes* 13 (1950): 285–315; Momigliano, "The Rise of Antiquarian Research," in Momigliano, *The Classical Foundations of Modern Historiography* (Berkeley, 1990), chap. 3; Blandine Barret-Kriegel, *Les historiens et la monarchie,* 4 vols. (Paris, 1988); Chantal Grell, *L'histoire entre érudition et philosophie: Étude sur la connaissance historique à l'âge des Lumières* (Paris, 1993); Anthony Grafton, *The Footnote: A Curious History* (Cambridge, Mass., 1997); Grafton, "Jean Hardouin: The Antiquary as Pariah," *Journal of the Warburg and Courtauld Institutes* 62 (1999): 241–267; Dmitri Levitin, *Ancient Wisdom in the Age of the New Science: Histories of Philosophy in England, c. 1640–1700* (Cambridge, 2015).

8. Simon Ockley, *The Conquest of Syria, Persia, and Ægypt, by the Saracens: Containing the Lives of Abubeker, Omar and Othman, the immediate Successors of Mahomet. Giving an Account of their most remarkable Battles, Sieges, &c. particularly those of Aleppo, Antioch, Damascus, Alexandria and Jerusalem. Illustrating the Religion, Rites, Customs and Manner of Living of that Warlike People. Collected from the most Authentick Arabick Authors, especially Manuscripts, not hitherto publish'd in any European Language* (London, 1708).

9. The 1718 *History of the Saracens* appeared in two volumes, the first of which reproduced the 1708 publication. Simon Ockley, *The History of the Saracens: Containing the lives of Abubeker, Omar, Othman, Ali, Hasan, Moawiyah I. Yezid I. Moawiyah II. Abdolla, Merwan I. and Abdòl mélick, the immediate Successors of Mahomet. Giving an Account of their most remarkable Battles, Sieges, &c. particularly those of Aleppo, Antioch, Damascus, Alexandria and Jerusalem. Illustrating the Religion, Rites, Customs and Manner of Living of that Warlike People. Collected from the most Authentick Arabick Authors, especially Manuscripts, not hitherto publish'd in any European Language,* 2 vols., 2nd ed. (London, 1718).

10. Ockley's life has been well told in *ODNB,* s.v. "Ockley, Simon (*bap.* 1679, *d.* 1720)"; and in A. J. Arberry, *Oriental Essays: Portraits of Seven Scholars* (London, 1960), 11–47. His Judaic interest was reflected in his English translation of Richard Simon's French version of the Venetian rabbi Leone Modena's *Historia de' riti hebraici,* published as *History of the Present Jews throughout the World being an ample tho succinct account of their customs, ceremonies, and manner of living at this time* (London, 1707).

11. The first four holders were Abraham Wheelock, Edmund Castell, John Luke, and Charles Wright. The Collège Royal in Paris and Leiden University both preceded Cambridge in establishing an Arabic chair, in 1587 and 1613 respectively.

12. Simon Ockley, *Saracens,* xlvii–xlviii. Ockley's fate was sorry enough to earn him posthumous inclusion in Isaac Disraeli, *Calamities of Authors: Including Some Inquiries Respecting their Moral and Literary Characters* (London, 1812).

13. An awareness awakened by the example of Humphrey Prideaux, whose English-language life of the prophet Muhammad was a best-selling work in early eighteenth-century England: Humphrey Prideaux, *The True Nature of Imposture Fully Displayed in the Life of Mahomet* (London, 1697).

14. J. G. A. Pocock, *Barbarism and Religion,* vol. 2, *Narratives of Civil Government* (Cambridge, 1999), 38.

15. Dutch: *De verovering van Syrien, Perzien en Egypten door de Saracenen* (Amsterdam, 1741). Vol. 2 was entitled *Historie der Saracenen.* German: *Geschichte der Saracenen, oder ihre Eroberung der Länder Syrien, Persien u. Ægypten,* trans. Th. Arnold (Leipzig and Altona, 1745). French: *Histoire des Sarrasins,* trans. A. F. Jault (Paris, 1748).

16. Cambridge, 1757. All the nineteenth-century editions were published in London.

17. Niccolò Machiavelli, *Discorsi,* bk. 2, preface. See Machiavelli, *The Chief Works and Others,* 3 vols., trans. Allan Gilbert (1965; repr., Durham, N.C., 1989), 1:322.

18. Ockley, *Conquest,* ix.

19. Ibid.

20. Ibid., xvi.

21. Ibid., xi.

22. Ibid., xvii.

23. Beinecke Rare Book and Manuscript Library, Yale University, Gen Mss. File 80, letter from J. Hilldrop of 16 January [1709?]. Hilldrop reports on the authority of an acquaintance that "[your performance] has procured you no contemptible interest at Lambeth," and expects that Ockley will "soon receive some very particular acknowledgements."

24. Ockley, *Saracens,* xv.

25. Johann Jacob Reiske, *D. Johann Jacob Reiskens von ihm selbst aufgesetzte Lebensbeschreibung* (Leipzig, 1783), 9.

26. Such works as do address his life and works are in German. He was lionized by Johann Fück, but has not been studied much even in his native land. See Johann Fück, *Die arabischen Studien in Europa bis in den Anfang des 20. Jahrhunderts* (Leipzig, 1955), 108–124; Gotthard Strohmaier, "Johann Jacob Reiske, Der Märtyrer der arabischen Literatur," *Das Altertum* 20 (1974): 166–179; Strohmaier, "Johann Jacob Reiske—Byzantinist und Arabist der Aufklärung" and "Johann Jacob Reiske über die Aufgaben der Arabistik," both in Strohmaier, *Von Demokrit bis Dante: Die Bewahrung antiken Erbes in der arabischen Kultur* (Hildesheim, 1996), 501–511, 512–515; Hans-Georg Ebert and Thoralf Hanstein, eds., *Johann Jacob Reiske: Leben und Wirkung: Ein Leipziger Byzantinist und Begründer der Orientalistik im 18. Jahrhundert* (Leipzig, 2005), esp. the essay by Jan Loop, "Kontroverse Bemühungen um den Orient," 45–85.

27. Reiske, *Lebensbeschreibung,* 44.

28. On Reiske's years at the Nikolaischule, see Otto Kaemmel, *Geschichte des Leipziger Schulwesens vom Anfange des 13. bis gegen die Mitte des 19. Jahrhunderts (1214–1846)* (Leipzig, 1909), 370–416.

29. Reiske, *Lebensbeschreibung,* 11.

30. In Leipzig in 1766 (the work is dated 23 March 1765), he attached two writings to a book by Johann Bernhard Köhler, which was an edition of a geographic table of Syria from Abū'l-Fidāʾ. Johann Bernhard Köhler, *Abulfedae Tabula Syriae cum Excerpto Geographico ex Ibn ol Wardii. Accessere Io. Iacobi Reiskii V.C. Animadversiones ad Abulfedam et Prodidagmata ad Historiam et Geographiam Orientalem* (Leipzig, 1766). See Fück, *Die arabischen Studien,* 113. Reiske, "Prodidagmata ad Hagji Chalifae librum memorialem rerum a Muhammedanis gestarum exhibentia introductionem generalem in historiam sic dictam orientalem," in Köhler, *Abulfedae Tabula Syriae,* 193–240. The essay was reprinted

twice, first in the second edition of Köhler's *Tabula* (Leipzig, 1786), and then by J. G. Meusel in the *Bibliotheca Historica,* vol. 2 (Leipzig, 1785), 107–204, under the title "Scriptores de Rebus Arabicis." Meusel, however, removes the concluding section of the "Prodidagmata," which is 238–240 in Köhler's edition.

31. Reiske, "Prodidagmata ad Hagji Chalifae librum," 215.

32. Ibid., 238. For the contrast between Reiske's view of the subject and that of his German predecessors and contemporaries, see Asaph Ben Tov, "The Academic Study of Arabic in Seventeenth- and Early Eighteenth-Century Protestant Germany," *History of Universities* 28, no. 2 (2015): 93–135.

33. Reiske, "Prodidagmata," 238.

34. Ibid.

35. Ibid.

36. Ockley, *Saracens,* xxxii.

37. Petrarch, *De viris illustribus,* ed. Guido Martellotti (Florence, 1964). For an introduction, see Ronald G. Witt, "The Rebirth of the Romans as Models of Character: *De viris illustribus,*" in *Petrarch: A Critical Guide to the Complete Works,* ed. Victoria Kirkham and Armando Maggi (Chicago, 2009), chap. 4.

38. Robert Lamberton, "Plutarch," in *The Classical Tradition,* ed. Anthony Grafton et al. (Cambridge, Mass., 2010), 747–750.

39. John D. Lyons, *Exemplum: The Rhetoric of Example in Early Modern France and Italy* (Princeton, N.J., 1989).

40. Pococke, *Specimen,* 6.

41. Ibid., "Notae," 165.

42. Ibid., 166.

43. Ibid.

44. Ibid.

45. Ibid.

46. Ibid. 166–67.

47. Ibid. 167.

48. Ibid.

49. Ockley, *Conquest,* xii.

50. Ibid., xiii.

51. Ibid.

52. Ibid., xx.

53. Ibid. xiii.

54. Pococke, *Specimen,* 166. In this respect at least it seems hard to argue, as John Pocock does, that Ockley's work represented a "philosophical" advance over Edward Pococke. See J. G. A. Pocock, *Barbarism and Religion,* vol. 1, *The Enlightenments of Edward Gibbon, 1737–1764* (Cambridge, 1999), 42.

55. Ockley, *Conquest,* xiii–xiv.

56. The impact of translations from Arabic was widely recognized in Europe at this time, even outside the circles of Arabic scholars. In other words, this was not a controversial claim to make. See the discussion of *historia literaria* in Chapter 4.

57. Ockley, *Conquest,* xiv.

58. There is not an enormous amount of modern scholarship on Renaudot. See Antoine Villien, *L'abbé Eusèbe Renaudot: Essai sur sa vie et sur son oeuvre liturgique* (Paris, 1904); J. M. Hussey, "L'Abbé Eusèbe Renaudot," in E. Renaudot, *Liturgiarum Orientalium Collectio,* 2 vols., rev. ed. (1847; repr., Farnborough, 1970); Jean Sgard, ed., *Dictionnaire des journalistes, 1600–1789* (Grenoble, 1976), s.v. "Eusèbe Renaudot"; Pierre-François Burger, "Pierre Nicole, La Perpétuité et l'abbé Eusèbe Renaudot," in *Pierre Nicole (1625–1695),* special issue, *Chroniques de Port-Royal* 45 (1996): 135–153; *Dictionnaire des orientalistes de langue française,* s.v. "Renaudot, Eusèbe."

59. Eusèbe Renaudot, *Historia Patriarcharum Alexandrinorum* (Paris, 1713); *Liturgiarum Orientalium Collectio,* 2 vols. (Paris, 1715–1716).

60. Eusèbe Renaudot, *Anciennes relations des Indes et de la Chine de deux voyageurs mahométans qui y allèrent dans le neuviéme siècle; traduites d'arabe: avec des Remarques sur les principaux endroits de ces Relations* (Paris, 1718). This was translated into English as *Ancient Accounts of India and China, by two Mohammedan Travellers, Who went to those Parts in the 9th Century; translated from the Arabic, by the late learned Eusebius Renaudot* (London, 1733).

61. BnF, Ms. NAF 7477 and 7478. Upon his death they passed to Dom Berthereau, a Benedictine scholar who turned the materials over to the French Royal Library in 1773. By contrast, Renaudot, at his death, left his Oriental manuscripts to the library of Saint-Germain-des-Prés; they were transferred to the (freshly renamed) Bibliothèque nationale in 1794.

62. Ms. NAF 7477 contains a continuous history that stretches for roughly 160 folios (300 pages at about 25 lines of text to a page, though there are blank pages and crossed-out passages) entitled simply "Histoire de Saladin." A blank margin occupies about a third of each page; Renaudot uses this for occasional additions or corrections, but above all to list his sources, as well as the calendar years to which the chronicle refers. Renaudot's history is divided into seven parts: "Livre premier," fols. 47r–61r; "Livre second," fols. 61v–92v; "Livre troisieme," fols. 93r–110r; "Livre quatrieme," fols. 110v–146v; "Livre sixieme," fols. 148r–185v; "Livre septieme," fols. 188r–217r. (A heading for "Livre cinquième" does not appear.)

63. Ms. NAF 7477, fol. 47r: "J'entreprens d'ecrire l'histoire d'un fameux conquerant, qui s'estant rendu illustre par l'establissement d'un puissant Empire acheva de se signaler contre les Chrestiens par la ruine du Royaume de Jerusalem. Quoy que son elevation a une souveraine puissance enferme des evenemens fort extraordi-

naires, on peut dire neantmoins que ce grand Royaume composé des plus belles provinces de l'Asie fut un ouvrage ou la fortune eut moins de part, que le merite du Sultan Saladin. Sa valeur & toutes ses vertus Royales ayant paru particulierement dans les guerres d'Outremer, il a eu l'avantage d'estre loüé non seulement par les siens, qui le mettent au dessus de tous leurs grands hommes, mais aussi par les Chrestiens, qui en ont rendu un illustre temoignage."

64. Ms. NAF 7477, fol. 47v: "Heros Mahometan."

65. Ibid., fol. 185r: "On ne peut pas soupconner de flatter ny les Francois, ny les Anglois, puis qu'ils temoignent par tout une egale aversion des uns & des autres, [et] que les choses qu'ils raportent sont a leur honte, & a la gloire des chrestiens, dont ils ne decrivent les victoires qu'avec douleur & lors que la verité les empeche de les dissimuler."

66. Ibid., fols. 213r–v: "Sa table estoit servie proprement, mais sans aucune magnificence: il ne s'habilla jamais depuis qu'il fut parvenu a la dignite de Sultan que d'etoffes de laine, de coton ou de lin. & son secretaire qui le temoigne, assure que souvent ceux qui venoient à l'audiance avoient peine a le reconnoistre, tant ses habits & ses manieres estoient simples quoy que sans aucune affectation."

67. Ibid., 214r: "Il est tres difficile de trouver un exemple plus illustre d'une patience & d'une bonte singuliere." Ibid., 215r: "Son humanite estoit si grande que les Chrestiens mesmes en rendent d'illustres temoignages, & si on excepte les malheurs inevitables de la guerre jamais on ne vit d'ennemy plus traitable ny moins de dureté dans un Prince victorieux."

68. Ibid., 216r: "ceux qui passerent pour les plus habiles dans la Theologie Mahometane . . . Il les faisoit parler, sur quelque point de religion ou sur l'Alcoran. Alors il faisoit venir ses enfans & les domestiques, & il les faisoit asseoir autor de luy pour ecouter les instructions de ces Theologiens, ou la lecture de quelque bon livre."

69. Ibid., fol. 217r: ". . . il ne paroit pas qu'il ait fait pendant son regne aucune action indigne de l'exemple qu'il devoit a ses sujets. Il faisoit de grandes aumones il recompensoit la vertu, il punissoit le vice, il aimoit son peuple & en estoit aimé comme un bon pere. Enfin si on excepte quelques endroits de sa vie ou il a temoigné trop d'ingratitude pour la maison de Nouraddin son maistre & son bienfacteur, & quelques autres choses qui font voir que les plus grands hommes vivant dans les tenebres d'une fausse religion ne sont pas exemts [sic] de vices ny de foiblesses il doit estre consideré comme un Prince dont l'histoire peut servir d'instruction a ceux qui cherchent la veritable grandeur."

70. On this normative concept and its history, see Michael Cook, *Commanding Right and Forbidding Wrong in Islamic Thought* (Cambridge, 2000).

71. Ms. NAF 7477, fol. 47r: "Un Prince reglé dans ses moeurs, occupé tousjours de la felicité de ses peuples, enfin un conquerant dont les victoires ne furent pas

comme ces deluges de sang dont la memoire funeste fait l'eloge des premiers heros de l'antiquité. Cette histoire fournira peut estre un modele plus parfait, que ne sont celles de ces illustres payens dont la vie a esté souillée de toute sorte de crimes."

72. On shifting notions of civilization in France, see Jonathan Dewald, *Aristocratic Experience and the Origins of Modern Culture: France, 1570–1715* (Berkeley, 1993); Larry F. Norman, *The Shock of the Ancient: Literature and History in Early Modern France* (Chicago, 2011).

73. Johann Jacob Reiske, *Dissertatio de Principibus Muhammedanis Qui aut Eruditione aut ab Amore Literarum et Literatorum Claruerunt* (Leipzig, 1747).

74. Reiske, *Dissertatio,* ix–x.

75. Ibid., xi.

76. Ibid.

77. Hugh Kennedy, *The Prophet and the Age of the Caliphates: The Islamic Near East from the Sixth to the Eleventh Century,* 2nd ed. (Harlow, 2004), 76–80.

78. Reiske, *Dissertatio,* xii.

79. Reiske, *Animadversionum ad Graecos Auctores Volumen Primum [-quintum],* 5 vols. (Leipzig, 1757–1766); Reiske, *Oratorum Græcorum, Quorum Princeps Est Demosthenes, Quae Supersunt, Monumenta Ingenii, e Bonis Libris,* 12 vols. (Leipzig, 1770–1775).

80. Loop, "Divine Poetry," 455–488.

81. Reiske, *Dissertatio,* xii.

82. Ibid., xii–xiii.

83. Ibid., xiii.

84. Ibid.

85. Ibid.

86. Ibid., xv.

87. Ibid., xx.

88. Moreover, his pension was paid irregularly, and after 1755 not at all. Reiske, *Lebensbeschreibung,* 43–44; Fück, *Die arabischen Studien,* 117.

89. For a recent perspective on Abbasid patronage, see Dimitri Gutas, *Greek Thought, Arabic Culture: The Graeco-Arabic Translation Movement in Baghdad and Early 'Abbāsid Society (2nd–4th / 8th–10th Centuries)* (London, 1998).

90. Gutas, *Greek Thought, Arabic Culture,* 95–104, quotation at 100.

91. Ockley, *Saracens,* xlv; Thomas Hearne, *Remarks and Collections of Thomas Hearne,* ed. C. E. Doble (Oxford, 1885), 3:286, as quoted in *ODNB,* s.v. "Ockley."

92. Ockley, *Conquest,* xviii–xx. Bod., MSS Laud Num A. 118; modern shelfmark MS. Laud Or. 163.

93. Reiske, *Lebensbeschreibung,* 15.

94. Ibid., 16.

95. Johann Jacob Reiske, *Tharaphae Moallakah: Cum Scholiis Nahas e Mss. Leidensibus* (Leiden, 1742).

96. Reiske, *Lebensbeschreibung,* 29. Ibn Qutayba, a medieval Persian scholar; Ibn Abī Uṣaibiʿaʾs biographies of doctors; both works of Abūʾl-Fidāʾ; Ḥamza al-Iṣbahanī, a medieval Persian historian and geographer; Ibn al-Shiḥna, who epitomized Abūʾl-Fidāʾ's history.

97. Ockley, *Conquest,* xx.

98. On al-Wāqidī and early Islamic historiography, see *EI2,* s.v. "al-Maghāzī"; *EQ,* s.v. "Sīra and the Qurʾān." On the pseudo-Wāqidī, see Franz Rosenthal, *A History of Muslim Historiography,* 2nd ed. (Leiden, 1968), 186–193; Chase F. Robinson, *Islamic Historiography* (Cambridge, 2003), 42–43.

99. Ockley, *Conquest,* xx.

100. Ibid., xxi.

101. Ibid., xxii.

102. Ibid., xxi–xxii.

103. Ibid., xix, xxiii.

104. Hendrik Arens Hamaker, *Incerti Auctoris Liber de Expugnatione Memphidis et Alexandriae, Vulgo Adscriptus Abou Abdallae Mohammedi Omari Filio, Wakidaeo, Medinensi* (Leiden, 1825). Hamaker's proofs include the mention of a historical figure who was al-Wāqidī's junior and the use of geographical terminology from a later period. He concludes that the book is no older than the late eleventh century.

105. Hamaker, *De Expugnatione Memphidis et Alexandriae,* viii–xi. By the time of Uri's catalog of the Bodleian, there were four copies in Oxford, numbered 655, 684, 736, and 795. Ockley had known two of these: in addition to his MSS Laud Num A. 118, he also identified Pococke Ms. 326 as a copy of the same book. See Ockley, *Conquest,* xxiii.

106. Aḥmad b. Muḥammad b. ʿAbd al-Rabbihi's *al-ʿIqd,* al-Suyūṭī's *Ithāf al-akhiṣṣāʾ bi-faḍāʾil al-masjid al-aqṣā;* Ibrāhīm b. Muḥammad b. Duqmāq's *al-Jawhar al-thamīn fī siyar al-khulafāʾ waʾl-salāṭīn,* and al-Thaʿlabī al-Nīsābūrī's *al-Ajāz fīʾl-ijāz.* See Shereen Nagib Khairallah, "Arabic Studies in England in the Late Seventeenth and Early Eighteenth Centuries" (PhD diss., University of London, 1972), 164–165.

107. Ockley, *Saracens,* 2:xxxii–xxxiii.

108. On Abūʾl-Fidāʾ, see *EI2,* s.v. "Abu ʾl-Fidå"; *EI3,* s.v. "Abū l-Fidā"; *The Memoirs of a Syrian Prince: Abu ʾl-Fidāʾ, Sultan of Ḥamāh (672–732 / 1273–1331),* trans. and intro. P. M. Holt (Wiesbaden, 1983); D. P. Little, *An Introduction to Mamlūk Historiography: An Analysis of Arabic Annalistic and Biographical Sources for the Reign of al-Malik an-Nāsir Muhammad ibn Qalāʾūn* (Wiesbaden, 1970), 142ff.

109. Robinson, *Islamic Historiography,* 98–99.

110. Ibid., 148.

111. Johann Jacob Reiske, *Abilfedae Annales Moslemici Latinos Ex Arabicis Fecit Io. Iacobus Reiske* (Leipzig, 1754), viii–ix.

112. Ibid., ix.

113. Ibid., viii.

114. Ibid., iv.

115. Ibid.

116. John Gagnier, *De Vita et Rebus Gestis Mohammedis* (Oxford, 1723); Albert Schultens, *Vita et Res Gestæ Sultani, Almalichi Alnasiri, Saladini, Abi Modaffiri Josephi f. Jobi, f. Sjadsi. Auctore Bohadino f. Sjeddadi. Nec Non Excerpta ex Historia Universali Abulfedæ, Easdem Res Gestas, Reliquamque Historiam Temporis, Compendiose Exhibentia* (Leiden, 1732).

117. The edition never appeared, but Reiske's extensive work on it survives in manuscript and is held in DKB (uncataloged Reiske manuscripts).

118. The visit took place in 1701. Villien, *Renaudot,* 119–121.

119. Henry Laurens, *Aux sources de l'orientalisme: La* Bibliothèque Orientale *de Barthélemi d'Herbelot* (Paris, 1978), 15–16.

120. On the two men's friendship, see Villien, *Renaudot,* 26, 168.

121. Robinson, *Islamic Historiography,* 18.

122. On the origins of Islamic historiography, see Rosenthal, *A History of Muslim Historiography;* Tarif Khalidi, *Arabic Historical Thought in the Classical Period* (Cambridge, 1994); Fred M. Donner, *Narratives of Islamic Origins: The Beginnings of Islamic Historical Writing* (Princeton, N.J., 1998); Julie Scott Meisami, *Persian Historiography to the End of the Twelfth Century* (Edinburgh, 1999); Robinson, *Islamic Historiography.*

123. Ockley, *Conquest,* xiv–xv.

124. Ibid., xv.

125. Ibid., xvi.

126. Ibid., xxii.

127. For the Middle Ages, see the references in Chapters 2 and 3. For the Renaissance, see, e.g., Pier Mattia Tommasino, *L'Alcorano di Macometto: Storia di un libro del Cinquecento europeo* (Bologna, 2013).

128. Nancy Bisaha, *Creating East and West: Renaissance Humanists and the Ottoman Turks* (Philadelphia, 2004); Margaret Meserve, *Empires of Islam in Renaissance Historical Thought* (Cambridge, Mass., 2008); Paula S. Fichtner, "Austrian Historians in the Renaissance and Islam: Pathways to Stereotyping" (conference paper, University of Copenhagen, 27 August 2010); Anders Ingram, *Writing the Ottomans: Turkish History in Early Modern England* (London, 2015).

129. Hendrik Johannes Erasmus, *The Origins of Rome in Historiography from Petrarch to Perizonius* (Assen, 1962); William McCuaig, *Carlo Sigonio: The Changing World of the Late Renaissance* (Princeton, N.J., 1989); William Stenhouse, *Reading Inscriptions and Writing Ancient History: Historical Scholarship in the Late Renaissance* (London, 2005). The writing of histories of ancient Greece began in the early seventeenth century: Ubbo Emmius, *Vetus Graecia Illustrata* (Leiden, 1626). See also Giovanna Ceserani, "Narrative, Interpretation, and Plagiarism in Mr. Robertson's 1778 *History of Ancient Greece*," *Journal of the History of Ideas* 66 (2005): 413–436; Ceserani, "Modern Histories of Ancient Greece: Genealogies, Contexts, and Eighteenth-Century Narrative Histories," in *The Western Time of Ancient History: Historiographical Encounters with the Greek and Roman Pasts*, ed. Alexandra Lianeri (Cambridge, 2011), chap. 6.

130. Ockley, *Saracens*, viii.

131. Ibid., vii–viii.

132. Ibid., viii–ix.

133. Ibid., xiii.

134. Ibid., xiv.

135. Cf. Lionel Gossman, *Medievalism and the Ideologies of the Enlightenment: The World and Work of La Curne de Sainte-Palaye* (Baltimore, 1968).

136. Ockley, *Saracens*, vii.

137. Ibid., xi.

138. Ockley's approach recalls that of the French eighteenth-century medievalist Jean-Baptiste La Curne de Sainte-Palaye. See Gossman, *Medievalism and the Ideologies of the Enlightenment*.

139. Around 1738, Reiske was invited to edit the history of Abū'l-Fidāʾ in Arabic and Latin. For circumstantial reasons, the history never appeared. See Reiske, *Lebensbeschreibung*, 46–48; Fück, *Die arabischen Studien*, 117–118. Yet Reiske completed much work on Abū'l-Fidāʾ, the bulk of which survives in manuscript, and even published a lengthy excerpt in Latin translation: Reiske, *Annales Moslemici*. A full edition of Abū'l-Fidāʾ based on Reiske's work would be published after his death: Jacob Georg Christian Adler, ed., *Abulfedae Annales Muslemici Arabice et Latine*, 5 vols. (Copenhagen, 1789–1794). See Reiske, *Lebensbeschreibung*, 68.

140. Adler, in Reiske, *Annales Moslemici* [1789], "Lecturis," vii.

141. Reiske, *Annales Moslemici*, xviii–xix.

142. Ockley, *Conquest*, xxiv. He provided further explanations for the shortcomings of his two books in comparison with his ambitions in 1718: Ockley, *Saracens*, xl–xlii.

143. Beinecke, Gen Mss. File 80, letter from Humphrey Prideaux of 20 December 1708.

144. Ockley, *Conquest,* xi.

145. Ockley, *Saracens,* v–vi.

146. Ibid., v–vi.

147. Ibid., vi.

148. Ibid., xliv.

149. Ibid., xxxix. Arberry, *Oriental Essays,* 44: "His second volume thus draws on better sources than his first." See also Khairallah, "Arabic Studies in England," 169–170.

150. Ockley, *Saracens,* xlvi.

151. BnF, Ms. NAF 7478, fol. 2v: "un corps d'histoire parfait qui conduira jusques au temps des premieres Croisades."

152. Ms. NAF 7478, fol. 2r: "il est difficile en traduisant les auteurs d'eviter un detail ennuyeux des miracles des Prophetes, et de superstitions dont la connoissance exacte n'est pas fort utile. Il suffit d'en choisir quelqu'un qui soit exacte, comme il y en a un assez grand nombre."

153. Ibid., fol. 3r: "Il faudra alors se servir des livres Turcs qui sont originaux sur cette matiere, au lieu que pour les temps precedens, on ne les doit considerer que comme des meschantes copies. Il y a des histoires generales en chaque langue qui renfirment assez exactement l'histoire ancienne et moderne comme sont celles d'Abulfeda, Nuiri, Ebn Chekena, et plusieurs autres qu'on pourroit utilement traduite; mais il est necessaire de remarquer que les historiens Arabes sont ordinairement peu exacts sur les affaires de la Haute Asie; que les Persiens les ecrivent plus exactement, mais aussy ils sont moins exacts que les Arabes en ce qui regarde les affaires de Syrie et d'Egypte. L'histoire d'Afrique est fort obscure; et peu d'Auteurs l'ont eclaircie parceque l'Afrique a presque toujours esté soumise a des Princes particuliers, qui n'ont eu aucun commerce avec les autres Princes Mahometans."

154. Ibid., fol. 2v: "Ce temps des Croisades est un Epoque considerable dans l'histoire Orientale."

155. Ibid., fol. 3r: "La plus exacte est celle de Makrisi, qui commence quelques années avant Saladin, et comprend l'histoire de la pluspart des Sultans d'Egypte appellées Mamelucs. On peut joindre a cet histoire plusieurs autres histoires particulieres d'Egypte, et de Syrie. Ensuite avec le secours de quelques histoires modernes, on conduira l'histoire Orientale, jusqu'à l'établissement de la maison Ottomane."

156. Ibid., fol. 3v: "On ajoutera a chaque traduction des marques courtes tirées des auteurs Mahometans pour eclaircir les principaux faits historiques, les coutumes, les moeurs, et en general tout ce qui ne peut estre connu par ceux qui n'ont pas fait une estude particuliere de cette histoire."

157. Ibid., fol. 3v: "Il ne sera pas inutile d'y joindre des remarques tirées des Auteurs Grecs, et Latins, et mesme des plus anciens en langue vulgaire pour faire voir la conformité de l'histoire."

158. Ibid., fol. 3v–4r: "On y joindra des notices des principales dignitez charges et emplois. Un Index Geographique des lieux dont il sera fait mention dans l'histoire. Des Tables Chronologiques pour raporter toutes dates aux années de Jesus Christ. On pourra joindre aussy aux remarques des medailles antiques des monnoyes des inscriptions qui se trouvent dans les cabinets des Curieux, et qui peuvent eclaircir plusieurs difficultez. Il sera aussy tres utile, que quelques uns de ceux qui travailleront a cet ouvrage composent une preface generale, qui puisse servir a tout ce corps d'histoire."

159. On the Magdeburg Centuries, see Anthony Grafton, "Where Was Salomon's House? Ecclesiastical History and the Intellectual Origins of Bacon's *New Atlantis*," in Grafton, *Worlds Made by Words: Scholarship and Community in the Modern West* (Cambridge, Mass., 2009), 98–113.

160. Reiske, *Annales Moslemici*, xxviii.

161. Reiske would have an opportunity to publish another excerpt from Abū'l-Fidā' as late as 1770 in the periodical edited by Anton Friedrich Büsching: Reiske, "Abilfedae Opus Geographicum," *Magazin für die neue Historie und Geographie,* pt. 4 (1770); this was a version of Abū'l-Fidā''s *Taqwīm al-Buldān* (Survey of countries). Abū'l-Fidā''s other major work, the *Taqwīm al-Buldān,* was a geography with tables of data such as geographical coordinates drawn from other sources. The *Taqwīm* had already caught the attention of John Greaves in 1650: John Greaves, *Chorasmiae et Mawaralnahrae: Hoc Est Regionum extra Fluvium Oxum Descriptio ex Tabulis Abulfedae Ismaelis* (London, 1650).

6 · ISLAM AND THE ENLIGHTENMENT

1. Denis Diderot and Jean Le Rond d'Alembert, eds., *Encyclopédie, ou, Dictionnaire raisonné des sciences, des arts et des métiers,* 17 vols. (Paris, 1765), 9:864.

2. For an example of how the writings of the Republic of Arabic Letters were absorbed into the *Encyclopédie,* see Alexander Bevilacqua, "How to Organise the Orient: D'Herbelot and the *Bibliothèque Orientale,*" *Journal of the Warburg and Courtauld Institutes* 79 (2016): 259–260.

3. Ernst Cassirer, *The Philosophy of the Enlightenment,* trans. Fritz C. A. Koelln and James P. Pettegrove (1932; trans., Princeton, N.J., 1951); Peter Gay, *The Enlightenment: An Interpretation,* 2 vols. (New York, 1966–1969); Jonathan Israel, *Radical Enlightenment: Philosophy and the Making of Modernity, 1650–1750* (Oxford, 2001) and sequels. For the argument that deism, not atheism, was more in line with the scientific understandings of the day, see Winfried

Schröder, *Ursprünge des Atheismus: Untersuchungen zur Metaphysik-und Religionskritik des 17. und 18. Jahrhunderts* (Stuttgart, 1998). For an overview of the current state of the historiography on the Enlightenment, see William J. Bulman, "Introduction: Enlightenment for the Culture Wars," in *God in the Enlightenment,* ed. William J. Bulman and Robert G. Ingram (Oxford, 2016), 1–41. For references on the "religious Enlightenment," see the conclusion to this chapter.

4. Hichem Djaït, *L'Europe et l'Islam* (Paris, 1978); Maxime Rodinson, *La fascination de l'Islam* (Paris, 1980); Thierry Hentsch, *L'Orient imaginaire: La vision politique occidentale de l'est méditerranéen* (Paris, 1988); Ahmad Gunny, *Images of Islam in Eighteenth-Century Writings* (London, 1996); Ann Thomson, "Les Lumières et le monde islamique," in *Les Lumières et la solidarité internationale,* ed. Michel Baridon (Dijon, 1997), 101–111; Alastair Hamilton, "Western Attitudes to Islam in the Enlightenment," *Middle Eastern Lectures* 3 (1999): 69–85; Israel, *Radical Enlightenment,* chap. 36; Sadek Neaimi, *L'Islam au siècle des Lumières: Image de la civilisation islamique chez les philosophes français du XVIIIe siècle* (Paris, 2003); Jonathan Israel, *Enlightenment Contested: Philosophy, Modernity, and the Emancipation of Man, 1670–1752* (Oxford, 2006), chap. 24; Ziad Elmarsafy, *The Enlightenment Qur'an: The Politics of Translation and the Construction of Islam* (Oxford, 2009); Lynn Hunt, Margaret C. Jacob, and Wijnand Mijnhardt, *The Book That Changed Europe: Picart and Bernard's Religious Ceremonies of the World* (Cambridge, Mass., 2010), chap. 10; Humberto Garcia, *Islam and the English Enlightenment, 1670–1840* (Baltimore, 2012).

5. See Chapter 3 and references there. The word "civilization" was coined in the 1760s, but much earlier Europeans conceived the notion that the cultural and intellectual achievements of Muslims could be assessed and assigned an overall evaluation. On civilization, see Lucien Febvre et al., *Civilisation, le mot et l'idée* (Paris, 1930); E. de Dampierre, "Note sur 'Culture' et 'Civilisation,'" *Comparative Studies in Society and History* 3 (1961): 328–340; Émile Benveniste, *Problèmes de linguistique générale,* 2 vols. (Paris, 1966), vol. 1, chap. 28; *Europäische Schlüsselwörter,* vol. 3, *Kultur und Zivilisation* (Munich, 1967); Jean Starobinski, *Blessings in Disguise; or, the Morality of Evil,* trans. Arthur Goldhammer (Cambridge, Mass., 1993), chap. 1.

6. Voltaire, *Questions sur l'Encyclopédie, par des amateurs,* vol. 7, *Langues-Prières,* ed. Nicholas Cronk and Christiane Mervaud (Oxford, 2012) (= *Oeuvres complètes de Voltaire,* vol. 42b), 119.

7. Montesquieu, *De l'esprit des lois,* in *Oeuvres complètes,* 2 vols., ed. Roger Caillois (Paris, 1951), 2:229. Translation from Montesquieu, *The Spirit of the Laws,* ed. and trans. Anne M. Cohler et al. (Cambridge, 1989), xliii.

8. Catherine Volpilhac-Auger, *Tacite et Montesquieu* (Oxford, 1985) (= *Studies on Voltaire and the Eighteenth Century,* vol. 232).

9. Jean Ehrard and Catherine Volpilhac-Auger, eds., *Oeuvres complètes de Montesquieu,* vol. 1, *Lettres persanes* (Oxford, 2004) (hereafter cited as *Lettres persanes*). On the immediate success, see the introduction, 16–17, and note 12 there.

10. Gian Paolo Marana, *L'espion du Grand-Seigneur et ses relations secrètes, envoyées au divan de Constantinople. Découvertes à Paris pendant le règne de Louys Le Grand,* 3 vols., 2nd ed. (1684; 2nd ed., Paris, 1686); *DBI,* s.v. "Gian Paolo Marana" and the comprehensive bibliography there.

11. *Lettres persanes,* letter 1, 140–141.

12. Ibid., letter 51, 329–323.

13. Ibid., letter 96, 400–402, here 400; and letter 97, 403–405, here 403.

14. Ibid., letter 94, 392–396, here 395.

15. Ibid., letter 73, 333–335; letter 55, 280–282; letter 78, 353.

16. Ibid., letter 44, 248. See also the condemnation of superstition in *Lettres persanes,* letter 137, 518–520.

17. Ibid., letter 54, 279.

18. Ibid., letter 16, 175–176.

19. Ibid., letter 58, 291.

20. Ibid., letter 83, 367.

21. Ibid.

22. Montesquieu also treats despotism in *Lettres persanes,* letters 99–100; in letters 111–112 he analyzes why Muslim states are depopulated. On the political thought of *Persian Letters,* see Jean Ehrard, "La signification politique des *Lettres persanes,*" *Archives des lettres modernes* 116 (1969): 33–50; Jean-Marie Goulemot, "Questions sur la signification politique des *Lettres persanes,*" in *Approches des Lumières: Mélanges offerts à Jean Fabre* (Paris, 1974), 213–225.

23. *Lettres persanes,* letter 87 and passim.

24. Ibid., letter 9, 157.

25. Muriel Dodds, *Les récits de voyages: Sources de l'Esprit des lois de Montesquieu* (Paris, 1929); Paul Vernière, "Montesquieu et le monde musulman, d'après *L'Esprit des lois,*" in *Actes du Congrès Montesquieu réuni à Bordeaux du 23 mai au 26 mai 1955 pour commémorer le deuxième centenaire de la mort de Montesquieu* (Bordeaux, 1956), 175–190; Parvine Mahmoud, "Les Persans de Montesquieu," *French Review* 34 (1960): 44–50; *Lettres persanes,* introduction, 52–54.

26. *Lettres persanes,* introduction, 47–48 on Montesquieu's "syncretism."

27. Montesquieu's evolving thoughts on the association of Islam and despotism can be traced in his *Pensées,* collections of notes kept from the 1720s until just before his death. See Vernière, "Montesquieu et le monde musulman," 179.

28. Aristotle, *The Politics,* ed. and trans. Carnes Lord (Chicago, 1984), 3.7.96, 3.14.109.

29. Franco Venturi, "Oriental Despotism," *Journal of the History of Ideas* 24 (1963): 133–142; Rolando Minuti, "Mito e realtà del dispotismo ottomano: Note in margine ad una discussione settecentesca," *Studi settecenteschi* 1 (1981): 35–59; Lucette Valensi, *The Birth of the Despot: Venice and the Sublime Porte,* trans. Arthur Denner (Ithaca, N.Y., 1993); Jürgen Osterhammel, *Die Entzauberung Asiens: Europa und die asiatischen Reiche im 18. Jahrhundert* (Munich, 1998); Thomas Kaiser, "The Evil Empire? The Debate on Turkish Despotism in Eighteenth-Century French Political Culture," *Journal of Modern History* 72 (2000): 6–34; Joan-Pau Rubiès, "Oriental Despotism and European Orientalism: Botero to Montesquieu," *Journal of Early Modern History* 9 (2005): 109–180; Rolando Minuti, "Oriental Despotism," *European History Online (EGO)* (2012), http://ieg-ego.eu/en/threads/models-and-stereotypes/the-wild-and-the-civilized/rolando-minuti-oriental-despotism/. On the concept of despotism in the eighteenth century, see R. Koebner, "Despot and Despotism: Vicissitudes of a Political Term," *Journal of the Warburg and Courtauld Institutes* 14 (1951): 275–302; Derek Beales, "Philosophical Kingship and Enlightened Despotism," in *The Cambridge History of Eighteenth-Century Political Thought,* ed. Mark Goldie and Robert Wokler (Cambridge, 2006), chap. 17, esp. 512–521.

30. John J. Hurt, *Louis XIV and the Parlements: The Assertion of Royal Authority* (Oxford, 2002).

31. Lionel Rothkrug, *Opposition to Louis XIV: The Political and Social Origins of the French Enlightenment* (Princeton, N.J., 1965).

32. See *Lettres persanes,* letter 134, 503, on the role of the *parlements.*

33. Ibid., letter 99, 408.

34. Montesquieu, *The Spirit of the Laws,* vol. 5, chap. 14, 59.

35. Ibid., 61.

36. Paul Rycaut, *The Present State of the Ottoman Empire* (London, 1667). The latter two books covered the periods 1623–1677 and 1679–1699, respectively. On Rycaut: B. H. Beck, *From the Rising of the Sun: English Images of the Ottoman Empire to 1715* (New York, 1987); Sonia P. Anderson, *An English Consul in Turkey: Paul Rycaut at Smyrna, 1667–1678* (Oxford, 1989); Linda T. Darling, "Ottoman Politics through British Eyes: Paul Rycaut's 'The Present State of the Ottoman Empire,'" *Journal of World History* 5 (1994): 71–97; *ODNB,* s.v. "Rycaut, Sir Paul (1629–1700)."

37. Anderson, *English Consul,* append. 1.

38. Rycaut, *Present State,* 4.

39. Darling, "Ottoman Politics through British Eyes."

40. Rycaut, *Histoire de l'etat présent de l'Empire ottoman: Contenant les maximes Politiques des Turcs; les principaux points de la Religion Mahometane, ses Sectes,*

ses Heresies, et des diverses sortes de Religieux; etc., traduit de l'Anglois . . . (Paris, 1670).

41. C[onstantin]-F[rançois] Volney, *Considérations sur la guerre actuelle des Turcs* (London [i.e., Paris], 1788), 67n1.

42. Other writers in this tradition included the British diplomat James Porter, and the French diplomat François Baron de Tott. See Rolando Minuti, *Orientalismo e idee di tolleranza nella cultura francese del primo '700* (Florence, 2006), chap. 2.

43. For instance, Montesquieu cites the Qur'an on incest prohibition and the law of retaliation: Montesquieu, *The Spirit of the Laws,* bk. 6, chap. 19, 93; bk. 24, chap. 17, 471; bk. 26, chap. 14, 508.

44. Prideaux: Montesquieu, *The Spirit of the Laws,* bk. 24, chap. 16, 471. Boulainvilliers: Montesquieu, *The Spirit of the Laws,* bk. 24, chap. 24, 477. Hyde and Renaudot: Montesquieu, *The Spirit of the Laws,* bk. 24, chap. 20, 474.

45. Rubiès, "Oriental Despotism and European Orientalism."

46. Rycaut, *Present State;* François Bernier, *Voyage dans les États du Grand Mogol* (Paris, 1671); Jean-Baptiste Tavernier, *Les six voyages* (Paris, 1676–1677); Jean Chardin, *Journal du voyage du Chevalier Chardin en Perse* (Paris, 1686); Charles-Jacques Poncet, *Relation abrégée du voyage que M. Charles Jacques Poncet . . . fit en Ethiopie en 1698, 1699 et 1700* (Paris, 1704); Jacques Philippe Laugier de Tassy, *Histoire du Royaume d'Alger* (Amsterdam, 1725); Thomas Shaw, *Travels, or Observations relating to several parts of Barbery and the Levant,* 2 vols. (Oxford, 1738–1746).

47. See Vernière, "Montesquieu et le monde musulman," 186–190.

48. Alexandre-Louis-Marie Pétis de la Croix, *Canon du sultan Suleiman II, représenté au sultan Mourad IV pour son instruction, ou état politique et militaire, tiré des archives . . . des princes ottomans . . . trad. du turc* (Paris, 1725). On Ebū's-suʿūd, see Colin Imber, *Ebu's-su'ud: The Islamic Legal Tradition* (Stanford, 1997); *EI3,* s.v. "Abū l-Suʿūd." The translator was the third of a dynasty of interpreters. See *Dictionnaire des orientalistes de langue française,* s.v. "Pétis de la Croix François."

49. Review of "Canon de Sultan Suleiman II," *Journal des sçavans* (Sept. 1725): 541–546.

50. Vernière, "Montesquieu et le monde musulman," 177; Louis Desgraves, ed., *Catalogue de la bibliothèque de Montesquieu* (Geneva, 1954); Louis Desgraves and Catherine Volpilhac-Auger, eds., *Catalogue de la bibliothèque de Montesquieu à La Brède* (Naples, 1999). Among the works he owned were (catalog nos. are in parentheses): *L'Alcorano di Macometto* (Venice, 1547) (584); André Du Ryer, *L'Alcoran de Mahomet* (Paris, 1647) (585); Barthélemy d'Herbelot, *Bibliothèque Orientale* (Paris, 1697) (2487); Antoine Galland, *La mort du*

sultan Osman (Paris, 1978) (3118); Henri de Boulainvilliers, *La vie de Mahomed* (London, 1730) (3124); Adriaan Reland, *La Religion des Mahométans* (The Hague, 1721) (3126).

51. Abraham-Hyacinthe Anquetil-Duperron, *Zend-Avesta: Ouvrage de Zoroastre, contenant les idées théologiques, physiques & morales de ce législateur, les cérémonies du culte religieux qu'il a établi, & plusieurs traits importans relatifs à l'ancienne histoire des Perses* (Paris, 1771). On Anquetil-Duperron, see Siep Stuurman, "Cosmopolitan Egalitarianism in the Enlightenment: Anquetil Duperron on India and America," *Journal of the History of Ideas* 68 (2007): 255–278; Urs App, *The Birth of Orientalism* (Philadelphia, 2010), chap. 7.

52. Anquetil-Duperron, *Législation orientale* (Amsterdam, 1778). Venturi, "Oriental Despotism," 137–139.

53. Voltaire, *Commentaire sur l'esprit des loix de Montesquieu* ([Paris], 1778) (hereafter *Commentaire*), para. 3, 9–11; para. 34, 50. Voltaire and Montesquieu's relationship has been discussed by Robert Shackleton, "Allies and Enemies: Voltaire and Montesquieu," in Shackleton, *Essays on Montesquieu and on the Enlightenment,* ed. David Gilson and Martin Smith (Oxford, 1988), 153–169; Jean Ehrard, "Voltaire vu par Montesquieu," in *Voltaire et ses combats,* 2 vols., ed. Ulla Kölving and Christiane Mervaud (Oxford, 1997), 2:939–951.

54. Voltaire, *Commentaire*, 73–77.

55. Ibid., para. 11, 22; para. 12, 23.

56. Ibid., para. 23, 36–37.

57. Ibid., para. 13, 24. On inheritance: para. 25, 38–39.

58. Ibid., para. 31, 45.

59. Ibid., 46–47.

60. Ibid., para. 13, 23–24.

61. See Koebner, "Despot and Despotism."

62. Voltaire, *Commentaire,* para. 26, 39; para. 35, 50–51.

63. Ibid., para. 13, 25. The Italian naturalist and diplomat Luigi Ferdinando Marsigli (1658–1730) had written a treatise based on his time in the Ottoman Empire. Luigi Ferdinando Marsigli, *Stato militare dell'Imperio Ottomanno, incremento et decremento del medesimo: L'Etat militaire de l'Empire Ottoman, ses progrès et sa décadence* (The Hague, 1732). The book was published in a bilingual Italian and French ed. On Marsigli, see *DBI*, s.v. "Marsili, Luigi Ferdinando."

64. Koebner, "Despot and Despotism."

65. In the nineteenth century, Montesquieu's arguments were again attacked, this time by the great Antoine-Isaac Silvestre de Sacy, "Mémoires sur la nature et les révolutions du droit de propriété territoriale en Égypte, depuis la conquête de ce pays par les Musulmans jusqu'à l'expédition des Français," *Académie des in-*

scriptions et belles-lettres, mémoires de l'Institut royal de France, 1 (1815): 1–165; 5 (1821): 1–175; 7 (1824): 55–124. For episodes in the later history of the concept, see Osterhammel, *Entzauberung Asiens;* Chen Tzoref-Ashkenazi, "Romantic Attitudes toward Oriental Despotism," *Journal of Modern History* 85 (2013): 280–320; Robert Travers, *Ideology and Empire in Eighteenth Century India: The British in Bengal* (Cambridge, 2007). See also Minuti, "Oriental Despotism."

66. A salient example is the German Arabic scholar and Göttingen professor Johann David Michaelis, who acknowledged an explicit debt to Montesquieu: Johann David Michaelis, *Mosaisches Recht,* 6 vols. (Frankfurt am Main, 1770–1775), 1:2.

67. Rousseau makes brief references to episodes in Islamic history in his "Discourse on the Moral Effects of the Arts and Sciences" (1750); *The Social Contract* (1762); and *Essay on the Origin of Languages* (published posthumously). See Rousseau, *Oeuvres complètes,* 5 vols., ed. B. Gagnebin and M. Raymond (Paris, 1959–1995), 3:28; 3:462–463; 5:409–410.

68. David Hume, "Of the Standard of Taste" [1757], in Hume, *Essays, Moral and Literary,* ed. Eugene F. Miller (Indianapolis, 1987), essay 23, 226–249.

69. Adam Ferguson, *An Essay on the History of Civil Society,* ed. Fania Oz-Salzberger (Cambridge, 1995), 111; Adam Smith, *Lectures on Jurisprudence,* ed. R. L. Meek et al. (Oxford, 1978), passim; Smith, *An Inquiry into the Nature and Causes of the Wealth of Nations,* 2 vols., ed. R. H. Campbell and A. S. Skinner (Oxford, 1976), passim; Smith, "The History of Astronomy," in Smith, *Essays on Philosophical Subjects,* ed. W. P. D. Wightman and J. C. Bryce (Oxford, 1980), 353.

70. Voltaire, *Essai sur les mœurs et l'esprit des nations,* vol. 2, *Avant-propos et chapitres 1–37,* ed. Bruno Bernard, John Renwick, Nicholas Cronk, and Janet Gooden (Oxford, 2009) (= *Oeuvres complètes de Voltaire,* vol. 22), 16. Part of Voltaire, *Essai sur les mœurs et l'esprit des nations,* 9 vols. (Oxford, 2009–2017) (= *Oeuvres complètes de Voltaire,* vols. 21A–27). Voltaire had dedicated an earlier work to the age of the Sun King: Voltaire, *Le siècle de Louis XIV* (Berlin, 1751).

71. Catherine Volpilhac-Auger, "Comment lire l'*Essai sur les mœurs*?," *Storia della storiografia* 38 (2000): 3–16.

72. Voltaire, *Essai,* 1–2. See also the passage in Voltaire, *Remarques pour servir de supplément à l'Essai sur les mœurs* ([Geneva], 1763). See Pierre Force, "Voltaire and the Necessity of Modern History," *Modern Intellectual History* 6 (2009): 457–484.

73. Voltaire, *Essai,* 5.

74. Jacques-Bénigne Bossuet, "Discours sur l'histoire universelle," in *Oeuvres de Bossuet,* 4 vols., ed. Saint-Marc Girardin and Henri Patin (Paris, 1852), 1:170–171. Bossuet had planned a sequel in which he would discuss the rise of Islam,

but this never appeared. See Bossuet, "Discours," 298. On Bossuet, see Arnaldo Momigliano, "La formazione della moderna storiografia sull'impero romano," in Momigliano, *Contributo alla storia degli studi classici* (Rome, 1955), 107–164.

75. Voltaire, *Essai,* 4.

76. René Pomeau, *La religion de Voltaire,* 2nd ed. (Paris, 1969).

77. Voltaire's views of Islam have been the object of several studies: see Pomeau, *Religion de Voltaire,* 146–156; Magdy G. Badir, *Voltaire et l'Islam* (Oxford, 1974); Djavad Hadidi, *Voltaire et l'Islam* (Paris, 1974); Ahmad Gunny, *Images of Islam in Eighteenth-Century Writings* (London, 1996), 132–162; Diego Venturino, "Un prophète 'philosophe'? Une *Vie de Mahomed* à l'aube des Lumières," *Dix-huitième siècle* 24 (1992): 321–331; Venturino, "Imposteur ou législateur? Le Mahomet des Lumières (vers 1750–1789)," in *Religions en transition dans la seconde moitié du XVIIIe siècle,* ed. Louis Châtellier (Oxford, 2000), 243–262; *Encyclopaedia of the Enlightenment,* s.v. "Islam."

78. Voltaire, *Le fanatisme, ou, Mahomet le prophète,* ed. Christopher Todd and Ahmad Gunny (Geneva, 2002) (=*Oeuvres complètes de Voltaire,* vol. 20B). See Badir, *Voltaire et l'Islam,* 71–146. *Mahomet* was begun in 1739 and first performed in Lille in 1741 and in Paris the following year. The first authorized edition appeared in print in 1743.

79. Hadidi, *Voltaire et l'Islam.*

80. Voltaire, *Essai,* 117.

81. Letter of 14 August 1738, quoted in *Corpus des notes marginales de Voltaire,* vol. 4, ed. N. Elaguina (Oxford, 2011) (= *Oeuvres complètes de Voltaire,* vol. 139), 724n599.

82. Hadidi, *Voltaire et l'Islam,* 76.

83. Boulainvilliers, *Vie de Mahomed;* John Gagnier, *De Vita et Rebus Gestis Mohammedis* (Oxford, 1723).

84. The new Voltaire Foundation critical edition of the *Essai sur les mœurs et l'esprit des nations,* ed. Bruno Bernard, John Renwick, Nicholas Cronk, and Janet Godden (Oxford, 2009–) (= *Oeuvres complètes de Voltaire,* vols. 21A–27) has done much to clarify Voltaire's use of sources, especially the many sources that he did not cite. See also the review by Saul Anton in *H-France Review* 12 (April 2012): n54, and references there.

85. Voltaire, *Oeuvres complètes de Voltaire,* 20B:334.

86. Elaguina, *Corpus des notes marginales,* 4:724.

87. These are reproduced in *Corpus des notes marginales,* bk. 814, 4:654–664.

88. George Sale, *Koran,* chap. 2, 30n. Of the famous Throne Verse, Sale wrote: "It must not be supposed the translation comes up to the dignity of the original."

89. Voltaire, *Essai,* chap. 5, 97; 98.

90. Ibid., chap. 6, 122.

91. Ibid., 123.
92. Sale, "Preliminary Discourse," 30.
93. Voltaire, *Essai,* chap. 7, 148.
94. Ibid., 149.
95. Ibid., chap. 6, 129.
96. Ibid., chap. 7, 159.
97. Ibid., chap. 6, 131.
98. See Chapter 5.
99. Ibid., chap. 7, 153.
100. Ibid., 158.
101. Ibid., chap. 6, 143.
102. Rousseau, *Oeuvres complètes,* 5 vols., ed. B. Gagnebin and M. Raymond (Paris, 1964), 3:462–463.
103. Voltaire, *Essai,* chap. 6, 133.
104. Ibid., 143–144.
105. Ibid., chap. 7, 159–160.
106. Ibid., chap. 6, 132.
107. Ibid. See, for instance, Adam Sutcliffe, *Judaism and Enlightenment* (Cambridge, 2003), chap. 12, and references there. On attitudes toward Judaism among the *philosophes* in general, see David Nirenberg, *Anti-Judaism: The Western Tradition* (New York, 2013), 343–55.
108. Voltaire, *Essai,* chap. 6, 132–133. On Voltaire's anthropology, see Michèle Duchet, *Anthropologie et histoire au siècle des Lumières: Buffon, Voltaire, Rousseau, Helvétius, Diderot* (Paris, 1971), 281–321.
109. Voltaire, *Essai,* chap. 6, 138. The editors suggest that this is a reference to the damage wrought on the Parthenon by the Ottoman-Venetian war of 1687.
110. Ibid.
111. Ibid., 139.
112. Ibid., 141.
113. Ibid., 145, 145–146.
114. Ibid., 146, 146n.
115. Anon., *Critique de l'Histoire universelle de M. de Voltaire, au sujet de Mahomet et du Mahométisme* ([n.p., n.d.]) appeared after 1756 and before 1759.
116. Ibid., 3.
117. Ibid., 7 (chronology), 32 (Caliphs), 15–16 (five pillars), 11 (controversialists), 26 (Shiites).
118. Ibid., 16–18.
119. Ibid., 18–19.
120. Ibid., 27.
121. Ibid., 11–12.

122. Ibid., 12–13.
123. Ibid., 27–29.
124. Ibid., 32–34.
125. Voltaire, *Lettre civile et honnête à l'auteur malhonnête de la Critique de l'histoire universelle* (n.p., [1760]), 1.
126. Ibid., 4.
127. Ibid., 15.
128. Ibid., 16.
129. Ibid., 12.
130. Ibid., 22–23.
131. Ibid., 23.
132. Voltaire also dismissed the critic's reference to Boulainvilliers as a Muslim as an inaccurate libel: ibid., 26–28.
133. See Chapter 3.
134. App, *Birth of Orientalism,* chap. 1. On the role of forgeries in advancing scholarship, see Anthony Grafton, *Forgers and Critics: Creativity and Duplicity in Western Scholarship* (Princeton, N.J., 1990).
135. The question of the *Encyclopédie*'s overall treatment of Islam, and its use of the Republic of Arabic Letters and of other sources, merits a longer treatment than I have space for here. Other entries that treat Islam include "Alcoran ou Al-Coran"; "Fanatisme"; "Imam"; "Islam"; "Mecque, la"; "Médine"; "Sarrasins ou Arabes, philosophie des."
136. Jaucourt, "Mahométisme," in *Encyclopédie,* 9:864–868, here 864.
137. E.g., Arnaldo Momigliano, "Ancient History and the Antiquarian," *Journal of the Warburg and Courtauld Institutes* 13 (1950): 285–315.
138. Voltaire did not reveal his sources or research process to his reader, but Gibbon's footnotes bear testimony both to his research and to his weighing of the evidence. On the comparison of Voltaire and Gibbon, see J. G. A. Pocock, *Barbarism and Religion,* vol. 2, *Narratives of Civil Government* (Cambridge, 1999), chaps. 5–10, esp. chap. 10; Pierre Force, "The 'Exasperating Predecessor': Pocock on Gibbon and Voltaire," *Journal of the History of Ideas* 77 (2016): 129–145.
139. Or, at least, that is how he chose to describe the work's origin. See Gibbon, *Memoirs,* 143.
140. Patricia B. Craddock, *Edward Gibbon, Luminous Historian, 1772–1794* (Baltimore, 1989), 213. Treatments of Gibbon's discussion of Islam: Bernard Lewis, "Gibbon on Muhammad," *Daedalus* 105 (1976): 89–101, also published in *Edward Gibbon and the Decline and Fall of the Roman Empire,* ed. G. W. Bowersock et al. (Cambridge, Mass., 1977), 61–73. Lewis primarily asserts the influence on Gibbon of Boulain-villiers's vision of Muhammad as a wise deist, 98. Jeremy Toner, *Homer's Turk:*

How Classics Shaped Ideas of the East (Cambridge, Mass., 2013), 117–132; Garth Fowden, "Gibbon on Islam," *English Historical Review* 131 (2016): 261–292. While Fowden's account is preferable to Lewis's, Fowden also overstates Gibbon's originality at the expense of the tradition that made possible his work on Islamic history, and treats the writers whom Gibbon consulted merely as sources, rather than as scholars in their own right.

141. Gibbon, *Memoirs,* 67–68.

142. Ibid., 71. *An Universal History from the Earliest Account of Time to the Present, compiled from Original Authors* (London, 1736–1744).

143. William Howell, *An Institution of General History, or the History of the World,* 2 vols., 2nd ed. (London, 1680–1685).

144. Gibbon, *Memoirs,* 72. Pocock, *Barbarism and Religion,* vol. 1, *The Enlightenments of Edward Gibbon, 1737–1764* (Cambridge, 1999), discusses the sources of Gibbon's discovery of Islamic history, 28–42. See also A. J. Arberry, *Oriental Essays* (London, 1960), 33, on this passage.

145. Gibbon, *Memoirs,* 80–82.

146. Ibid., 185n. Ovid, *Metamorphoses,* 4:428.

147. Niccolò Machiavelli, *Discorsi,* bk. 2, preface. See Machiavelli, *The Chief Works and Others,* 3 vols., trans. Allan Gilbert (Durham, N.C., 1989), 1:322.

148. Gibbon, *Memoirs,* 168.

149. Craddock, *Edward Gibbon,* 213.

150. Gibbon, *The Decline and Fall of the Roman Empire* (1788), 6 vols., ed. David Womersley (New York, 1994), 5:85. I have followed the punctuation and spelling of the 1788 edition.

151. Ibid., 5:85.

152. Ibid., 5:230.

153. Ibid., 5:85.

154. Carsten Niebuhr, *Beschreibung von Arabien aus eigenen Beobachtungen und im Lande selbst gesammleten Nachrichten* (Copenhagen, 1772). French trans.: *Description de l'Arabie faite sur des observations propres et des avis recueillis dans les lieux mêmes* (Amsterdam, 1774).

155. Gibbon, *Decline and Fall,* 5:230n.

156. Ibid., 5:270.

157. Ibid., 5:310n1, 331–332, 332n3.

158. Ibid., 5:310n1.

159. Ibid., 5:251.

160. Ibid., 5:234.

161. Ibid., 5:242.

162. Ibid., 5:242n1. Even so, like Reiske, he admired the sentences attributed to ʿAlī b. Abī Ṭālib, which Ockley had translated into English: Simon Ockley,

Sentences of Ali, son-in-law of Mahomet, and his fourth successor: Translated from an authentick Arabick manuscript in the Bodleian library at Oxford (London, 1717).

163. Fowden, "Gibbon on Islam," 275.

164. Gibbon, *Decline and Fall*, 5:305–306.

165. Ibid., 5:258.

166. Ibid., 5:259.

167. Ibid., 5:304.

168. Ibid., 5:260.

169. Ibid., 5:261.

170. Ibid., 5:262.

171. Ibid., 5:262–263.

172. Ibid., 5:263.

173. Ibid., 5:458.

174. Gibbon paraphrased a viewpoint expressed in Edward Pococke, *Specimen Historiæ Arabum: Sive, Gregorii Abul Farajii Malatiensis, de Origine & Moribus Arabum Succincta Narratio, in Linguam Latinam Conversa, Notisque è Probatissimis apud Ipsos Authoribus, Fusiùs Illustrat* (Oxford, 1650), "Notae," 166. See the discussion in Chapter 5.

175. Gibbon, *Decline and Fall*, 6:441.

176. Ibid., 5:458–465.

177. Gibbon cited the "Prodidagmata" elsewhere. See Gibbon, *Decline and Fall*, 5:344n2: "Till something better shall be found [than al-Wāqidī], [Simon Ockley] will not deserve the petulant animadversion of Reiske (Prodidagmata ad Hagji Chalifae Tabulas, p. 236)."

178. Gibbon, *Decline and Fall*, 5:425.

179. Ibid., 5:464. "Freedom of thought" here is to be understood as a view of the opening of the mind occasioned by the reading of the classics—a humanist trope—rather than a more modern notion associated with a liberal, democratic state.

180. Johann Joachim Winckelmann, *Gedanken über die Nachahmung der griechischen Werke in der Malerey und Bildhauerkunst*, 2nd ed. (Dresden, 1756), 21.

181. Gibbon, *Decline and Fall*, 5:465.

182. On Jones, see Garland Cannon, *The Life and Mind of Oriental Jones: Sir William Jones, the Father of Modern Linguistics* (Cambridge, 1990); *ODNB*, s.v. "Jones, Sir William"; Michael J. Franklin, *Orientalist Jones: Sir William Jones, Poet, Lawyer, and Linguist, 1746–1794* (Oxford, 2011).

183. Gibbon, *Decline and Fall*, 5:465n1. The work to which Gibbon refers is William Jones, *Poeseos Asiaticae Commentariorum Libri Sex* (London, 1774).

184. Gibbon, *Decline and Fall,* 5:246n1. The statement is reminiscent of Voltaire's appraisal of Sale's "Preliminary Discourse," above. To Voltaire and Gibbon, the interpretations and the historical context mattered more than the actual literary texts.

185. Gibbon, *Decline and Fall,* 5:465.

186. Ibid.

187. Ibid., 5:332–333.

188. Anna A. Akasoy and Alexander Fidora, eds., *Aristotle: The Arabic Version of the Nicomachean Ethics,* trans. Douglas M. Dunlop (Leiden, 2005). More broadly, see Gutas, *Greek Thought, Arabic Culture,* and the up-to-date bibliography in *EI3,* s.v. "Aristotle and Aristotelianism."

189. Fowden, "Gibbon on Islam," 292, seeks to exculpate Gibbon by blaming "Gibbon's translated sources and the secondary scholarship," but this judgment, as we have seen, gets the relationship exactly wrong.

190. App, *Birth of Orientalism,* chap. 1.

191. Craddock, *Edward Gibbon,* 216.

192. See Dmitri Levitin, "From Sacred History to the History of Religion: Paganism, Judaism, and Christianity in European Historiography from Reformation to 'Enlightenment,'" *Historical Journal* 55 (2012): 1117–1160; Bulman, "Enlightenment for the Culture Wars." See also J. G. A. Pocock, *Barbarism and Religion,* 6 vols. (Cambridge, 1999–2015); Jonathan Sheehan, *The Enlightenment Bible: Translation, Scholarship, Culture* (Princeton, N.J., 2005); David Sorkin, *The Religious Enlightenment: Protestants, Jews, and Catholics from London to Vienna* (Princeton, N.J., 2008); G. J. Toomer, *John Selden: A Life in Scholarship,* 2 vols. (Oxford, 2009); Dan Edelstein, *The Enlightenment: A Genealogy* (Chicago, 2010); Guy G. Stroumsa, *A New Science: The Discovery of Religion in the Age of Reason* (Cambridge, Mass., 2010); Anthony Ossa-Richardson, *The Devil's Tabernacle: The Pagan Oracles in Early Modern Thought* (Princeton, N.J., 2013); William J. Bulman, *Anglican Enlightenment: Orientalism, Religion, and Politics in England and Its Empire, 1648–1715* (Cambridge, 2015); Dmitri Levitin, *Ancient Philosophy in the Age of the New Science: Histories of Philosophy in England, c. 1640–1700* (Cambridge, 2015); William J. Bulman and Robert G. Ingram, eds., *God in the Enlightenment* (Oxford, 2016); Anthony Grafton, "Spinoza's Hermeneutics: Some Heretical Thoughts," in *Scriptural Authority and Biblical Criticism in the Dutch Golden Age: God's Word Questioned* (Oxford, forthcoming).

193. See, e.g., Stroumsa, *New Science;* Levitin, *Ancient Philosophy.*

194. Bulman, "Enlightenment for the Culture Wars," 6.

195. In J. G. A. Pocock's interpretation, the fruits of English clerical learning (the work of Pococke and Ockley) were to nourish Gibbon's engagement with

philosophical history. Pocock, *Barbarism and Religion,* i, 42. These stylized distinctions, however, occlude the fact that, for instance, Pococke and Ockley's statements about Islamic learning were adopted wholesale by Gibbon.

196. Sebastian Conrad, "Enlightenment in Global History: A Historiographical Critique," *American Historical Review* 117 (2012): 999–1027.

EPILOGUE

1. Among others, see Norbert Elias, *The Civilizing Process: Sociogenetic and Psychogenetic Investigations,* rev. ed., trans. E. Jephcott (1939; repr., Malden, Mass., 2000); Jean Dagen, *L'histoire de l'esprit humain dans la pensée française de Fontenelle à Condorcet* (Paris, 1977); Ann Thomson, *Barbary and Enlightenment: European Attitudes towards the Maghreb in the 18th Century* (Leiden, 1987); Jonathan Dewald, *Aristocratic Experience and the Origins of Modern Culture in France, 1500–1715* (Berkeley, 1993); J. G. A. Pocock, *Barbarism and Religion,* vol. 1, *The Enlightenments of Edward Gibbon, 1737–1764* (Cambridge, 1999), chap. 8; Larry F. Norman, *The Shock of the Ancient: Literature and History in Early Modern France* (Chicago, 2011). "Europe" was not a united block, of course, and the sense of superiority created fissures even within the continent: see, e.g., Michael Broers, "Cultural Imperialism in a European Context? Political Culture and Cultural Politics in Napoleonic Italy," *Past and Present* 170 (2001): 152–180.

2. On coffee, see Robert Paris, *De 1660 à 1789: Le Levant,* vol. 5 of *Histoire du commerce de Marseille,* ed. Gaston Rambert (Paris, 1957), 450, 464; Edhem Eldem, *French Trade in Istanbul in the Eighteenth Century* (Leiden, 1999), 75–80.

3. Rifaat Abou-El-Haj, "The Formal Closure of the Ottoman Frontier in Europe, 1699–1703," *Journal of the American Oriental Society* 89 (1969): 467–475; Immanuel Wallerstein, "The Ottoman Empire and the Capitalist World-Economy: Some Questions for Research," in *Social and Economic History of Turkey, 1071–1920,* ed. O. Okyar and H. Inalcik (Ankara, 1980), 117–122; Immanuel Wallerstein et al., *Incorporation of the Ottoman Empire into the World-Economy: An Overview* (Berlin, 1982); Murat Çizakça, "Incorporation of the Middle East into the European World-Economy," *Review* 8 (1985): 353–377; Bruce A. Masters, *The Origins of Western Economic Dominance in the Middle East: Mercantilism and the Islamic Economy in Aleppo, 1600–1750* (New York, 1988); Michel Fontenay, "The Mediterranean, 1500–1800: Social and Economic Perspectives," in *Venice and Hospitaller Malta, 1530–1798: Aspects of a Relationship,* ed. Victor Mallia-Milanes (Msida, Malta, 1993), 43–110; Edhem Eldem, "Capitulations and Western Trade," in *The Cambridge History of Turkey,* vol. 3, *The Later Ottoman Empire, 1603–1839,* ed. Suraiya Faroqhi (Cambridge, 2006), chap. 14; Molly Greene, "Islam and Europe," in *A Companion to Eighteenth-Century Europe,* ed. Peter H. Wilson (Oxford, 2009), chap. 24.

4. Johann David Michaelis, *Arabische Grammatik. Nebst einer arabischen Chrestomathie, und Abhandlung vom arabischen Geschmack, sonderlich in der poetischen und historischen Schreibart,* 2nd ed. (Göttingen, 1781), "Vorrede zur ersten Ausgabe;" Olaus Domey, *Nova Versio Partis Surae II. Corani, cum Illustrationibus Subiectis: Specimen Novae Versionis Totius Corani* (Göttingen, 1754); Jan Loop, "Kontroverse Bemühungen um den Orient," in *Johann Jacob Reiske: Leben und Wirkung: Ein Leipziger Byzantinist und Begründer der Orientalistik im 18. Jahrhundert,* ed. Hans-Georg Ebert and Thoralf Hanstein (Leipzig, 2005), 45–85.

5. Alastair Hamilton, " 'To Rescue the Honour of the Germans': Qur'an Translations by Eighteenth and Early Nineteenth-Century German Protestants," *Journal of the Warburg and Courtauld Institutes* 77 (2014): 173–209.

6. Peter van Rooden, "Willem Surenhuys' Translation of the Mishna and the Strange Death of Christian Hebraism," in *Reuchlin und seine Erben: Forscher, Denker, Ideologen und Spinner,* ed. Peter Schäfer and Irina Wandrey (Ostfildern, 2005), 97–111.

7. Jean Gaulmier, "A la découverte du Proche-Orient: Barthélemy d'Herbelot et sa *Bibliothèque Orientale,*" *Bulletin de la Faculté des Lettres de Strasbourg* 48 (1969): 4–6.

8. Antoine-Isaac Silvestre de Sacy, "Mémoire sur quelques événemens de l'Histoire des Arabes avant Mahomet," *Mémoires de littérature, tirés des registres de l'Académie royale des inscriptions et belles lettres* 48 (1808): 484–626; Silvestre de Sacy, "Mémoire sur l'origine et les anciens monumens de la littérature parmi les Arabes," *Mémoires de littérature, tirés des registres de l'Académie royale des inscriptions et belles lettres* 50 (1808): 247–412.

Selected Bibliography

This bibliography does not list all sources cited in the notes, but only the most important unpublished materials and secondary works. It is intended especially for those who wish to pursue this subject further.

1. Archival Sources

BATH, CENTRAL LIBRARY
SAL 1 / 1

CAMBRIDGE UNIVERSITY LIBRARY
Ms. Add. 3466, 7513
SPCK MS. A1 / 12; Ms. A32 / 1; Ms. D5 / 4

COPENHAGEN, DET KONGELIGE BIBLIOTEK
Bøll. Brevs. U 2° 251
Cod. Arab. 172
NKS 133 20
Uncatalogued Reiske papers

COPENHAGEN, RIGSARKIVET
Reviderede regnskaber, Videnskabelige Institutioner m.m. Kaptajn C. Niebuhrs rejse
    1760–1767

FLORENCE, BIBLIOTECA NAZIONALE CENTRALE
Magl. VIII, 572; Magl. VIII, 388; Magl. VIII, serie 3, vol. 1; Magl. VIII, 1356.
    II, II, 115

GÖTTINGEN, NIEDERSÄCHSISCHE STAATS-UND UNIVERSITÄTSBIBLIOTHEK
Mich. 294; Ms. Pers. 8

THE HAGUE, KONINKLIJKE BIBLIOTHEEK
72 G 5, 72 G 6

SELECTED BIBLIOGRAPHY

LEIDEN UNIVERSITY LIBRARY

Cod. Or. 554

LONDON, BRITISH LIBRARY

Ms Add. 34727, Harleian MS 1876

LONDON, METROPOLITAN ARCHIVE

CLC / 180 Ms. 20185 / 11

OXFORD, BODLEIAN LIBRARY

Mss. Sale 41, 48–49, 56, 67, 68, 69, 70, 77, 78, 82
MS. Laud Or. 163

PADUA, ARCHIVIO DEL SEMINARIO MAGGIORE DI PADOVA

Archivio del Seminario Maggiore, vol. 122

PARIS, BIBLIOTHÈQUE NATIONALE DE FRANCE

Estampes, Od. 5–4
Ms. Arabe 4458; 4844–4849
Ms. Français 6130, 25280
Ms. Ital. 478, 480
Ms. Nouvelles Acquisitions Françaises 5384, 5408, 5764, 5765, 7477, 7478, 8943, 8972
Ms. Supplément grec 932

PARIS, BIBLIOTHÈQUE MAZARINE

Ms. 1587 pièce 85

ROME, ARCHIVIO STORICO DI PROPAGANDA FIDE

SOCG (Scritture originali riferite nelle Congregazioni Generali) 502, 504
 Congressi Stamperia I

ROME, ORDINE DELLA MADRE DI DIO

Marracci Mss. I, II, III, IV, XI, XII, XIII

VATICAN CITY, BIBLIOTECA APOSTOLICA VATICANA

Archivio della Biblioteca 26, 27, 34
Cod. vaticano Arabo 206; Cod. vaticano siriaco 446

VENICE, ARCHIVIO DEL SEMINARIO PATRIARCALE

Ms. 1168; Ms. 1169; Ms. 1170 (già 586); Ms. 1171 (già 587); Ms. 1172 (già 588)

SELECTED BIBLIOGRAPHY

VENICE, BIBLIOTECA MARCIANA
Cod. CLXXVII (= 202); CLXXVIII (= 134); CLXXXIII (= 160)

VIENNA, ÖSTERREICHISCHE NATIONALBIBLIOTHEK
Altprunk 12.C.9

YALE UNIVERSITY, BEINECKE RARE BOOK & MANUSCRIPT LIBRARY
General Collection, Gen Mss. File 80

2. Annotated Printed Books

Cambridge University Library, shelfmark C.1.22
Columbia University, Rare Book & Manuscript Library, shelfmark B893.7K84.J81
Harvard University, Houghton Library, shelfmark OL 2482.2F
Lucca, Biblioteca Statale, shelfmark S.M.N. 332.9
Madrid, Biblioteca Nacional de España, shelfmark 2 / 41438
Paris, Bibliothèque nationale de France, shelfmark Fol-O2G-126 (2)

3. Printed Sources before 1800

Adler, Jacob Georg Christian, ed. *Abulfedae Annales Muslemici Arabice et Latine.* 5 vols. Copenhagen: F. W. Thiele, C. G. Proft, 1789–1794.

Agapitus a valle Flemmarum. *Flores Grammaticales Arabici Idiomatis Collecti ex Optimis Quibusque Grammaticis.* Padua: Ex Typographia Seminarii, 1687.

Agnellini, Timoteo. *Adagii turcheschi con la parafrase latina et italiana.* Padua: Nella stamperia del Seminario, 1688.

———. *Libro della Penitenza e Passione di Gesù Christo e di sua santissima madre, in arabo e italiano.* 3 vols. Padua: Nella stamperia del Seminario, 1693.

———. *Proverbii utili, e virtuosi in lingua araba, persiana, e turca, gran parte in versi, con la loro ispiegatione in Lingua Latina, e Italiana.* Padua: Nella stamperia del Seminario, 1688.

Andrès, Juan. *Confusion de la secta mahomatica y del alcoran.* Valencia: Juan Joffre, 1515.

Anquetil-Duperron, Abraham-Hyacinthe. *Législation orientale.* Amsterdam: Chez Marc-Michel Rey, 1778.

Assemani, Giuseppe Simonio. *Bibliotheca Orientalis Clementino-Vaticana.* 4 vols. Rome: Typis Sacræ Congregationis de Propaganda Fide, 1719–1728 [–1730].

Assemani, Stefano Evodio. *Bibliothecae Mediceae Laurentianae et Palatinae Codicum Mss. Orientalium Catalogus.* Florence: Ex Typographio Albiziniano, 1742.

Assemani, Stefano Evodio, and Giuseppe Simonio Assemani. *Bibliothecae Apostolicae Vaticanae Codicum Manuscriptorum Catalogus.* 3 vols. Rome: Ex Typographia

Linguarum Orientalium apud Hæredes Barbiellini ad Forum Pasquini, 1756–1758 [–1759].

Bacon, Francis. *New Atlantis: A Worke unfinished,* published together with *Sylva sylvarum, or, a naturall history in ten centuries.* London: Printed by J. H. for William Lee, 1626.

Bandini, Angelo Maria. *Dei princìpi e progressi della Real Biblioteca Mediceo Laurenziana: Ms. Laur. Acquisti e Doni 142.* Edited by Rosario Pintaudi, Mario Tesi, and Anna Rita Fantoni. Florence, 1990.

Biblia Sacra Arabica, Sacræ Congregationis de Propaganda Fide Iussu Edita ad Usum Ecclesiarum Orientalium. 3 vols. Rome: Typis Sacræ Congregationis de Propaganda Fide, 1671.

Bibliotheca Schultensiana, sive Catalogus Librorum Quos Collegit Vir Clarissimus Johannes Jacobus Schultensius. Leiden: H. Mostert, 1780.

Bogdanus, Pietro. *Cuneus Prophetarum.* Padua: Ex Typographia Seminarii, 1685.

Boulainvilliers, Henri de. *La vie de Mahomed: Avec des réflexions sur la religion mahometane, et les coutumes des musulmans.* London [i.e., Amsterdam]: Chez Pierre Humbert, 1731.

Brerewood, Edward. *Recherches cvrievses svr la diversité des langves et religions: Par toutes les principales parties du monde . . . et mises en françois par I. de Montagne.* Paris: chez Olivier de Varennes, 1640.

Buchmann, Theodor, ed. *Machumetis Saracenorum Principis, Eiusque Successorum Vitae, ac Doctrina, Ipseque Alcoran.* Basel: Ioannes Oporinus, 1543.

Casiri, Miguel. *Bibliotheca Arabico-Hispana Escurialensis.* 2 vols. Madrid: Antonius Perez de Soto Matriti, 1760–1770.

Castell, Edmund. *Lexicon Heptaglotton Hebraicum, Chaldaicum, Syriacum, Samaritanum, Aethiopicum, Arabicum, Conjunctim, et Persicum, Separatim.* London: Thomas Roycroft, 1669.

Catalogus Bibliothecae Quam Reliquit Henricus Albertus Schultens. Leiden: A. and J. Honkoop, 1794.

Chardin, Jean. *Journal du voyage du Chevalier Chardin en Perse.* London: Moses Pitt, 1686.

Critique de l'Histoire universelle de M. de Voltaire, au sujet de Mahomet et du Mahométisme. [n.p., n.d.]

Diderot, Denis, and Jean Le Rond d'Alembert, eds. *Encyclopédie, ou, Dictionnaire raisonné des sciences, des arts et des métiers.* 17 vols. Paris: Chez Briasson, David l'aîné, Le Breton, Durand, 1751–1765.

Dieu, Lodewijk de. *Rudimenta linguae persicae.* Leiden: Ex officina Elseviriana, 1639.

Disegno dello Stendardo del Primo Visire levato sotto Vienna dal Serenissimo e Invittissimo Giovanni Terzo Rè di Polonia, e da Sua Maestà Mandato alla Santità di nostro Signore Papa Innocenzo Undecimo, Aggiuntavi la vera interpretatione delle parole Arabiche, che in detto Stendardo sono artificiosamente intessute. Rome and Bologna: Per Giacomo Monti, 1683.

Domey, Olaus. *Nova versio partis surae II Corani.* Göttingen: P. Ch. Hager, 1754.

Du Ryer, André. *Gulistan, ou l'empire des roses, composé par Sadi.* Paris: Chez Anthoine de Sommaville, 1634.

Ecchellensis, Abraham, and Giovanni Alfonso Borelli. *Apollonii Pergæi conicorum lib. V, VI, VII, paraphraste Abalphato Aspahahanensi. . . .* Florence: Iosephi Cocchini ad insigne Stellæ, 1661.

Erpenius, Thomas. *Grammatica arabica.* Leiden: Officina Raphelengiana, 1613.

Gagnier, John. *De vita et rebus gestis Mohammedis.* Oxford: E Theatro Sheldoniano, 1723.

Galland, Antoine. *Journal d'Antoine Galland pendant son séjour à Constantinople (1672–1673).* 2 vols. Edited by Charles Schefer. Paris, 1881.

———. *Les Paroles remarquables, les bons mots et les maximes des orientaux.* Paris: Simon Benard et Michel Brunet, 1694.

Gentius, George. *Musladini Sadi Rosarium politicum: Sive Amoenum sortis humanae theatrum.* Amsterdam: Ex Typographeio Joannis Blaeu, 1651.

Gessner, Conrad. *Bibliotheca universalis.* Zurich: Apud Christophorum Froschouerum, 1545.

Gibbon, Edward. *The Decline and Fall of the Roman Empire.* 6 vols. Edited by David Womersley. 1788; repr., New York, 1994.

———. *Memoirs of My Life.* Edited by B. Radice. 1795; repr., London, 1984.

Giggi, Antonio. *Thesaurus linguae Arabicae.* Milan: Ex Ambrosiani Collegii Typographia, 1632.

Golius, Jacobus. *Arabicae Linguae Tyrocinium.* Leiden: Ioannis Maire, 1656.

———. *Lexicon Arabico-Latinum Contextum ex Probatioribus Orientis Lexicographis: Accedit Index Latinus Copiosissimus, Qui Lexici Latino-Arabici Vicem Explere Possit.* Leiden: Typis Bonaventurae et Abrahami Elseviriorum, 1653.

González de Santalla, Tirso. *Manuductio ad Conversionem Mohametanorum.* 2 vols. Madrid, [Ex officina Bernardi de Villa-Diego], 1687.

Greaves, John. *Chorasmiae et Mawaralnahrae: Hoc Est Regionum extra Fluvium Oxum Descriptio ex Tabulis Abulfedae Ismaelis.* London: s.n., 1650.

———. *Elementa Linguae Persicae.* London: Typis Jacobi Flesher, 1649.

Grelot, Guillaume-Joseph. *Relation nouvelle d'un voyage de Constantinople.* Paris: Chez la veuve de Damien Foucault, 1680.

Grotius, Hugo. *De Veritate Religionis Christianae.* 2nd ed. Leiden: Ex officina Ioannis Maire, 1629.

Guadagnoli, Filippo. *Breves Arabicae Linguae Institutiones.* Rome: Ex Typographia Sacræ Congregationis de Propaganda Fide, 1642.

Guignes, Joseph de. *Essai historique sur la typographie orientale et grecque de l'Imprimerie royale.* Paris: s.n., 1787.

Hamerton, William. *A Choice Collection of Most Curious and Inestimable Manuscripts, In the Turkish, Arabic and Persian Languages, from the Library of the late Learned and Ingenious Mr. George Sale.* London: Hamerton, [1736].

d'Herbelot de Molainville, Barthélemy. *Bibliothèque Orientale, Ou, Dictionaire Universel: Contenant Généralement Tout ce qui regarde la connoissance des Peuples de l'Orient. Leurs Histoires et Traditions Véritables Ou Fabuleuses. Leurs Religions, Sectes et Politique. Leurs Gouvernement, Loix, Coûtumes, Mœurs, Guerres, et les Révolutions de leurs Empires. Leurs Sciences, et Leurs Arts. Leurs Théologie, Mythologie, Magie, Physique, Morale, Médecine, Mathématiques, Histoire naturelle, Chronologie, Géographie, Observations Astronomiques, Grammaire, et Réthorique. Les Vies et Actions Remarquables de Tous Leurs Saints, Docteurs, Philosophes, Historiens, Poëtes, Capitaines, et de tous ceux qui se sont rendus illustres parmi eux, par leur Vertu, ou par leur Savoir. Des Jugemens Critiques, et des Extraits de Tous Leurs Ouvrages, De leurs Traitez, Traductions, Commentaires, Abregez, Recüeils de Fables, de Sentences, de Maximes, de Proverbes, de Contes, de bons Mots, et de tous leurs Livres écrits en Arabe, en Persan, ou en Turc, sur toutes sortes de Sciences, d'Arts, et de Professions.* Paris: La Compagnie des libraires, 1697.

———. *Bibliothèque Orientale.* Maastricht: J. E. Dufour et P. Roux, 1776.

———. *Bibliothèque Orientale.* 4 vols. Rev. ed. The Hague: J. Neaulme and N. van Daalen, 1777–1779.

———. *Bibliothèque Orientale.* 6 vols. Edited by Nicolas-Toussaint Lemoyne des Essarts. Rev. ed. Paris: Moutard, 1781–1783.

———. *Orientalische Bibliothek: Universalwörterbuch, welches alles enthält, was zur Kenntniss des Orients nothwendig ist.* 4 vols. Translated by J. C. F. Schulz. Halle: J. J. Gebauer, 1785–1790.

Hinckelmann, Abraham. *Al-Coranus S. Lex Islamitica Muhammedis, Filii Abdallæ Pseudoprophetæ.* Hamburg: Ex officina Schultzio-Schilleriana, 1694.

Hoornbeeck, Johannes. *Summa Controversiarum Religionis cum Infidelibus, Hæreticis, Schismaticis.* Utrecht: Ex officina Johannis Waesberge, 1653.

Hottinger, Johann Heinrich. *Historia Orientalis.* Zurich: Typis Joh. Jacobi Bodmeri, 1651.

Hume, David. *Essays, Moral and Literary.* Edited by Eugene F. Miller. Indianapolis, 1987.

Hyde, Thomas. *Historia Religionis Veterum Persarum, Eorumque Magorum.* Oxford: E Theatro Sheldoniano, 1700.

Index Librorum Prohibitorum Clementis X. Rome: Ex Typographia Rev. Cam. Apost., 1670.

Jones, William. *A Grammar of the Persian Language.* London: W. A. J. Richardson, 1771.

————. *Poeseos Asiaticae Commentariorum Libri Sex.* London: E typographeo Rich-ardsoniano, 1774.

Köhler, Johann Bernhard. *Abulfedae Tabula Syriae cum Excerpto Geographico ex Ibn ol Wardii: Accessere Io. Iacobi Reiskii V. C. Animadversiones ad Abulfedam et Pro-didagmata ad Historiam et Geographiam Orientalem.* Leipzig: Litteris Schoener-markii, 1766.

Machiavelli, Niccolò. *The Chief Works and Others.* 3 vols. Translated by Allan Gilbert. 1965; repr., Durham, N.C., 1989.

Marracci, Lodovico. *Alcorani Textus Universus: ex Correctioribus Arabum Exemplar-ibus Summa Fide, atque Pulcherrimis Characteribus Descriptus: Eademque Fide, ac Pari Diligentia ex Arabico Idiomate in Latinum Translatus: Appositis Unicuique Capiti Notis, atque Refutatione: His Omnibus Praemissus Est Prodromus Totum Priorem Tomum Implens, in Quo Contenta Indicantur Pagina Sequenti.* 2 vols. Padua: Ex Typographia Seminarii, 1698.

————. *L'ebreo preso per le buone, o vero discorsi familiari, et amichevoli fatti con i Rab-bini di Roma intorno al Messia.* Rome: Per gli Eredi del Corbelletti, 1701.

————. *Prodromus ad Refutationem Alcorani in Quo per Quatuor Praecipuas Verae Religionis Notas Mahumetanae Sectae Falsitas Ostenditur: Christianae Religionis Veritas Comprobatur.* 4 vols. Rome: Typis Sacræ Congregationis de Propaganda Fide, 1691.

————. "Vita Innocentii Papae Exarata a P. Ludovico Marracci Qui Ipsi Fuit a Con-fessionibus." In Mattia Giuseppe Lippi, *Vita di Papa Innocenzo XI raccolta in tre libri.* Rome, 1889.

Martelotto, Francesco. *Institutiones Linguae Arabicae.* Rome: Stephanus Paulinus, 1620.

Mehmed Efendi. *Relation de l'ambassade de Mehemet-Effendi à la cour de France en 1721, écrite par lui-même et trad. du turc.* Translated by Julien-Claude Galland. Constantinople [i.e., Paris], Chez Ganeau, 1757. Reprinted as *Le paradis des in-fidèles: Relation de Yirmisekiz Çelebi Mehmed efendi, ambassadeur ottoman en France sous la Régence.* Paris, 1981.

Meninski, Franciscus à Mesgnien. *Linguarum Orientalium Turcicae, Arabicae, Persicae Institutiones, seu Grammatica Turcica.* Vienna: Printed by author, 1680.

————. *Thesaurus Linguarum Orientalium Turcicae, Arabicae et Persicae.* 4 vols. Vi-enna: Printed by author, 1680.

Michaelis, Johann David. *Arabische Grammatik: Nebst einer arabischen Chrestoma-thie, und Abhandlung vom arabischen Geschmack, sonderlich in der poetischen und historischen Schreibart,* 2nd ed. Göttingen: Verlegt von Victorin Bossiegel, ge-druckt bey Johann Christian Dieterich, 1781.

————. *Lebensbeschreibung von ihm selbst aufgefasst.* Leipzig: Johann Ambrosius Barth, 1793.

———. *Mosaisches Recht.* 6 vols. Frankfurt am Main: Johann Gottlieb Garbe, 1770–1775.

Montesquieu. *De l'esprit des lois.* In *Oeuvres complètes,* 2 vols., edited by Roger Caillois. Paris, 1951.

———. *Lettres persanes.* In *Oeuvres complètes de Montesquieu,* vol. 1, edited by Jean Ehrard and Catherine Volpilhac-Auger. Oxford, 2004.

———. *The Spirit of the Laws.* Edited and translated by Anne M. Cohler et al. Cambridge, 1989.

Moréri, Louis. *Le grand dictionnaire historique.* 10 vols. 20th ed. Paris: Les libraires associés, 1759.

Mylaeus, C. *De Scribenda Universitatis Rerum Historia.* Basel: Ex off. J. Oporini, 1551.

Naudé, Gabriel. *Advis pour dresser une bibliothèque.* Paris: F. Targa, 1627.

Nicholas of Cusa. *Nicolai de Cusa Opera Omnia.* Vol. 8, *Cribratio Alkorani* (1460–1461). Edited by Louis Hagemann. Hamburg, 1932.

Ockley, Simon. *The Conquest of Syria, Persia, and Ægypt, by the Saracens: Containing the Lives of Abubeker, Omar and Othman, the immediate Successors of Mahomet. Giving an Account of their most remarkable Battles, Sieges, &c. particularly those of Aleppo, Antioch, Damascus, Alexandria and Jerusalem. Illustrating the Religion, Rites, Customs and Manner of Living of that Warlike People. Collected from the most Authentick Arabick Authors, especially Manuscripts, not hitherto publish'd in any European Language.* London: Printed for R. Knaplock in St. Paul's Church-Yard, J. Sprint in Little Britain, R. Smith in Cornhill, B. Lintott in Fleetstreet, and J. Round in Exchange-Alley, 1708.

———. *The History of the Saracens: Containing the lives of Abubeker, Omar, Othman, Ali, Hasan, Moawiyah I, Yezid I, Moawiyah II, Abdolla, Merwan I, and Abdòl mélick, the immediate Successors of Mahomet. Giving an Account of their most remarkable Battles, Sieges, &c. particularly those of Aleppo, Antioch, Damascus, Alexandria and Jerusalem. Illustrating the Religion, Rites, Customs and Manner of Living of that Warlike People. Collected from the most Authentick Arabick Authors, especially Manuscripts, not hitherto publish'd in any European Language.* 2 vols. 2nd ed. London: Printed for R. Knaplock in St. Paul's Church-Yard, J. Sprint in Little Britain, R. Smith in Cornhill, B. Lintot in Fleetstreet, and J. Round in Exchange-Alley, 1718.

———. *Sentences of Ali, son-in-law of Mahomet, and his fourth successor. Translated from an authentick Arabick manuscript in the Bodleian library at Oxford.* London: B. Lintot, 1717.

Olearius, Adam. *Persianischer Rosenthal: In welchem viel lustige Historien, scharffsinnige Reden und nützliche Regeln / vor 400. Jahren von einem sinnreichen Poeten Schich Saadi in Persischer Sprach beschrieben.* Schleswig: Johann Holwein, 1654.

Peter the Venerable. "Epistola de Translatione Sua." In *Bibliotheca Cluniacensis,* edited by Martin Marrier and Andreas Quercetanus. 1614; repr., Brussels and Paris, 1915.

———. *Petrus Venerabilis Schriften zum Islam.* Edited and translated by Reinhold F. Glei. Altenberge, 1985.

Prideaux, Humphrey. *The True Nature of Imposture Fully Display'd in the Life of Mahomet. With a discourse annexed, for the vindicating of Christianity from this charge; offered to the consideration of the deists of the present age.* London: Printed by J. H. for William Rogers, 1697.

Pococke, Edward. *Appendix Notarum Miscellanea.* Oxford: Excudebat H. Hall, 1654.

———. *Historia Compendiosa Dynastiarum.* Oxford: Excudebat H. Hall, impensis R. Davis, 1663.

———. *Porta Mosis.* Oxford: Excudebat H. Hall, impensis R. Davis, 1655.

———. *Specimen Historiæ Arabum: Sive, Gregorii Abul Farajii Malatiensis, de origine & moribus Arabum succincta narratio, in linguam latinam conversa, notisque è probatissimis apud ipsos authoribus, fusiùs illustrat.* Oxford: Excudebat H. Hall, impensis Humph. Robinson, 1650.

Le Prince, N[icolas]-T[homas]. *Essai historique sur la Bibliothèque du Roi.* Paris: Bibliothèque du Roi, 1782.

Raphelengius, Franciscus. *Lexicon Arabicum.* Leiden: Officina Raphelengiana, 1613.

Reiske, Johann Jacob. *Abilfedae Annales Moslemici Latinos Ex Arabicis Fecit. . . .* Leipzig: Officina Gleditschiana, 1754.

———. "Abilfedae Opus Geographicum." *Magazin für die neue Historie und Geographie,* pt. 4 (1770).

———. *D. Johann Jacob Reiskens von ihm selbst aufgesetzte Lebensbeschreibung.* Leipzig: Buchhandlung der Gelehrten, 1783.

———. *Dissertatio de Principibus Muhammedanis Qui aut Eruditione aut ab Amore Literarum et Literatorum Claruerunt.* Leipzig: Breitkopf, 1747.

———. "Prodidagmata ad Hagji Chalifae Librum Memorialem." In Johann Bernhard Köhler, *Abulfedae Tabula Syriae cum Excerpto Geographico ex Ibn ol Wardii.* Leipzig: Litteris Schoenermarkii, 1766.

———. *Tharaphae Moallakah: Cum Scholiis Nahas e Mss. Leidensibus.* Leiden: Apud Joannem Luzac, 1742.

Reland, Adriaan. *De Religione Mohammedica Libri Duo: Quorum Prior Exhibet Compendium Theologiae Mohammedicae . . . Posterior Examinat Nonnulla, quae Falso Mohammedanis Tribuuntur.* Utrecht: Broedelet, 1705.

———. *De Religione Mohammedica Libri Duo.* 2nd ed. Utrecht: G. Broedelet, 1717.

———. *Four Treatises concerning the Doctrine, Discipline and Worship of the Mahometans.* London: J. Darby for B. Lintott, and E. Sanger, 1712.

———. *La religion des Mahométans: Exposée par leurs propres Docteurs avec des éclaircissemens sur les opinions qu'on leur a faussement attribuées.* Translated by David Durand. The Hague: Isaac Vaillant, 1721.

———. *Palaestina, ex Monumentis Veteribus Illustrata.* Utrecht: G. Broedelet, 1714.

"Relation abrégée du voyage litteraire que M. l'Abbé Fourmont a fait dans le Levant par ordre du Roy, dans les années 1719 et 1730." *Histoire de l'Académie royale des Inscriptions et Belles-Lettres* 7 (1738): 344–358.

Renaudot, Eusèbe. *Anciennes relations des Indes et de la Chine de deux voyageurs mahométans qui y allèrent dans le neuviéme siècle; traduites d'arabe: avec des Remarques sur les principaux endroits de ces Relations.* Paris: Jean-Baptiste Coignard, 1718.

———. *Historia Patriarcharum Alexandrinorum Jacobitarum.* Paris: Francis Fournier, 1713.

———. *Liturgiarum Orientalium Collectio.* 2 vols. Paris: Jean-Baptiste Coignard, 1715–1716.

Rousseau, Jean-Jacques. *The Social Contract and Other Later Political Writings.* Edited and translated by Victor Gourevitch. Cambridge, 1997.

———. *Oeuvres complètes.* 5 vols. Edited by B. Gagnebin and M. Raymond. Paris, 1959–1995.

Rycaut, Paul. *The Present State of the Ottoman Empire.* London: Printed for John Starkey and Henry Brome, 1667.

Sale, George. *The Koran, Commonly Called the Alcoran of Mohammed, Translated into English immediately from the Original Arabic; with Explanatory Notes, taken from the Most Approved Commentators. To which is prefixed A Preliminary Discourse.* London: Printed by C. Ackers for J. Wilcox, 1734 [1733].

———. *Observations historiques et critiques sur le Mahométisme, ou Traduction du discours préliminaire mis à la tête de la version anglaise de l'*Alcoran, *publiée par George Sale.* Geneva: Chez Barrillot et Fils, 1751.

Schultens, Albert. *Vita et Res Gestæ Sultani, Almalichi Alnasiri, Saladini, Abi Modaffiri Josephi f. Jobi, f. Sjadsi. Auctore Bohadino f. Sjeddadi. Nec Non Excerpta ex Historia Universali Abulfedæ, Easdem Res Gestas, Reliquamque Historiam Temporis, Compendiose Exhibentia.* Leiden: Apud Samuelem Luchtmans, 1732.

Selden, John, and Edward Pococke. *Contextio Gemmarum sive, Eutychii Patriarchae Alexandrini Annales.* 2 vols. Oxford: Excudebat H. Hall, 1654, 1656.

Silvestre de Sacy, Antoine-Isaac. "Mémoire sur l'origine et les anciens monumens de la littérature parmi les Arabes." *Mémoires de littérature, tirés des registres de l'Académie royale des inscriptions et belles lettres* 50 (1808): 247–412.

———. "Mémoire sur quelques événemens de l'Histoire des Arabes avant Mahomet." *Mémoires de littérature, tirés des registres de l'Académie royale des inscriptions et belles lettres* 48 (1808): 484–626.

Simon, Richard. *Additions aux "Recherches curieuses sur la diversité des langues et religions" d'Edward Brerewood.* Edited by Jacques Le Brun and John D. Woodbridge. Paris, 1983.

———. *Bibliothèque critique.* 4 vols. Amsterdam: Jean Louis de Lormes, 1708–1710.

———. *Cérémonies et coutumes qui s'observent aujourd'hui parmi les Juifs.* Paris: Louis Billaine, 1674.

———. *Histoire critique de la créance et des coutumes des nations du Levant.* Frankfurt: F. Arnaud, 1684.

———. *Histoire critique du Vieux Testament.* Paris: Imprimé par M. Clark, 1678.

———. *Lettres choisies.* 3 vols. Rotterdam: R. Leers, 1705.

———[Nicolas Barat, pseud.]. *Nouvelle Bibliothèque Choisie.* 2 vols. Amsterdam: David Mortier, 1714.

———. *Voyage du Mont Liban traduit de l'italien du R. P. Jérôme Dandini, nonce en ce pais-la, où il est traité tant de la créance & des coûtumes des Maronites que de pleusieurs particularitez touchant les Turcs, et de quelques lieux considérables de l'Orient, avec des remarques sur la théologie des Chrétiens du Levant et sur celle des Mahométans. Par R.S.P.* Paris: Chez Louis Billaine, 1675.

Spanheim, Friedrich. *Opera Omnia.* 3 vols. Leiden: Apud C. Boutestein, J. Luchtmans, 1701–1703.

Stubbe, Henry. *An Account of the Rise and Progress of Mahometanism: With the Life of Mahomet and a Vindication of Him and His Religion from the Calumnies of the Christians; from a Manuscript Copied by Charles Hornby of Pipe Office, in 1705, with Some Variations and Additions.* Edited by Mahmud Khan Shairani. London, 1911.

———. *Henry Stubbe and the Beginnings of Islam: The Originall & Progress of Mahometanism.* Edited by Nabil Matar. New York, 2014.

Thévenot, Jean de. *Les voyages aux Indes Orientales.* Edited by Françoise de Valence. 1689; repr., Paris, 2008.

———. *Relation d'un voyage fait au Levant. . . .* Paris: Thomas Joly, 1664.

Toderini, Gian Battista. *Letteratura turchesca.* Vol. 3, *Tipografia turca.* Venice: G. Storti, 1787.

Toland, John. *Mangoneutes.* London: J. Brotherton and W. Meadows et al., 1720.

———. *Nazarenus, or Jewish, Gentile, and Mahometan Christianity.* London: J. Brown, J. Roberts, and J. Brotherton, 1718.

Voltaire. *Commentaire sur l'esprit des loix de Montesquieu.* [Paris]: s.n., 1778.

———. *Corpus des notes marginales de Voltaire.* 10 vols. Edited by Natalia Elaguina. Oxford, 2008–.

———. *Essai sur les mœurs et l'esprit des nations.* 9 vols. Edited by Bruno Bernard, John Renwick, Nicholas Cronk, and Janet Godden. Oxford, 2009–2017. (= *Oeuvres complètes de Voltaire,* vols. 21A–27.)

———. *Le fanatisme, ou, Mahomet le prophète.* Edited by Christopher Todd and Ahmad Gunny. Geneva, 2002. (= *Oeuvres complètes de Voltaire,* vol. 20B.)

———. *Lettre civile et honnête à l'auteur malhonnête de la Critique de l'histoire universelle.* n.p., n.d. [1760].

———. *Questions sur l'Encyclopédie, par des amateurs.* 8 vols. Edited by Nicholas Cronk and Christiane Mervaud. Oxford, 2007–2018. (= *Oeuvres complètes de Voltaire,* vols. 37–43.)

4. Sources after 1800

Abdel-Halim, Mohamed. *Antoine Galland: Sa vie et son oeuvre.* Paris, 1964.

———. "Correspondance d'Antoine Galland." Thèse complémentaire, University of Paris, 1964. Held in Sorbonne University Bibliothèque Georges-Ascoli et Paul-Hazard.

Ageron, Pierre, and Mustapha Jaouhari. "Le programme pédagogique d'un arabisant du Collège royal, François Pétis de La Croix (1653–1713)." *Arabica* 61 (2014): 396–453.

d'Alverny, Marie-Thérèse. "Deux traductions latines du Coran au moyen age." *Archives d'histoire doctrinale et littéraire du Moyen Age* 16 (1947–1948): 69–131.

Arberry, A. J. *Oriental Essays.* London, 1960.

Babinger, Franz. "Die türkischen Studien in Europa bis zum Auftreten Josef von Hammer-Purgstalls." *Die Welt des Islams* 7 (1919): 103–129.

Badir, Magdy G. *Voltaire et l'Islam.* Oxford, 1974.

Behzad, Faramarz. *Adam Olearius' "Persianischer Rosenthal": Untersuchungen zur Übersetzung von Saadis "Golestan" im 17. Jahrhundert.* Göttingen, 1970.

Bellini, Giuseppe. *Storia della Tipografia del Seminario di Padova, 1684–1938.* 2nd ed. Padua, 1938.

Ben Tov, Asaph. "The Academic Study of Arabic in Seventeenth- and Early Eighteenth-Century Protestant Germany." *History of Universities* 28 (2015): 93–135.

———. "Johann Zechendorff (1580–1662) and Arabic Studies at Zwickau's Latin School." In *The Teaching and Learning Arabic in Early Modern Europe,* edited by Jan Loop, Alastair Hamilton, and Charles Burnett, 57–92. Leiden, 2017.

Bevilacqua, Alexander. "How to Organise the Orient: D'Herbelot and the *Bibliothèque Orientale.*" *Journal of the Warburg and Courtauld Institutes* 79 (2016): 213–260.

———. "The Qur'an Translations of Marracci and Sale." *Journal of the Warburg and Courtauld Institutes* 76 (2013): 93–130.

Bevilacqua, Alexander, and Helen Pfeifer. "Turquerie: Culture in Motion, 1650–1750." *Past and Present* 221 (2013): 75–118.

Bisaha, Nancy. *Creating East and West: Renaissance Humanists and the Ottoman Turks.* Philadelphia, 2004.

Blair, Ann M. *Too Much to Know: Managing Scholarly Information before the Modern Age*. New Haven, Ct., 2010.

Bobzin, Hartmut. *Der Koran im Zeitalter der Reformation: Studien zur Frühgeschichte der Arabistik und Islamkunde in Europa*. Beirut, 1995.

———. "Von Venedig nach Kairo: Zur Geschichte arabischer Korandrucke (16. bis frühes 20. Jarhundert)." In *Sprachen des Nahen Ostens und die Druckrevolution: Eine interkulturelle Begegnung*, edited by E. Hanebutt-Benz et al., 151–176. Westhofen, 2002.

Borrmans, Maurice. "Marracci et sa traduction latine du Coran." *Islamochristiana* 28 (2002): 73–86.

Bots, Hans, and Françoise Waquet. *La République des lettres*. Paris, 1997.

Brentjes, Sonja. *Travellers from Europe in the Ottoman and Safavid Empires, 16th–17th Centuries*. Burlington, Vt., 2010.

Brockway, Duncan. "The Second Edition of Volume I of Marracci's *Alcorani Textus Universus*." *Muslim World* 64 (1972): 141–144.

Brogi, Stefano. *Il cerchio dell'universo: Libertinismo, spinozismo e filosofia della natura in Boulainvilliers*. Florence, 1993.

Brolis, Maria Teresa. "La crociata di Pietro il Venerabile: Guerra di armi o guerra di idee?" *Aevum* 61 (1987): 327–354.

Bulman, William J. *Anglican Enlightenment: Orientalism, Religion, and Politics in England and Its Empire, 1648–1715*. Cambridge, 2015.

———. "Introduction: Enlightenment for the Culture Wars." In *God in the Enlightenment*, edited by William J. Bulman and Robert G. Ingram, 1–41. Oxford, 2016.

Burman, Thomas E. *Reading the Qur'an in Latin Christendom, 1140–1560*. Philadelphia, 2007.

Burnett, Charles. "Arabic into Latin: The Reception of Arabic Philosophy into Western Europe." In *The Cambridge Companion to Arabic Philosophy*, edited by Peter Adamson and Richard Taylor, 370–404. Cambridge, 2005.

Champion, Justin. " 'I Remember a Mahometan Story of Ahmed Ben Edris': Freethinking Uses of Islam from Stubbe to Toland." *Al-Qantara* 31 (2010): 443–480.

———. "Legislators, Impostors, and the Politic Origins of Religion: English Theories of 'Imposture' from Stubbe to Toland." In *Heterodoxy, Spinozism and Free Thought in Early Eighteenth-Century Europe: Studies on the* Traité des trois imposteurs, edited by Silvia Berti, Françoise Charles-Daubert, and Richard Popkin, chap. 11. Dordrecht, 1996.

——— *The Pillars of Priestcraft Shaken: The Church of England and Its Enemies, 1660–1730*. Cambridge, 1992.

———. *Republican Learning: John Toland and the Crisis of Christian Culture, 1696–1722*. Manchester, 2003.

Clarke, Jack A. "Abbé Jean-Paul Bignon: 'Moderator of the Academies' and Royal Librarian." *French Historical Studies* 8 (1973): 213–235.

Colas, Gérard. "Les manuscrits envoyés de l'Inde par les jésuites français entre 1729 et 1735." In *Scribes et manuscrits du Moyen-Orient,* edited by François Déroche and Francis Richard, 345–362. Paris, 1997.

Colombo, Emanuele. *Convertire i musulmani: L'esperienza di un gesuita spagnolo del Seicento.* Milan, 2007.

Conrad, Sebastian. "Enlightenment in Global History: A Historiographical Critique." *American Historical Review* 117 (2012): 999–1027.

Craddock, Patricia B. *Edward Gibbon, Luminous Historian, 1772–1794.* Baltimore, Md., 1989.

Daniel, Norman. *Islam and the West: The Making of an Image.* Edinburgh, 1960.

D'Errico, Gian Luca, ed. *Il Corano e il pontefice: Ludovico Marracci fra cultura islamica e Curia papale.* Rome, 2015.

Dew, Nicholas. "The Order of Oriental Knowledge: The Making of d'Herbelot's *Bibliothèque Orientale.*" In *Debating World Literature,* edited by Christopher Prendergast, chap. 11. London, 2004.

———. *Orientalism in Louis XIV's France.* Oxford, 2009.

Dunkelgrün, Theodor W. "The Multiplicity of Scripture: The Confluence of Textual Traditions in the Making of the Antwerp Polyglot Bible (1568–1573)." PhD dissertation, University of Chicago, 2012.

Ebert, Hans-Georg, and Thoralf Hanstein, eds. *Johann Jacob Reiske: Leben und Wirkung: Ein Leipziger Byzantinist und Begründer der Orientalistik im 18. Jahrhundert.* Leipzig, 2005.

Elmarsafy, Ziad. *The Enlightenment Qur'an: The Politics of Translation and the Construction of Islam.* Oxford, 2009.

Erünsal, İsmail E. "Osmanlılarda sahhaflık ve sahhaflar: Yeni bazı belge ve bilgiler (Secondhand Bookselling and Booksellers in the Ottoman Period: New Documents and Information)." In *Türk kitap medeniyeti,* edited by Alper Çeker, 133–180. Istanbul, 2008.

Fedalto, Giorgio. "Il Cardinale Gregorio Barbarigo e l'Oriente." In *Gregorio Barbarigo: Patrizio veneto, vescovo e cardinale nella tarda Controriforma (1625–1697): Atti del convegno di studi, Padova, 7–10 novembre 1996,* edited by Liliana Billanovich and Pierantonio Gios, 977–1001. Padua, 1999.

Feingold, Mordechai. "Oriental Studies." In *Seventeenth-Century Oxford,* vol. 4 of *The History of the University of Oxford,* edited by Nicholas Tyacke, 449–503. Oxford, 1997.

———. "Patrons and Professors: The Origins and Motives for the Endowment of University Chairs: In Particular the Laudian Professorship of Arabic." In *The

"Arabick" Interest of the Natural Philosophers in Seventeenth-Century England, edited by G. A. Russell, 109–127. Leiden, 1994.

———. "'The Turkish Alcoran': New Light on the 1649 English Translation of the Koran." *Huntington Library Quarterly* 75 (2012): 475–501.

Fleischer, Cornell H. *Bureaucrat and Intellectual in the Ottoman Empire: The Historian Mustafa Ali (1541–1600).* Princeton, N.J., 1986.

Force, Pierre. "The 'Exasperating Predecessor': Pocock on Gibbon and Voltaire." *Journal of the History of Ideas* 77 (2016): 129–145.

———. "Voltaire and the Necessity of Modern History." *Modern Intellectual History* 6 (2009): 457–484.

Fowden, Garth. "Gibbon on Islam." *English Historical Review* 131 (2016): 261–292.

Fück, Johann. *Die arabischen Studien in Europa bis in den Anfang des 20. Jahrhunderts.* Leipzig, 1955.

Games, Alison. *The Web of Empire: English Cosmopolitans in an Age of Expansion, 1560–1660.* Oxford, 2008.

Garcia, Humberto. *Islam and the English Enlightenment, 1670–1840.* Baltimore, Md., 2011.

García-Arenal, Mercedes, ed. *After Conversion: Iberia and the Emergence of Modernity.* Leiden, 2016.

———. "The Religious Identity of the Arabic Language and the Affair of the Lead Books of the Sacromonte of Granada." *Arabica* 56 (2009): 495–528.

García-Arenal, Mercedes, and Fernando Rodríguez Mediano, *The Orient in Spain: Converted Muslims, the Forged Lead Books of Granada, and the Rise of Orientalism.* Leiden, 2013.

Gaulmier, Jean. "A la découverte du Proche-Orient: Barthélemy d'Herbelot et sa *Bibliothèque Orientale*." *Bulletin de la Faculté des Lettres de Strasbourg* 48 (1969): 1–6.

Ghobrial, John-Paul. "The Archive of Orientalism and Its Keepers: Re-imagining the Histories of Arabic Manuscripts in Early Modern Europe." *Past and Present,* suppl. 11 (2016): 90–111.

———. *The Whispers of Cities: Information Flows in Istanbul, London, and Paris in the Age of William Trumbull.* Oxford, 2013.

Girard, Aurélien. "Des manuels de langue entre mission et érudition orientaliste au XVIIe siècle: Les grammaires de l'arabe des *Caracciolini*." In *L'Ordine dei Chierici Regolari Minori (Caracciolini): Religione e cultura in età postridentina: Atti del Convegno (Chieti, 11–12 aprile 2008),* edited by Irene Fosi and Giovanni Pizzorusso. *Studi Medievali e Moderni* 14 (2010): 279–296.

———. "Le christianisme oriental (XVIIe–XVIIIe siècles): Essor de l'orientalisme catholique en Europe et construction des identités confessionnelles au Proche-Orient." PhD dissertation, École Pratique des Hautes Études, Paris, 2011.

———. "L'enseignement de l'arabe à Rome au XVIIIe siècle." In *Maghreb-Italie: Des passeurs médiévaux à l'orientalisme moderne, XIIIe–milieu XXe siècle,* edited by Benoît Grévin, 209–234. Rome, 2010.

———. "Les manuels d'arabe en usage en France à la fin de l'ancien régime." In *Manuels d'arabe d'hier et d'aujourd'hui: France-Maghreb, XIXe–XXIe siècle,* edited by Sylvette Larzul and Alain Messaoudi, 12–26. Paris, 2013.

Glei, Reinhold F. *"Arabismus Latine Personatus:* Die Koranübersetzung von Ludovico Marracci (1698) und die Funktion des Lateinischen." *Jahrbuch für Europäische Wissenschaftskultur* 5 (2009 / 2010): 93–115.

Glei, Reinhold F., and Roberto Tottoli. *Ludovico Marracci at Work: The Evolution of His Latin Translation of the Qur'an in the Light of His Newly Discovered Manuscripts.* Leipzig, 2016.

Gossman, Lionel. *Medievalism and the Ideologies of the Enlightenment: The World and Work of La Curne de Sainte-Palaye.* Baltimore, Md., 1968.

Grafton, Anthony. "Christianity's Jewish Origins Rediscovered: The Roles of Comparison in Early Modern Ecclesiastical Scholarship." *Erudition and the Republic of Letters* 1 (2016): 13–42.

———. *The Footnote: A Curious History.* Cambridge, Mass., 1997.

———. *Forgers and Critics: Creativity and Duplicity in Western Scholarship.* Princeton, N.J., 1990.

———. "Jean Hardouin: The Antiquary as Pariah." *Journal of the Warburg and Courtauld Institutes* 62 (1999): 241–267.

———. "Spinoza's Hermeneutics: Some Heretical Thoughts." In *Scriptural Authority and Biblical Criticism in the Dutch Golden Age: God's Word Questioned.* Oxford, forthcoming.

———. "Where Was Salomon's House? Ecclesiastical History and the Intellectual Origins of Bacon's *New Atlantis.*" In *Worlds Made by Words: Scholarship and Community in the Modern West,* 98–113. Cambridge, Mass., 2009.

Grafton, Anthony, and Joanna Weinberg. *"I Have Always Loved the Holy Tongue": Isaac Casaubon, the Jews, and a Forgotten Chapter in Renaissance Scholarship.* Cambridge, Mass., 2011.

Greene, Molly. "Islam and Europe." In *A Companion to Eighteenth-Century Europe,* edited by Peter H. Wilson, chap. 24. Oxford, 2009.

Gunny, Ahmad. *Images of Islam in Eighteenth-Century Writings.* London, 1996.

Günther, Sebastian, Todd Lawson, and Christian Mauder, eds. *Roads to Paradise: Eschatology and Concepts of the Hereafter in Islam.* 2 vols. Leiden, 2017.

Hadidi, Djavad. *Voltaire et l'Islam.* Paris, 1974.

Hagen, Gottfried. "Katib Çelebi." In the online database *Historians of the Ottoman Empire,* edited by Cemal Kafadar, Hakan Karateke, and Cornell Fleischer. https://ottomanhistorians.uchicago.edu/en/historians/65.

Hamaker, Hendrik Arens. *Incerti Auctoris Liber de Expugnatione Memphidis et Alexandriae, Vulgo Adscriptus Abou Abdallae Mohammedi Omari Filio, Wakidaeo, Medinensi. Textum Arabicum ex Codice Bibliothecae L. B. Descripsit, Plurimisque Vitiis Purgatum, Edidit, et Annotationem Adjecit.* . . . Leiden, 1825.

Hamilton, Alastair. "Adrianus Reland (1676–1718): Outstanding Orientalist." In *Zes keer zestig: 360 jaar universitaire geschiedenis in zes biografieën,* edited by Hervé Jamin, 22–31. Utrecht, 1996.

———. *Arab Culture and Ottoman Magnificence in Antwerp's Golden Age.* Oxford, 2001.

———. "Arabists and Cartesians at Utrecht." In *Leven na Descartes: Zeven opstellen over ideeëngeschiedenis in Nederland in de tweede helft van de zeventiende eeuw: Uitgegeven ter gelegenheid van de vijftigste verjaardag van het verschijnen van Nederlands cartesianisme van dr. C. Louise Thijssen-Schoute,* edited by P. G. Hoftijzer and Theo Verbeek, 97–105. Hilversum, 2005.

———. "An Egyptian Traveller in the Republic of Letters: Josephus Barbatus or Abudacnus the Copt." *Journal of the Warburg and Courtauld Institutes* 57 (1994): 123–50.

———. *The Forbidden Fruit: The Koran in Early Modern Europe.* London, 2008.

———. "From a 'Closet at Utrecht': Adriaan Reland and Islam." *Nederlands Archief voor Kerkgeschiedenis* 78 (1998): 243–250.

———. "Humanists and the Bible." In *The Cambridge Companion to Renaissance Humanism,* edited by Jill Kraye, 100–117. Cambridge, 1996.

———. "Lutheran Islamophiles in Eighteenth-Century Germany." In *For the Sake of Learning: Essays in Honor of Anthony Grafton,* 2 vols., edited by A. Blair and A.-S. Goeing, 1:327–343. Leiden, 2016.

———. "A Lutheran Translator for the Quran: A Late Seventeenth-Century Quest." In *The Republic of Letters and the Levant,* edited by Alastair Hamilton, Maurits H. van den Boogert, and Bart Westerweel, 197–221. Leiden, 2005.

———. " 'Nam Tirones sumus': Franciscus Raphelengius' Lexicon Arabico-Latinum (Leiden 1613)." In *Ex Officina Plantiniana: Studia in Memoriam Christophori Plantini (ca. 1520–1589),* edited by Marcus de Schepper and Francine de Nave, 557–589. Antwerp, 1989.

———. " 'To Divest the East of All Its Manuscripts and All Its Rarities': The Unfortunate Embassy of Henri Gournay de Marcheville." In *The Republic of Letters and the Levant,* edited by Alastair Hamilton, Maurits H. van den Boogert, and Bart Westerweel, 123–150. Leiden, 2005.

———. " 'To Rescue the Honour of the Germans': Qur'an Translations by Eighteenth- and Early Nineteenth-Century German Protestants." *Journal of the Warburg and Courtauld Institutes* 77 (2014): 173–209.

———. "Western Attitudes to Islam in the Enlightenment." *Middle Eastern Lectures* 3 (1999): 69–85.

———. *William Bedwell, the Arabist (1563–1632)*. Leiden, 1985.

Hamilton, Alastair, Maurits H. van den Boogert, and Bart Westerweel, eds. *The Republic of Letters and the Levant*. Leiden, 2005.

Hamilton, Alastair, and Francis Richard. *André du Ryer and Oriental Studies in Seventeenth-Century France*. Oxford, 2004.

Hankins, James. "Renaissance Crusaders: Humanist Crusade Literature in the Age of Mehmed II." *Dumbarton Oaks Papers* 49 (1995): 111–207.

Hansen, Anne Haslund, and Stig T. Rasmussen, eds. *Min Sundheds Forliis: Frederik Christian von Havens Rejsejournal fra Den Arabiske Rejse, 1760–1763*. Copenhagen, 2005.

Hayes, Kevin J. "How Thomas Jefferson Read the Qur'ān." *Early American Literature* 39 (2004): 247–261.

Hershenzon, Daniel. "Traveling Libraries: The Arabic Manuscripts of Muley Zidan and the Escorial Library." *Journal of Early Modern History* 18 (2014): 535–558.

Heyberger, Bernard. "Abraham Ecchellensis dans la 'République des Lettres.'" In *Orientalisme, science et controverse: Abraham Ecchellensis (1605–1664)*, edited by Bernard Heyberger, 9–51. Turnhout, 2010.

———. "Chrétiens orientaux dans l'Europe catholique (XVIIe–XVIIIe siècles)." In *Hommes de l'entre-deux: Parcours individuels et portraits de groupes sur la frontière de la Méditerranée (XVIe–XXe siècle)*, edited by Bernard Heyberger and Chantal Verdeil, 61–92. Paris, 2009.

———. "La carrière manquée d'un ecclésiastique oriental en Italie: Timothée Karnûsh, archevêque syrien catholique de Mardîn." *Bulletin de la faculté des lettres de Mulhouse* 19 (1995): 31–47.

———. *Les chrétiens du Proche-Orient au temps de la Réforme catholique (Syrie, Liban, Palestine, XVIIe–XVIIIe siècles)*. Rome, 1994.

———. "L'islam et les Arabes chez un érudit maronite au service de l'Eglise catholique (Abraham Ecchellensis)." *Al-Qantara* 31 (2010): 481–512.

———, ed. *Orientalisme, science et controverse: Abraham Ecchellensis (1605–1664)*. Turnhout, 2010.

———. "'Pro nunc, nihil respondendum': Recherche d'information et prise de décision à la Propagande: L'exemple du levant (XVIIIe siècle)." *Mélanges de l'École française de Rome—Italie et Méditerranée* 109 (1997): 539–554.

Hitzel, Frédéric. "Manuscrits, livres et culture livresque à Istanbul." In *Livres et lecture dans le monde ottoman*, edited by Frédéric Hitzel. Special issue, *Revue des mondes musulmans et de la Méditerannée* 87–88 (1999): 19–38.

Holt, P. M. *A Seventeenth-Century Defender of Islam: Henry Stubbe (1632–76) and His Book*. London, 1972.

———. *Studies in the History of the Near East.* London, 1973.

Hunt, Lynn, Margaret Jacob, and Wijnand Mijnardt. *The Book That Changed Europe: Picart and Bernard's Religious Ceremonies of the World.* Cambridge, Mass., 2010.

Irwin, Robert. *For Lust of Knowing: The Orientalists and Their Enemies.* London, 2006.

Jones, Robert. "Learning Arabic in Renaissance Europe (1505–1624)." PhD dissertation, School of Oriental and African Studies, University of London, 1988.

———. "The Medici Oriental Press (Rome, 1584–1614) and the Impact of Its Arabic Publications on Northern Europe." In *The "Arabick" Interest of the Natural Philosophers in Seventeenth-Century England,* edited by G. A. Russell, chap. 5. Leiden, 1994.

Khairallah, Shereen Nagib. "Arabic Studies in England in the Late Seventeenth and Early Eighteenth Centuries." PhD dissertation, University of London, 1972.

Kimmel, Seth. *Parables of Coercion: Conversion and Knowledge at the End of Islamic Spain.* Chicago, 2015.

Kritzeck, James. *Peter the Venerable and Islam.* Princeton, N.J., 1964.

Lange, Christian. *Paradise and Hell in Islamic Traditions.* Cambridge, 2016.

Laurens, Henri. *Aux sources de l'orientalisme: La Bibliothèque Orientale de Barthélemi d'Herbelot.* Paris, 1978.

Levi della Vida, Giorgio. "Ludovico Marracci e la sua opera negli studi islamici." In *Aneddoti e svaghi arabi e non arabi,* 193–210. Milan, 1959.

———. *Ricerche sulla formazione del più antico fondo dei manoscritti orientali della Biblioteca Vaticana.* Vatican City, 1939.

Levinus Warner and His Legacy: Three Centuries Legatum Warnerianum in the Leiden University Library. Leiden, 1970.

Levitin, Dmitri. *Ancient Wisdom in the Age of the New Science: Histories of Philosophy in England, c. 1640–1700.* Cambridge, 2015.

———. "From Sacred History to the History of Religion: Paganism, Judaism, and Christianity in European Historiography from Reformation to 'Enlightenment.'" *Historical Journal* 55 (2012): 1117–1160.

———. "John Spencer's *De Legibus Hebraeorum* (1683–85) and 'Enlightened' Sacred History: A New Interpretation." *Journal of the Warburg and Courtauld Institutes* 76 (2013): 49–92.

Lewis, Bernard. "Gibbon on Muhammad." *Daedalus* 105 (1976): 89–101. Also published in *Edward Gibbon and the Decline and Fall of the Roman Empire,* edited by G. W. Bowersock et al., 61–73. Cambridge, Mass., 1977.

Loop, Jan. "Divine Poetry? Early Modern European Orientalists on the Beauty of the Koran." *Church History and Religious Culture* 89 (2009): 455–488.

———. "Johann Heinrich Hottinger (1620–1667) and the 'Historia Orientalis.'" *Church History and Religious Culture* 88 (2008): 169–203.

———. *Johann Heinrich Hottinger: Arabic and Islamic Studies in the Seventeenth Century.* Oxford, 2013.

———. "Kontroverse Bemühungen um den Orient." In *Johann Jacob Reiske: Leben und Wirkung: Ein Leipziger Byzantinist und Begründer der Orientalistik im 18. Jahrhundert,* edited by Hans-Georg Ebert and Thoralf Hanstein, 45–85. Leipzig, 2005.

Loop, Jan, Alastair Hamilton, and Charles Burnett, eds. *The Teaching and Learning of Arabic in Early Modern Europe.* Leiden, 2017.

Löfgren, Oscar, and Renato Traini, eds. *Catalogue of the Arabic Manuscripts in the Biblioteca Ambrosiana.* Vol. 1. Vicenza, 1975.

Malcolm, Noel. "The Crescent and the City of the Sun: Islam and the Renaissance Utopia of Tommaso Campanella." *Proceedings of the British Academy* 125 (2004): 41–67.

———. "The 1649 English Translation of the Koran: Its Origins and Significance." *Journal of the Warburg and Courtauld Institutes* 75 (2012): 261–295.

———. "The Study of Islam in Early Modern Europe: Obstacles and Missed Opportunities." In *Antiquarianism and Intellectual Life in Europe and China, 1500–1800,* edited by Peter N. Miller and François Louis, 265–288. Ann Arbor, Mich., 2012.

Marchand, Suzanne L. *German Orientalism in the Age of Empire: Religion, Race, and Scholarship.* Cambridge, 2009.

Marenbon, John. *Pagans and Philosophers: The Problem of Paganism from Augustine to Leibniz.* Princeton, N.J., 2015.

Meggitt, Justin J. *Early Quakers and Islam: Slavery, Apocalyptic and Christian-Muslim Encounters in the Seventeenth Century.* Uppsala, 2013.

Meserve, Margaret. *Empires of Islam in Renaissance Historical Thought.* Cambridge, Mass., 2008.

Miller, Peter N. "The 'Antiquarianization' of Biblical Scholarship and the London Polyglot Bible (1653–57)." *Journal of the History of Ideas* 62 (2001): 463–482.

———. "Making the Paris Polyglot Bible: Humanism and Orientalism in the Early Seventeenth Century." In *Die europäische Gelehrtenrepublik im Zeitalter des Konfessionalismus,* edited by Herbert Jaumann, 59–85. Wiesbaden, 2001.

———. *Peiresc's Mediterranean World.* Cambridge, Mass., 2015.

———. *Peiresc's Orient: Antiquarianism as Cultural History in the Seventeenth Century.* Burlington, Vt., 2012.

———. "Peiresc, the Levant and the Mediterranean." In *The Republic of Letters and the Levant,* edited by Alastair Hamilton, Maurits H. van den Boogert, and Bart Westerweel, 103–122. Leiden, 2005.

Mills, Simon. *A Commerce of Knowledge: Trade, Religion, and Scholarship between England and the Ottoman Empire.* Oxford, forthcoming.

Minuti, Rolando. *Orientalismo e idee di tolleranza nella cultura francese del primo '700.* Florence, 2006.

Momigliano, Arnaldo. "Ancient History and the Antiquarian." *Journal of the Warburg and Courtauld Institutes* 13 (1950): 285–315.

———. *The Classical Foundations of Modern Historiography.* Berkeley, 1990.

Monroe, James T. *Islam and the Arabs in Spanish Scholarship (Sixteenth Century to the Present).* Leiden, 1970.

Mulsow, Martin. "Mobilität und Vigilanz: Zur Informationsgeschichte von Numismatik und Orientreise unter Ludwig XIV." In *Prekäres Wissen: Eine andere Ideengeschichte der Frühen Neuzeit,* 342–366. Berlin, 2012.

———. "Orientalistik im Kontext der sozinianischen und deistischen Debatten um 1700." *Scientia Poetica* 2 (1998): 27–57.

———. "Socinianism, Islam and the Radical Uses of Arabic Scholarship." *Al-Qantara* 31 (2010): 549–586.

Nallino, Carlo Alfonso. "Le fonti arabe manoscritte." In *Raccolta di scritti editi e inediti a cura di Maria Nallino.* Rome, 1940.

Neveu, Bruno. "La vie érudite à Paris à la fin du XVIIe siècle d'après les papiers du P. Léonard de Sainte-Catherine (1695–1706)." *Bibliothèque de l'École de Chartes* 124 (1966): 478–480. Reprinted in Bruno Neveu, *Érudition et religion aux XVIIe et XVIIIe siècles,* 25–92. Paris, 1994.

Nuovo, Angela. "Il Corano arabo ritrovato." *La Bibliofilia* 89 (1987): 237–271.

Omont, Henri. *Missions archéologiques françaises en Orient aux XVIIe et XVIIIe siècles.* 2 vols. Paris, 1902.

Osterhammel, Jürgen. *Die Entzauberung Asiens: Europa und die asiatischen Reiche im 18. Jahrhundert.* Munich, 1998.

Pedani Fabris, Maria Pia. "Intorno alla questione della traduzione del Corano." In *Gregorio Barbarigo: Patrizio veneto, vescovo e cardinale nella tarda Controriforma (1625–1697): Atti del convegno di studi, Padova, 7–10 Novembre 1996,* edited by Liliana Billanovich and Pierantonio Gios, 353–365. Padua, 1999.

Pizzorusso, Giovanni. "Filippo Guadagnoli, i Caracciolini e lo studio delle lingue orientali e della controversia con l'Islam a Roma nel XVII secolo." In *L'Ordine dei Chierici Regolari Minori (Caracciolini): Religione e cultura in età postridentina: atti del Convegno (Chieti, 11–12 aprile 2008),* edited by Irene Fosi e Giovanni Pizzorusso. *Studi Medievali e Moderni* 14 (2010): 268–273.

———. "La preparazione linguistica e controversistica dei missionari per l'Oriente islamico: Scuole, testi, insegnanti a Roma e in Italia." In *L'Islam visto da Occidente: Cultura e religione del Seicento europeo di fronte all'Islam,* edited by Bernard Heyberger et al., 253–288. Genoa, 2009.

———. "Tra cultura e missione: La congregazione *De Propaganda Fide* e le scuole di lingua araba nel XVII secolo." In *Rome et la science moderne entre Renaissance et Lumières,* edited by Antonella Romano, 121–152. Rome, 2008.

Pocock, J. G. A. *Barbarism and Religion*. Vol. 1, *The Enlightenments of Edward Gibbon, 1737–1764*. Cambridge, 1999.

———. *Barbarism and Religion*. Vol. 2, *Narratives of Civil Government*. Cambridge, 1999.

Pomeau, René. *La religion de Voltaire*. 2nd ed. Paris, 1969.

Pouillon, François, ed. *Dictionnaire des orientalistes de langue française*. Paris, 2008.

Quinn, Meredith Moss. "Books and Their Readers in Seventeenth-Century Istanbul." PhD dissertation, Harvard University, 2016.

Richard, Francis. "Aux origines de la connaissance de la langue persane en France." *Luqmân: Annales des Presses universitaires d'Iran* 3 (1986–1987): 23–42.

———. *Catalogue des manuscrits persans*. Vol. 1, *Ancien Fonds*. Paris, 1989.

———. "Le dictionnaire de d'Herbelot." In *Istanbul et les langues orientales*, edited by Frédéric Hitzel, 79–88. Paris, 1997.

———. "Les Frères Vecchietti, diplomates, érudits et aventuriers." In *The Republic of Letters and the Levant*, edited by Alastair Hamilton, Maurits H. van den Boogert, and Bart Westerweel, 11–26. Leiden, 2005.

———. "Les manuscrits persans rapportés par les frères Vecchietti et conservés aujourd'hui à la Bibliothèque nationale." *Studia Iranica* 9 (1980): 291–300.

———. "Une traduction française méconnue du XVIIème siècle: Celle du *Ṣifāt al-'āshiqīn* de Helālī par Claude Bérault." *Luqmân: Annales des Presses universitaires d'Iran* 19 (2002–2003): 147–148.

Ricuperati, Giuseppe. "*Universal History:* Storia di un progetto europeo; Impostori, storici ed editori nella *Ancient Part*." *Studi settecenteschi* 1 (1981): 7–90.

Rizzardi, Giuseppe. "Il modello controversistico di Ludovico Marracci." In *Il Corano: Traduzioni, traduttori e lettori in Italia*, edited by Maurice Borrmans et al., 81–109. Milan, 2000.

Robinson, Chase F. *Islamic Historiography*. Cambridge, 2003.

Rodríguez Mediano, Fernando. "Fragmentos de orientalismo español del S. XVII." *Hispania—Revista Española de Historia* 66 (2006): 243–276.

Rooden, Peter van. "Willem Surenhuys' Translation of the Mishna and the Strange Death of Christian Hebraism." In *Reuchlin und seine Erben: Forscher, Denker, Ideologen und Spinner*, edited by Peter Schäfer and Irina Wandrey, 97–111. Ostfildern, 2005.

Rosenthal, Franz. *A History of Muslim Historiography*. 2nd ed. Leiden, 1968.

Ross, E. Denison. "Ludovico Marracci." *Bulletin of the School of Oriental Studies* 2 (1921): 117–123.

Rubiés, Joan-Pau. "Instructions for Travellers: Teaching the Eye to See." *History and Anthropology* 9 (1996): 139–190.

Secret, François. "Gilbert Gaulmin et l'histoire comparée des religions." *Revue de l'histoire des religions* 177 (1970): 35–63.

Serena, Sebastiano, ed. "Il Cardinale Gregorio Barbarigo e l'Oriente." In *S. Gregorio Barbarigo e la vita spirituale e culturale nel suo Seminario di Padova,* 2 vols., 1:137–171. Padua, 1963.

———, ed. *Quaranta Due Lettere del Cardinale Beato Gregorio Barbarigo a Giovanni Pastrizio.* Padua, 1938.

Shellabear, W. G. "Is Sale's Koran Reliable?" *Muslim World* 21 (1931): 126–142.

Sheehan, Jonathan. *The Enlightenment Bible: Translation, Scholarship, Culture.* Princeton, N.J., 2005.

Smith, Jonathan Z. *Drudgery Divine: On the Comparison of Early Christianities and the Religions of Late Antiquity.* Chicago, 1990.

Southern, R. W. *Western Views of Islam in the Middle Ages.* Cambridge, Mass., 1962.

Spellberg, Denise A. *Thomas Jefferson's Qur'an: Islam and the Founders.* New York, 2013.

Stagl, Justin. *A History of Curiosity: The Theory of Travel, 1550–1800.* Chur, Switzerland, 1995.

Stolzenberg, Daniel. *Egyptian Oedipus: Athanasius Kircher and the Secrets of Antiquity.* Chicago, 2013.

Strohmaier, Gotthard. "Johann Jacob Reiske: Byzantinist und Arabist der Aufklärung." In *Von Demokrit bis Dante: Die Bewahrung antiken Erbes in der arabischen Kultur,* edited by Gotthard Strohmaier, 501–511. Hildesheim, 1996.

———. "Johann Jacob Reiske, Der Märtyrer der arabischen Literatur." *Das Altertum* 20 (1974): 166–179.

———. "Johann Jacob Reiske über die Aufgaben der Arabistik." In *Von Demokrit bis Dante: Die Bewahrung antiken Erbes in der arabischen Kultur,* edited by Gotthard Strohmaier, 512–515. Hildesheim, 1996.

Stroumsa, Guy G. *A New Science: The Discovery of Religion in the Age of Reason.* Cambridge, Mass., 2010.

Subrahmanyam, Sanjay. *Europe's India: Words, People, Empires, 1500–1800.* Cambridge, Mass., 2017.

Thomson, Ann. *Barbary and Enlightenment: European Attitudes towards the Maghreb in the 18th Century.* Leiden, 1987.

Tolan, John. "Peter the Venerable on the 'Diabolical Heresy of the Saracens.'" In *The Devil, Heresy and Witchcraft in the Middle Ages: Essays in Honor of Jeffrey B. Russell,* edited by Alberto Ferreiro, 345–367. Leiden, 1998.

———. *Saracens: Islam in the Medieval European Imagination.* New York, 2002.

———. *Sons of Ishmael: Muslims through European Eyes in the Middle Ages.* Gainesville, Fla., 2008.

Tommasino, Pier Mattia. "Giovanni Battista Castrodardo bellunese traduttore dell'Alcorano di Macometto." *Oriente Moderno* 88 (2008): 15–40.

———. *L'Alcorano di Macometto: Storia di un libro del Cinquecento europeo.* Bologna, 2013.

Toomer, G. J. *Eastern Wisedome and Learning: The Study of Arabic in Seventeenth-Century England.* Oxford, 1995.

———. "Edward Pococke's Arabic Translation of Grotius, *De Veritate.*" *Grotiana* 33 (2012): 88–105.

Tottoli, Roberto. "I manoscritti di Ludovico Marracci conservati presso l'Ordine della Madre di Dio in Roma." In *Il Corano e il pontefice,* edited by Gian Luca D'Errico, 119–126. Rome, 2015.

———. "The Latin Translation of the Qurʾān by Johann Zechendorff (1580–1662) Discovered in Cairo Dār al-Kutub: A Preliminary Description." *Oriente Moderno* 95 (2015): 5–31.

———. "New Light on the Translation of the Qur'an of Ludovico Marracci from His Manuscripts Recently Discovered at the Order of the Mother of God in Rome." In *Books and Written Culture of the Islamic World: Studies Presented to Claude Gilliot on the Occasion of His 75th Birthday,* edited by Andrew Rippin and Roberto Tottoli, 91–130. Leiden, 2015.

Venturino, Diego. "Un prophète 'philosophe'? Une *Vie de Mahomed* à l'aube des Lumières." *Dix-huitième siècle* 24 (1992): 321–331.

Vernière, Paul. "Montesquieu et le monde musulman, d'après *L'Esprit des lois.*" In *Actes du Congrès Montesquieu réuni à Bordeaux du 23 mai au 26 mai 1955 pour commémorer le deuxième centenaire de la mort de Montesquieu,* 175–190. Bordeaux, 1956.

Volpilhac-Auger, Catherine. "Comment lire l'*Essai sur les moeurs?*" *Storia della storiografia* 38 (2000): 3–16.

Vrolijk, Arnoud. "The Prince of Arabists and His Many Errors: Thomas Erpenius's Image of Joseph Scaliger and the Edition of the *Proverbia Arabica* (1614)." *Journal of the Warburg and Courtauld Institutes* 73 (2010): 297–325.

———. "Scaliger and the Dutch Expansion in Asia: An Arabic Translation for an Early Voyage to the East Indies (1600)." *Journal of the Warburg and Courtauld Institutes* 78 (2015): 277–309.

———. " 'A Sublime Treasure of Pretious Manuscripts': The Schultens's Legacy in the Leiden University Library and the Elusive Purchase of 1806." *Journal of the Royal Asiatic Society of Great Britain and Ireland* 19 (2009): 281–292.

Vrolijk, Arnoud, and Richard van Leeuwen. *Arabic Studies in the Netherlands: A Short History in Portraits, 1580–1950.* Translated by A. Hamilton. Leiden, 2014.

Vrolijk, Arnoud, and Kasper van Ommen. *"All My Books in Foreign Tongues": Scaliger's Oriental Legacy in Leiden, 1609–2009: Catalogue of an Exhibition on the Quatercentenary of Scaliger's Death, 21 January 2009.* Leiden, 2009.

Wakefield, Colin. "The Arabic Collections in the Bodleian Library." In *A New Catalogue of Arabic Manuscripts in the Bodleian Library, University of Oxford.* Vol. 1, *Medicine,* edited by Emilie Savage-Smith, xxix–xxxvi. Oxford, 2011.

Witkam, Jan Just. "The Middle Eastern Holdings of the Library of the University of Leiden." *Bulletin—British Society for Middle Eastern Studies* 8 (1981): 60–64.

———. "Precious Books and Moments of Friendship in 17th-Century Istanbul." In *Essays in Honour of Ekmeleddin İhsanoğlu.* Vol. 1, *Societies, Cultures, Sciences: A Collection of Articles,* edited by Mustafa Kaçar and Zeynep Durukal, 464–474. Istanbul, 2006.

Acknowledgments

A number of institutions supported the research for this book, beginning with the History Department at Princeton, which generously funded a pan-European research project. At Princeton, I am also thankful to the Center for the Study of Religion, the Dean's Fund for Scholarly Travel, and the Institute for International and Regional Studies. In addition, I thank the American Council of Learned Societies, the American Historical Association, the Society for French Historical Studies, the American Society for Eighteenth-Century Studies, The Huntington, and the Warburg Institute.

In the United States, I am especially indebted to the staff at the Firestone Library, Princeton University; Widener, Houghton, and Andover-Harvard Theological Libraries, Harvard University; the Boston Athenæum; the Rare Book and Manuscript Library, Columbia University; Burke Library at Union Theological Seminary; the New York Public Library; and the Beinecke Rare Book and Manuscript Library, Yale University.

In Europe, I thank the staff of the Bibliothèque nationale de France, the Bibliothèque de l'Institut de France, the Bibliothèque Georges-Ascoli et Paul-Hazard at the Université Paris-Sorbonne, and the Library of the École normale supérieure, Paris; the Arcadian Library, the Manuscripts, Rare Books, and Asian and African Studies Reading Rooms at the British Library, the London Metropolitan Archive, the Royal Society Library, and the Warburg Institute Library, London; the University Library and the Wren Library of Trinity College, Cambridge; the Bodleian Library and the Codrington Library, Oxford; the Central Library, Bath; the Leiden University Library; the Utrecht University Library; the Royal Library, The Hague; the Royal Library and the State Archives, Copenhagen; the Göttingen University Library; the Austrian National Library, Vienna; the National Library, Madrid; the Seminary Library of the Bishopric of Padua; the Archive of the Patriarchal Seminary, the Biblioteca Marciana, and the State Archive, Venice; the Biblioteca Medicea Laurenziana and the National Central Library, Florence; the Biblioteca Apostolica Vaticana, Vatican City, the Historical Archive of the Propaganda Fide, and the Archive of Santa Maria in Campitelli, Rome.

ACKNOWLEDGMENTS

The Society of Fellows was a *locus amoenus* in which to write this book. Diana Morse, Kelly Katz, Yesim Erdmann, and Ana Novak smoothed my path throughout my time there. The William F. Milton Fund enabled follow-up research in Italy, France, Austria, and Britain. I thank Walter Gilbert and the senior and junior fellows for their sustaining feedback and intellectual exchange. Stephanie Dick, Alisha Holland, Abhishek Kaicker, Marika T. Knowles, Ya-Wen Lei, Adam Mestyan, Andrew Ollett, and Alma Steingart read and commented on several chapters.

A predecessor of Chapter 2 (with equal space given to Marracci and Sale) appeared in the *Journal of the Warburg and Courtauld Institutes* 76 (2013); a companion essay to Chapter 4 appeared in that *Journal* 79 (2016). I am most grateful to Jill Kraye and Jenny Boyle for their editorial work, and to the anonymous readers for their reports.

My debt is greater to no one than to Anthony T. Grafton. From our first conversation he saw further than I did; he believed in this project when I faltered. His labors on my behalf cannot be repaid, but I hope he will hear echoes of our many conversations in this book.

This work would likewise have been impossible without the watchful eyes of Michael Cook, whose teaching and advice made it possible for me to write on the history of Islamic studies. David A. Bell provided frequent sound counsel, suggested the writing of Chapter 6, and offered thoughtful feedback on an earlier version. David Nirenberg will find that I have been unable to do justice to his welcome perspectives as a medievalist and Hispanist.

I have long enjoyed the counsel of the choicest mentors, to whom I give warm thanks: David R. Armitage, Ann M. Blair, Alastair Hamilton, Bernard Heyberger, Mordechai Feingold, Molly Greene, and Suzanne L. Marchand. Professor Hamilton, as the bibliography reveals, has done more than anyone for the history of Arabic studies in Europe; his advice and support have been a true honor.

My learned friends and colleagues Jan Loop, Valeria López Fadul, Simon Mills, Andrei Pesic, Helen Pfeifer, Pier Mattia Tommasino, Roberto Tottoli, and Michael Tworek all read the entire manuscript and improved the final version with their lucid comments.

I am grateful to a number of colleagues and friends for encouragement and exchanges, and especially to those whose research made my own possible: Asaph Ben Tov, Charles Burnett, Mercedes García-Arenal, Aurélien Girard,

John-Paul Ghobrial, Maria Pia Pedani, Giovanni Pizzorusso, and Arnoud Vrolijk.

In addition, I thank Catherine Abou Nemeh, Adam Beaver, Jane Booth, William Bulman, Frederic N. Clark, Theodor Dunkelgrün, Yaacob Dweck, Kasper Risbjerg Eskildsen, Khaled Fahmy, Hussein Fancy, Noah Feldman, Pierre Force, Lionel Gossman, James Hankins, Margaret and Patrice Higonnet, Maya Jasanoff, Dmitri Levitin, Hannah Marcus, Peter N. Miller, Susan Gilson Miller, Yair Mintzker, Eric Nelson, Claudia Roth Pierpont, Meredith Quinn, Ahmed Ragab, Jerrold Seigel, Jack Tannous, Francesca Trivellato, Chris Waters, and Nurfadzilah Yahaya.

I thank Roberto Tottoli for permission to use his photographs of Marracci's manuscripts in Santa Maria in Campitelli, Rome, and Stefano Paradiso for allowing me to reproduce his photograph of Marracci's portrait. For their generous hospitality in Rome and crucial help, I thank Marco and Maria Antonia Bevilacqua.

In the production of the book, I have been fortunate to work with Sharmila Sen, Heather M. Hughes, Isabelle Lewis, Susan Miller, Carla M. Heelan, Han Hsien Liew, and everyone at Harvard University Press.

Finally, I thank my family: Guido Bevilacqua, Lois and Alan Hibberd, Lena and Ross Martin, Nerina and Pier Luigi Zampaglione, Leitha Martin and Fabio Bevilacqua, Catherine Bevilacqua. And, especially, Thomas Dolinger.

Index